JOHNNY RED

FALCON'S FIRST FLIGHT

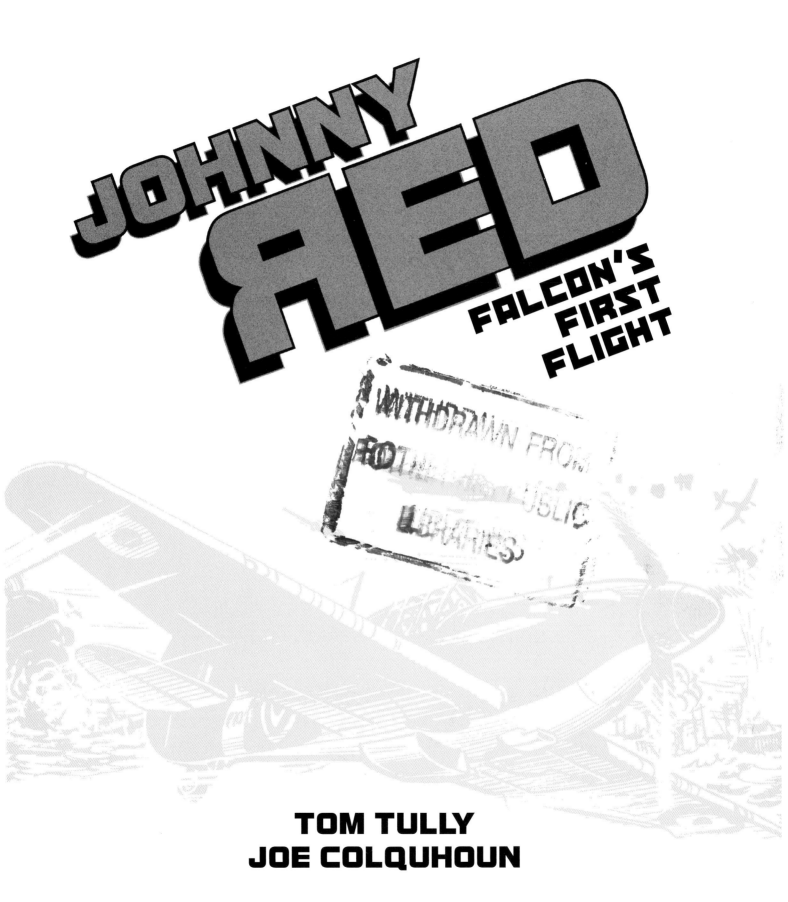

TOM TULLY
JOE COLQUHOUN

TITAN BOOKS

JOHNNY RED: FALCON'S FIRST FLIGHT

ISBN: 9781848560338

Published by
Titan Books
A division of Titan Publishing Group Ltd
144 Southwark Street
London SE1 0UP

A CIP catalogue record for this title is available from the British Library.

This edition first published: January 2011
2 4 6 8 10 9 7 5 3 1

Printed in China.

Also available from Titan Books:
Charley's War: 2 June 1916 – 1 August 1916 (ISBN: 9781840236279)
Charley's War: 1 August 1916 – 17 October 1916 (ISBN: 9781840239294)
Charley's War: 17 October 1916 – 21 February 1917 (ISBN: 9781845762704)
Charley's War: Blue's Story – 21 February 1917 (ISBN: 9781845763237)
Charley's War: Return to The Front – April 1917 (ISBN: 9781845767969)
Charley's War: Underground and Over the Top (ISBN: 9781845767976)

Grateful thanks to Pat Mills, Garth Ennis, Moose Harris, Jeremy Briggs and Paul Travers for their help and support in the production of this book.

What did you think of this book? We love to hear from our readers. Please email us at: readerfeedback@titanemail.com, or write to us at the above address.

To receive advance information, news, competitions, and exclusive Titan offers online, please register as a member by clicking the "sign up" button on our website: www.titanbooks.com

Much of the comic strip source material used by Titan Books in this edition is exceedingly rare. As such, we hope that readers appreciate that the quality of reproduction achievable can vary.

www.titanbooks.com

INTRODUCTION
GARTH ENNIS

You're waiting to die at the top of the world. You and the rest of Falcon Squadron, Fifth Air Brigade of the Soviet Air Force, rotting at a tiny forward airbase up above the Arctic Circle. When summer came, the Nazis smashed into your beloved Mother Russia like a pack of bloodthirsty demons, tore through the Ukraine at breakneck pace, encircled and destroyed whole armies, apparently at will. The Panzers made short work of what resistance could be mustered. You and your comrades did your damnedest, but the Messerschmitts clawed your aging biplanes from the sky. Now the foe is on his way to Moscow, and the order has been given: no surrender.

It's late September, 1941. You take another drag on your foul-tasting cigarette and peer into the gloom, well aware there's nothing to be seen but freezing fog and endless dark. But you know what's really out there, lurking in the night's black heart, gathering that dreadful strength. The Germans are coming. Which means you're as good as dead.

★ ★ ★

Johnny Red was the longest-running strip in *Battle Picture Weekly*, a British anthology comic that began in 1975 and lasted roughly thirteen years. Writer Tom Tully and artist Joe Colquhoun brought us the story of Johnny Redburn, a tough and often hot-headed young man from the back streets of Liverpool, who longs to be a fighter pilot but is instead kicked out of the Royal Air Force for striking an officer. Employed as a mess servant on a vessel bound for Murmansk, the nineteen-year-old gets his first taste of combat when German bombers attack the supply convoy his ship is assigned to defend. Johnny takes to the air in a stolen Hurricane fighter, skirmishes with the enemy long enough to score a couple of kills, and makes for the Russian coast with just enough fuel left to reach a local airbase. There he meets the forlorn survivors of Falcon Squadron, effectively goes native, and becomes a legend.

Ten years of the serial gave us three-and-a-half years of air war on the Eastern Front, with Tom Tully scripting very nearly everything and John Cooper – and eventually Carlos Pino – taking over from Colquhoun. Johnny and his Hurricane saw action over Leningrad and Murmansk, Stalingrad and Kursk, at first alongside and then leading the Falcons. The squadron took fearful losses but never stopped fighting, not until the Russian armies were kicking down the gates of Berlin in 1945. Johnny Red was with them all the way. He made friends like Rudi Vorishkin and the Night Witch Nina Petrova, and – of course – the bear-like Dimitri Yakob. He made enemies, too, with a succession of corrupt commanders and evil Commissars taking exception to the Englishman's (extreme) independent streak. As time went by Johnny got a little wilier, but no less eager for the fight, and certainly no less loyal to his comrades.

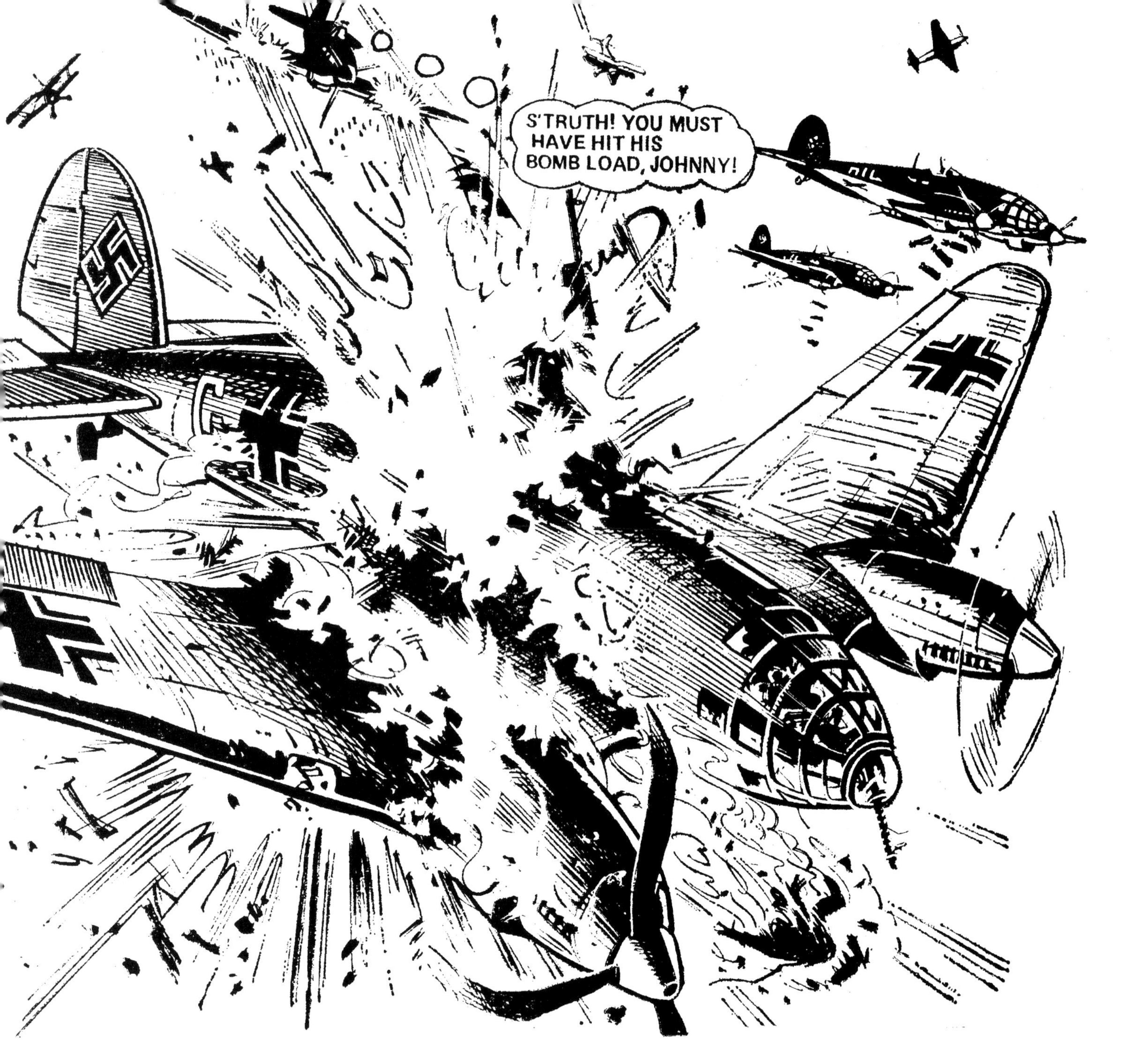
S'TRUTH! YOU MUST HAVE HIT HIS BOMB LOAD, JOHNNY!

For what might at first seem no more than a piece of 1970s juvenilia, *Johnny Red* achieves a level of historical detail that I still find remarkable today. The strip seldom shirks from depicting the savagery of warfare on the Russian Front; Colquhoun gives us scene after scene of pulverising destruction, as populations are obliterated, towns and cities become dust, and whole landscapes are rendered into desolation. Communist and Fascist juggernauts are shown engaged in total war, with soldiers and civilians alike dying at a rate that reduces them to little more than offal on a slaughterhouse floor. Yet even in the midst of utter carnage, Tully finds time to highlight elements that may still seem incredible to many readers: such as Russia's women warriors, thousands of whom fought on land or in the air as bravely as any man; or the catapult-armed merchant ships that Britain put to sea for want of sufficient aircraft carriers, the pilot of the single Hurricane taking on odds of up to thirty-to-one, and then – with no flight deck to return to – quite often parachuting into the icy Barents Sea in hope of naval rescue.

That said, there are aspects of the story that stretch credibility beyond the breaking point; no great surprise in a boys' adventure story of its time, perhaps, but worth mentioning when considering *Johnny Red* as history mixed with entertainment. The most obvious example is our hero's mount, the Hawker Hurricane that always took unspeakable punishment but returned to the skies again and again. The Hurricanes flown from the catapult ships were nearly all ageing Mark Ones, some even veterans of the Battle of Britain, with overhauled (not new) Merlin engines and patches aplenty. Johnny's would have been a scrapper from the start, an obsolete aircraft intended only for a one-way trip. Certainly, several thousand Hurricanes were supplied to the Russians, so replacement guns and engines would not have been a major problem – but the battered airframe would have lasted weeks, at best. Indeed, even a pristine Hurricane Mark Two was little improvement on the Soviet Rata it was intended to replace, and the British fighter's performance against the Messerschmitt 109F is perhaps best left unmentioned.

Johnny Red is one of my all-time favourite comic strips, and probably reigned supreme for a good chunk of 1978–80. I liked seeing the Falcons at the end of yet another mission, trudging away from their bullet-holed aircraft with their parachute packs slung over their shoulders. I liked Nina and her Angels of Death, flying deathtrap biplanes over and sometimes through the streets of bombed-out Stalingrad. I liked Johnny himself, his working-class manner and permanently grubby appearance a departure from the jolly-good-show toffs who had inhabited the fighter pilot stories I'd read up to that point. And most of all, I liked the Hurricane. Even at nine or ten I suspected something was amiss – *no* aircraft could survive such treatment – but I didn't mind. The old Hurri always looked so good, instantly recognisable at the head of all those soulless Yaks[1] and LaGGs[2], the RAF roundels as distinctive as the falcon symbol painted just beneath her cockpit.

I didn't mind then and I don't mind now. The indestructible Hurricane is more a source of gentle amusement than a major historical gaffe. At least for the first few years of its run, I think *Johnny Red* got more things right than it did wrong, testament to Tom Tully's depth of research and Joe Colquhoun's magnificent artwork. The episodes you're about to read have lain dormant for over thirty years, lost in limbo without hope of being reprinted before now. I for one am delighted to see them again; Johnny's story is not just one of my favourites but a British comics classic, instantly recognisable to the generation that read *Battle*. We know that Hurricane on sight, we know its scruffy Scouser of a pilot, we know his snarl of "Straight in and no messing" means that several German airmen won't be going home.

★ ★ ★

You're waiting to die at the top of the world. The night grows colder by the minute, and you pull your jacket tighter, turn to head inside. And that's when you hear it. Faint at first but growing louder, carried on the wind: an aircraft engine, coming from the north. You don't recognise the make, no more than you do the knife-edge silhouette that swims from the darkness just above the pines. You call to your friends as you watch the intruder's undercarriage drop and lock, realise this mystery 'plane is coming in to land. It's not a '109, nor does it resemble the Falcon Squadron relics dispersed along the runway. No, you still don't know the type. But you know what it is.

A *fighter*.

Garth Ennis

New York City, January 2010

Garth Ennis is the Eisner Award-winning creator of *The Boys*, *Preacher*, *Hitman* and more. He is also renowned on both sides of the Atlantic for his outstanding war comics, including DC/Vertigo's *War Stories* and his current series, *Battlefields*, for Dynamite Entertainment.

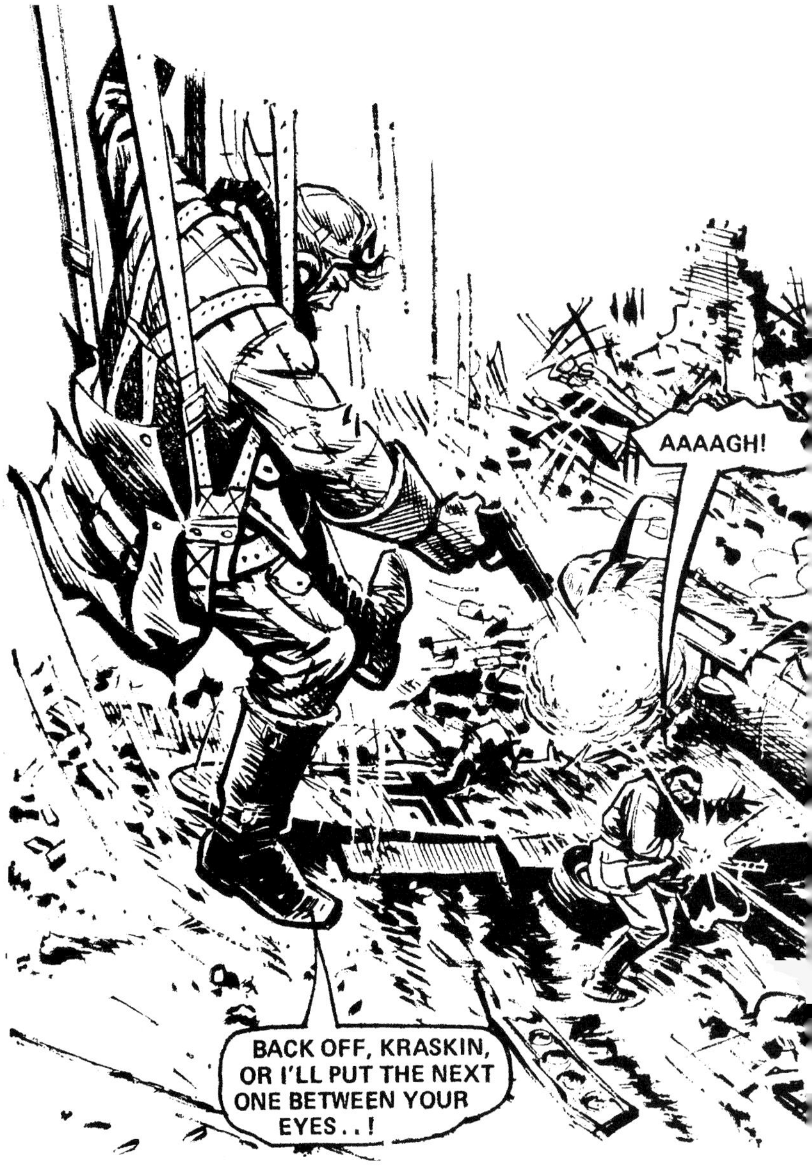
AAAAGH!
BACK OFF, KRASKIN, OR I'LL PUT THE NEXT ONE BETWEEN YOUR EYES..!

1 The "Yak" series was made by A.S. Yakovlev Design Bureau JSC.

2 The "LaGG" refers to manufacturer Lavochkin-Gorbunov-Goudkov.

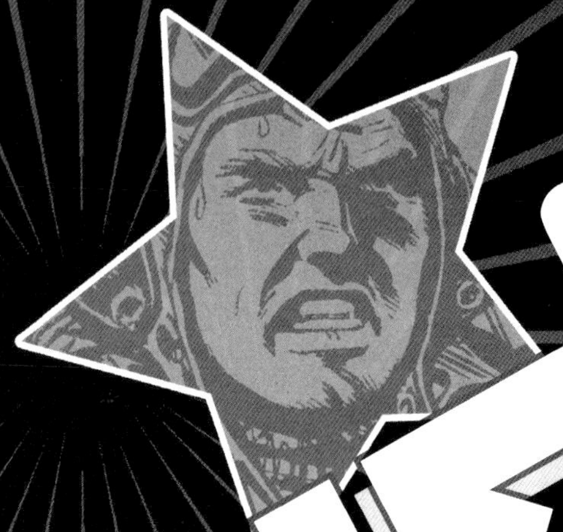

GENESIS OF A HERO

JEREMY BRIGGS

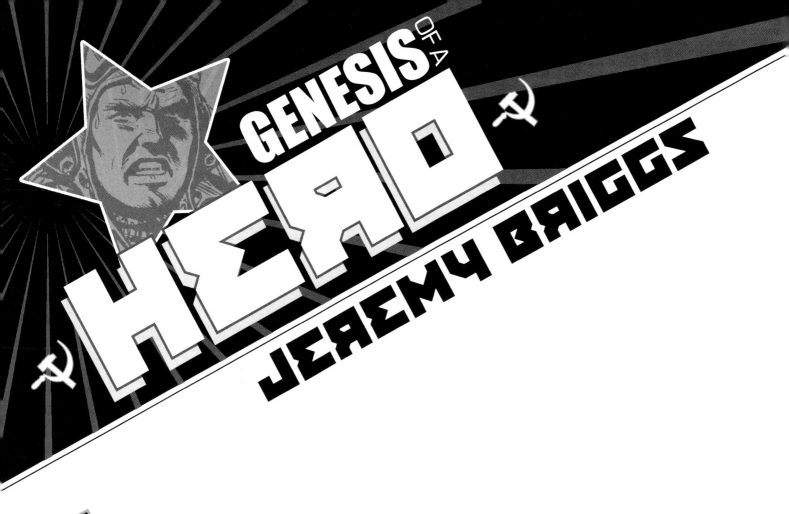

Battle Picture Weekly was first published in March 1975 as publisher IPC's reaction to DC Thomson's popular *Warlord* comic. With seven ongoing stories in each issue plus factual features, the comic, as its title suggests, was devoted exclusively to stories of combat. IPC merged the failing *Valiant* comic with it in October 1976 to create *Battle Picture Weekly and Valiant*, and it was into this combined title that the British pilot Johnny "Red" Redburn was introduced in January 1977, as part of an overhaul of stories for the comic's hundredth issue.

Johnny Red was created by two comic industry veterans: artist Joe Colquhoun and writer Tom Tully. Colquhoun was the original artist on *Roy of the Rovers* when it began in *Tiger* in 1954 and even took over the writing of the strip for four years. By the 1960s, he was illustrating the adventures of fighter pilot Paddy Payne in *Lion*, and in the 1970s he drew *Soldier Sharp: The Rat of the Rifles* for *Valiant*. This World War II strip continued in *Battle* when it was merged with *Valiant*, and Colquhoun moved over to *Johnny Red* when that strip ended. He continued to work on the strip for two years, before moving on to begin *Battle*'s new World War I strip, *Charley's War*.

In the 1960s, Tom Tully wrote *The Steel Claw* in *Valiant* and *Roy of the Rovers* in *Tiger*, while in the 1970s he wrote *Harlem Heroes* in *2000AD* and continued *Roy of the Rovers* through to its conclusion in 1993.

While *Johnny Red* is largely fictional, it draws on the plight of the Soviet Union and its people during World War II, and its hero is inspired by a real-life Royal Air Force pilot assigned to protect Britain's ships from German attack.

On 18 September 1942, on board the Catapult Armed Merchantmen SS *Empire Morn*, steaming between Loch Ewe, Scotland and Arkangel, in the Soviet Union, Flying Officer Arthur Henry Burr of the Royal Air Force Volunteer Reserve was strapped into the seat of his Hawker Sea Hurricane Mark 1A. At approximately 1150 hours local time, as the *Empire Morn* crested a wave, the ship's firing officer pressed his button and the thirteen rockets strapped to Burr's Hurricane burst into fiery life.

With its engine roaring and a tail of flame longer than the aircraft itself, the Hurricane was thrust forward down the seventy-five-foot-long launch ramp and climbed into the air at just seventy knots. Banking violently to avoid the cables of the barrage balloons attached to other ships in Allied Convoy PQ-18 somewhere in the Barents Sea, and some 'friendly' anti-aircraft fire directed at him, Burr could see the fifteen Heinkel He-111 torpedo bombers that were only three miles away. The German planes had formed into a line abreast attack formation and were flying at an altitude of only fifty feet above the waves towards the convoy. Burr turned his plane to attack.

At this point in World War II, aircraft carriers were in short supply. The big fleet carriers were too valuable to be used for convoy protection and the small escort carriers that were designed for the task were only just being commissioned. The Catapult Armed Merchantmen (CAM) were a stop-gap attempt to give Allied convoys at least some fighter cover.

These CAM ships were civilian freighters built for the Department of War Transport that, in addition to their cargoes, carried a single Hurricane fighter of the RAF's Merchant Ship Fighter Unit, formed on 5 May 1941. The MSFU was based at RAF Speke, now better known as Liverpool's John Lennon Airport, where the volunteer pilots were trained to fly their modified Hurricanes off the rocket-propelled catapult mechanism that was attached to the bow of the CAM ships. During training, the pilots were able to land their aircraft back at the airfield – but during a combat launch in the middle of the ocean there was no such option, as the plane could not land back on its mother ship.

Over the Barents Sea, Arthur Burr climbed to 700 feet, lined his Hurricane up on one of the oncoming bombers and dived on it, opening fire when he was at a range of 300 yards. He saw white smoke coming from the plane's starboard engine as his machine gun bullets bit into it. Banking away after this initial attack, he returned to finish off the bomber with the rest of his limited ammunition supply.

By this time, the Heinkels were in range of the convoy's anti-aircraft fire and Burr broke off his attack in time to see the wreckage of one of them in the sea as the ships took on the rest of the bomber formation. As well as shooting down one of the German aircraft his attack had forced another out of formation and, in trying to manoeuvre at too low an altitude, it too crashed into the sea.

With his ammunition finished and the Heinkel attack dispersed, Burr maintained position near the convoy in his Hurricane until it was apparent that no further coordinated attacks were forthcoming. Then he asked his shipboard colleagues where the nearest aerodrome was; perhaps to his dismay, they told him that it was some 240 miles due south.

Burr now had three options: parachute out of his plane and await pickup in the icy water; crash land his plane on the ocean and hope to clamber out before it sank and again await pickup, considered a very dangerous option; or attempt to fly to that distant Soviet aerodrome. With seventy gallons of fuel remaining, he decided to make for

Below: Johnny in action against German anti-tank units on the Eastern Front.

THE NAME'S JOHNNY 'RED' REDBURN, KRAUT! I'M FIGHTING WITH THE RUSSIANS BECAUSE MY OWN PEOPLE HAVE PUT A PRICE ON MY HEAD!

land – which was perhaps no surprise, considering the grisly fate of another CAM pilot, just six months earlier.

During the period the MSFU operated – just over two years, until there were enough escort carriers available that its services were no longer required – a total of nine combat launches took place, including Burr's. The unit shot down eight enemy aircraft and chased off others thanks to their presence. Of the nine combat launches, all made by different pilots, just one, twenty-one-year-old Welsh Pilot Officer John Bedford Kendal, died before being recovered.

On 25 May 1942, Kendal was launched as protection for Arctic convoy QP12, shooting down a Junkers Ju-88 bomber and chasing off a Blohm and Voss BV138 reconnaissance aircraft before dying of injuries sustained when he bailed out into the sea. Kendal's Hurricane had been launched from the SS *Empire Morn*, the same ship Burr was launched from – and the only CAM ship to perform two combat launches. His death could well have been a factor in Burr's decision to attempt to save his plane by making for a distant aerodrome – the least dangerous option available to him.

Fifteen minutes after turning south, Burr ran into a forty-mile-wide fogbank but despite this he managed to make landfall and pinpoint his position, allowing him to find the port of Arkangel and its Keg Ostov aerodrome. There, he fired his recognition flare to avoid being attacked and finally landed safely after almost two-and-a-half hours in the air, landing with just five gallons of fuel left in his reserve tank.

Convoy PQ18 from Britain to Russia lost thirteen of its forty-four merchant ships to German bombers and U-boats, but the SS *Empire Morn* survived all the attacks and entered the port of Arkangel three days later. Burr's Hurricane was taken to the port and reloaded onto the ship's catapult system. In saving his aircraft, he had provided the next convoy with fighter cover and was awarded the Distinguished Flying Cross on 30 October 1942 for his actions.

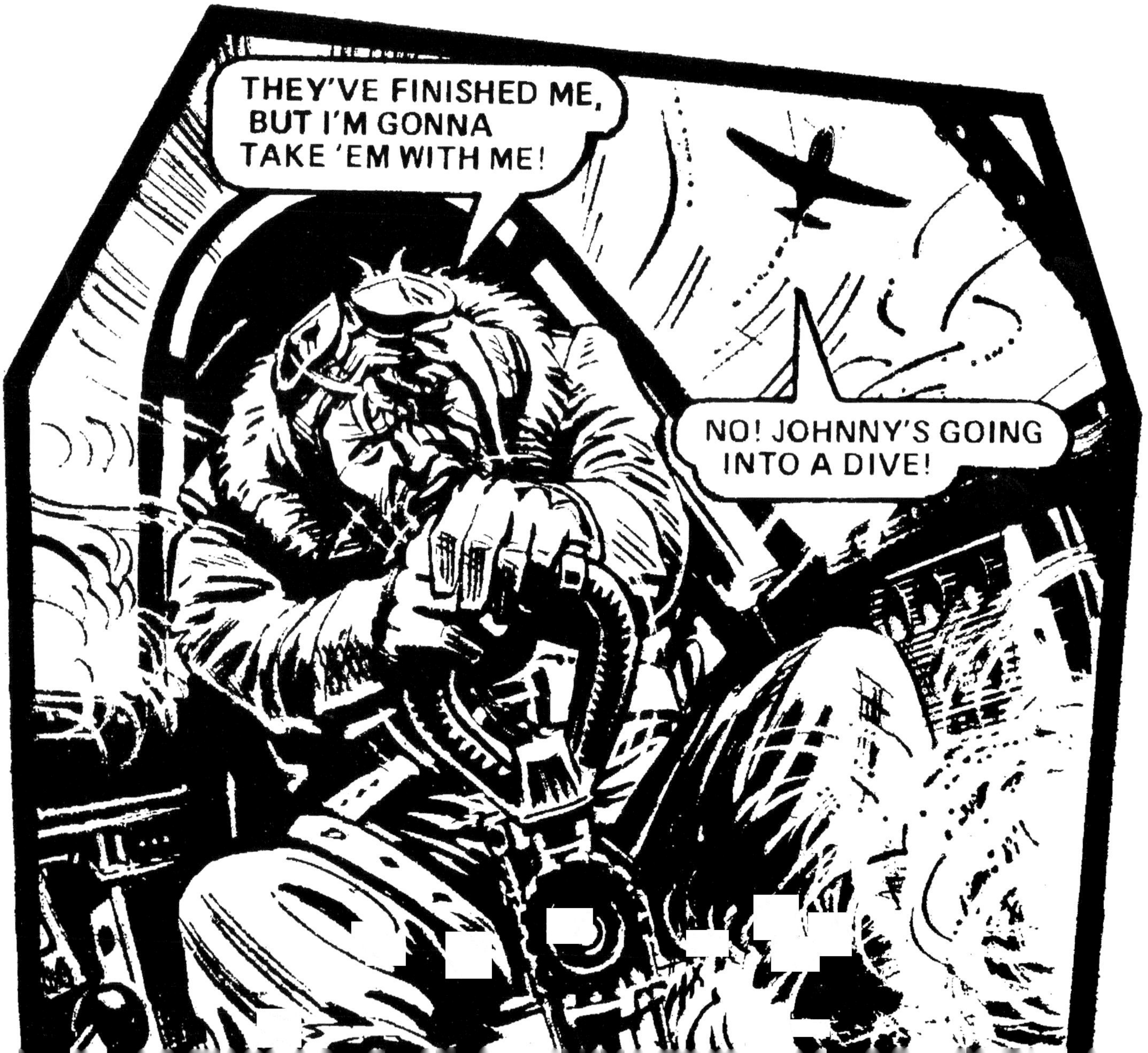
THEY'VE FINISHED ME, BUT I'M GONNA TAKE 'EM WITH ME!
NO! JOHNNY'S GOING INTO A DIVE!

British pilots also flew Hurricanes in the Soviet Union, for a short while at least. In the immediate aftermath of the 1941 Nazi invasion, Britain and Canada began to ship over 3,000 Hawker Hurricane fighters to the Soviet Air Force. To help defend the Kola Peninsula area, which included the strategic port of Murmansk, the RAF also formed 151 Wing, consisting of No. 81 and 134 Squadrons, to operate as a training unit. Their first Hurricanes arrived at Murmansk's Vianga airfield in August 1941, and the Wing remained there for three months defending the region from German attacks and training Soviet pilots.

In November 1941 they handed their remaining aircraft over to their Soviet hosts and returned to Britain. Within a year, the Soviet Air Force had twenty-nine fighter regiments equipped with Hurricanes in the fighter and ground attack roles.

The RAF's 151 Wing were not the only Western pilots to fly in defence of the Soviet Union. Free-French leader General de Gaulle wanted his forces to serve on all fronts during the war and so Fighter Group 3, named Normandie, was formed and dispatched to the Eastern Front to fly Soviet fighters under Soviet markings. The Group entered combat in March 1943 and would eventually shoot down 273 enemy aircraft. For their courageous part in the fighting around the Nieman River on the Soviet–German border in 1944, Soviet Leader Joseph Stalin ordered the Group to add Niemen to its name.

The highest scoring ace of Normandie-Niemen was Marcel Albert, who scored twenty-one of his twenty-three aerial victories flying Soviet Yak-3 and Yak-9 fighters. Like Johnny Red, Marcel Albert was a fighter pilot who rose to command a squadron on the Eastern Front and, also like Johnny, the Soviet Union decorated him for his actions in defence of the Motherland. After the war Albert moved to the United States and in November 2009 was made a Grand Officer of the French Legion d'Honneur when he was ninety-two years old.

Despite there being only nine combat launches, the CAM ships and their catapult Hurricanes, nicknamed 'Hurricats', have been a favourite of war writers over the years. In addition to *Johnny Red*, they have appeared in many British comic strips from digests like *Commando* to weekly comics such as *Warlord* and *Battle Picture Weekly*,

AAAAAAGH !

Left: More gritty dogfight action from superb artist Joe Colquhoun.

while writer Garth Ennis included a Hurricat tale, 'Archangel', in his *War Stories* collection.

While the decision of one pilot to try and save his Hurricane inspired the beginning of the *Johnny Red* saga, Tom Tully was able to continue it by using other ideas taken from the reality of air combat on the Eastern Front.

The story of *Johnny Red* continued in *Battle* for ten years, a long run for a strip that had been inspired by a quick decision made above the Barents Sea in 1942. The pilot who made that decision, Flying Officer Arthur Burr DFC, was promoted to Flight Lieutenant in March 1943 and went on to become an RAF flying instructor but, sadly, he did not live to see the end of the war. Killed on 25 March 1945, he is buried in the St. Leonard churchyard at Heston near London's Heathrow Airport. However, Johnny Red, the character that he inspired, continues to fly on in our imaginations.

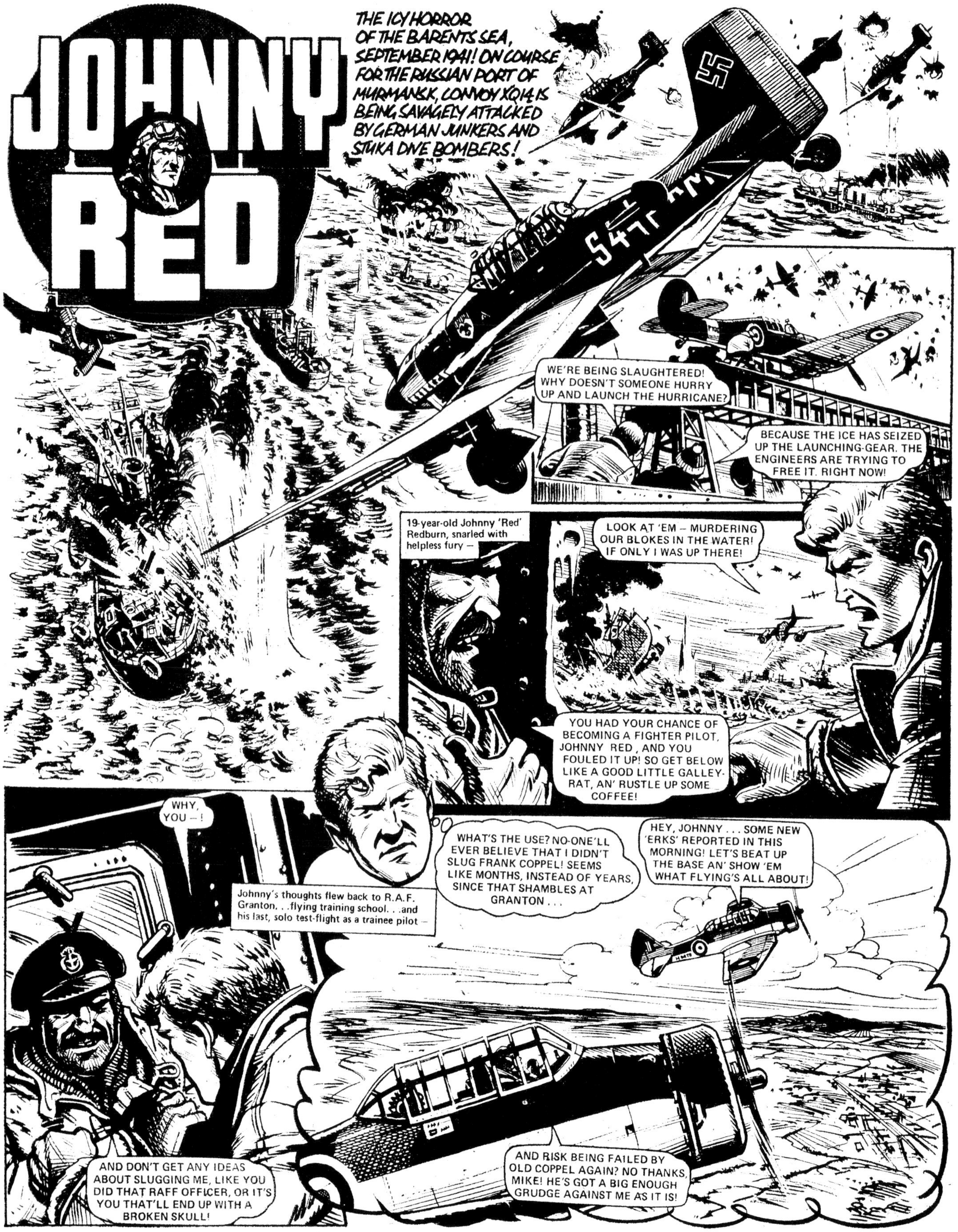
JOHNNY RED
THE ICY HORROR OF THE BARENTS SEA, SEPTEMBER 1941! ON COURSE FOR THE RUSSIAN PORT OF MURMANSK, CONVOY XQ14 IS BEING SAVAGELY ATTACKED BY GERMAN JUNKERS AND STUKA DIVE BOMBERS!
WE'RE BEING SLAUGHTERED! WHY DOESN'T SOMEONE HURRY UP AND LAUNCH THE HURRICANE?
BECAUSE THE ICE HAS SEIZED UP THE LAUNCHING-GEAR. THE ENGINEERS ARE TRYING TO FREE IT. RIGHT NOW!
19-year-old Johnny 'Red' Redburn, snarled with helpless fury –
LOOK AT 'EM – MURDERING OUR BLOKES IN THE WATER! IF ONLY I WAS UP THERE!
YOU HAD YOUR CHANCE OF BECOMING A FIGHTER PILOT, JOHNNY RED, AND YOU FOULED IT UP! SO GET BELOW LIKE A GOOD LITTLE GALLEY-RAT, AN' RUSTLE UP SOME COFFEE!
WHY, YOU –!
AND DON'T GET ANY IDEAS ABOUT SLUGGING ME, LIKE YOU DID THAT RAFF OFFICER, OR IT'S YOU THAT'LL END UP WITH A BROKEN SKULL!
WHAT'S THE USE? NO-ONE'LL EVER BELIEVE THAT I DIDN'T SLUG FRANK COPPEL! SEEMS LIKE MONTHS, INSTEAD OF YEARS, SINCE THAT SHAMBLES AT GRANTON . . .
Johnny's thoughts flew back to R.A.F. Granton. . .flying training school. . .and his last, solo test-flight as a trainee pilot –
HEY, JOHNNY . . . SOME NEW 'ERKS' REPORTED IN THIS MORNING! LET'S BEAT UP THE BASE AN' SHOW 'EM WHAT FLYING'S ALL ABOUT!
AND RISK BEING FAILED BY OLD COPPEL AGAIN? NO THANKS, MIKE! HE'S GOT A BIG ENOUGH GRUDGE AGAINST ME AS IT IS!

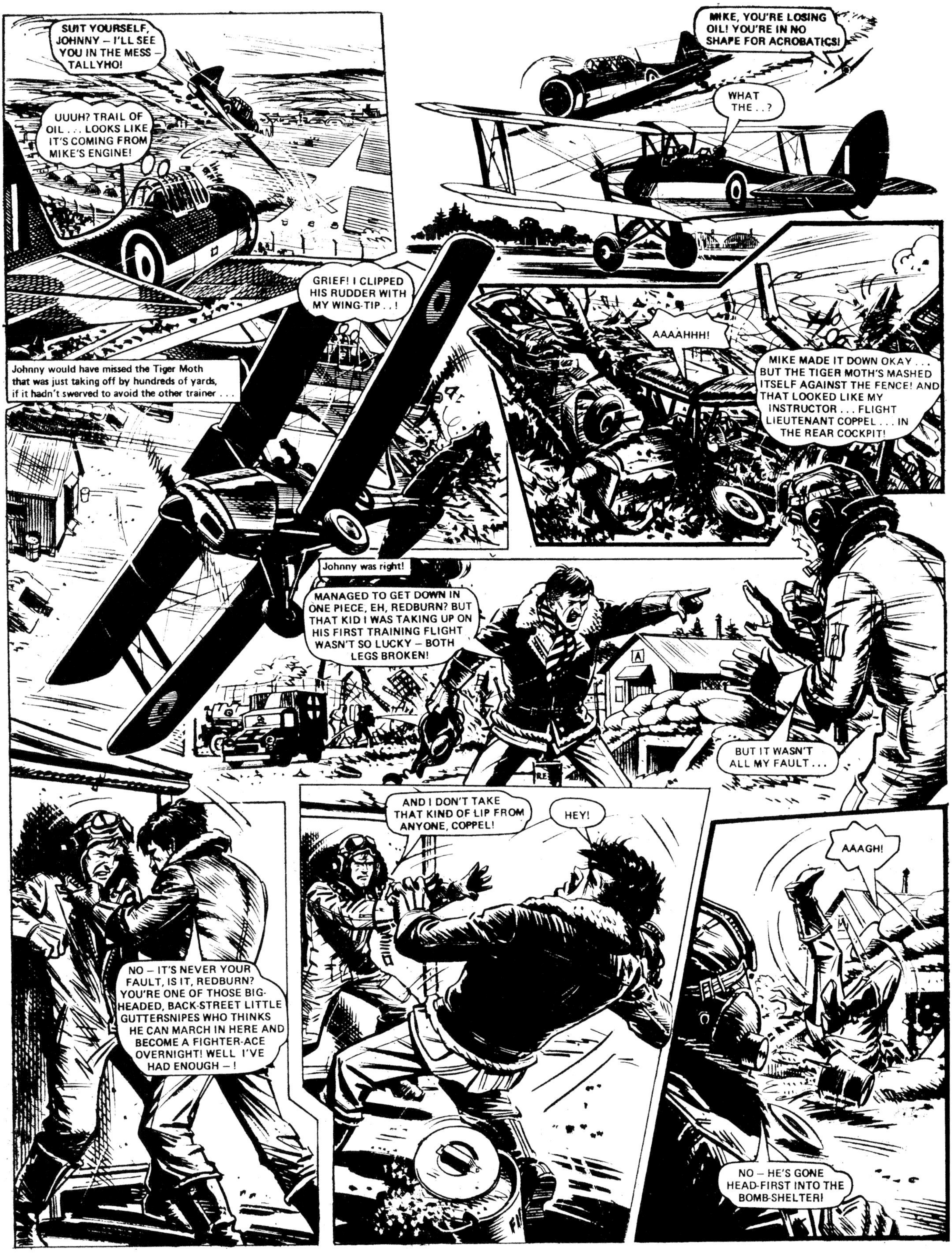

SUIT YOURSELF, JOHNNY – I'LL SEE YOU IN THE MESS – TALLYHO!
UUUH? TRAIL OF OIL . . . LOOKS LIKE IT'S COMING FROM MIKE'S ENGINE!
MIKE, YOU'RE LOSING OIL! YOU'RE IN NO SHAPE FOR ACROBATICS!
WHAT THE . . ?
Johnny would have missed the Tiger Moth that was just taking off by hundreds of yards, if it hadn't swerved to avoid the other trainer . . .
GRIEF! I CLIPPED HIS RUDDER WITH MY WING-TIP . . !
AAAAHHH!
MIKE MADE IT DOWN OKAY . . . BUT THE TIGER MOTH'S MASHED ITSELF AGAINST THE FENCE! AND THAT LOOKED LIKE MY INSTRUCTOR . . . FLIGHT LIEUTENANT COPPEL . . . IN THE REAR COCKPIT!
Johnny was right!
MANAGED TO GET DOWN IN ONE PIECE, EH, REDBURN? BUT THAT KID I WAS TAKING UP ON HIS FIRST TRAINING FLIGHT WASN'T SO LUCKY – BOTH LEGS BROKEN!
BUT IT WASN'T ALL MY FAULT . . .
NO – IT'S NEVER YOUR FAULT, IS IT, REDBURN? YOU'RE ONE OF THOSE BIG-HEADED, BACK-STREET LITTLE GUTTERSNIPES WHO THINKS HE CAN MARCH IN HERE AND BECOME A FIGHTER-ACE OVERNIGHT! WELL I'VE HAD ENOUGH – !
AND I DON'T TAKE THAT KIND OF LIP FROM ANYONE, COPPEL!
HEY!
AAAGH!
NO – HE'S GONE HEAD-FIRST INTO THE BOMB-SHELTER!

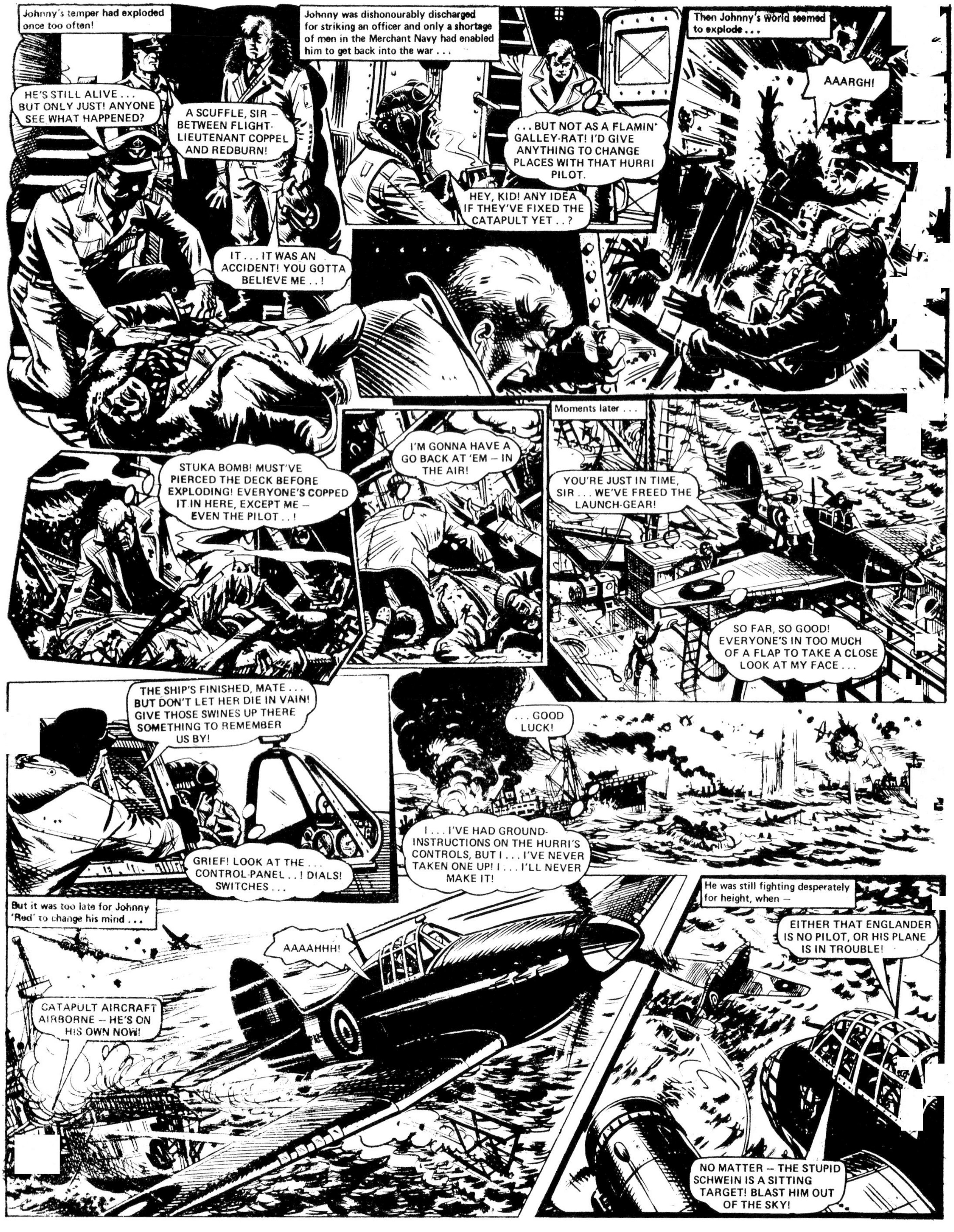

Johnny's temper had exploded once too often!
HE'S STILL ALIVE . . . BUT ONLY JUST! ANYONE SEE WHAT HAPPENED?
A SCUFFLE, SIR – BETWEEN FLIGHT-LIEUTENANT COPPEL AND REDBURN!
IT . . . IT WAS AN ACCIDENT! YOU GOTTA BELIEVE ME . . !
Johnny was dishonourably discharged for striking an officer and only a shortage of men in the Merchant Navy had enabled him to get back into the war . . .
. . . BUT NOT AS A FLAMIN' GALLEY-RAT! I'D GIVE ANYTHING TO CHANGE PLACES WITH THAT HURRI PILOT.
HEY, KID! ANY IDEA IF THEY'VE FIXED THE CATAPULT YET . . ?
Then Johnny's world seemed to explode . . .
AAARGH!
STUKA BOMB! MUST'VE PIERCED THE DECK BEFORE EXPLODING! EVERYONE'S COPPED IT IN HERE, EXCEPT ME – EVEN THE PILOT . . !
I'M GONNA HAVE A GO BACK AT 'EM – IN THE AIR!
Moments later . . .
YOU'RE JUST IN TIME, SIR . . . WE'VE FREED THE LAUNCH-GEAR!
SO FAR, SO GOOD! EVERYONE'S IN TOO MUCH OF A FLAP TO TAKE A CLOSE LOOK AT MY FACE . . .
THE SHIP'S FINISHED, MATE . . . BUT DON'T LET HER DIE IN VAIN! GIVE THOSE SWINES UP THERE SOMETHING TO REMEMBER US BY!
GRIEF! LOOK AT THE . . . CONTROL-PANEL . . ! DIALS! SWITCHES . . .
. . . GOOD LUCK!
I . . . I'VE HAD GROUND-INSTRUCTIONS ON THE HURRI'S CONTROLS, BUT I . . . I'VE NEVER TAKEN ONE UP! I . . . I'LL NEVER MAKE IT!
But it was too late for Johnny 'Red' to change his mind . . .
AAAAHHH!
CATAPULT AIRCRAFT AIRBORNE – HE'S ON HIS OWN NOW!
He was still fighting desperately for height, when –
EITHER THAT ENGLANDER IS NO PILOT, OR HIS PLANE IS IN TROUBLE!
NO MATTER – THE STUPID SCHWEIN IS A SITTING TARGET! BLAST HIM OUT OF THE SKY!

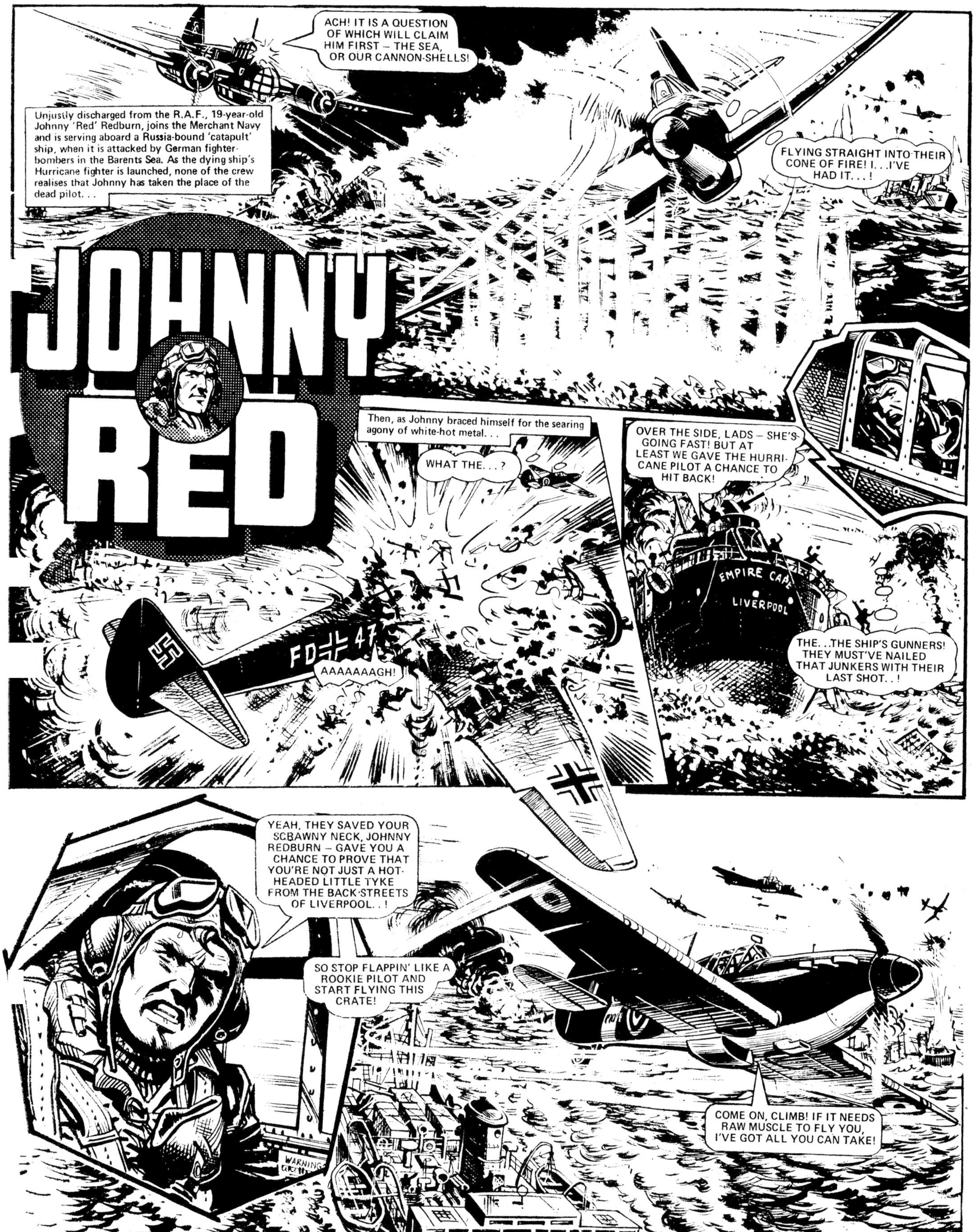

ACH! IT IS A QUESTION OF WHICH WILL CLAIM HIM FIRST – THE SEA, OR OUR CANNON-SHELLS!
Unjustly discharged from the R.A.F., 19-year-old Johnny 'Red' Redburn, joins the Merchant Navy and is serving aboard a Russia-bound 'catapult' ship, when it is attacked by German fighter-bombers in the Barents Sea. As the dying ship's Hurricane fighter is launched, none of the crew realises that Johnny has taken the place of the dead pilot. . .
FLYING STRAIGHT INTO THEIR CONE OF FIRE! I. . .I'VE HAD IT. . . !
JOHNNY RED
Then, as Johnny braced himself for the searing agony of white-hot metal. . .
WHAT THE. . . ?
FD 47
AAAAAAAGH!
OVER THE SIDE, LADS – SHE'S GOING FAST! BUT AT LEAST WE GAVE THE HURRICANE PILOT A CHANCE TO HIT BACK!
EMPIRE CAPE
LIVERPOOL
THE. . .THE SHIP'S GUNNERS! THEY MUST'VE NAILED THAT JUNKERS WITH THEIR LAST SHOT. . !
YEAH, THEY SAVED YOUR SCRAWNY NECK, JOHNNY REDBURN – GAVE YOU A CHANCE TO PROVE THAT YOU'RE NOT JUST A HOT-HEADED LITTLE TYKE FROM THE BACK-STREETS OF LIVERPOOL. . !
SO STOP FLAPPIN' LIKE A ROOKIE PILOT AND START FLYING THIS CRATE!
COME ON, CLIMB! IF IT NEEDS RAW MUSCLE TO FLY YOU, I'VE GOT ALL YOU CAN TAKE!

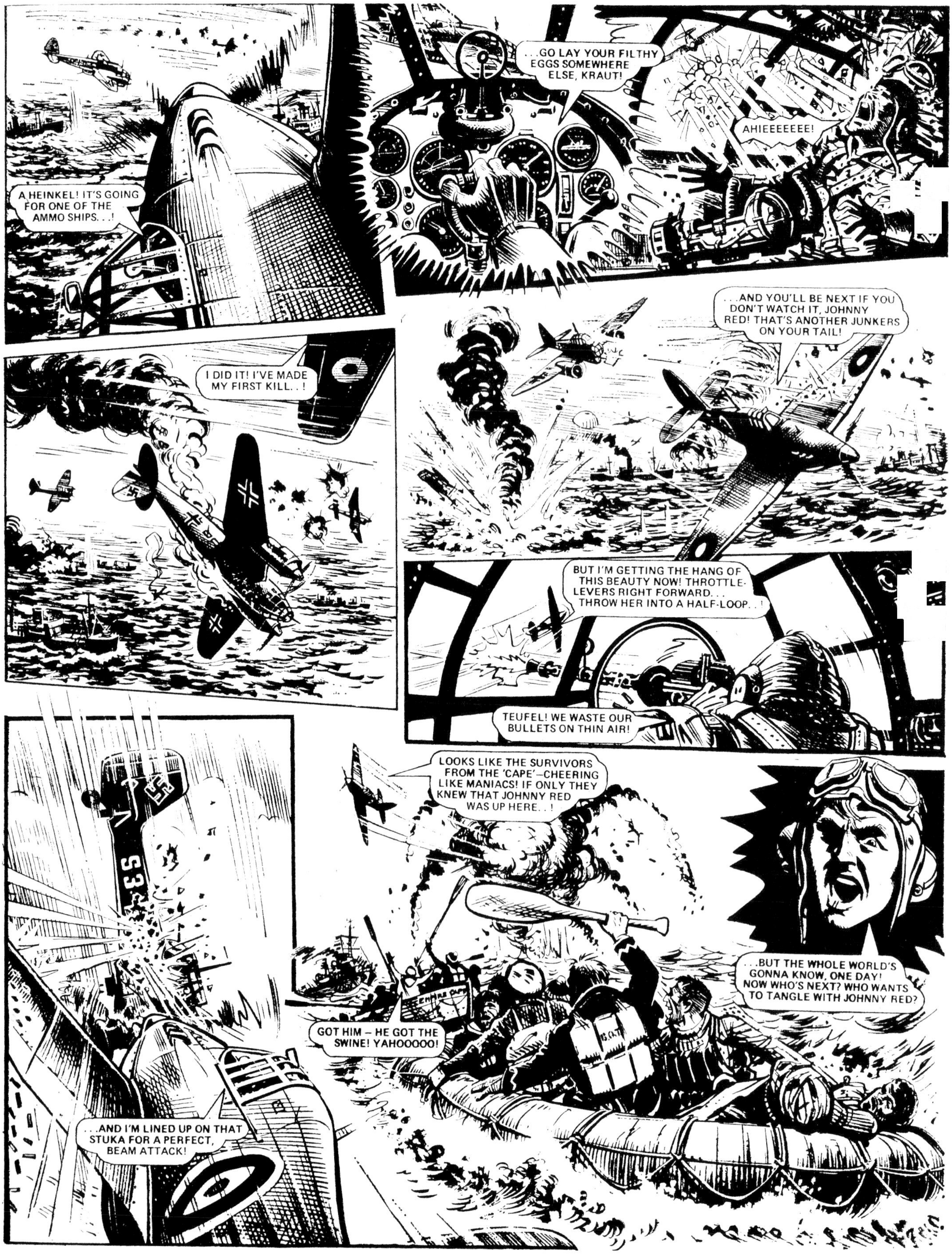
A HEINKEL! IT'S GOING FOR ONE OF THE AMMO SHIPS. . .!
. . .GO LAY YOUR FILTHY EGGS SOMEWHERE ELSE, KRAUT!
AHIEEEEEEE!
I DID IT! I'VE MADE MY FIRST KILL. . !
. . .AND YOU'LL BE NEXT IF YOU DON'T WATCH IT, JOHNNY RED! THAT'S ANOTHER JUNKERS ON YOUR TAIL!
BUT I'M GETTING THE HANG OF THIS BEAUTY NOW! THROTTLE-LEVERS RIGHT FORWARD. . . THROW HER INTO A HALF-LOOP. . !
TEUFEL! WE WASTE OUR BULLETS ON THIN AIR!
. . .AND I'M LINED UP ON THAT STUKA FOR A PERFECT, BEAM ATTACK!
GOT HIM – HE GOT THE SWINE! YAHOOOOO!
LOOKS LIKE THE SURVIVORS FROM THE 'CAPE'–CHEERING LIKE MANIACS! IF ONLY THEY KNEW THAT JOHNNY RED WAS UP HERE. . !
. . .BUT THE WHOLE WORLD'S GONNA KNOW, ONE DAY! NOW WHO'S NEXT? WHO WANTS TO TANGLE WITH JOHNNY RED?

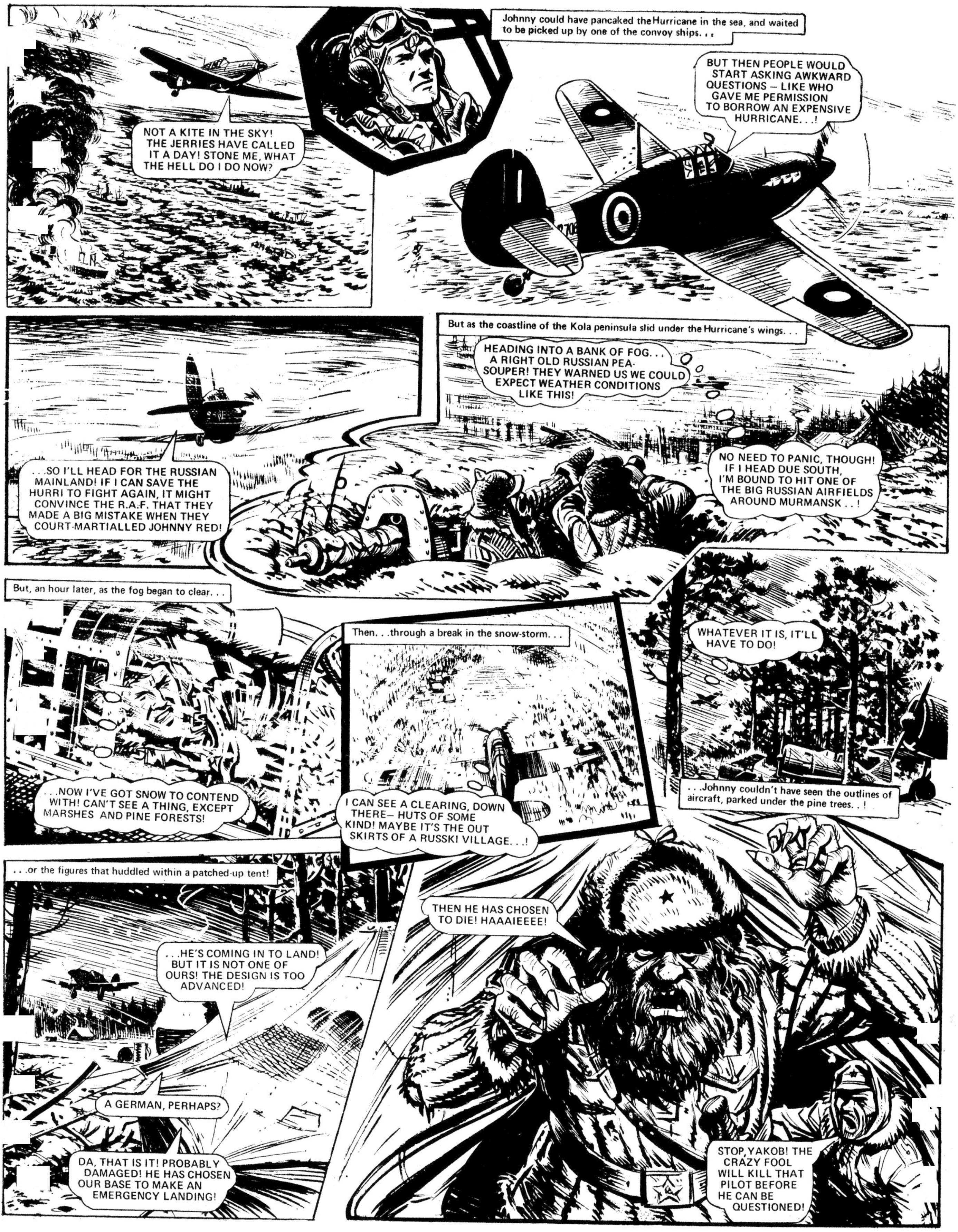
NOT A KITE IN THE SKY! THE JERRIES HAVE CALLED IT A DAY! STONE ME, WHAT THE HELL DO I DO NOW?
Johnny could have pancaked the Hurricane in the sea, and waited to be picked up by one of the convoy ships. . .
BUT THEN PEOPLE WOULD START ASKING AWKWARD QUESTIONS — LIKE WHO GAVE ME PERMISSION TO BORROW AN EXPENSIVE HURRICANE. . .!
. . .SO I'LL HEAD FOR THE RUSSIAN MAINLAND! IF I CAN SAVE THE HURRI TO FIGHT AGAIN, IT MIGHT CONVINCE THE R.A.F. THAT THEY MADE A BIG MISTAKE WHEN THEY COURT-MARTIALLED JOHNNY RED!
But as the coastline of the Kola peninsula slid under the Hurricane's wings. . .
HEADING INTO A BANK OF FOG. . . A RIGHT OLD RUSSIAN PEA-SOUPER! THEY WARNED US WE COULD EXPECT WEATHER CONDITIONS LIKE THIS!
NO NEED TO PANIC, THOUGH! IF I HEAD DUE SOUTH, I'M BOUND TO HIT ONE OF THE BIG RUSSIAN AIRFIELDS AROUND MURMANSK . .!
But, an hour later, as the fog began to clear. . .
. . .NOW I'VE GOT SNOW TO CONTEND WITH! CAN'T SEE A THING, EXCEPT MARSHES AND PINE FORESTS!
Then. . .through a break in the snow-storm. . .
I CAN SEE A CLEARING, DOWN THERE— HUTS OF SOME KIND! MAYBE IT'S THE OUT SKIRTS OF A RUSSKI VILLAGE. . .!
WHATEVER IT IS, IT'LL HAVE TO DO!
. . .Johnny couldn't have seen the outlines of aircraft, parked under the pine trees. . !
. . .or the figures that huddled within a patched-up tent!
. . .HE'S COMING IN TO LAND! BUT IT IS NOT ONE OF OURS! THE DESIGN IS TOO ADVANCED!
A GERMAN, PERHAPS?
DA, THAT IS IT! PROBABLY DAMAGED! HE HAS CHOSEN OUR BASE TO MAKE AN EMERGENCY LANDING!
THEN HE HAS CHOSEN TO DIE! HAAAIEEEE!
STOP, YAKOB! THE CRAZY FOOL WILL KILL THAT PILOT BEFORE HE CAN BE QUESTIONED!

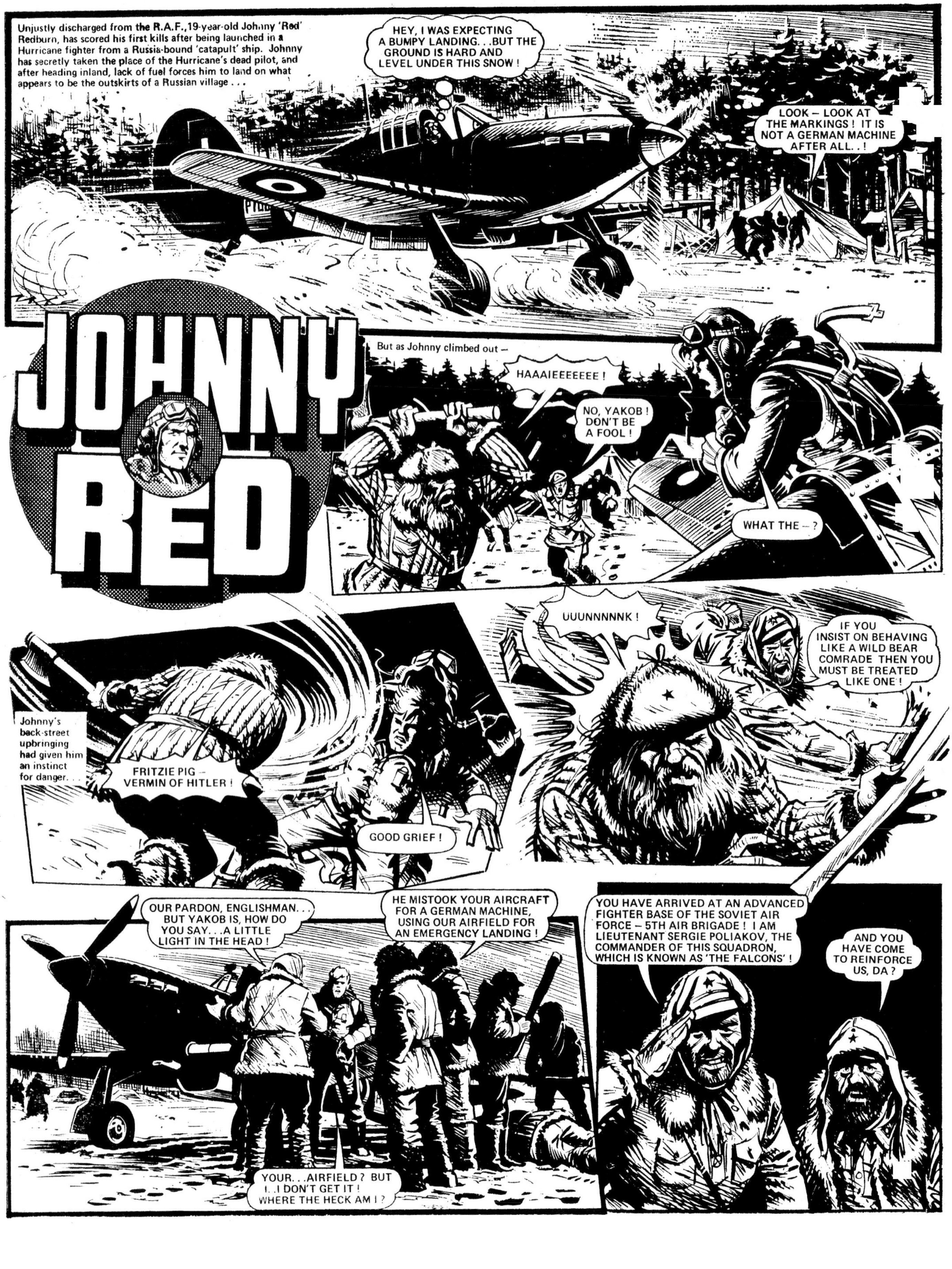

Unjustly discharged from the R.A.F., 19-year-old Johnny 'Red' Redburn, has scored his first kills after being launched in a Hurricane fighter from a Russia-bound 'catapult' ship. Johnny has secretly taken the place of the Hurricane's dead pilot, and after heading inland, lack of fuel forces him to land on what appears to be the outskirts of a Russian village . . .
HEY, I WAS EXPECTING A BUMPY LANDING. . .BUT THE GROUND IS HARD AND LEVEL UNDER THIS SNOW !
LOOK – LOOK AT THE MARKINGS ! IT IS NOT A GERMAN MACHINE AFTER ALL. . !
JOHNNY RED
But as Johnny climbed out –
HAAAIEEEEEEE !
NO, YAKOB ! DON'T BE A FOOL !
WHAT THE – ?
Johnny's back-street upbringing had given him an instinct for danger. . .
FRITZIE PIG – VERMIN OF HITLER !
GOOD GRIEF !
UUUNNNNNK !
IF YOU INSIST ON BEHAVING LIKE A WILD BEAR COMRADE THEN YOU MUST BE TREATED LIKE ONE !
OUR PARDON, ENGLISHMAN. . . BUT YAKOB IS, HOW DO YOU SAY. . .A LITTLE LIGHT IN THE HEAD !
HE MISTOOK YOUR AIRCRAFT FOR A GERMAN MACHINE, USING OUR AIRFIELD FOR AN EMERGENCY LANDING !
YOUR. . .AIRFIELD ? BUT I. . I DON'T GET IT ! WHERE THE HECK AM I ?
YOU HAVE ARRIVED AT AN ADVANCED FIGHTER BASE OF THE SOVIET AIR FORCE – 5TH AIR BRIGADE ! I AM LIEUTENANT SERGIE POLIAKOV, THE COMMANDER OF THIS SQUADRON, WHICH IS KNOWN AS 'THE FALCONS' !
AND YOU HAVE COME TO REINFORCE US, DA ?

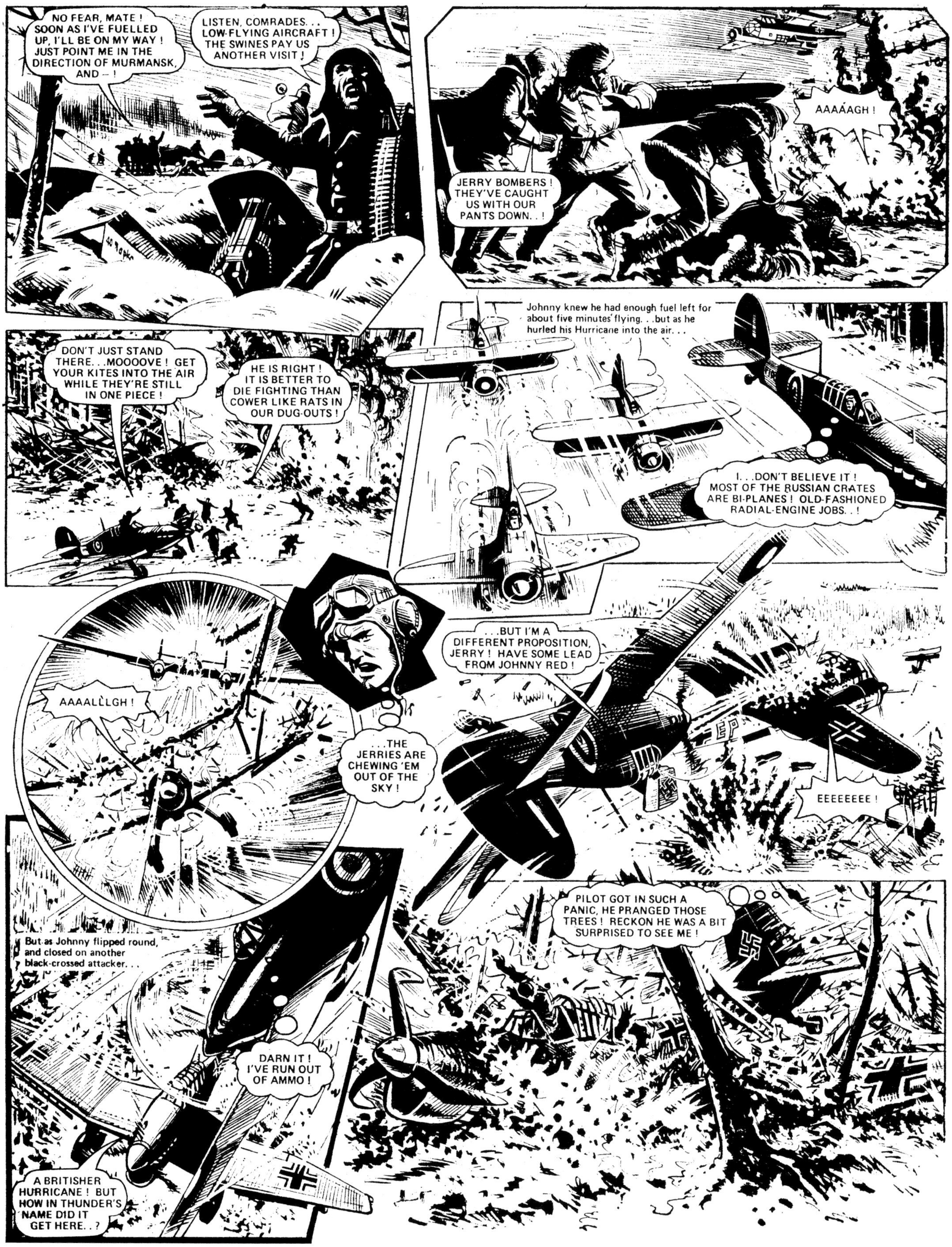
NO FEAR, MATE ! SOON AS I'VE FUELLED UP, I'LL BE ON MY WAY ! JUST POINT ME IN THE DIRECTION OF MURMANSK, AND — !
LISTEN, COMRADES. . . LOW-FLYING AIRCRAFT ! THE SWINES PAY US ANOTHER VISIT !
JERRY BOMBERS ! THEY'VE CAUGHT US WITH OUR PANTS DOWN. . !
AAAÁAGH !
DON'T JUST STAND THERE. . .MOOOOVE ! GET YOUR KITES INTO THE AIR WHILE THEY'RE STILL IN ONE PIECE !
HE IS RIGHT ! IT IS BETTER TO DIE FIGHTING THAN COWER LIKE RATS IN OUR DUG-OUTS !
Johnny knew he had enough fuel left for about five minutes' flying. . .but as he hurled his Hurricane into the air. . .
I. . .DON'T BELIEVE IT ! MOST OF THE RUSSIAN CRATES ARE BI-PLANES ! OLD-FASHIONED RADIAL-ENGINE JOBS. . !
AAAALLLGH !
. . .THE JERRIES ARE CHEWING 'EM OUT OF THE SKY !
. . .BUT I'M A DIFFERENT PROPOSITION, JERRY ! HAVE SOME LEAD FROM JOHNNY RED !
EEEEEEEE !
But as Johnny flipped round, and closed on another black-crossed attacker. . .
DARN IT ! I'VE RUN OUT OF AMMO !
A BRITISHER HURRICANE ! BUT HOW IN THUNDER'S NAME DID IT GET HERE. . ?
PILOT GOT IN SUCH A PANIC, HE PRANGED THOSE TREES ! RECKON HE WAS A BIT SURPRISED TO SEE ME !

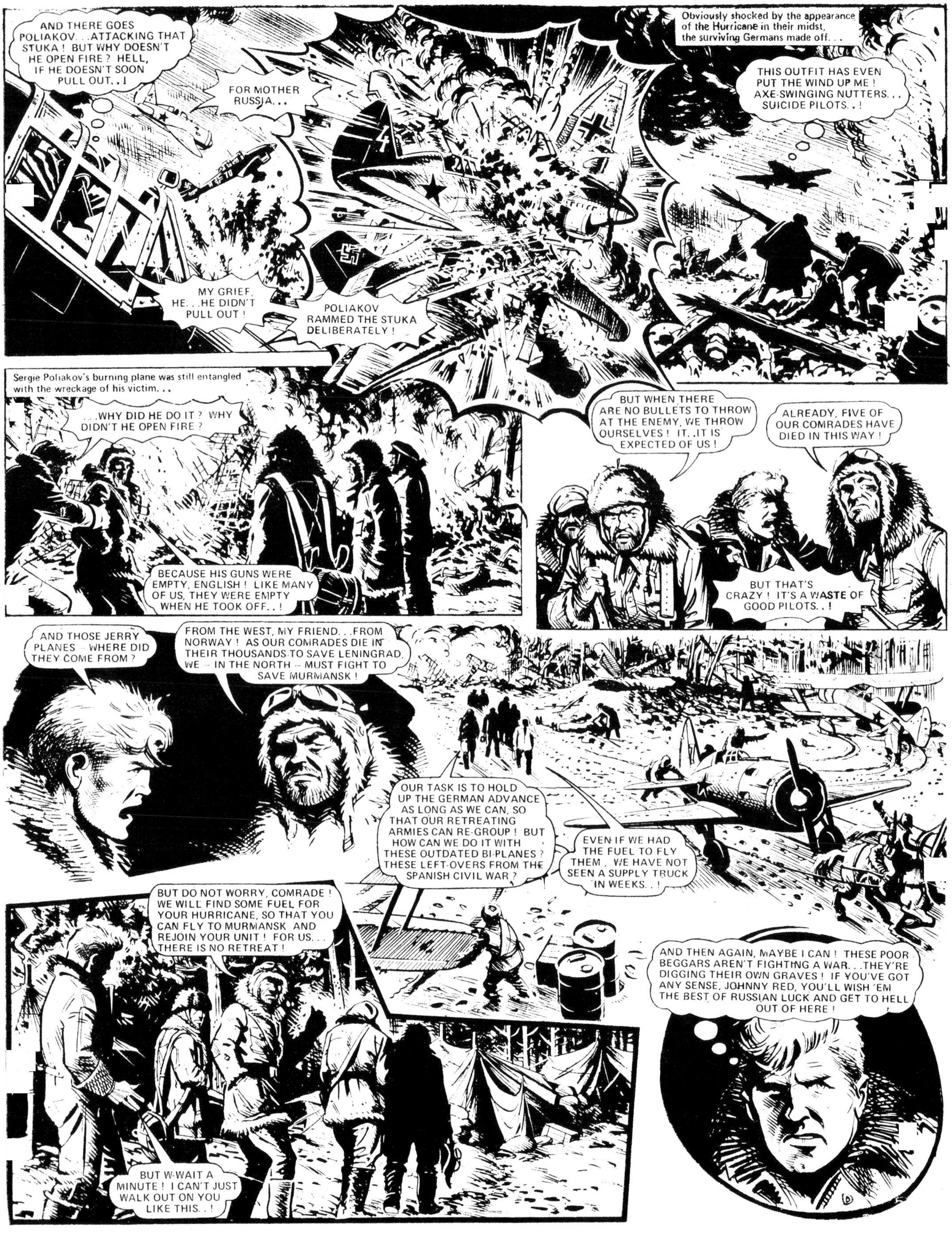
AND THERE GOES POLIAKOV. . .ATTACKING THAT STUKA ! BUT WHY DOESN'T HE OPEN FIRE ? HELL, IF HE DOESN'T SOON PULL OUT. . !
FOR MOTHER RUSSIA. . .
MY GRIEF, HE. . .HE DIDN'T PULL OUT !
POLIAKOV RAMMED THE STUKA DELIBERATELY !
Obviously shocked by the appearance of the Hurricane in their midst, the surviving Germans made off. . .
THIS OUTFIT HAS EVEN PUT THE WIND UP ME ! AXE-SWINGING NUTTERS. . . SUICIDE PILOTS. . !
Sergie Poliakov's burning plane was still entangled with the wreckage of his victim. . .
. . .WHY DID HE DO IT ? WHY DIDN'T HE OPEN FIRE ?
BECAUSE HIS GUNS WERE EMPTY, ENGLISH ! LIKE MANY OF US, THEY WERE EMPTY WHEN HE TOOK OFF. . !
BUT WHEN THERE ARE NO BULLETS TO THROW AT THE ENEMY, WE THROW OURSELVES ! IT. .IT IS EXPECTED OF US !
ALREADY, FIVE OF OUR COMRADES HAVE DIED IN THIS WAY !
BUT THAT'S CRAZY ! IT'S A WASTE OF GOOD PILOTS. . !
AND THOSE JERRY PLANES – WHERE DID THEY COME FROM ?
FROM THE WEST, MY FRIEND. . .FROM NORWAY ! AS OUR COMRADES DIE IN THEIR THOUSANDS TO SAVE LENINGRAD, WE – IN THE NORTH – MUST FIGHT TO SAVE MURMANSK !
OUR TASK IS TO HOLD UP THE GERMAN ADVANCE AS LONG AS WE CAN, SO THAT OUR RETREATING ARMIES CAN RE-GROUP ! BUT HOW CAN WE DO IT WITH THESE OUTDATED BI-PLANES ? THESE LEFT-OVERS FROM THE SPANISH CIVIL WAR ?
EVEN IF WE HAD THE FUEL TO FLY THEM, WE HAVE NOT SEEN A SUPPLY TRUCK IN WEEKS. . !
BUT DO NOT WORRY, COMRADE ! WE WILL FIND SOME FUEL FOR YOUR HURRICANE, SO THAT YOU CAN FLY TO MURMANSK AND REJOIN YOUR UNIT ! FOR US. . . THERE IS NO RETREAT !
BUT W-WAIT A MINUTE ! I CAN'T JUST WALK OUT ON YOU LIKE THIS. . !
AND THEN AGAIN, MAYBE I CAN ! THESE POOR BEGGARS AREN'T FIGHTING A WAR. . .THEY'RE DIGGING THEIR OWN GRAVES ! IF YOU'VE GOT ANY SENSE, JOHNNY RED, YOU'LL WISH 'EM THE BEST OF RUSSIAN LUCK AND GET TO HELL OUT OF HERE !

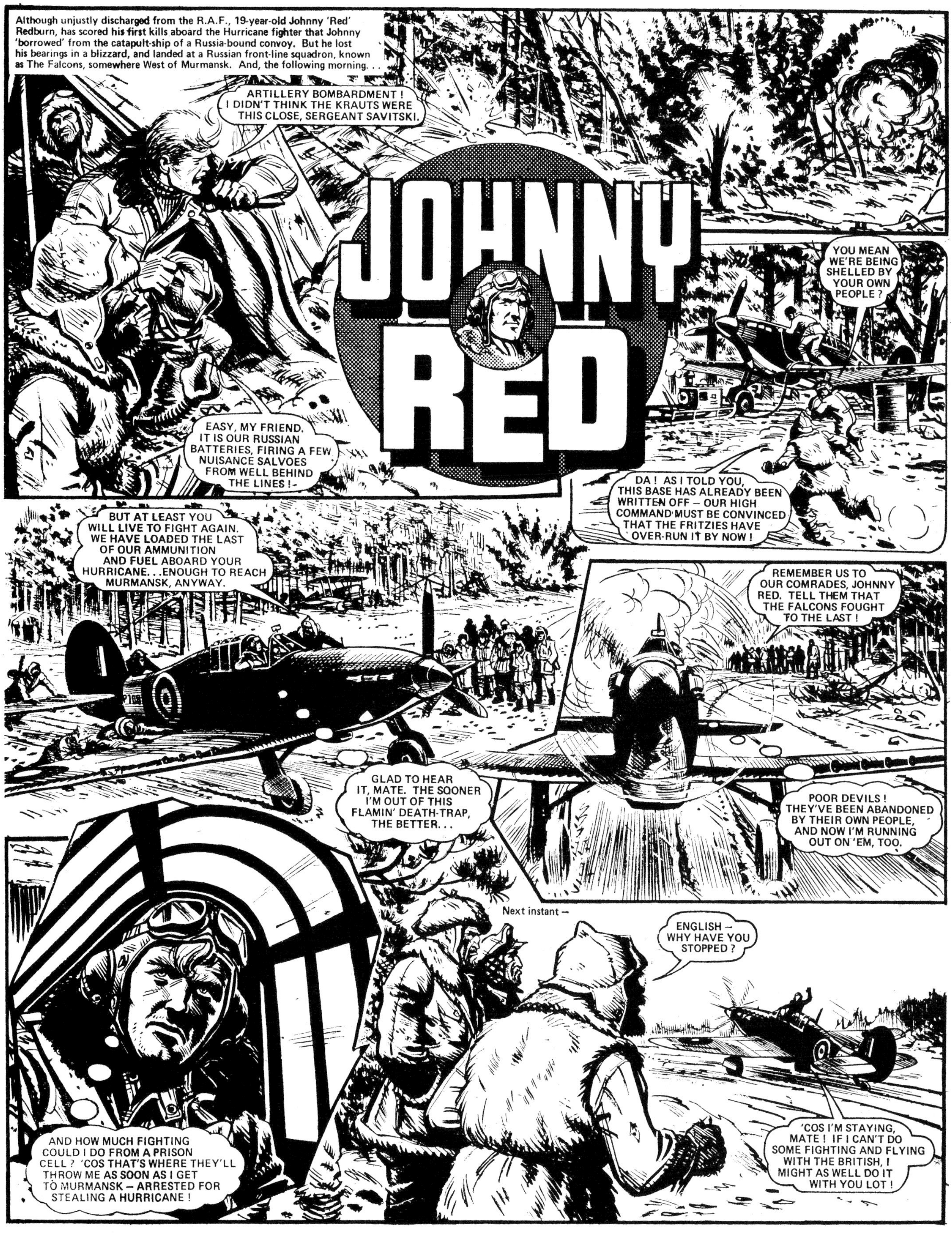

Although unjustly discharged from the R.A.F., 19-year-old Johnny 'Red' Redburn, has scored his first kills aboard the Hurricane fighter that Johnny 'borrowed' from the catapult-ship of a Russia-bound convoy. But he lost his bearings in a blizzard, and landed at a Russian front-line squadron, known as The Falcons, somewhere West of Murmansk. And, the following morning. . .
JOHNNY RED
ARTILLERY BOMBARDMENT! I DIDN'T THINK THE KRAUTS WERE THIS CLOSE, SERGEANT SAVITSKI.
EASY, MY FRIEND. IT IS OUR RUSSIAN BATTERIES, FIRING A FEW NUISANCE SALVOES FROM WELL BEHIND THE LINES!–
YOU MEAN WE'RE BEING SHELLED BY YOUR OWN PEOPLE?
DA! AS I TOLD YOU, THIS BASE HAS ALREADY BEEN WRITTEN OFF – OUR HIGH COMMAND MUST BE CONVINCED THAT THE FRITZIES HAVE OVER-RUN IT BY NOW!
BUT AT LEAST YOU WILL LIVE TO FIGHT AGAIN. WE HAVE LOADED THE LAST OF OUR AMMUNITION AND FUEL ABOARD YOUR HURRICANE. . . ENOUGH TO REACH MURMANSK, ANYWAY.
GLAD TO HEAR IT, MATE. THE SOONER I'M OUT OF THIS FLAMIN' DEATH-TRAP, THE BETTER. . .
REMEMBER US TO OUR COMRADES, JOHNNY RED. TELL THEM THAT THE FALCONS FOUGHT TO THE LAST!
POOR DEVILS! THEY'VE BEEN ABANDONED BY THEIR OWN PEOPLE, AND NOW I'M RUNNING OUT ON 'EM, TOO.
Next instant –
ENGLISH – WHY HAVE YOU STOPPED?
AND HOW MUCH FIGHTING COULD I DO FROM A PRISON CELL? 'COS THAT'S WHERE THEY'LL THROW ME AS SOON AS I GET TO MURMANSK – ARRESTED FOR STEALING A HURRICANE!
'COS I'M STAYING, MATE! IF I CAN'T DO SOME FIGHTING AND FLYING WITH THE BRITISH, I MIGHT AS WELL DO IT WITH YOU LOT!

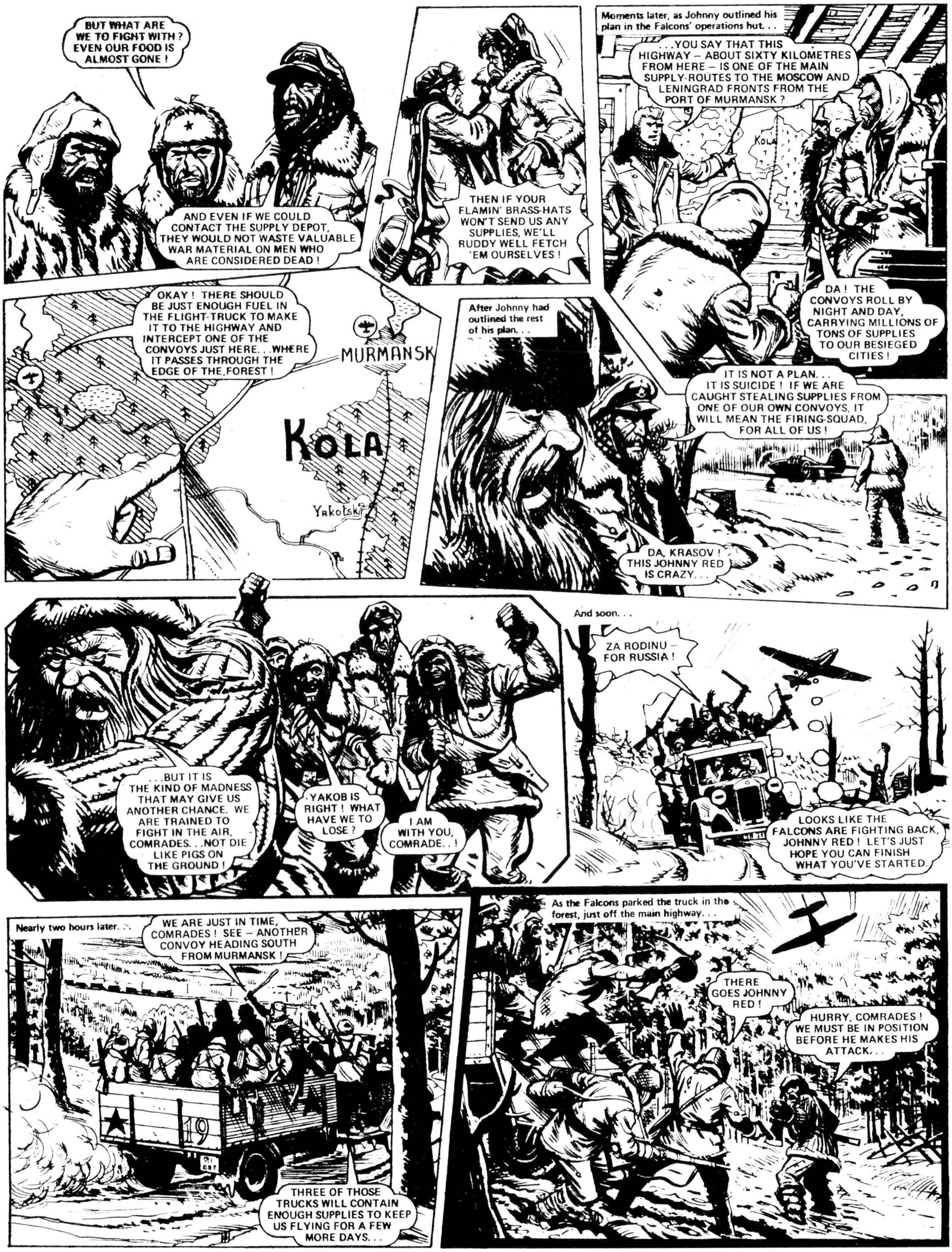

BUT WHAT ARE WE TO FIGHT WITH? EVEN OUR FOOD IS ALMOST GONE!
AND EVEN IF WE COULD CONTACT THE SUPPLY DEPOT, THEY WOULD NOT WASTE VALUABLE WAR MATERIAL ON MEN WHO ARE CONSIDERED DEAD!
THEN IF YOUR FLAMIN' BRASS-HATS WON'T SEND US ANY SUPPLIES, WE'LL RUDDY WELL FETCH 'EM OURSELVES!
Moments later, as Johnny outlined his plan in the Falcons' operations hut...
...YOU SAY THAT THIS HIGHWAY – ABOUT SIXTY KILOMETRES FROM HERE – IS ONE OF THE MAIN SUPPLY-ROUTES TO THE MOSCOW AND LENINGRAD FRONTS FROM THE PORT OF MURMANSK?
KOLA
DA! THE CONVOYS ROLL BY NIGHT AND DAY, CARRYING MILLIONS OF TONS OF SUPPLIES TO OUR BESIEGED CITIES!
OKAY! THERE SHOULD BE JUST ENOUGH FUEL IN THE FLIGHT-TRUCK TO MAKE IT TO THE HIGHWAY AND INTERCEPT ONE OF THE CONVOYS JUST HERE...WHERE IT PASSES THROUGH THE EDGE OF THE FOREST!
MURMANSK
KOLA
Yakotsk
After Johnny had outlined the rest of his plan...
IT IS NOT A PLAN... IT IS SUICIDE! IF WE ARE CAUGHT STEALING SUPPLIES FROM ONE OF OUR OWN CONVOYS, IT WILL MEAN THE FIRING-SQUAD, FOR ALL OF US!
DA, KRASOV! THIS JOHNNY RED IS CRAZY...
...BUT IT IS THE KIND OF MADNESS THAT MAY GIVE US ANOTHER CHANCE. WE ARE TRAINED TO FIGHT IN THE AIR, COMRADES...NOT DIE LIKE PIGS ON THE GROUND!
YAKOB IS RIGHT! WHAT HAVE WE TO LOSE?
I AM WITH YOU, COMRADE...!
And soon...
ZA RODINU – FOR RUSSIA!
LOOKS LIKE THE FALCONS ARE FIGHTING BACK, JOHNNY RED! LET'S JUST HOPE YOU CAN FINISH WHAT YOU'VE STARTED.
Nearly two hours later...
WE ARE JUST IN TIME, COMRADES! SEE – ANOTHER CONVOY HEADING SOUTH FROM MURMANSK!
19
THREE OF THOSE TRUCKS WILL CONTAIN ENOUGH SUPPLIES TO KEEP US FLYING FOR A FEW MORE DAYS...
As the Falcons parked the truck in the forest, just off the main highway...
THERE GOES JOHNNY RED!
HURRY, COMRADES! WE MUST BE IN POSITION BEFORE HE MAKES HIS ATTACK...

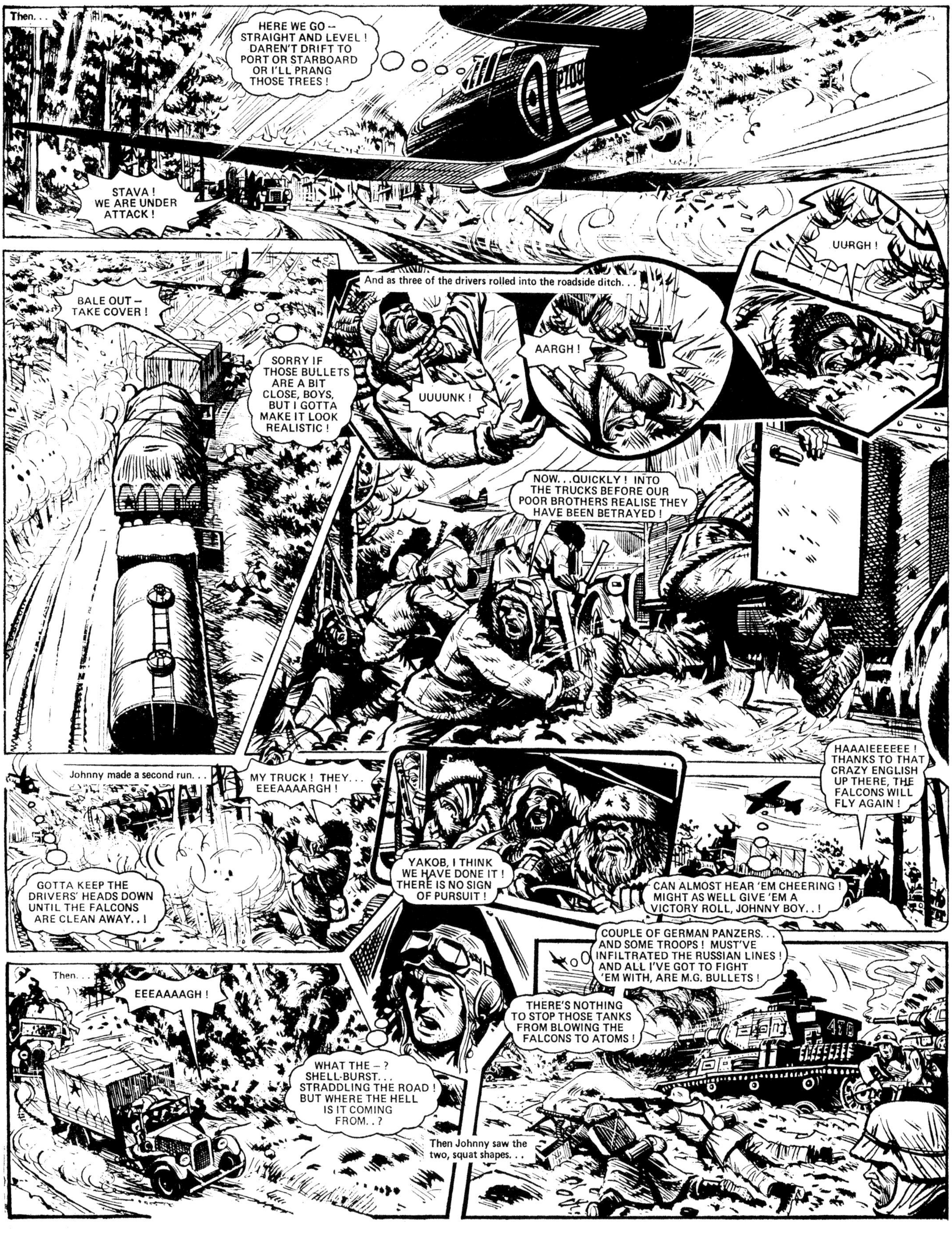
Then. . .
HERE WE GO – STRAIGHT AND LEVEL ! DAREN'T DRIFT TO PORT OR STARBOARD OR I'LL PRANG THOSE TREES !
STAVA ! WE ARE UNDER ATTACK !
BALE OUT – TAKE COVER !
SORRY IF THOSE BULLETS ARE A BIT CLOSE, BOYS, BUT I GOTTA MAKE IT LOOK REALISTIC !
And as three of the drivers rolled into the roadside ditch. . .
UUUUNK !
AARGH !
UURGH !
NOW. . .QUICKLY ! INTO THE TRUCKS BEFORE OUR POOR BROTHERS REALISE THEY HAVE BEEN BETRAYED !
Johnny made a second run. . .
MY TRUCK ! THEY. . . EEEAAAAARGH !
GOTTA KEEP THE DRIVERS' HEADS DOWN UNTIL THE FALCONS ARE CLEAN AWAY. . !
YAKOB, I THINK WE HAVE DONE IT ! THERE IS NO SIGN OF PURSUIT !
HAAAIEEEEEE ! THANKS TO THAT CRAZY ENGLISH UP THERE, THE FALCONS WILL FLY AGAIN !
CAN ALMOST HEAR 'EM CHEERING ! MIGHT AS WELL GIVE 'EM A VICTORY ROLL, JOHNNY BOY. . !
Then. . .
EEEAAAAGH !
WHAT THE – ? SHELL-BURST. . . STRADDLING THE ROAD ! BUT WHERE THE HELL IS IT COMING FROM. . ?
COUPLE OF GERMAN PANZERS. . . AND SOME TROOPS ! MUST'VE INFILTRATED THE RUSSIAN LINES ! AND ALL I'VE GOT TO FIGHT 'EM WITH, ARE M.G. BULLETS !
THERE'S NOTHING TO STOP THOSE TANKS FROM BLOWING THE FALCONS TO ATOMS !
Then Johnny saw the two, squat shapes. . .

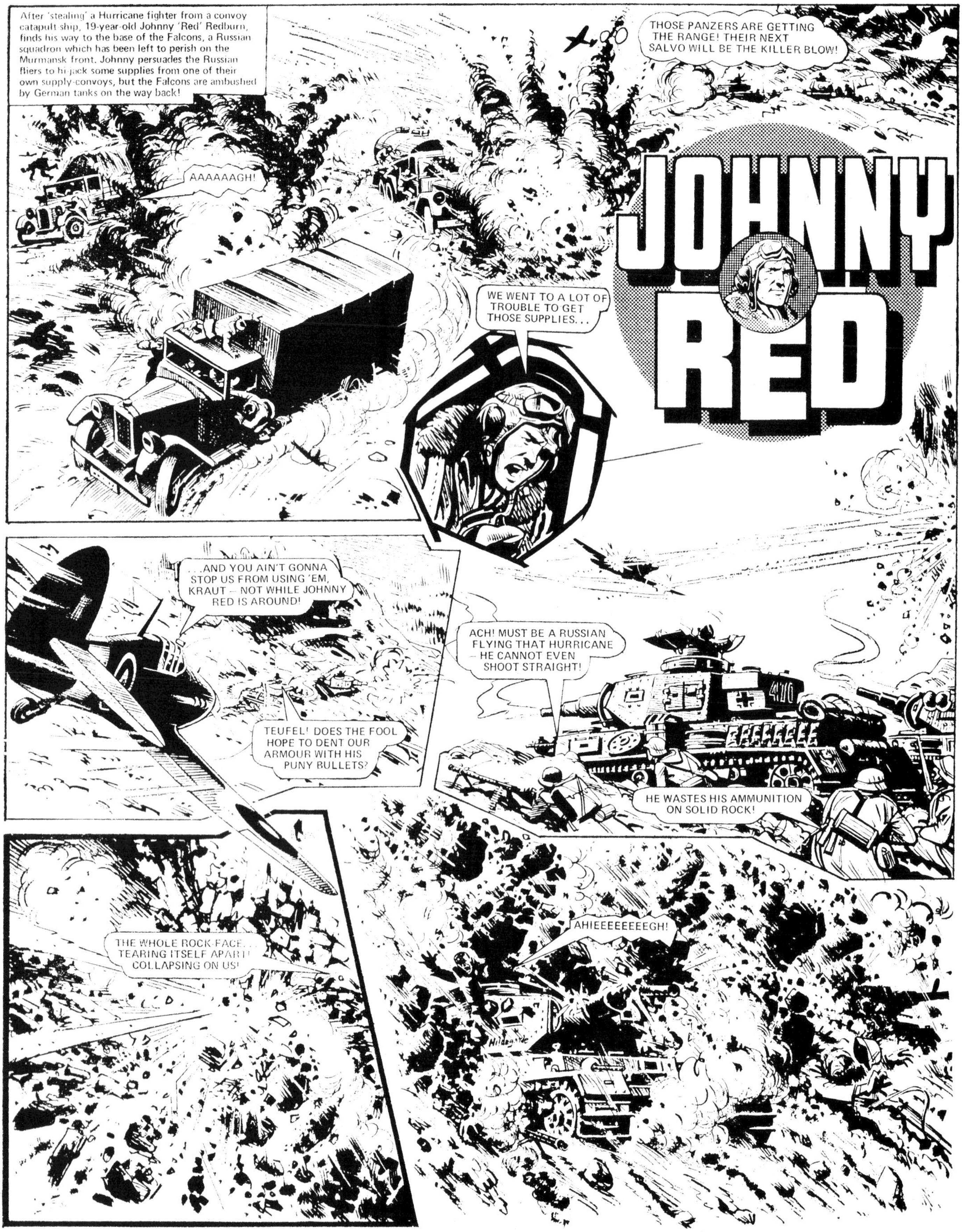

After 'stealing' a Hurricane fighter from a convoy catapult ship, 19-year-old Johnny 'Red' Redburn, finds his way to the base of the Falcons, a Russian squadron which has been left to perish on the Murmansk front. Johnny persuades the Russian fliers to hi-jack some supplies from one of their own supply-convoys, but the Falcons are ambushed by German tanks on the way back!
THOSE PANZERS ARE GETTING THE RANGE! THEIR NEXT SALVO WILL BE THE KILLER BLOW!
JOHNNY RED
AAAAAAGH!
WE WENT TO A LOT OF TROUBLE TO GET THOSE SUPPLIES...
...AND YOU AIN'T GONNA STOP US FROM USING 'EM, KRAUT – NOT WHILE JOHNNY RED IS AROUND!
TEUFEL! DOES THE FOOL HOPE TO DENT OUR ARMOUR WITH HIS PUNY BULLETS?
ACH! MUST BE A RUSSIAN FLYING THAT HURRICANE – HE CANNOT EVEN SHOOT STRAIGHT!
HE WASTES HIS AMMUNITION ON SOLID ROCK!
THE WHOLE ROCK-FACE... TEARING ITSELF APART! COLLAPSING ON US!
AHIEEEEEEEEGH!

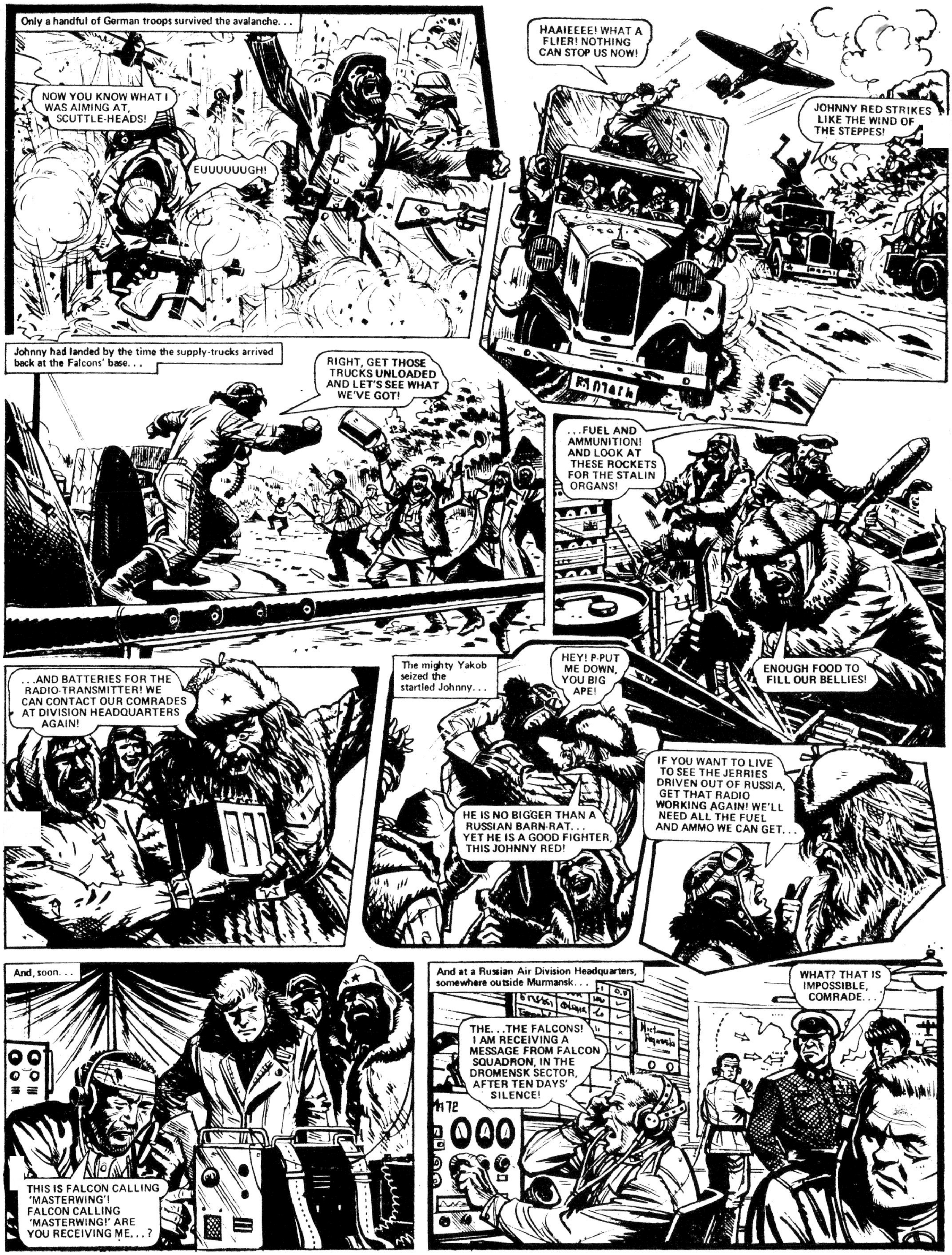

Only a handful of German troops survived the avalanche. . .
NOW YOU KNOW WHAT I WAS AIMING AT, SCUTTLE-HEADS!
EUUUUUUGH!
HAAIEEEE! WHAT A FLIER! NOTHING CAN STOP US NOW!
JOHNNY RED STRIKES LIKE THE WIND OF THE STEPPES!
Johnny had landed by the time the supply-trucks arrived back at the Falcons' base. . .
RIGHT, GET THOSE TRUCKS UNLOADED AND LET'S SEE WHAT WE'VE GOT!
. . .FUEL AND AMMUNITION! AND LOOK AT THESE ROCKETS FOR THE STALIN ORGANS!
ENOUGH FOOD TO FILL OUR BELLIES!
. . .AND BATTERIES FOR THE RADIO-TRANSMITTER! WE CAN CONTACT OUR COMRADES AT DIVISION HEADQUARTERS AGAIN!
The mighty Yakob seized the startled Johnny. . .
HEY! P-PUT ME DOWN, YOU BIG APE!
HE IS NO BIGGER THAN A RUSSIAN BARN-RAT. . . YET HE IS A GOOD FIGHTER, THIS JOHNNY RED!
IF YOU WANT TO LIVE TO SEE THE JERRIES DRIVEN OUT OF RUSSIA, GET THAT RADIO WORKING AGAIN! WE'LL NEED ALL THE FUEL AND AMMO WE CAN GET. . .
And, soon. . .
THIS IS FALCON CALLING 'MASTERWING'! FALCON CALLING 'MASTERWING!' ARE YOU RECEIVING ME. . .?
And at a Russian Air Division Headquarters, somewhere outside Murmansk. . .
THE. . .THE FALCONS! I AM RECEIVING A MESSAGE FROM FALCON SQUADRON, IN THE DROMENSK SECTOR, AFTER TEN DAYS' SILENCE!
WHAT? THAT IS IMPOSSIBLE, COMRADE. . .

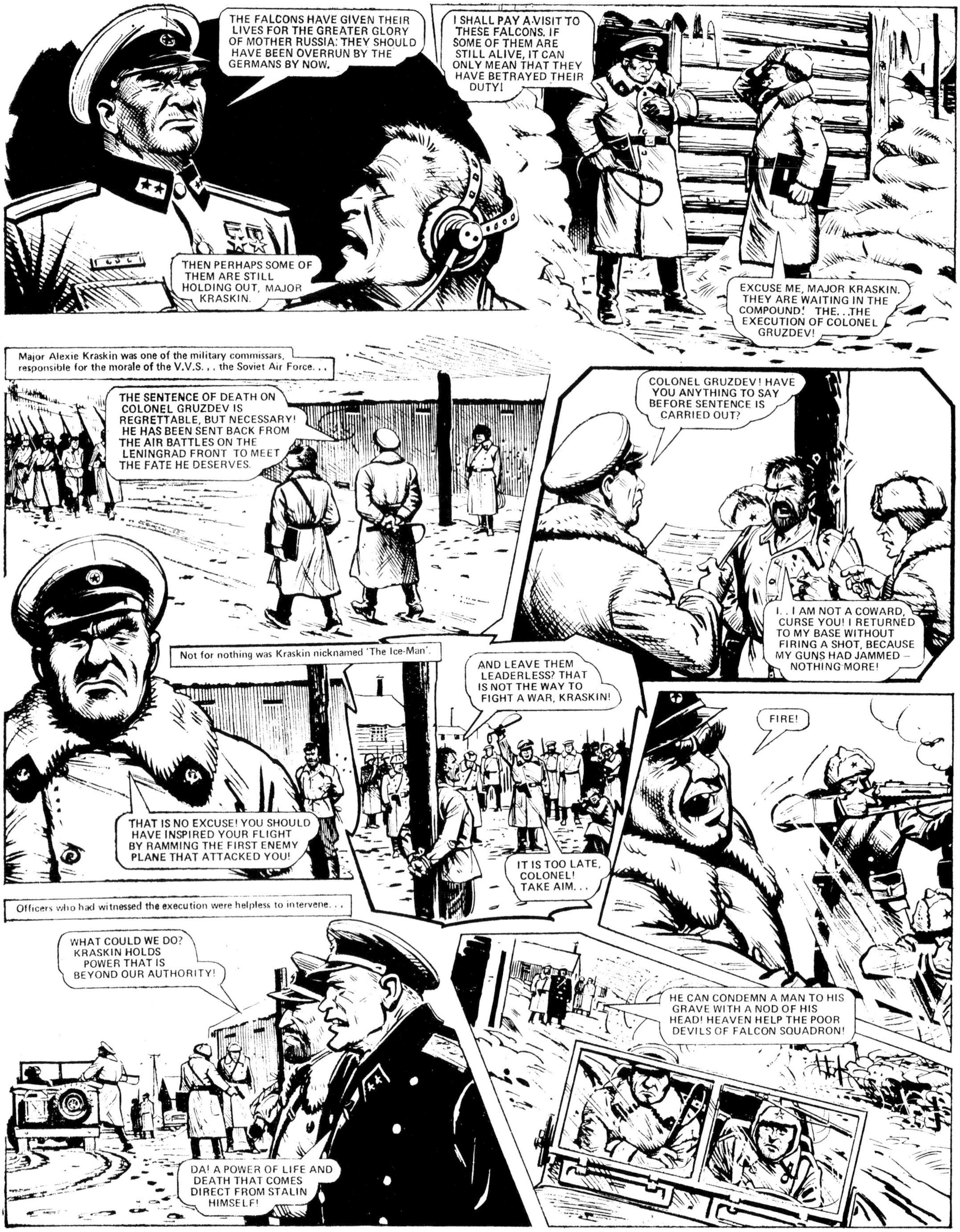
THE FALCONS HAVE GIVEN THEIR LIVES FOR THE GREATER GLORY OF MOTHER RUSSIA: THEY SHOULD HAVE BEEN OVERRUN BY THE GERMANS BY NOW.
THEN PERHAPS SOME OF THEM ARE STILL HOLDING OUT, MAJOR KRASKIN.
I SHALL PAY A VISIT TO THESE FALCONS. IF SOME OF THEM ARE STILL ALIVE, IT CAN ONLY MEAN THAT THEY HAVE BETRAYED THEIR DUTY!
EXCUSE ME, MAJOR KRASKIN. THEY ARE WAITING IN THE COMPOUND! THE. . .THE EXECUTION OF COLONEL GRUZDEV!
Major Alexie Kraskin was one of the military commissars, responsible for the morale of the V.V.S. . . the Soviet Air Force. . .
THE SENTENCE OF DEATH ON COLONEL GRUZDEV IS REGRETTABLE, BUT NECESSARY! HE HAS BEEN SENT BACK FROM THE AIR BATTLES ON THE LENINGRAD FRONT TO MEET THE FATE HE DESERVES.
COLONEL GRUZDEV! HAVE YOU ANYTHING TO SAY BEFORE SENTENCE IS CARRIED OUT?
I. . I AM NOT A COWARD, CURSE YOU! I RETURNED TO MY BASE WITHOUT FIRING A SHOT, BECAUSE MY GUNS HAD JAMMED — NOTHING MORE!
Not for nothing was Kraskin nicknamed 'The Ice-Man'.
THAT IS NO EXCUSE! YOU SHOULD HAVE INSPIRED YOUR FLIGHT BY RAMMING THE FIRST ENEMY PLANE THAT ATTACKED YOU!
AND LEAVE THEM LEADERLESS? THAT IS NOT THE WAY TO FIGHT A WAR, KRASKIN!
IT IS TOO LATE, COLONEL! TAKE AIM. . .
FIRE!
Officers who had witnessed the execution were helpless to intervene. . .
WHAT COULD WE DO? KRASKIN HOLDS POWER THAT IS BEYOND OUR AUTHORITY!
DA! A POWER OF LIFE AND DEATH THAT COMES DIRECT FROM STALIN HIMSELF!
HE CAN CONDEMN A MAN TO HIS GRAVE WITH A NOD OF HIS HEAD! HEAVEN HELP THE POOR DEVILS OF FALCON SQUADRON!

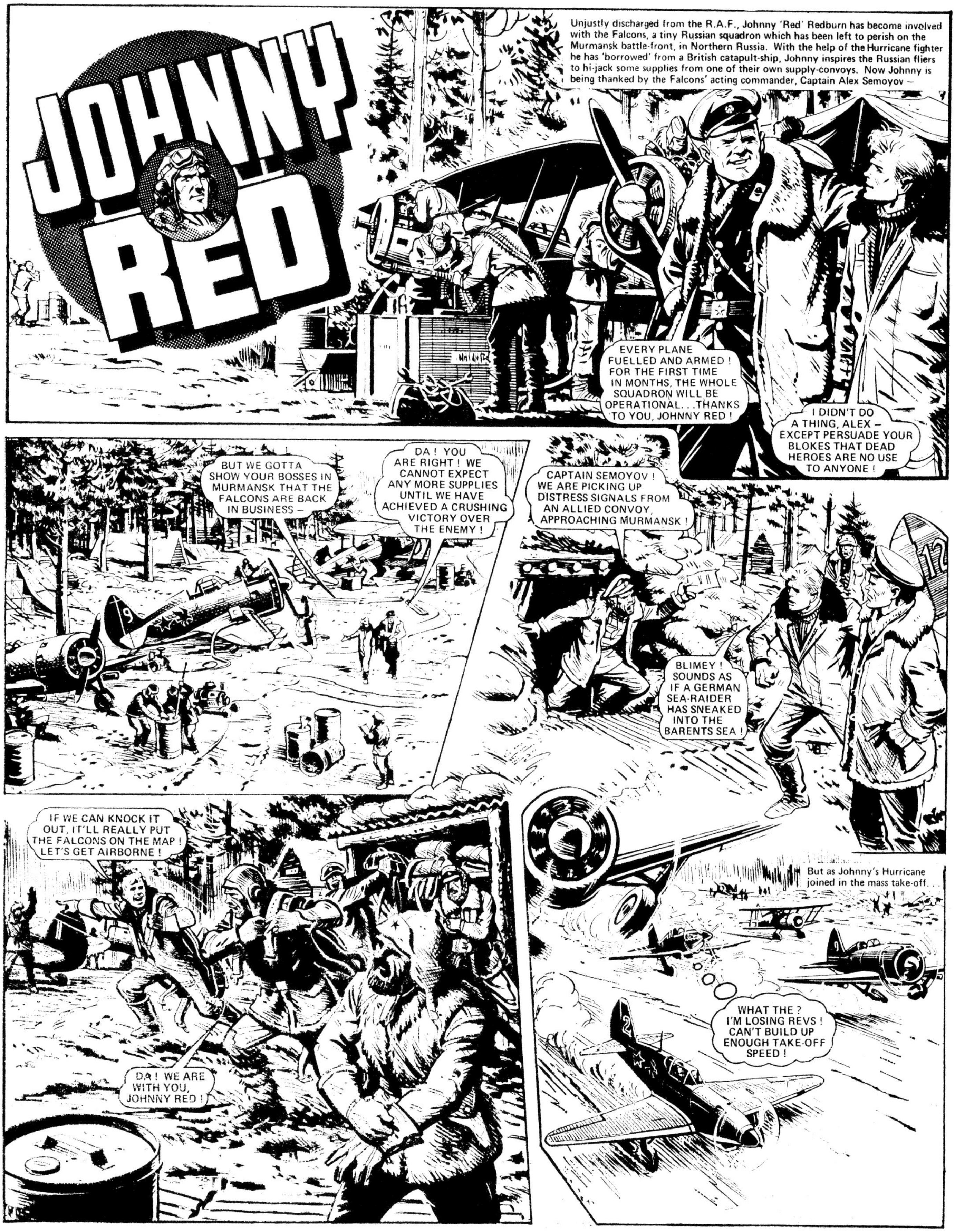
JOHNNY RED
Unjustly discharged from the R.A.F., Johnny 'Red' Redburn has become involved with the Falcons, a tiny Russian squadron which has been left to perish on the Murmansk battle-front, in Northern Russia. With the help of the Hurricane fighter he has 'borrowed' from a British catapult-ship, Johnny inspires the Russian fliers to hi-jack some supplies from one of their own supply-convoys. Now Johnny is being thanked by the Falcons' acting commander, Captain Alex Semoyov –
EVERY PLANE FUELLED AND ARMED! FOR THE FIRST TIME IN MONTHS, THE WHOLE SQUADRON WILL BE OPERATIONAL. . .THANKS TO YOU, JOHNNY RED!
I DIDN'T DO A THING, ALEX – EXCEPT PERSUADE YOUR BLOKES THAT DEAD HEROES ARE NO USE TO ANYONE!
BUT WE GOTTA SHOW YOUR BOSSES IN MURMANSK THAT THE FALCONS ARE BACK IN BUSINESS –
DA! YOU ARE RIGHT! WE CANNOT EXPECT ANY MORE SUPPLIES UNTIL WE HAVE ACHIEVED A CRUSHING VICTORY OVER THE ENEMY!
CAPTAIN SEMOYOV! WE ARE PICKING UP DISTRESS SIGNALS FROM AN ALLIED CONVOY, APPROACHING MURMANSK!
BLIMEY! SOUNDS AS IF A GERMAN SEA-RAIDER HAS SNEAKED INTO THE BARENTS SEA!
IF WE CAN KNOCK IT OUT, IT'LL REALLY PUT THE FALCONS ON THE MAP! LET'S GET AIRBORNE!
DA! WE ARE WITH YOU, JOHNNY RED!
But as Johnny's Hurricane joined in the mass take-off. . .
WHAT THE? I'M LOSING REVS! CAN'T BUILD UP ENOUGH TAKE-OFF SPEED!

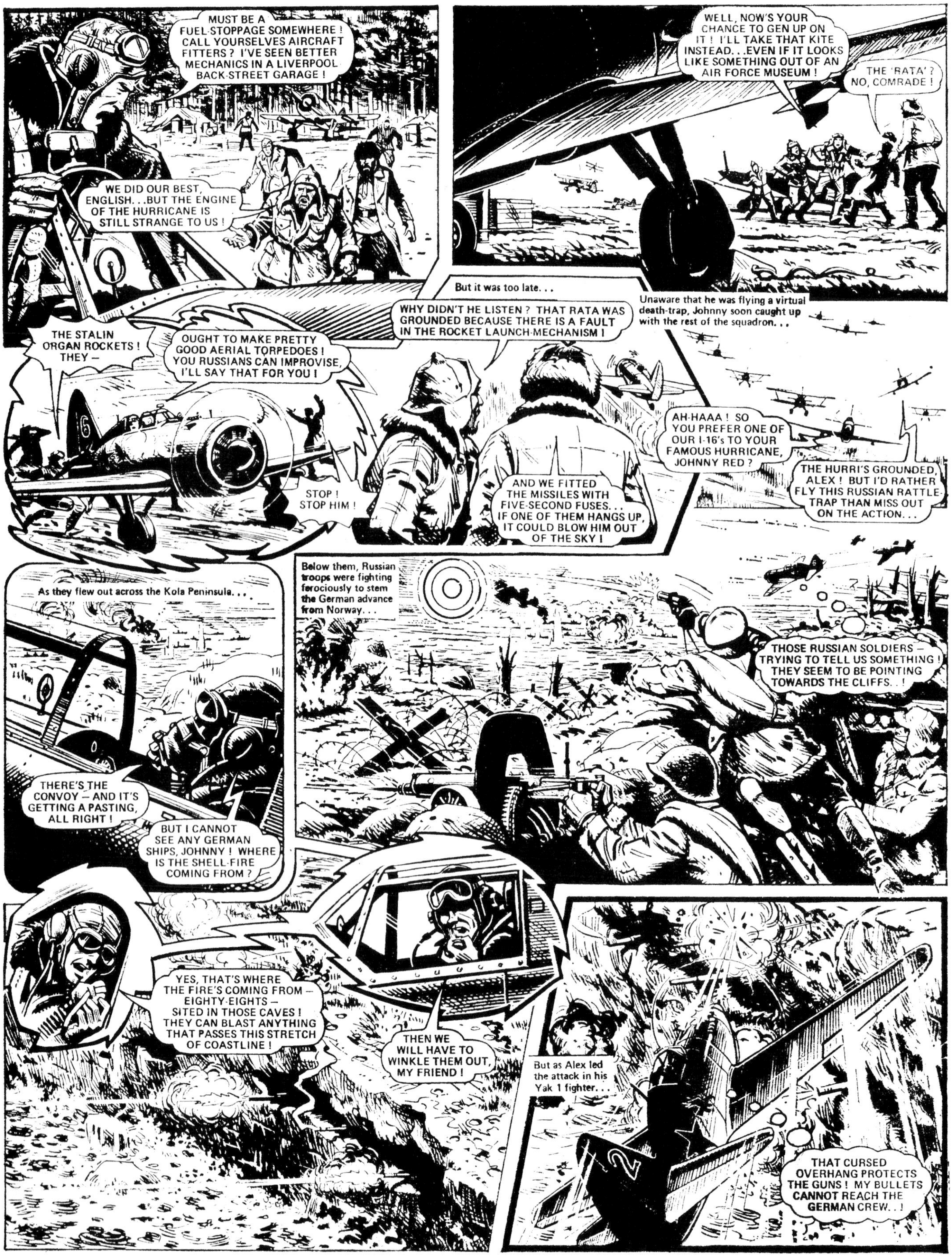

MUST BE A FUEL-STOPPAGE SOMEWHERE! CALL YOURSELVES AIRCRAFT FITTERS? I'VE SEEN BETTER MECHANICS IN A LIVERPOOL BACK-STREET GARAGE!
WE DID OUR BEST, ENGLISH... BUT THE ENGINE OF THE HURRICANE IS STILL STRANGE TO US!
WELL, NOW'S YOUR CHANCE TO GEN UP ON IT! I'LL TAKE THAT KITE INSTEAD... EVEN IF IT LOOKS LIKE SOMETHING OUT OF AN AIR FORCE MUSEUM!
THE 'RATA'? NO, COMRADE!
THE STALIN ORGAN ROCKETS! THEY –
OUGHT TO MAKE PRETTY GOOD AERIAL TORPEDOES! YOU RUSSIANS CAN IMPROVISE, I'LL SAY THAT FOR YOU!
STOP! STOP HIM!
But it was too late...
WHY DIDN'T HE LISTEN? THAT RATA WAS GROUNDED BECAUSE THERE IS A FAULT IN THE ROCKET LAUNCH-MECHANISM!
AND WE FITTED THE MISSILES WITH FIVE-SECOND FUSES... IF ONE OF THEM HANGS UP, IT COULD BLOW HIM OUT OF THE SKY!
Unaware that he was flying a virtual death-trap, Johnny soon caught up with the rest of the squadron...
AH-HAAA! SO YOU PREFER ONE OF OUR I-16's TO YOUR FAMOUS HURRICANE, JOHNNY RED?
THE HURRI'S GROUNDED, ALEX! BUT I'D RATHER FLY THIS RUSSIAN RATTLE-TRAP THAN MISS OUT ON THE ACTION...
As they flew out across the Kola Peninsula...
THERE'S THE CONVOY – AND IT'S GETTING A PASTING, ALL RIGHT!
BUT I CANNOT SEE ANY GERMAN SHIPS, JOHNNY! WHERE IS THE SHELL-FIRE COMING FROM?
Below them, Russian troops were fighting ferociously to stem the German advance from Norway...
THOSE RUSSIAN SOLDIERS – TRYING TO TELL US SOMETHING! THEY SEEM TO BE POINTING TOWARDS THE CLIFFS..!
YES, THAT'S WHERE THE FIRE'S COMING FROM – EIGHTY-EIGHTS – SITED IN THOSE CAVES! THEY CAN BLAST ANYTHING THAT PASSES THIS STRETCH OF COASTLINE!
THEN WE WILL HAVE TO WINKLE THEM OUT, MY FRIEND!
But as Alex led the attack in his Yak 1 fighter...
THAT CURSED OVERHANG PROTECTS THE GUNS! MY BULLETS CANNOT REACH THE GERMAN CREW..!

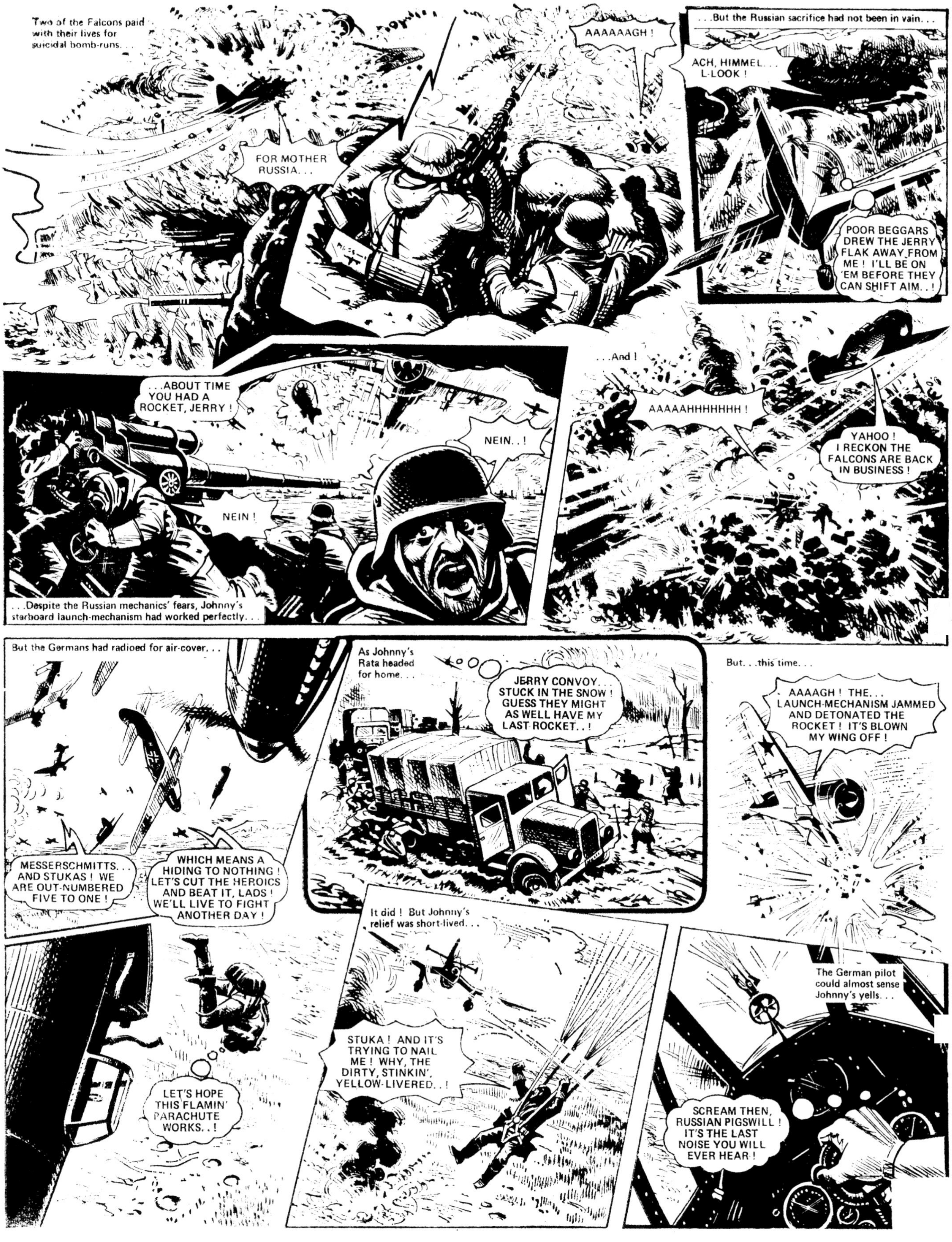
Two of the Falcons paid with their lives for suicidal bomb-runs. . .
FOR MOTHER RUSSIA. . .
AAAAAAGH !
. . .But the Russian sacrifice had not been in vain. . .
ACH, HIMMEL. . . L-LOOK !
POOR BEGGARS DREW THE JERRY FLAK AWAY FROM ME ! I'LL BE ON 'EM BEFORE THEY CAN SHIFT AIM. . !
. . .ABOUT TIME YOU HAD A ROCKET, JERRY !
NEIN. . !
NEIN !
. . .Despite the Russian mechanics' fears, Johnny's starboard launch-mechanism had worked perfectly. . .
. . .And !
AAAAAHHHHHHH !
YAHOO ! I RECKON THE FALCONS ARE BACK IN BUSINESS !
But the Germans had radioed for air-cover. . .
MESSERSCHMITTS. . . AND STUKAS ! WE ARE OUT-NUMBERED FIVE TO ONE !
WHICH MEANS A HIDING TO NOTHING ! LET'S CUT THE HEROICS AND BEAT IT, LADS ! WE'LL LIVE TO FIGHT ANOTHER DAY !
As Johnny's Rata headed for home. . .
JERRY CONVOY. . . STUCK IN THE SNOW ! GUESS THEY MIGHT AS WELL HAVE MY LAST ROCKET. . !
But. . .this time. . .
AAAAGH ! THE. . . LAUNCH-MECHANISM JAMMED AND DETONATED THE ROCKET ! IT'S BLOWN MY WING OFF !
LET'S HOPE THIS FLAMIN' PARACHUTE WORKS. . !
It did ! But Johnny's relief was short-lived. . .
STUKA ! AND IT'S TRYING TO NAIL ME ! WHY, THE DIRTY, STINKIN', YELLOW-LIVERED. . !
The German pilot could almost sense Johnny's yells. . .
SCREAM THEN, RUSSIAN PIGSWILL ! IT'S THE LAST NOISE YOU WILL EVER HEAR !

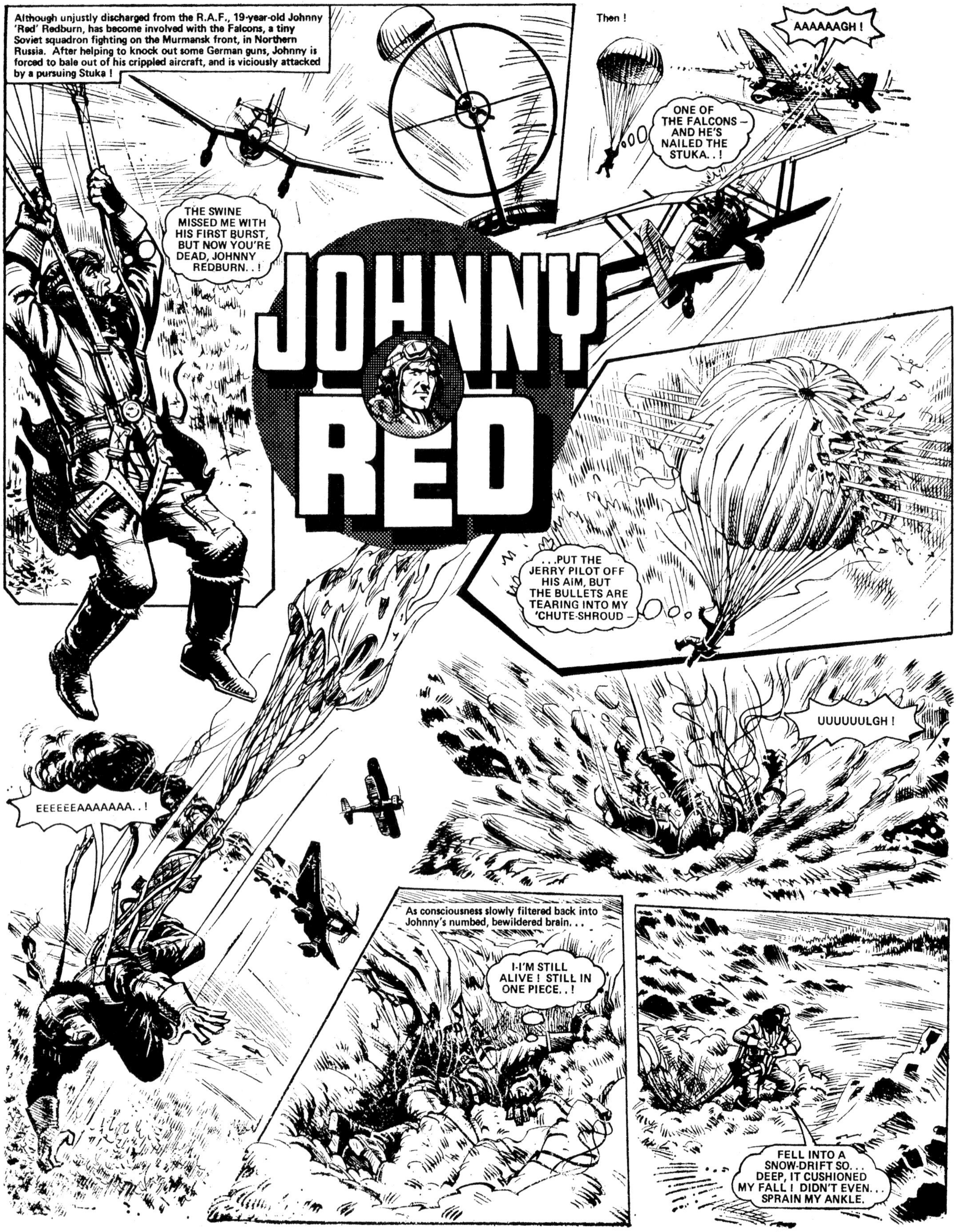
Although unjustly discharged from the R.A.F., 19-year-old Johnny 'Red' Redburn, has become involved with the Falcons, a tiny Soviet squadron fighting on the Murmansk front, in Northern Russia. After helping to knock out some German guns, Johnny is forced to bale out of his crippled aircraft, and is viciously attacked by a pursuing Stuka !
THE SWINE MISSED ME WITH HIS FIRST BURST, BUT NOW YOU'RE DEAD, JOHNNY REDBURN. . !
JOHNNY RED
Then !
AAAAAAGH !
ONE OF THE FALCONS – AND HE'S NAILED THE STUKA. . !
. . .PUT THE JERRY PILOT OFF HIS AIM, BUT THE BULLETS ARE TEARING INTO MY 'CHUTE-SHROUD –
EEEEEEAAAAAAA. . !
UUUUUULGH !
As consciousness slowly filtered back into Johnny's numbed, bewildered brain. . .
I-I'M STILL ALIVE ! STILL IN ONE PIECE. . !
FELL INTO A SNOW-DRIFT SO. . . DEEP, IT CUSHIONED MY FALL ! DIDN'T EVEN. . . SPRAIN MY ANKLE.

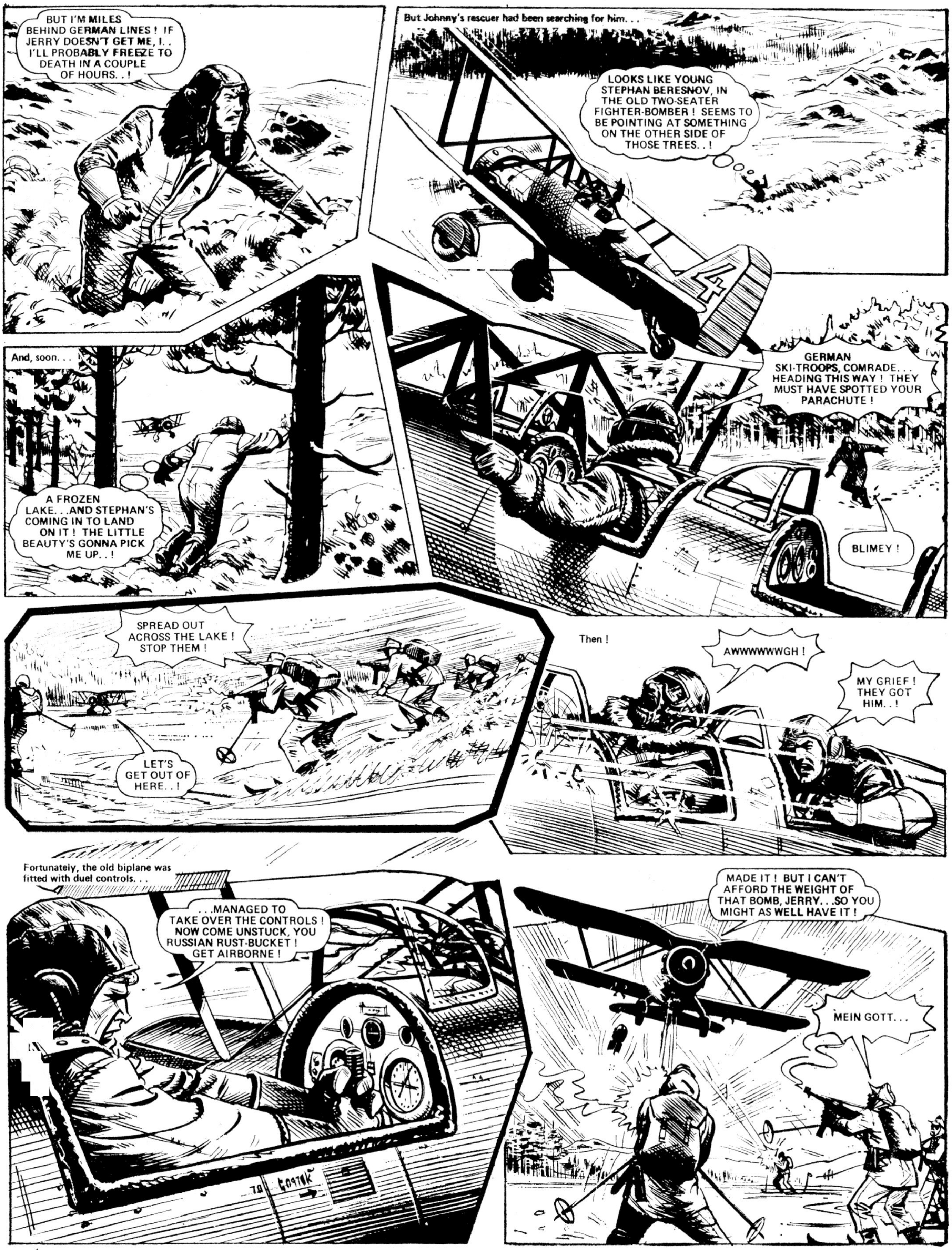

BUT I'M MILES BEHIND GERMAN LINES ! IF JERRY DOESN'T GET ME, I. . I'LL PROBABLY FREEZE TO DEATH IN A COUPLE OF HOURS. . !
But Johnny's rescuer had been searching for him. . .
LOOKS LIKE YOUNG STEPHAN BERESNOV, IN THE OLD TWO-SEATER FIGHTER-BOMBER ! SEEMS TO BE POINTING AT SOMETHING ON THE OTHER SIDE OF THOSE TREES. . !
And, soon. . .
A FROZEN LAKE. . .AND STEPHAN'S COMING IN TO LAND ON IT ! THE LITTLE BEAUTY'S GONNA PICK ME UP. . !
GERMAN SKI-TROOPS, COMRADE. . . HEADING THIS WAY ! THEY MUST HAVE SPOTTED YOUR PARACHUTE !
BLIMEY !
SPREAD OUT ACROSS THE LAKE ! STOP THEM !
LET'S GET OUT OF HERE. . !
Then !
AWWWWWWGH !
MY GRIEF ! THEY GOT HIM. . !
Fortunately, the old biplane was fitted with duel controls. . .
. . .MANAGED TO TAKE OVER THE CONTROLS ! NOW COME UNSTUCK, YOU RUSSIAN RUST-BUCKET ! GET AIRBORNE !
MADE IT ! BUT I CAN'T AFFORD THE WEIGHT OF THAT BOMB, JERRY. . .SO YOU MIGHT AS WELL HAVE IT !
MEIN GOTT. . .

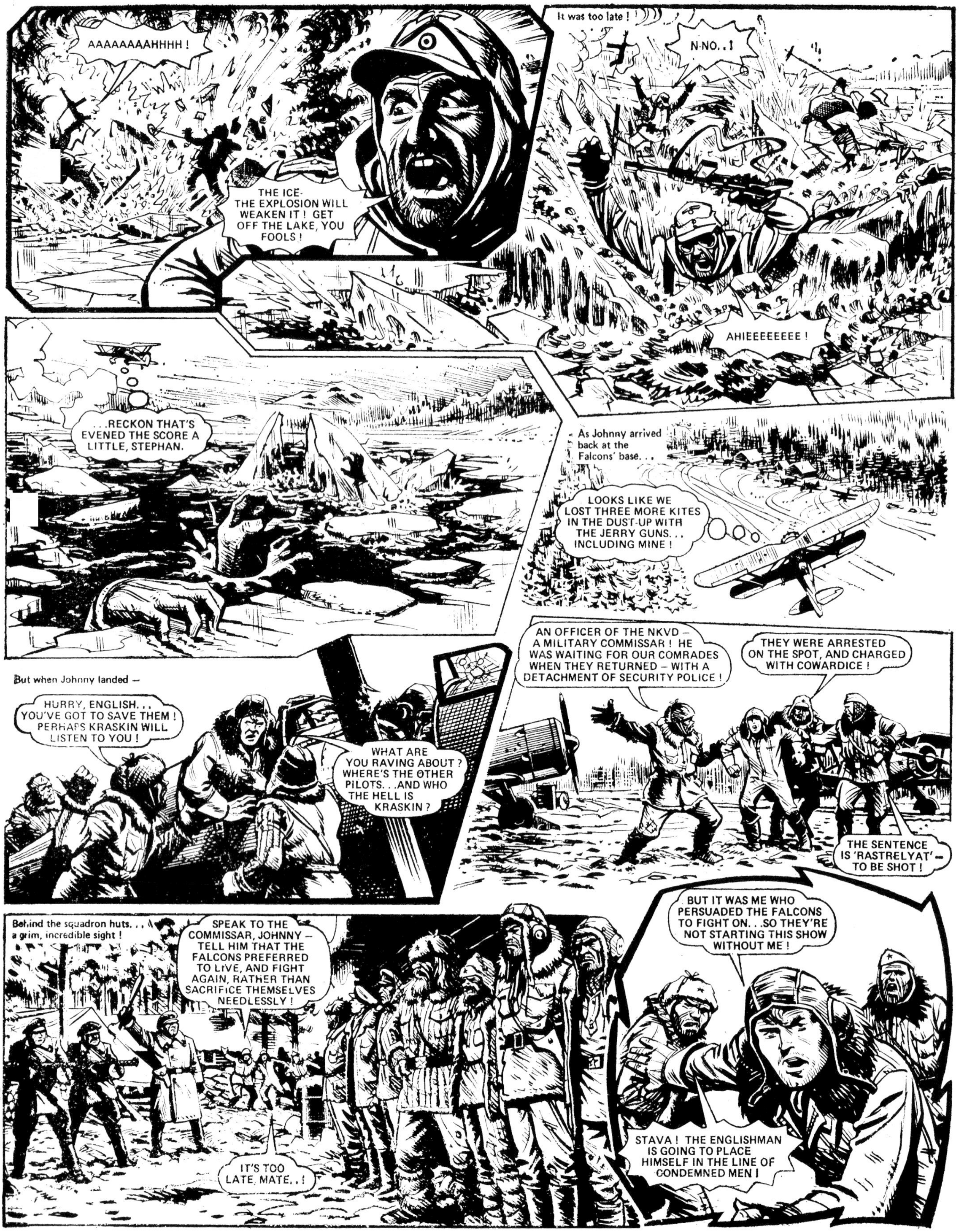
AAAAAAAAHHHH !
THE ICE- THE EXPLOSION WILL WEAKEN IT ! GET OFF THE LAKE, YOU FOOLS !
It was too late !
N-NO. . !
AHIEEEEEEEE !
. . .RECKON THAT'S EVENED THE SCORE A LITTLE, STEPHAN.
As Johnny arrived back at the Falcons' base. . .
LOOKS LIKE WE LOST THREE MORE KITES IN THE DUST-UP WITH THE JERRY GUNS. . . INCLUDING MINE !
But when Johnny landed –
HURRY, ENGLISH. . . YOU'VE GOT TO SAVE THEM ! PERHAPS KRASKIN WILL LISTEN TO YOU !
WHAT ARE YOU RAVING ABOUT ? WHERE'S THE OTHER PILOTS. . .AND WHO THE HELL IS KRASKIN ?
AN OFFICER OF THE NKVD – A MILITARY COMMISSAR ! HE WAS WAITING FOR OUR COMRADES WHEN THEY RETURNED – WITH A DETACHMENT OF SECURITY POLICE !
THEY WERE ARRESTED ON THE SPOT, AND CHARGED WITH COWARDICE !
THE SENTENCE IS 'RASTRELYAT' – TO BE SHOT !
Behind the squadron huts. . . a grim, incredible sight !
SPEAK TO THE COMMISSAR, JOHNNY – TELL HIM THAT THE FALCONS PREFERRED TO LIVE, AND FIGHT AGAIN, RATHER THAN SACRIFICE THEMSELVES NEEDLESSLY !
IT'S TOO LATE, MATE. . !
BUT IT WAS ME WHO PERSUADED THE FALCONS TO FIGHT ON. . .SO THEY'RE NOT STARTING THIS SHOW WITHOUT ME !
STAVA ! THE ENGLISHMAN IS GOING TO PLACE HIMSELF IN THE LINE OF CONDEMNED MEN !

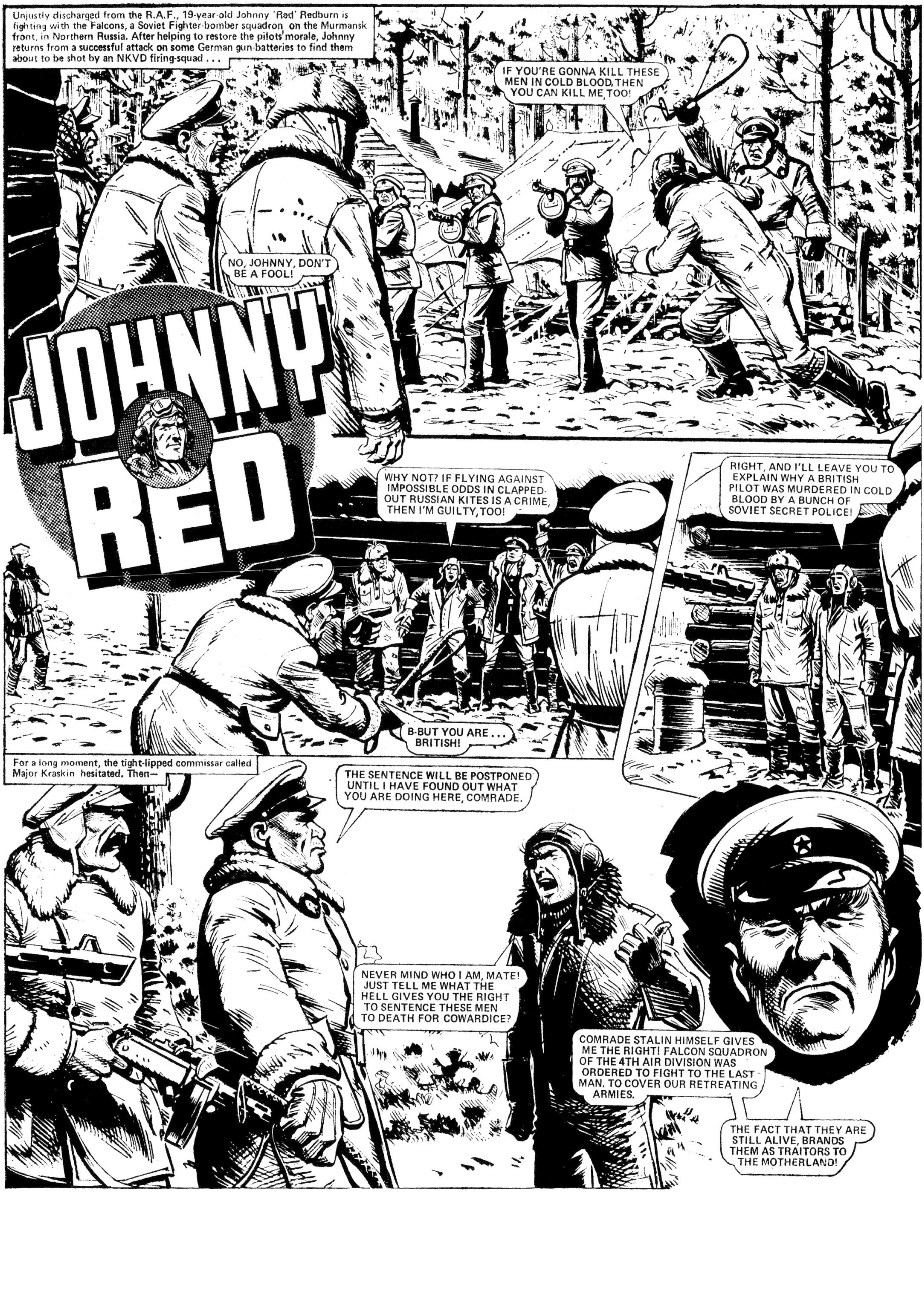
Unjustly discharged from the R.A.F., 19-year-old Johnny 'Red' Redburn is fighting with the Falcons, a Soviet Fighter-bomber squadron on the Murmansk front, in Northern Russia. After helping to restore the pilots' morale, Johnny returns from a successful attack on some German gun-batteries to find them about to be shot by an NKVD firing-squad . . .
IF YOU'RE GONNA KILL THESE MEN IN COLD BLOOD, THEN YOU CAN KILL ME, TOO!
NO, JOHNNY, DON'T BE A FOOL!
JOHNNY RED
WHY NOT? IF FLYING AGAINST IMPOSSIBLE ODDS IN CLAPPED-OUT RUSSIAN KITES IS A CRIME, THEN I'M GUILTY, TOO!
B-BUT YOU ARE . . . BRITISH!
RIGHT, AND I'LL LEAVE YOU TO EXPLAIN WHY A BRITISH PILOT WAS MURDERED IN COLD BLOOD BY A BUNCH OF SOVIET SECRET POLICE!
For a long moment, the tight-lipped commissar called Major Kraskin hesitated. Then—
THE SENTENCE WILL BE POSTPONED UNTIL I HAVE FOUND OUT WHAT YOU ARE DOING HERE, COMRADE.
NEVER MIND WHO I AM, MATE! JUST TELL ME WHAT THE HELL GIVES YOU THE RIGHT TO SENTENCE THESE MEN TO DEATH FOR COWARDICE?
COMRADE STALIN HIMSELF GIVES ME THE RIGHT! FALCON SQUADRON OF THE 4TH AIR DIVISION WAS ORDERED TO FIGHT TO THE LAST MAN, TO COVER OUR RETREATING ARMIES.
THE FACT THAT THEY ARE STILL ALIVE, BRANDS THEM AS TRAITORS TO THE MOTHERLAND!

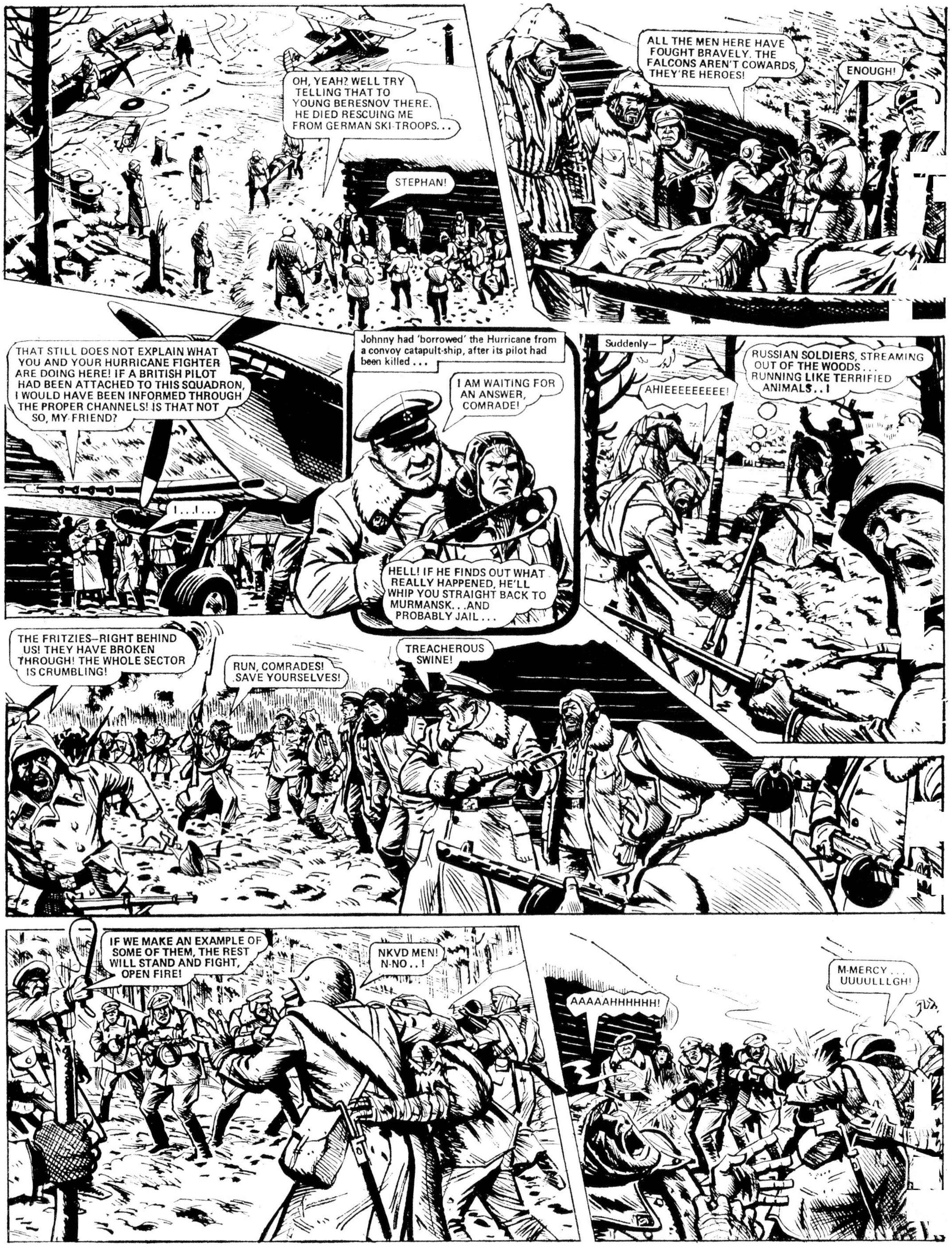
OH, YEAH? WELL TRY TELLING THAT TO YOUNG BERESNOV THERE. HE DIED RESCUING ME FROM GERMAN SKI-TROOPS . . .
STEPHAN!
ALL THE MEN HERE HAVE FOUGHT BRAVELY. THE FALCONS AREN'T COWARDS, THEY'RE HEROES!
ENOUGH!
THAT STILL DOES NOT EXPLAIN WHAT YOU AND YOUR HURRICANE FIGHTER ARE DOING HERE! IF A BRITISH PILOT HAD BEEN ATTACHED TO THIS SQUADRON, I WOULD HAVE BEEN INFORMED THROUGH THE PROPER CHANNELS! IS THAT NOT SO, MY FRIEND?
I . . I . . .
Johnny had 'borrowed' the Hurricane from a convoy catapult-ship, after its pilot had been killed . . .
I AM WAITING FOR AN ANSWER, COMRADE!
HELL! IF HE FINDS OUT WHAT REALLY HAPPENED, HE'LL WHIP YOU STRAIGHT BACK TO MURMANSK. . .AND PROBABLY JAIL . . .
Suddenly—
RUSSIAN SOLDIERS, STREAMING OUT OF THE WOODS . . . RUNNING LIKE TERRIFIED ANIMALS . . !
AHIEEEEEEEEE!
THE FRITZIES—RIGHT BEHIND US! THEY HAVE BROKEN THROUGH! THE WHOLE SECTOR IS CRUMBLING!
RUN, COMRADES! SAVE YOURSELVES!
TREACHEROUS SWINE!
IF WE MAKE AN EXAMPLE OF SOME OF THEM, THE REST WILL STAND AND FIGHT. OPEN FIRE!
NKVD MEN! N-NO . . !
AAAAAHHHHHH!
M-MERCY . . . UUUULLLGH!

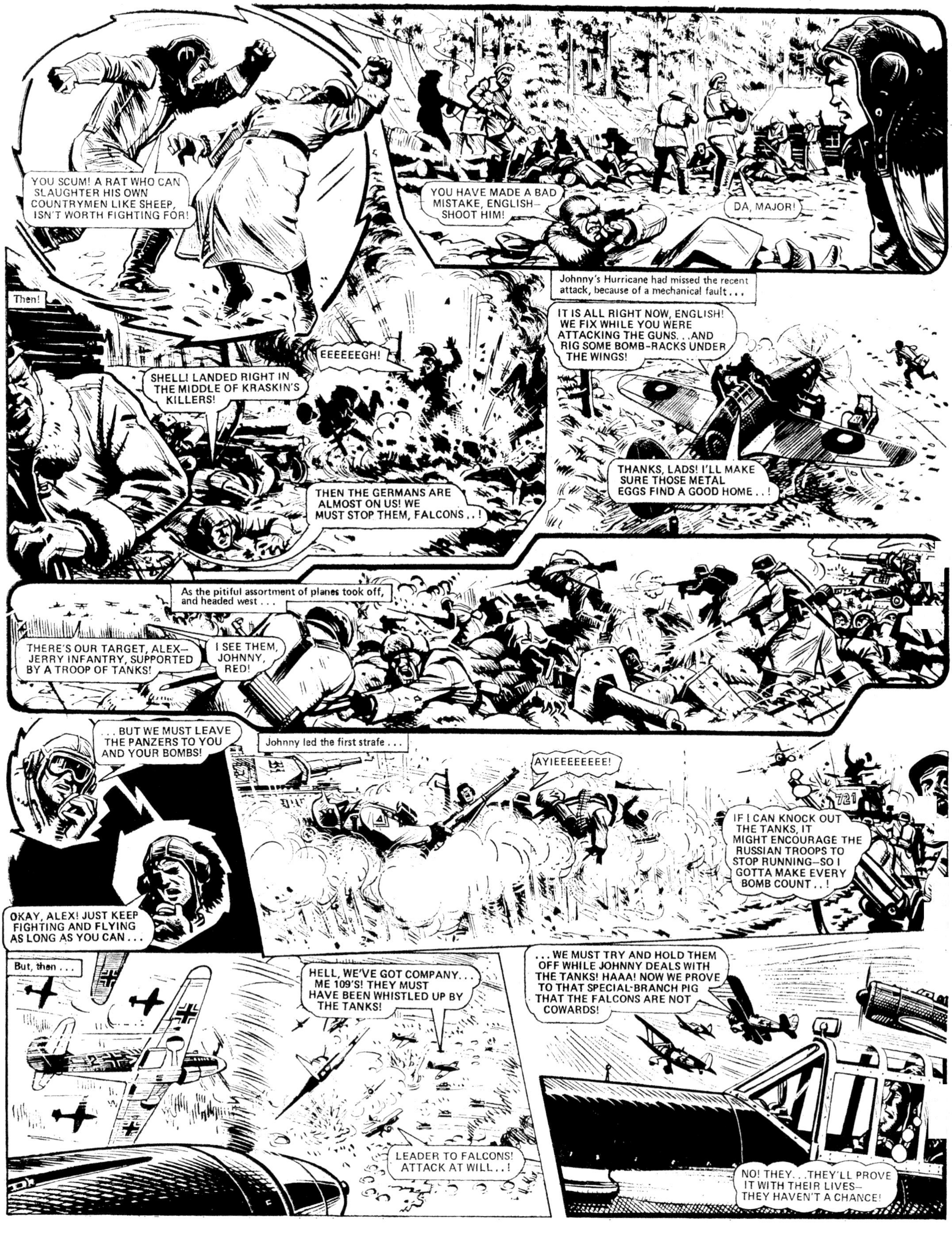

YOU SCUM! A RAT WHO CAN SLAUGHTER HIS OWN COUNTRYMEN LIKE SHEEP, ISN'T WORTH FIGHTING FOR!
YOU HAVE MADE A BAD MISTAKE, ENGLISH– SHOOT HIM!
DA, MAJOR!
Then!
SHELL! LANDED RIGHT IN THE MIDDLE OF KRASKIN'S KILLERS!
EEEEEEGH!
THEN THE GERMANS ARE ALMOST ON US! WE MUST STOP THEM, FALCONS . . !
Johnny's Hurricane had missed the recent attack, because of a mechanical fault . . .
IT IS ALL RIGHT NOW, ENGLISH! WE FIX WHILE YOU WERE ATTACKING THE GUNS. . .AND RIG SOME BOMB-RACKS UNDER THE WINGS!
THANKS, LADS! I'LL MAKE SURE THOSE METAL EGGS FIND A GOOD HOME . . !
As the pitiful assortment of planes took off, and headed west . . .
THERE'S OUR TARGET, ALEX– JERRY INFANTRY, SUPPORTED BY A TROOP OF TANKS!
I SEE THEM, JOHNNY, RED!
. . . BUT WE MUST LEAVE THE PANZERS TO YOU AND YOUR BOMBS!
OKAY, ALEX! JUST KEEP FIGHTING AND FLYING AS LONG AS YOU CAN . . .
Johnny led the first strafe . . .
AYIEEEEEEEE!
IF I CAN KNOCK OUT THE TANKS, IT MIGHT ENCOURAGE THE RUSSIAN TROOPS TO STOP RUNNING–SO I GOTTA MAKE EVERY BOMB COUNT . . !
But, then . . .
HELL, WE'VE GOT COMPANY. . . ME 109'S! THEY MUST HAVE BEEN WHISTLED UP BY THE TANKS!
LEADER TO FALCONS! ATTACK AT WILL . . !
. . . WE MUST TRY AND HOLD THEM OFF WHILE JOHNNY DEALS WITH THE TANKS! HAAA! NOW WE PROVE TO THAT SPECIAL-BRANCH PIG THAT THE FALCONS ARE NOT COWARDS!
NO! THEY. . .THEY'LL PROVE IT WITH THEIR LIVES– THEY HAVEN'T A CHANCE!

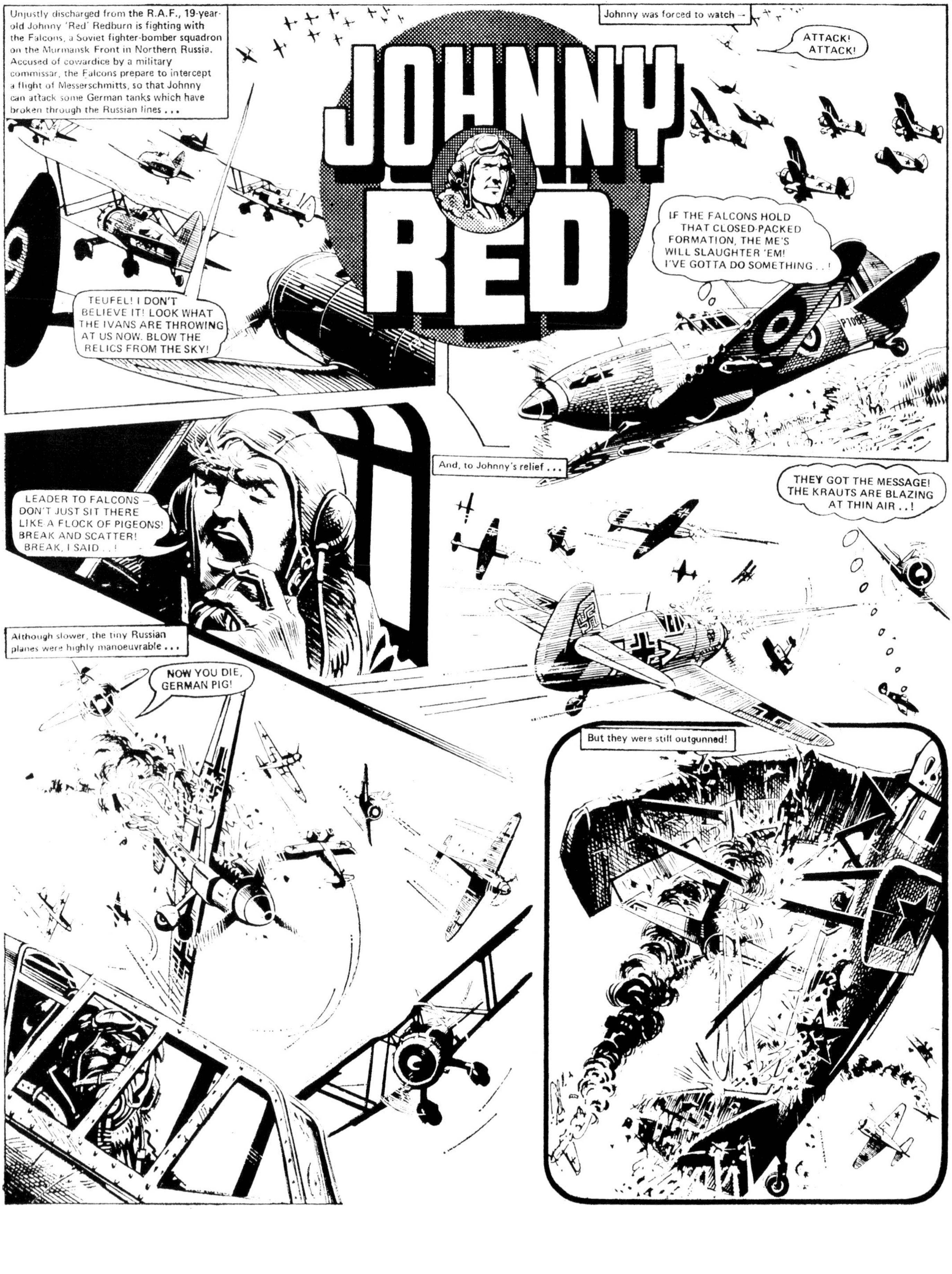

JOHNNY RED
Unjustly discharged from the R.A.F., 19-year-old Johnny 'Red' Redburn is fighting with the Falcons, a Soviet fighter-bomber squadron on the Murmansk Front in Northern Russia. Accused of cowardice by a military commissar, the Falcons prepare to intercept a flight of Messerschmitts, so that Johnny can attack some German tanks which have broken through the Russian lines . . .
TEUFEL! I DON'T BELIEVE IT! LOOK WHAT THE IVANS ARE THROWING AT US NOW. BLOW THE RELICS FROM THE SKY!
Johnny was forced to watch –
ATTACK! ATTACK!
IF THE FALCONS HOLD THAT CLOSED-PACKED FORMATION, THE ME'S WILL SLAUGHTER 'EM! I'VE GOTTA DO SOMETHING . . !
LEADER TO FALCONS – DON'T JUST SIT THERE LIKE A FLOCK OF PIGEONS! BREAK AND SCATTER! BREAK, I SAID . . !
And, to Johnny's relief . . .
THEY GOT THE MESSAGE! THE KRAUTS ARE BLAZING AT THIN AIR . . !
Although slower, the tiny Russian planes were highly manoeuvrable . . .
NOW YOU DIE, GERMAN PIG!
But they were still outgunned!

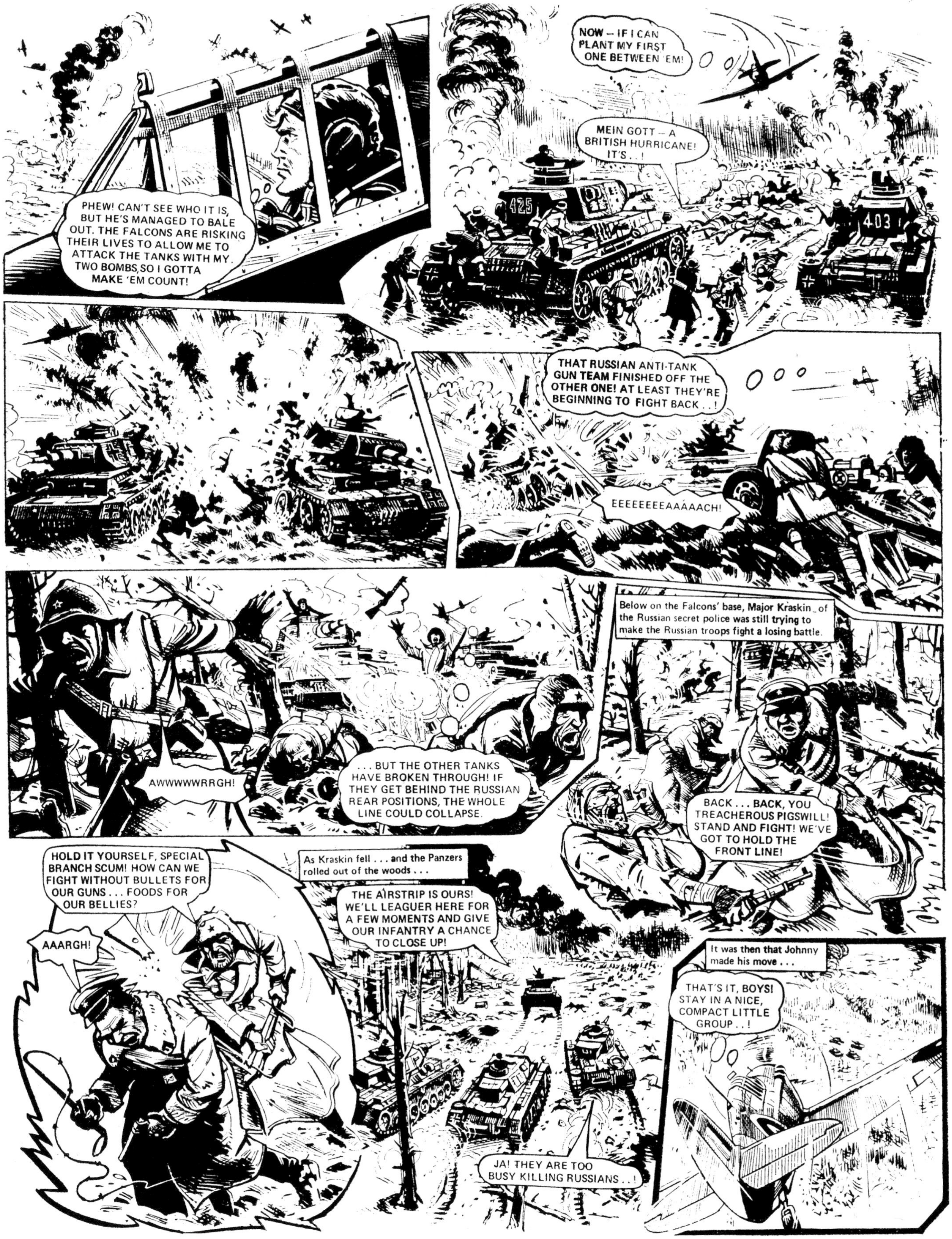
PHEW! CAN'T SEE WHO IT IS, BUT HE'S MANAGED TO BALE OUT. THE FALCONS ARE RISKING THEIR LIVES TO ALLOW ME TO ATTACK THE TANKS WITH MY TWO BOMBS, SO I GOTTA MAKE 'EM COUNT!
NOW – IF I CAN PLANT MY FIRST ONE BETWEEN 'EM!
MEIN GOTT – A BRITISH HURRICANE! IT'S . . !
425
403
THAT RUSSIAN ANTI-TANK GUN TEAM FINISHED OFF THE OTHER ONE! AT LEAST THEY'RE BEGINNING TO FIGHT BACK . . !
EEEEEEEEAAÁÁACH!
AWWWWWRRGH!
. . . BUT THE OTHER TANKS HAVE BROKEN THROUGH! IF THEY GET BEHIND THE RUSSIAN REAR POSITIONS, THE WHOLE LINE COULD COLLAPSE.
Below on the Falcons' base, Major Kraskin of the Russian secret police was still trying to make the Russian troops fight a losing battle.
BACK . . . BACK, YOU TREACHEROUS PIGSWILL! STAND AND FIGHT! WE'VE GOT TO HOLD THE FRONT LINE!
HOLD IT YOURSELF, SPECIAL BRANCH SCUM! HOW CAN WE FIGHT WITHOUT BULLETS FOR OUR GUNS . . . FOODS FOR OUR BELLIES?
AAARGH!
As Kraskin fell . . . and the Panzers rolled out of the woods . . .
THE AIRSTRIP IS OURS! WE'LL LEAGUER HERE FOR A FEW MOMENTS AND GIVE OUR INFANTRY A CHANCE TO CLOSE UP!
JA! THEY ARE TOO BUSY KILLING RUSSIANS . . !
It was then that Johnny made his move . . .
THAT'S IT, BOYS! STAY IN A NICE, COMPACT LITTLE GROUP . . !

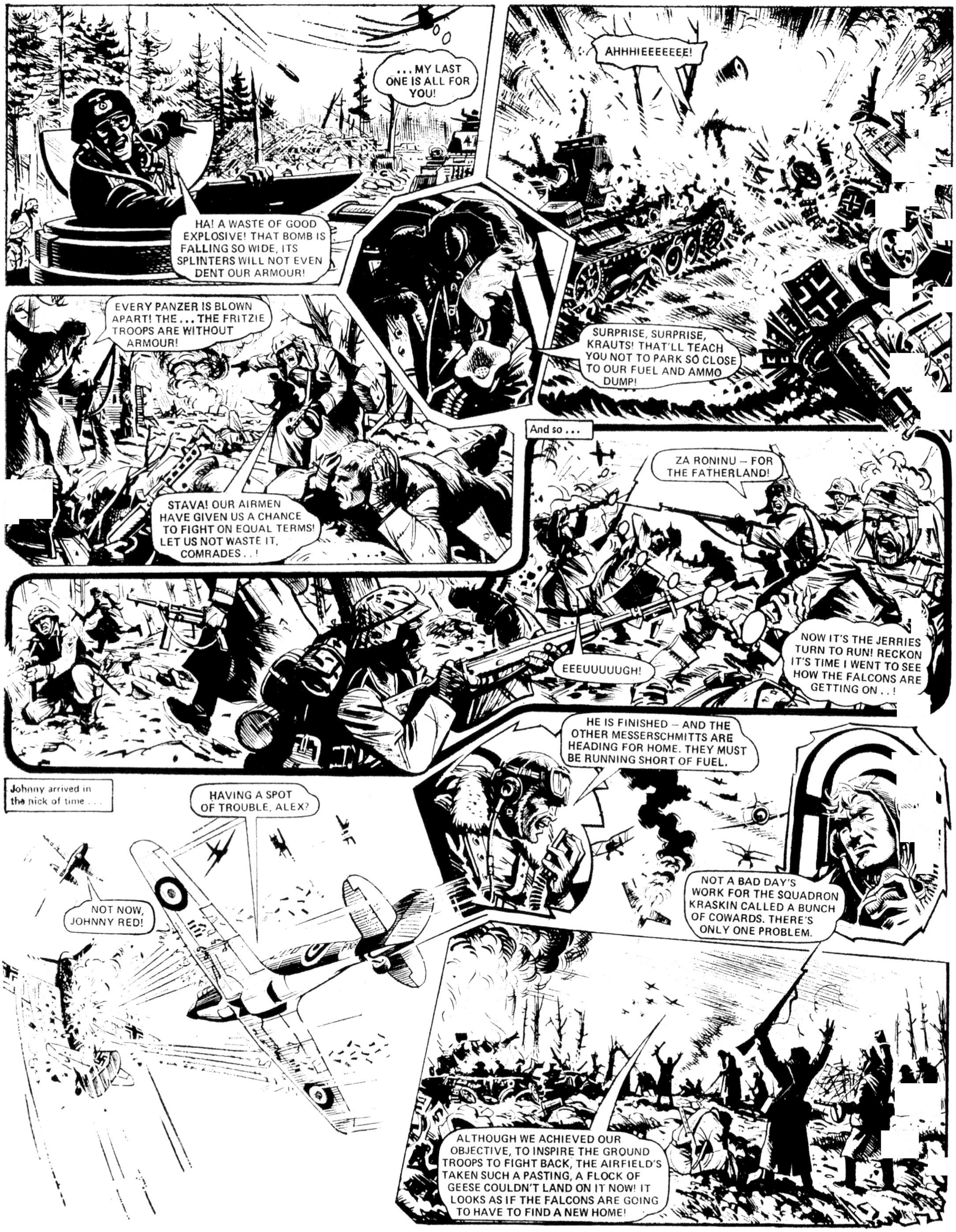
...MY LAST ONE IS ALL FOR YOU!
HA! A WASTE OF GOOD EXPLOSIVE! THAT BOMB IS FALLING SO WIDE, ITS SPLINTERS WILL NOT EVEN DENT OUR ARMOUR!
AHHHIEEEEEEE!
SURPRISE, SURPRISE, KRAUTS! THAT'LL TEACH YOU NOT TO PARK SO CLOSE TO OUR FUEL AND AMMO DUMP!
EVERY PANZER IS BLOWN APART! THE ... THE FRITZIE TROOPS ARE WITHOUT ARMOUR!
STAVA! OUR AIRMEN HAVE GIVEN US A CHANCE TO FIGHT ON EQUAL TERMS! LET US NOT WASTE IT, COMRADES..!
And so ...
ZA RONINU – FOR THE FATHERLAND!
EEEUUUUUGH!
NOW IT'S THE JERRIES TURN TO RUN! RECKON IT'S TIME I WENT TO SEE HOW THE FALCONS ARE GETTING ON..!
Johnny arrived in the nick of time ...
HAVING A SPOT OF TROUBLE, ALEX?
NOT NOW, JOHNNY RED!
HE IS FINISHED – AND THE OTHER MESSERSCHMITTS ARE HEADING FOR HOME. THEY MUST BE RUNNING SHORT OF FUEL.
NOT A BAD DAY'S WORK FOR THE SQUADRON KRASKIN CALLED A BUNCH OF COWARDS. THERE'S ONLY ONE PROBLEM.
ALTHOUGH WE ACHIEVED OUR OBJECTIVE, TO INSPIRE THE GROUND TROOPS TO FIGHT BACK, THE AIRFIELD'S TAKEN SUCH A PASTING, A FLOCK OF GEESE COULDN'T LAND ON IT NOW! IT LOOKS AS IF THE FALCONS ARE GOING TO HAVE TO FIND A NEW HOME!

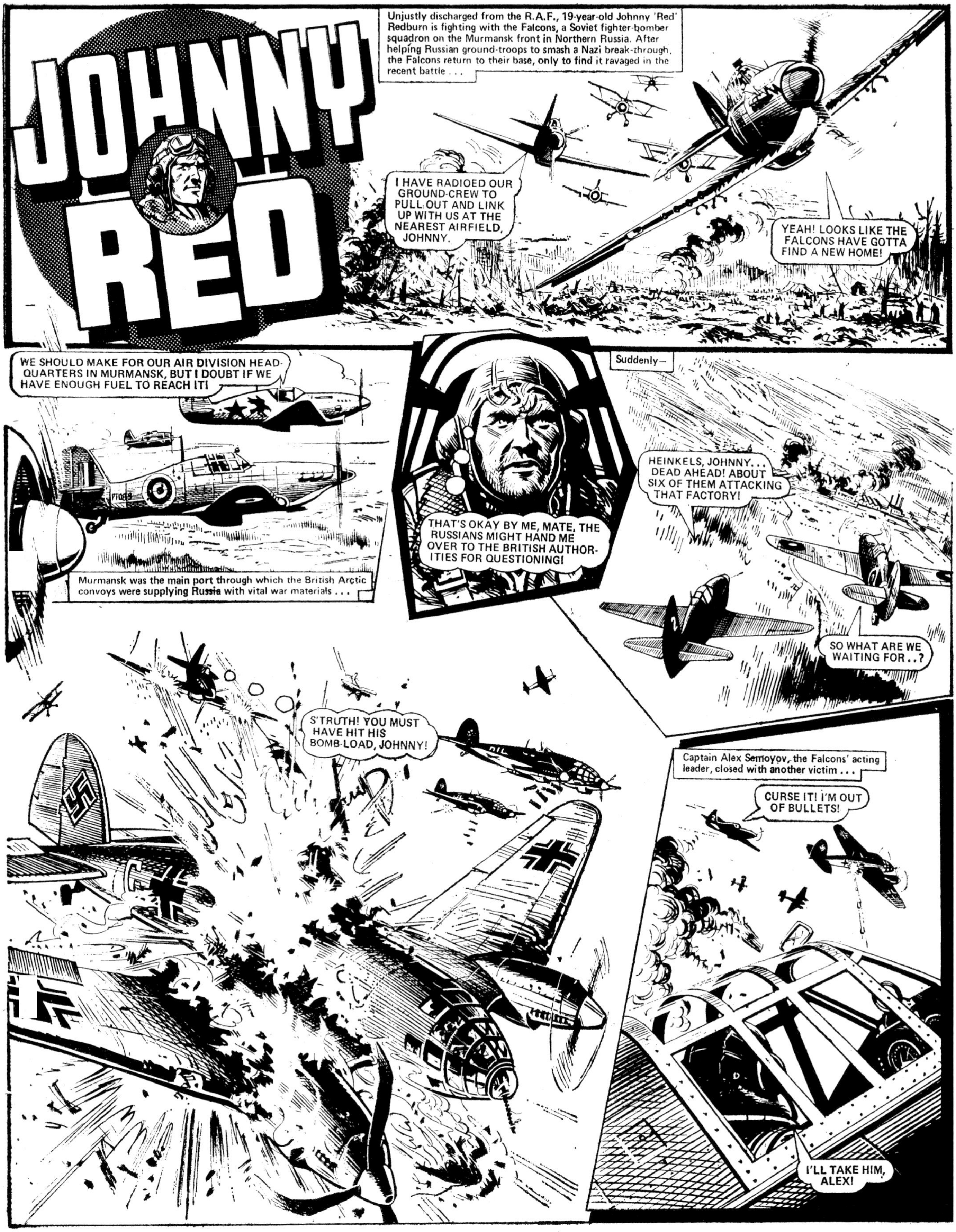

JOHNNY RED
Unjustly discharged from the R.A.F., 19-year-old Johnny 'Red' Redburn is fighting with the Falcons, a Soviet fighter-bomber squadron on the Murmansk front in Northern Russia. After helping Russian ground-troops to smash a Nazi break-through, the Falcons return to their base, only to find it ravaged in the recent battle . . .
I HAVE RADIOED OUR GROUND-CREW TO PULL-OUT AND LINK UP WITH US AT THE NEAREST AIRFIELD, JOHNNY.
YEAH! LOOKS LIKE THE FALCONS HAVE GOTTA FIND A NEW HOME!
WE SHOULD MAKE FOR OUR AIR DIVISION HEAD-QUARTERS IN MURMANSK, BUT I DOUBT IF WE HAVE ENOUGH FUEL TO REACH IT!
Murmansk was the main port through which the British Arctic convoys were supplying Russia with vital war materials . . .
THAT'S OKAY BY ME, MATE. THE RUSSIANS MIGHT HAND ME OVER TO THE BRITISH AUTHOR-ITIES FOR QUESTIONING!
Suddenly—
HEINKELS, JOHNNY... DEAD AHEAD! ABOUT SIX OF THEM ATTACKING THAT FACTORY!
SO WHAT ARE WE WAITING FOR ..?
S'TRUTH! YOU MUST HAVE HIT HIS BOMB-LOAD, JOHNNY!
Captain Alex Semoyov, the Falcons' acting leader, closed with another victim . . .
CURSE IT! I'M OUT OF BULLETS!
I'LL TAKE HIM, ALEX!

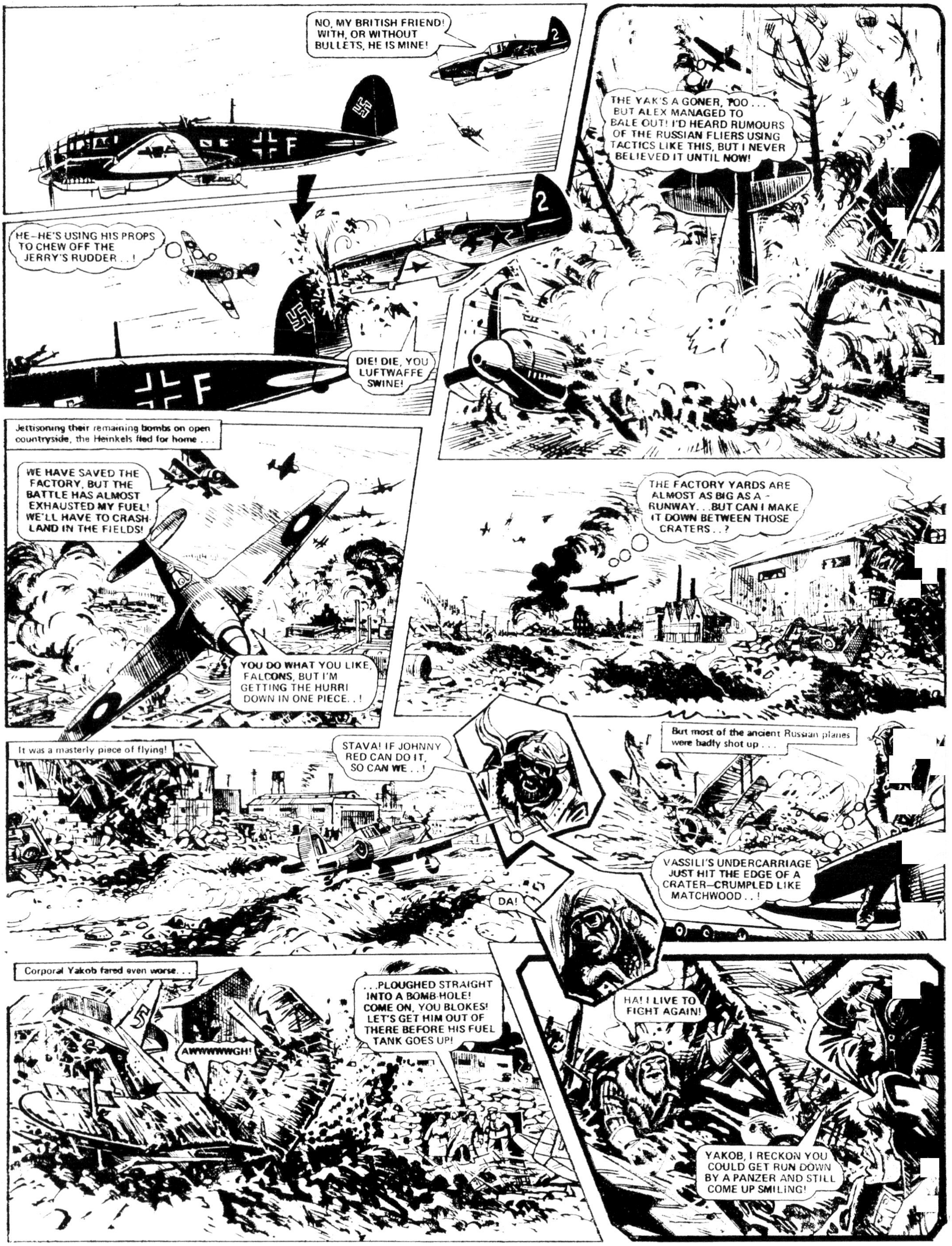
NO, MY BRITISH FRIEND! WITH, OR WITHOUT BULLETS, HE IS MINE!
HE–HE'S USING HIS PROPS TO CHEW OFF THE JERRY'S RUDDER . . !
DIE! DIE, YOU LUFTWAFFE SWINE!
THE YAK'S A GONER, TOO . . . BUT ALEX MANAGED TO BALE OUT! I'D HEARD RUMOURS OF THE RUSSIAN FLIERS USING TACTICS LIKE THIS, BUT I NEVER BELIEVED IT UNTIL NOW!
Jettisoning their remaining bombs on open countryside, the Heinkels fled for home . . .
WE HAVE SAVED THE FACTORY, BUT THE BATTLE HAS ALMOST EXHAUSTED MY FUEL! WE'LL HAVE TO CRASH-LAND IN THE FIELDS!
YOU DO WHAT YOU LIKE, FALCONS, BUT I'M GETTING THE HURRI DOWN IN ONE PIECE . . !
THE FACTORY YARDS ARE ALMOST AS BIG AS A RUNWAY . . . BUT CAN I MAKE IT DOWN BETWEEN THOSE CRATERS . . ?
It was a masterly piece of flying!
STAVA! IF JOHNNY RED CAN DO IT, SO CAN WE . . !
But most of the ancient Russian planes were badly shot up . . .
VASSILI'S UNDERCARRIAGE JUST HIT THE EDGE OF A CRATER–CRUMPLED LIKE MATCHWOOD . . !
DA!
Corporal Yakob fared even worse . . .
AWWWWWGH!
. . . PLOUGHED STRAIGHT INTO A BOMB-HOLE! COME ON, YOU BLOKES! LET'S GET HIM OUT OF THERE BEFORE HIS FUEL TANK GOES UP!
HA! I LIVE TO FIGHT AGAIN!
YAKOB, I RECKON YOU COULD GET RUN DOWN BY A PANZER AND STILL COME UP SMILING!

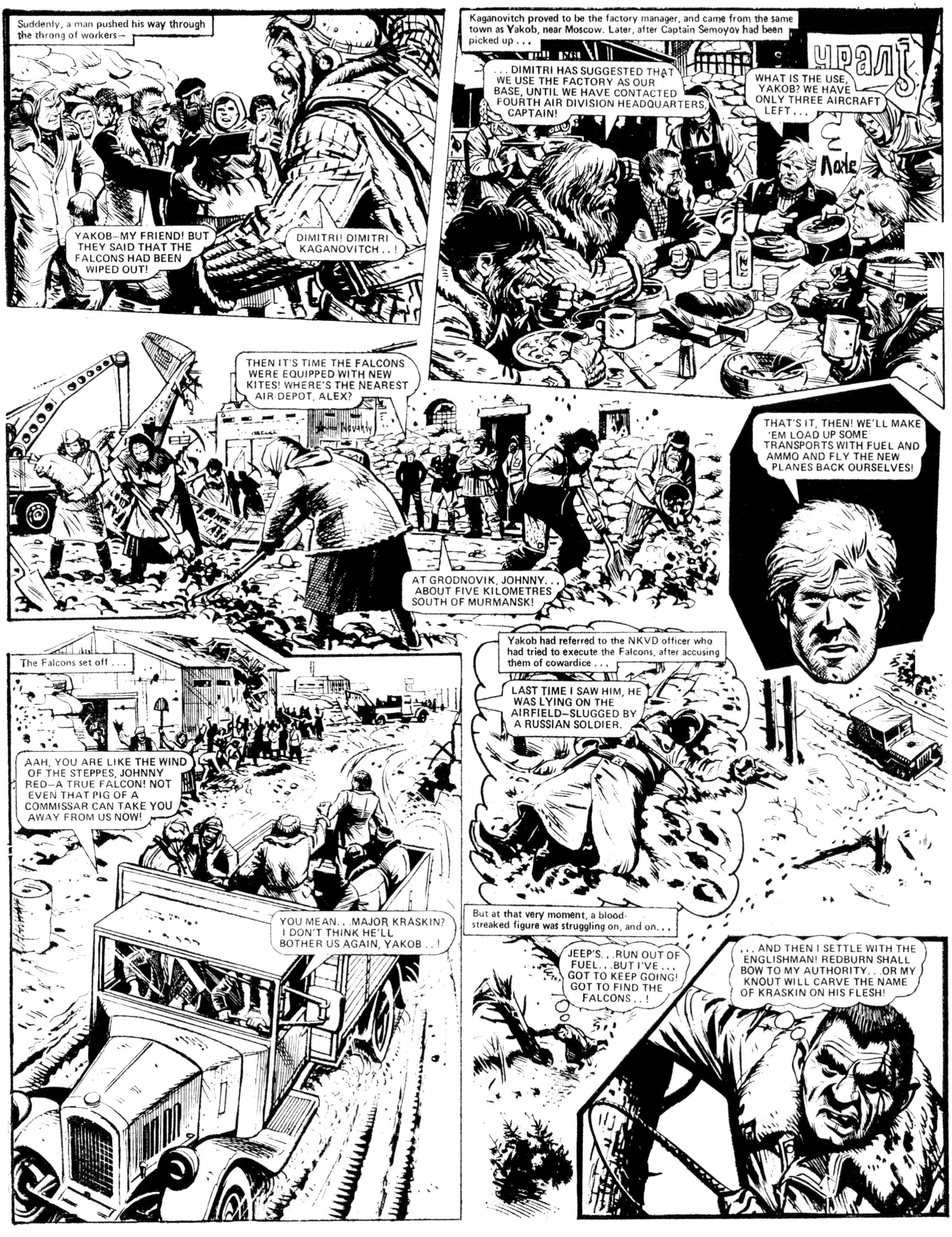
Suddenly, a man pushed his way through the throng of workers—
YAKOB—MY FRIEND! BUT THEY SAID THAT THE FALCONS HAD BEEN WIPED OUT!
DIMITRI! DIMITRI KAGANOVITCH . . !
Kaganovitch proved to be the factory manager, and came from the same town as Yakob, near Moscow. Later, after Captain Semoyov had been picked up . . .
. . . DIMITRI HAS SUGGESTED THAT WE USE THE FACTORY AS OUR BASE, UNTIL WE HAVE CONTACTED FOURTH AIR DIVISION HEADQUARTERS, CAPTAIN!
WHAT IS THE USE, YAKOB? WE HAVE ONLY THREE AIRCRAFT LEFT . . .
THEN IT'S TIME THE FALCONS WERE EQUIPPED WITH NEW KITES! WHERE'S THE NEAREST AIR-DEPOT, ALEX?
AT GRODNOVIK, JOHNNY. . ABOUT FIVE KILOMETRES SOUTH OF MURMANSK!
THAT'S IT, THEN! WE'LL MAKE 'EM LOAD UP SOME TRANSPORTS WITH FUEL AND AMMO AND FLY THE NEW PLANES BACK OURSELVES!
The Falcons set off . . .
AAH, YOU ARE LIKE THE WIND OF THE STEPPES, JOHNNY RED—A TRUE FALCON! NOT EVEN THAT PIG OF A COMMISSAR CAN TAKE YOU AWAY FROM US NOW!
YOU MEAN. . .MAJOR KRASKIN? I DON'T THINK HE'LL BOTHER US AGAIN, YAKOB . . !
Yakob had referred to the NKVD officer who had tried to execute the Falcons, after accusing them of cowardice . . .
LAST TIME I SAW HIM, HE WAS LYING ON THE AIRFIELD—SLUGGED BY A RUSSIAN SOLDIER.
But at that very moment, a blood-streaked figure was struggling on, and on. . .
JEEP'S. . .RUN OUT OF FUEL. . .BUT I'VE . . . GOT TO KEEP GOING! GOT TO FIND THE FALCONS . . !
. . . AND THEN I SETTLE WITH THE ENGLISHMAN! REDBURN SHALL BOW TO MY AUTHORITY. . .OR MY KNOUT WILL CARVE THE NAME OF KRASKIN ON HIS FLESH!

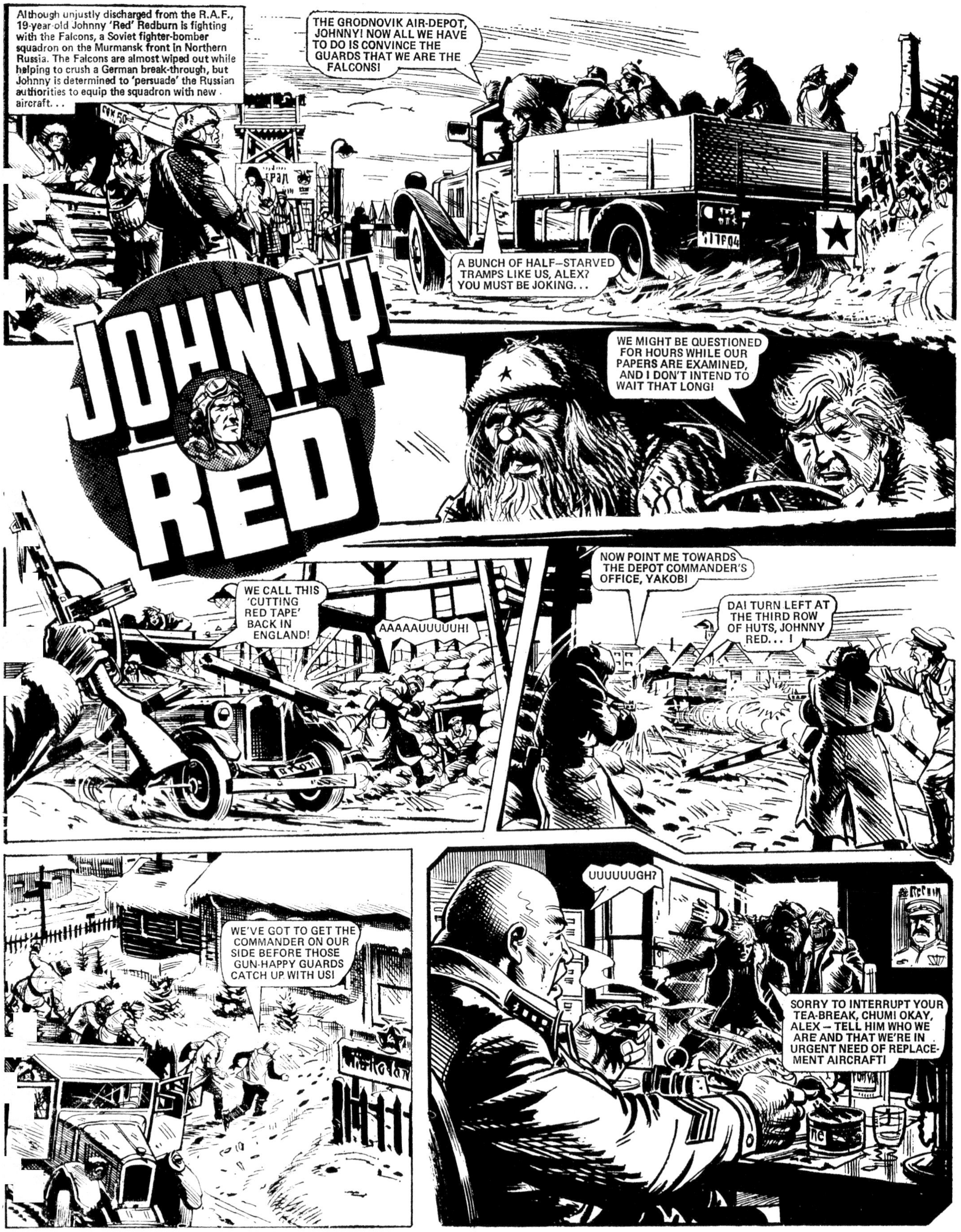

Although unjustly discharged from the R.A.F., 19-year-old Johnny 'Red' Redburn is fighting with the Falcons, a Soviet fighter-bomber squadron on the Murmansk front in Northern Russia. The Falcons are almost wiped out while helping to crush a German break-through, but Johnny is determined to 'persuade' the Russian authorities to equip the squadron with new aircraft. . .
THE GRODNOVIK AIR-DEPOT, JOHNNY! NOW ALL WE HAVE TO DO IS CONVINCE THE GUARDS THAT WE ARE THE FALCONS!
A BUNCH OF HALF-STARVED TRAMPS LIKE US, ALEX? YOU MUST BE JOKING. . .
JOHNNY RED
WE MIGHT BE QUESTIONED FOR HOURS WHILE OUR PAPERS ARE EXAMINED, AND I DON'T INTEND TO WAIT THAT LONG!
WE CALL THIS 'CUTTING RED TAPE' BACK IN ENGLAND!
AAAAAUUUUUH!
NOW POINT ME TOWARDS THE DEPOT COMMANDER'S OFFICE, YAKOB!
DAI TURN LEFT AT THE THIRD ROW OF HUTS, JOHNNY RED. . . !
WE'VE GOT TO GET THE COMMANDER ON OUR SIDE BEFORE THOSE GUN-HAPPY GUARDS CATCH UP WITH US!
UUUUUUGH?
SORRY TO INTERRUPT YOUR TEA-BREAK, CHUM! OKAY, ALEX — TELL HIM WHO WE ARE AND THAT WE'RE IN URGENT NEED OF REPLACEMENT AIRCRAFT!

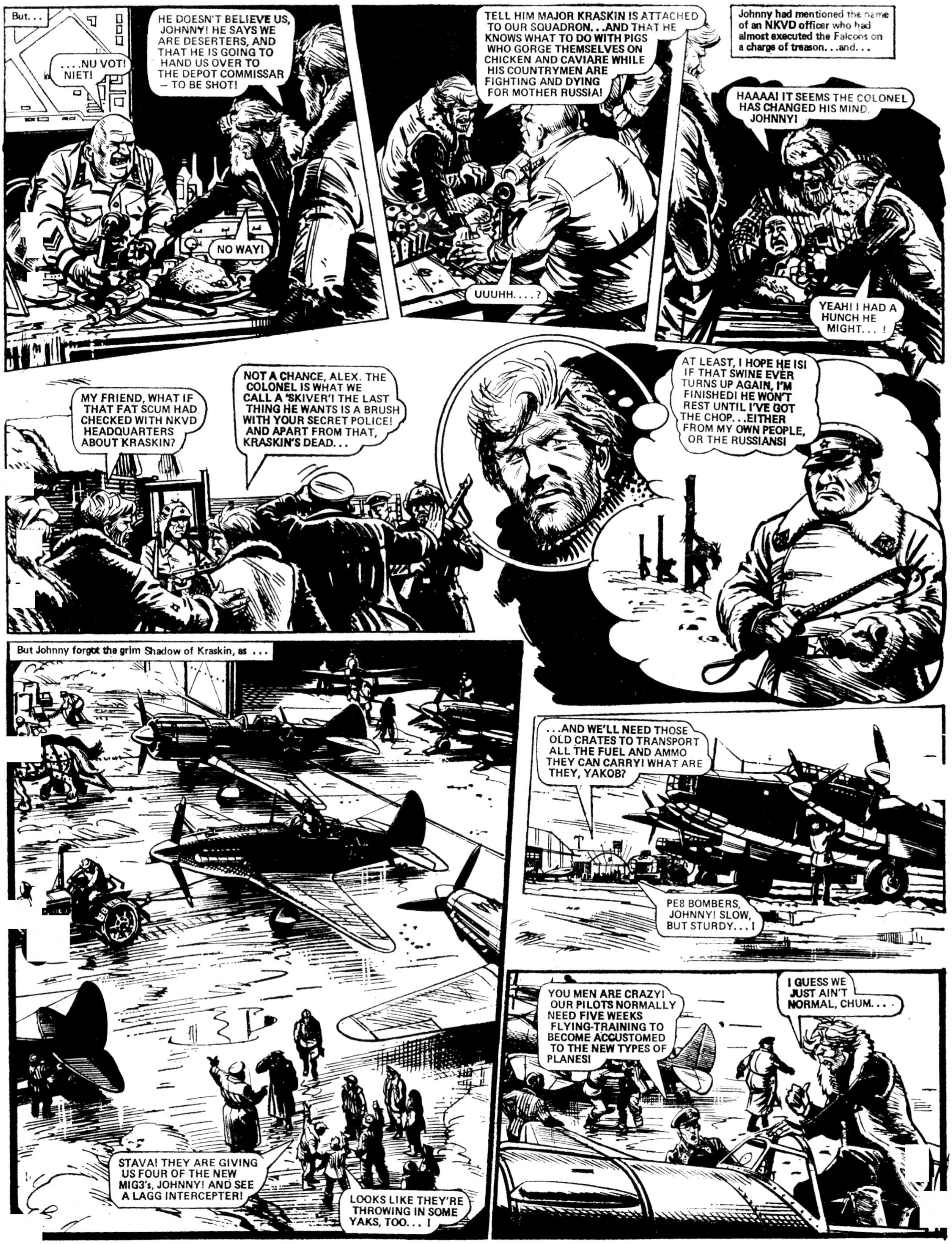

But...
....NU VOT! NIET!
HE DOESN'T BELIEVE US, JOHNNY! HE SAYS WE ARE DESERTERS, AND THAT HE IS GOING TO HAND US OVER TO THE DEPOT COMMISSAR – TO BE SHOT!
NO WAY!
TELL HIM MAJOR KRASKIN IS ATTACHED TO OUR SQUADRON...AND THAT HE KNOWS WHAT TO DO WITH PIGS WHO GORGE THEMSELVES ON CHICKEN AND CAVIARE WHILE HIS COUNTRYMEN ARE FIGHTING AND DYING FOR MOTHER RUSSIA!
UUUHH....?
Johnny had mentioned the name of an NKVD officer who had almost executed the Falcons on a charge of treason...and...
HAAAA! IT SEEMS THE COLONEL HAS CHANGED HIS MIND, JOHNNY!
YEAH! I HAD A HUNCH HE MIGHT... !
MY FRIEND, WHAT IF THAT FAT SCUM HAD CHECKED WITH NKVD HEADQUARTERS ABOUT KRASKIN?
NOT A CHANCE, ALEX. THE COLONEL IS WHAT WE CALL A 'SKIVER'! THE LAST THING HE WANTS IS A BRUSH WITH YOUR SECRET POLICE! AND APART FROM THAT, KRASKIN'S DEAD...
AT LEAST, I HOPE HE IS! IF THAT SWINE EVER TURNS UP AGAIN, I'M FINISHED! HE WON'T REST UNTIL I'VE GOT THE CHOP...EITHER FROM MY OWN PEOPLE, OR THE RUSSIANS!
But Johnny forgot the grim Shadow of Kraskin, as ...
STAVA! THEY ARE GIVING US FOUR OF THE NEW MIG3's, JOHNNY! AND SEE A LAGG INTERCEPTER!
LOOKS LIKE THEY'RE THROWING IN SOME YAKS, TOO... !
...AND WE'LL NEED THOSE OLD CRATES TO TRANSPORT ALL THE FUEL AND AMMO THEY CAN CARRY! WHAT ARE THEY, YAKOB?
PE8 BOMBERS, JOHNNY! SLOW, BUT STURDY... !
YOU MEN ARE CRAZY! OUR PILOTS NORMALLY NEED FIVE WEEKS FLYING-TRAINING TO BECOME ACCUSTOMED TO THE NEW TYPES OF PLANES!
I GUESS WE JUST AIN'T NORMAL, CHUM...

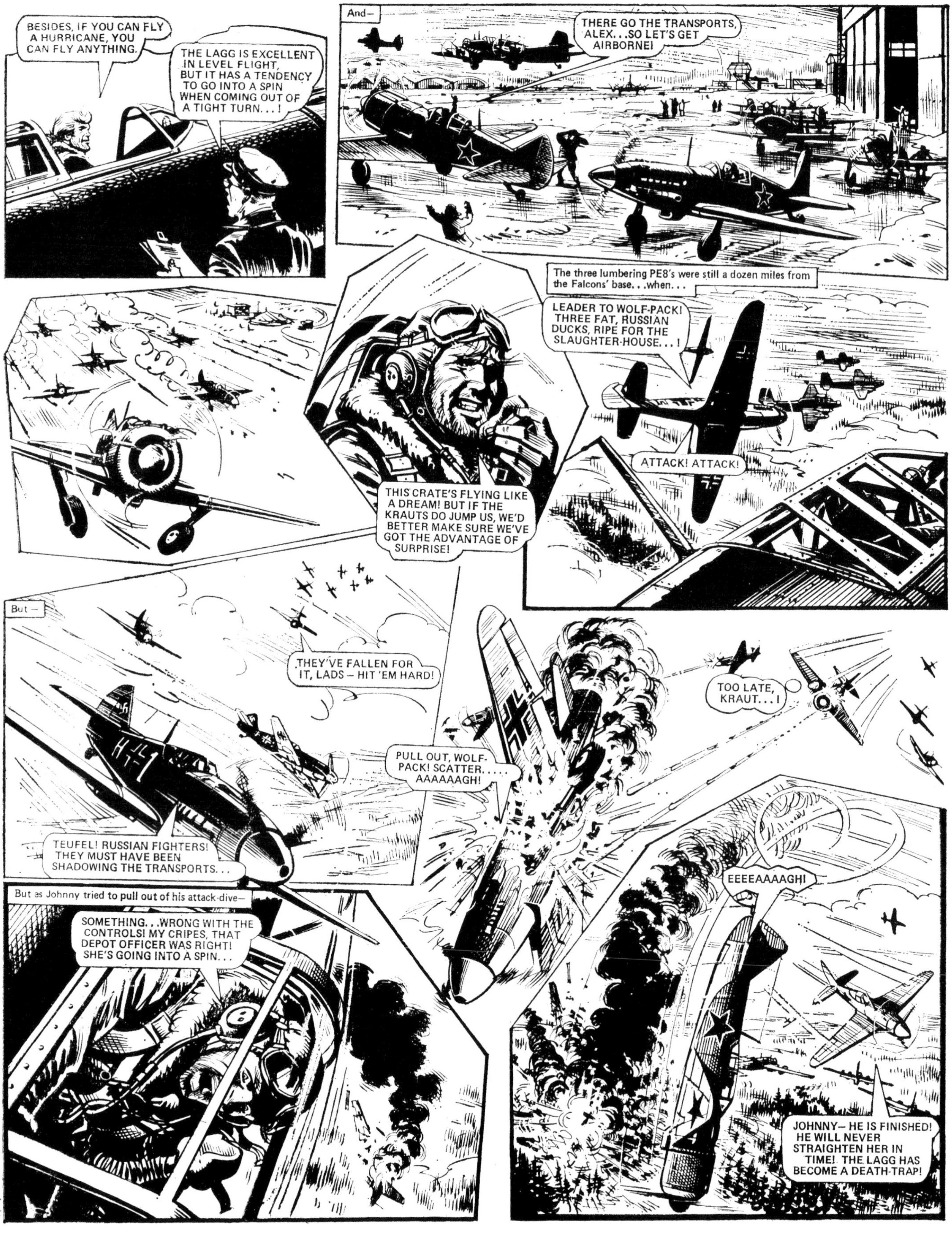
BESIDES, IF YOU CAN FLY A HURRICANE, YOU CAN FLY ANYTHING.
THE LAGG IS EXCELLENT IN LEVEL FLIGHT, BUT IT HAS A TENDENCY TO GO INTO A SPIN WHEN COMING OUT OF A TIGHT TURN...!
And—
THERE GO THE TRANSPORTS, ALEX...SO LET'S GET AIRBORNE!
THIS CRATE'S FLYING LIKE A DREAM! BUT IF THE KRAUTS DO JUMP US, WE'D BETTER MAKE SURE WE'VE GOT THE ADVANTAGE OF SURPRISE!
The three lumbering PE8's were still a dozen miles from the Falcons' base...when...
LEADER TO WOLF-PACK! THREE FAT, RUSSIAN DUCKS, RIPE FOR THE SLAUGHTER-HOUSE...!
ATTACK! ATTACK!
But —
THEY'VE FALLEN FOR IT, LADS – HIT 'EM HARD!
TEUFEL! RUSSIAN FIGHTERS! THEY MUST HAVE BEEN SHADOWING THE TRANSPORTS...
PULL OUT, WOLF-PACK! SCATTER..... AAAAAAGH!
TOO LATE, KRAUT...!
But as Johnny tried to pull out of his attack-dive—
SOMETHING...WRONG WITH THE CONTROLS! MY CRIPES, THAT DEPOT OFFICER WAS RIGHT! SHE'S GOING INTO A SPIN...
EEEEAAAAGH!
JOHNNY— HE IS FINISHED! HE WILL NEVER STRAIGHTEN HER IN TIME! THE LAGG HAS BECOME A DEATH-TRAP!

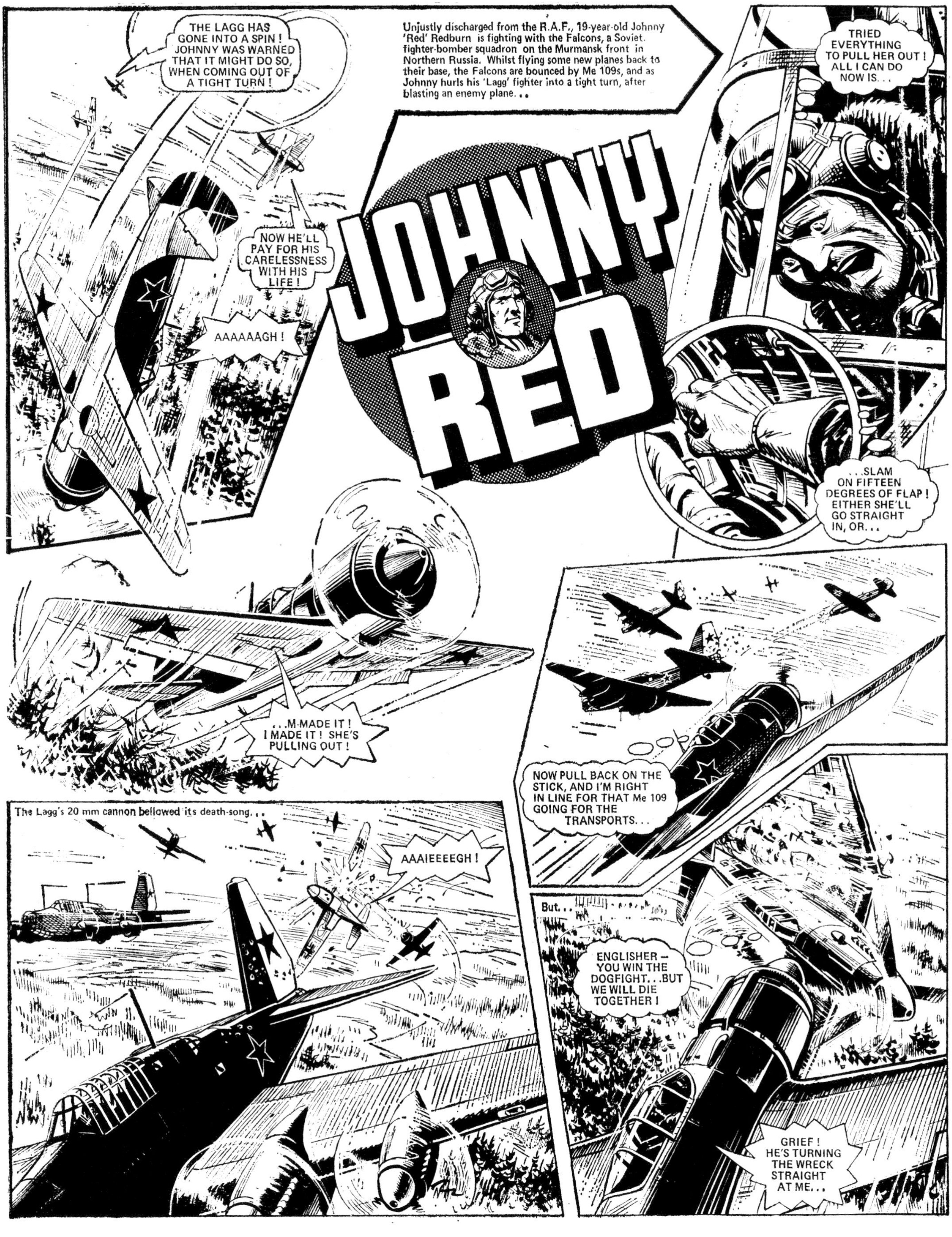
THE LAGG HAS GONE INTO A SPIN! JOHNNY WAS WARNED THAT IT MIGHT DO SO, WHEN COMING OUT OF A TIGHT TURN!
Unjustly discharged from the R.A.F., 19-year-old Johnny 'Red' Redburn is fighting with the Falcons, a Soviet fighter-bomber squadron on the Murmansk front in Northern Russia. Whilst flying some new planes back to their base, the Falcons are bounced by Me 109s, and as Johnny hurls his 'Lagg' fighter into a tight turn, after blasting an enemy plane...
JOHNNY RED
NOW HE'LL PAY FOR HIS CARELESSNESS WITH HIS LIFE!
AAAAAAGH!
TRIED EVERYTHING TO PULL HER OUT! ALL I CAN DO NOW IS...
...SLAM ON FIFTEEN DEGREES OF FLAP! EITHER SHE'LL GO STRAIGHT IN, OR...
...M-MADE IT! I MADE IT! SHE'S PULLING OUT!
NOW PULL BACK ON THE STICK, AND I'M RIGHT IN LINE FOR THAT Me 109 GOING FOR THE TRANSPORTS...
The Lagg's 20 mm cannon bellowed its death-song...
AAAIEEEEGH!
But...
ENGLISHER – YOU WIN THE DOGFIGHT...BUT WE WILL DIE TOGETHER!
GRIEF! HE'S TURNING THE WRECK STRAIGHT AT ME...

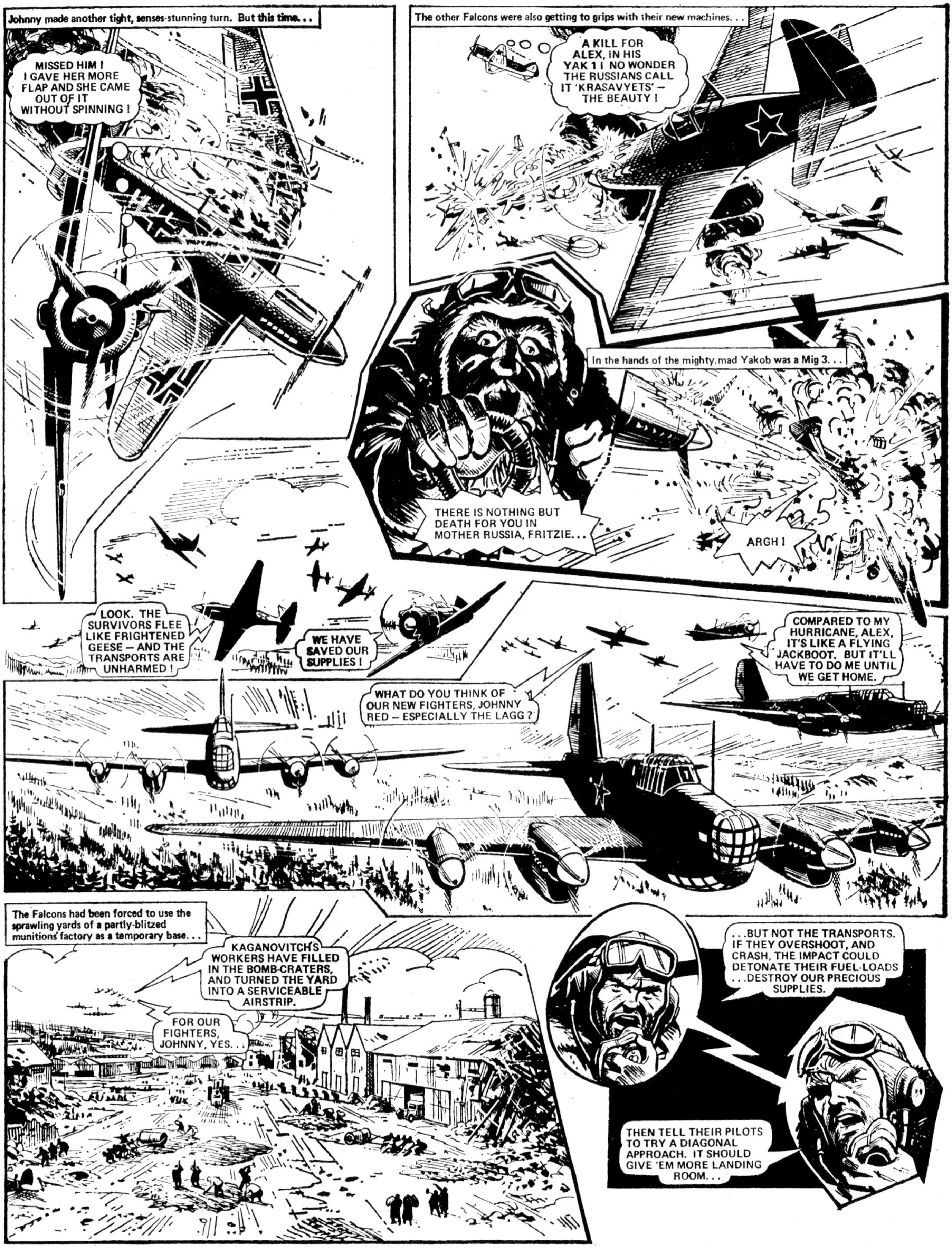
Johnny made another tight, senses-stunning turn. But this time...
MISSED HIM! I GAVE HER MORE FLAP AND SHE CAME OUT OF IT WITHOUT SPINNING!
The other Falcons were also getting to grips with their new machines...
A KILL FOR ALEX, IN HIS YAK 1! NO WONDER THE RUSSIANS CALL IT 'KRASAVYETS' — THE BEAUTY!
In the hands of the mighty, mad Yakob was a Mig 3...
THERE IS NOTHING BUT DEATH FOR YOU IN MOTHER RUSSIA, FRITZIE...
ARGH!
LOOK. THE SURVIVORS FLEE LIKE FRIGHTENED GEESE — AND THE TRANSPORTS ARE UNHARMED!
WE HAVE SAVED OUR SUPPLIES!
WHAT DO YOU THINK OF OUR NEW FIGHTERS, JOHNNY RED — ESPECIALLY THE LAGG?
COMPARED TO MY HURRICANE, ALEX, IT'S LIKE A FLYING JACKBOOT. BUT IT'LL HAVE TO DO ME UNTIL WE GET HOME.
The Falcons had been forced to use the sprawling yards of a partly-blitzed munitions factory as a temporary base...
KAGANOVITCH'S WORKERS HAVE FILLED IN THE BOMB-CRATERS, AND TURNED THE YARD INTO A SERVICEABLE AIRSTRIP.
FOR OUR FIGHTERS, JOHNNY, YES...
...BUT NOT THE TRANSPORTS. IF THEY OVERSHOOT, AND CRASH, THE IMPACT COULD DETONATE THEIR FUEL-LOADS ...DESTROY OUR PRECIOUS SUPPLIES.
THEN TELL THEIR PILOTS TO TRY A DIAGONAL APPROACH. IT SHOULD GIVE 'EM MORE LANDING ROOM...

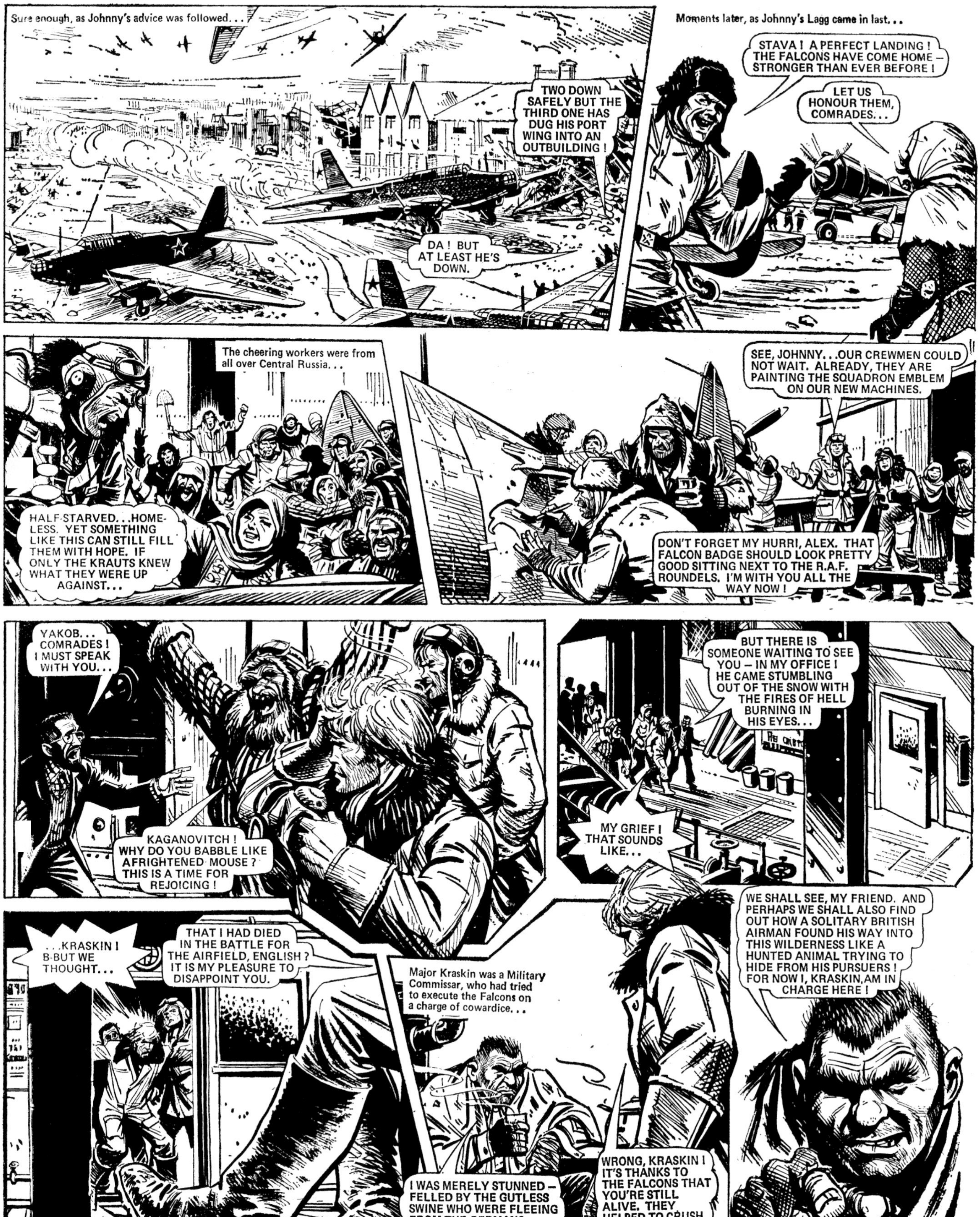
Sure enough, as Johnny's advice was followed...
TWO DOWN SAFELY BUT THE THIRD ONE HAS DUG HIS PORT WING INTO AN OUTBUILDING !
DA ! BUT AT LEAST HE'S DOWN.
Moments later, as Johnny's Lagg came in last...
STAVA ! A PERFECT LANDING ! THE FALCONS HAVE COME HOME – STRONGER THAN EVER BEFORE !
LET US HONOUR THEM, COMRADES...
The cheering workers were from all over Central Russia...
HALF-STARVED...HOME-LESS. YET SOMETHING LIKE THIS CAN STILL FILL THEM WITH HOPE. IF ONLY THE KRAUTS KNEW WHAT THEY WERE UP AGAINST...
SEE, JOHNNY...OUR CREWMEN COULD NOT WAIT. ALREADY, THEY ARE PAINTING THE SQUADRON EMBLEM ON OUR NEW MACHINES.
DON'T FORGET MY HURRI, ALEX. THAT FALCON BADGE SHOULD LOOK PRETTY GOOD SITTING NEXT TO THE R.A.F. ROUNDELS. I'M WITH YOU ALL THE WAY NOW !
YAKOB... COMRADES ! I MUST SPEAK WITH YOU...
KAGANOVITCH ! WHY DO YOU BABBLE LIKE A FRIGHTENED MOUSE ? THIS IS A TIME FOR REJOICING !
BUT THERE IS SOMEONE WAITING TO SEE YOU – IN MY OFFICE ! HE CAME STUMBLING OUT OF THE SNOW WITH THE FIRES OF HELL BURNING IN HIS EYES...
MY GRIEF ! THAT SOUNDS LIKE...
...KRASKIN ! B-BUT WE THOUGHT...
THAT I HAD DIED IN THE BATTLE FOR THE AIRFIELD, ENGLISH ? IT IS MY PLEASURE TO DISAPPOINT YOU.
Major Kraskin was a Military Commissar, who had tried to execute the Falcons on a charge of cowardice...
I WAS MERELY STUNNED – FELLED BY THE GUTLESS SWINE WHO WERE FLEEING FROM THE GERMANS. TRAITORS TO THE MOTHER-LAND – LIKE YOU.
WRONG, KRASKIN ! IT'S THANKS TO THE FALCONS THAT YOU'RE STILL ALIVE. THEY HELPED TO CRUSH THE GERMAN BREAK-THROUGH !
WE SHALL SEE, MY FRIEND. AND PERHAPS WE SHALL ALSO FIND OUT HOW A SOLITARY BRITISH AIRMAN FOUND HIS WAY INTO THIS WILDERNESS LIKE A HUNTED ANIMAL TRYING TO HIDE FROM HIS PURSUERS ! FOR NOW I, KRASKIN, AM IN CHARGE HERE !

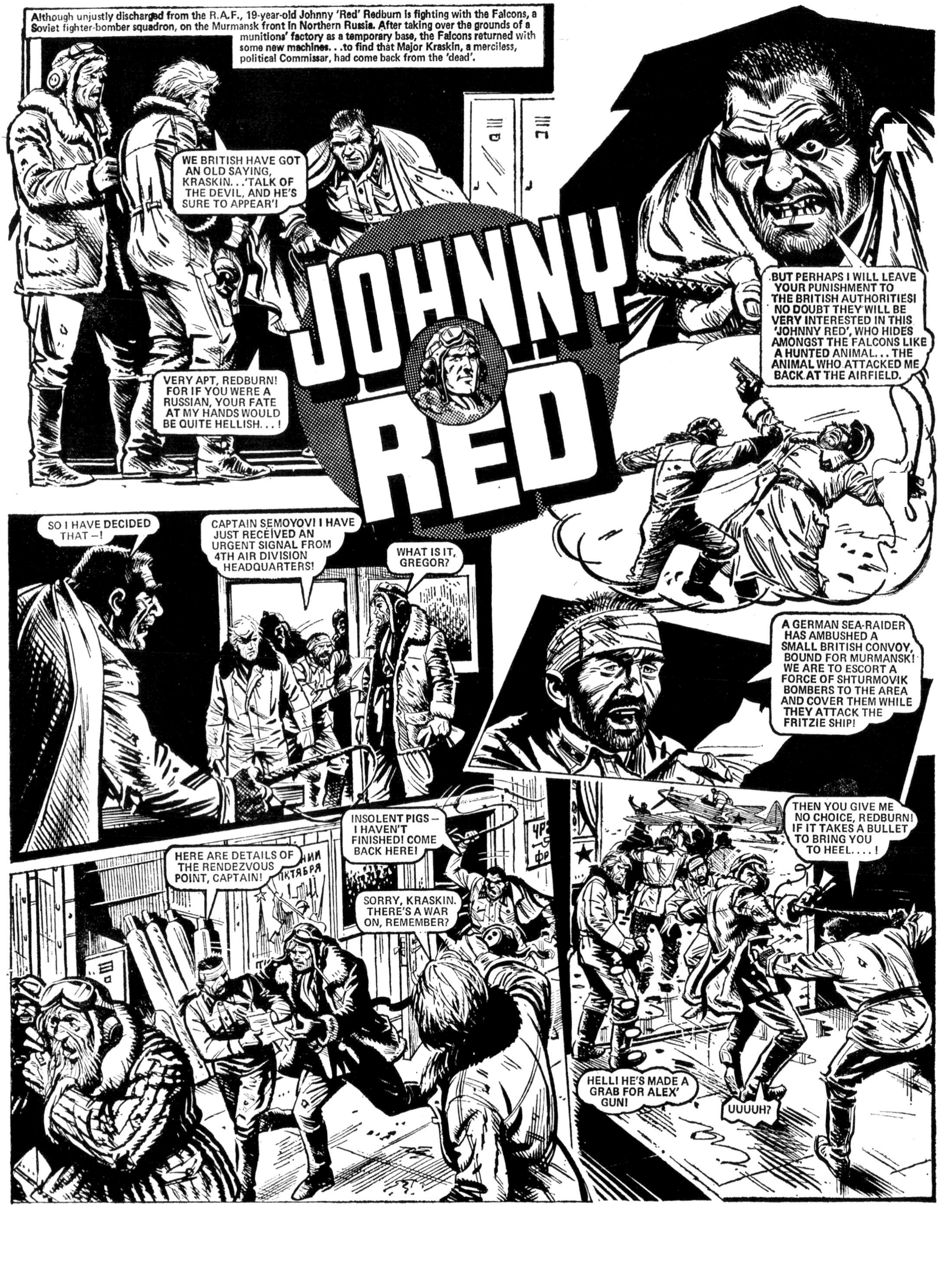
Although unjustly discharged from the R.A.F., 19-year-old Johnny 'Red' Redburn is fighting with the Falcons, a Soviet fighter-bomber squadron, on the Murmansk front in Northern Russia. After taking over the grounds of a munitions' factory as a temporary base, the Falcons returned with some new machines. . .to find that Major Kraskin, a merciless, political Commissar, had come back from the 'dead'.
JOHNNY RED
WE BRITISH HAVE GOT AN OLD SAYING, KRASKIN. . .'TALK OF THE DEVIL, AND HE'S SURE TO APPEAR'!
VERY APT, REDBURN! FOR IF YOU WERE A RUSSIAN, YOUR FATE AT MY HANDS WOULD BE QUITE HELLISH. . . !
.BUT PERHAPS I WILL LEAVE YOUR PUNISHMENT TO THE BRITISH AUTHORITIES! NO DOUBT THEY WILL BE VERY INTERESTED IN THIS 'JOHNNY RED', WHO HIDES AMONGST THE FALCONS LIKE A HUNTED ANIMAL. . . THE ANIMAL WHO ATTACKED ME BACK AT THE AIRFIELD.
SO I HAVE DECIDED THAT –!
CAPTAIN SEMOYOV! I HAVE JUST RECEIVED AN URGENT SIGNAL FROM 4TH AIR DIVISION HEADQUARTERS!
WHAT IS IT, GREGOR?
A GERMAN SEA-RAIDER HAS AMBUSHED A SMALL BRITISH CONVOY, BOUND FOR MURMANSK! WE ARE TO ESCORT A FORCE OF SHTURMOVIK BOMBERS TO THE AREA AND COVER THEM WHILE THEY ATTACK THE FRITZIE SHIP!
HERE ARE DETAILS OF THE RENDEZVOUS POINT, CAPTAIN!
INSOLENT PIGS – I HAVEN'T FINISHED! COME BACK HERE!
SORRY, KRASKIN. THERE'S A WAR ON, REMEMBER?
THEN YOU GIVE ME NO CHOICE, REDBURN! IF IT TAKES A BULLET TO BRING YOU TO HEEL. . . . !
HELL! HE'S MADE A GRAB FOR ALEX' GUN!
UUUUH?

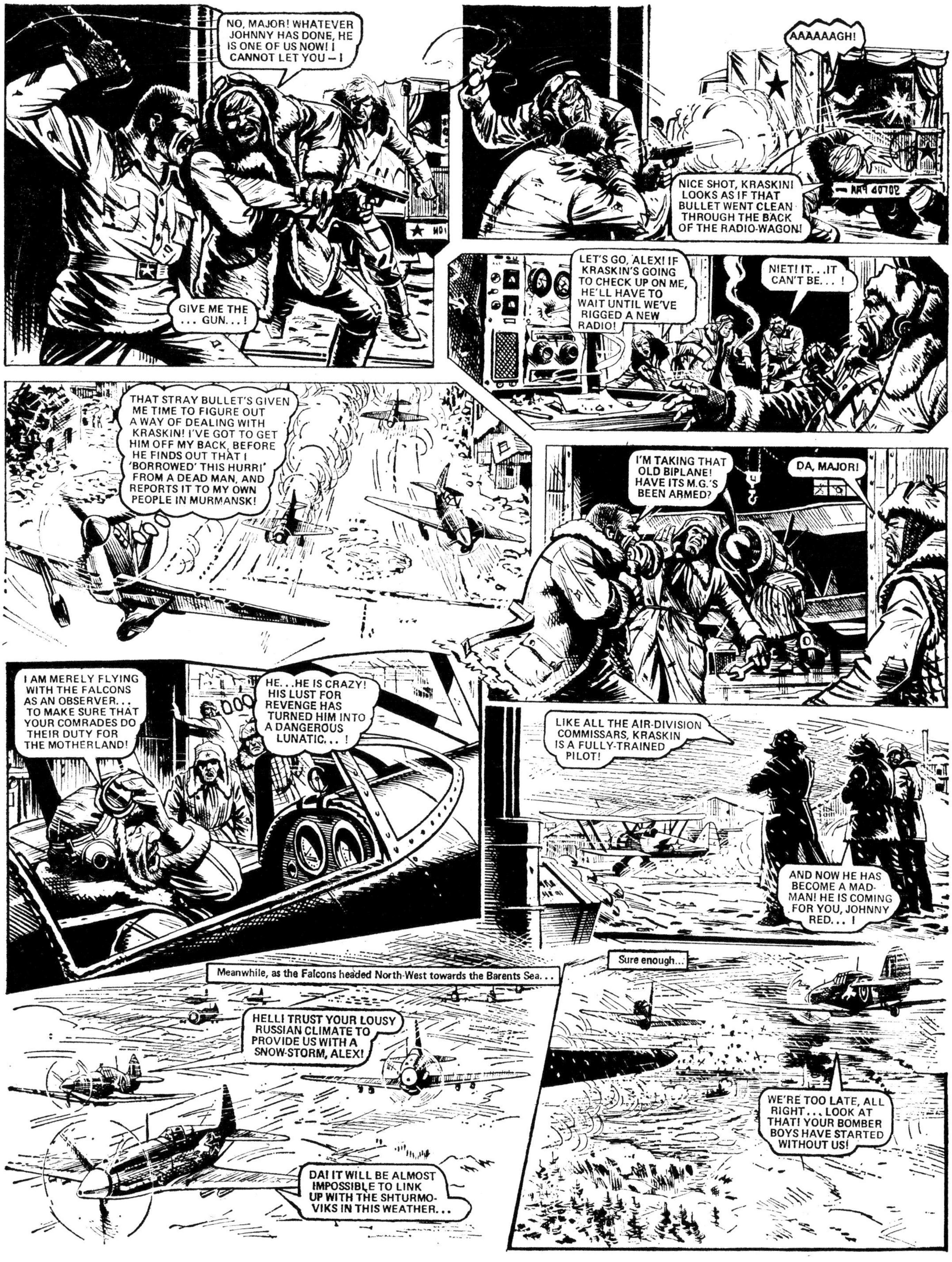

NO, MAJOR! WHATEVER JOHNNY HAS DONE, HE IS ONE OF US NOW! I CANNOT LET YOU – !
GIVE ME THE . . . GUN. . . !
AAAAAAGH!
NICE SHOT, KRASKIN! LOOKS AS IF THAT BULLET WENT CLEAN THROUGH THE BACK OF THE RADIO-WAGON!
LET'S GO, ALEX! IF KRASKIN'S GOING TO CHECK UP ON ME, HE'LL HAVE TO WAIT UNTIL WE'VE RIGGED A NEW RADIO!
NIET! IT. . . IT CAN'T BE. . . !
THAT STRAY BULLET'S GIVEN ME TIME TO FIGURE OUT A WAY OF DEALING WITH KRASKIN! I'VE GOT TO GET HIM OFF MY BACK, BEFORE HE FINDS OUT THAT I 'BORROWED' THIS HURRI' FROM A DEAD MAN, AND REPORTS IT TO MY OWN PEOPLE IN MURMANSK!
I'M TAKING THAT OLD BIPLANE! HAVE ITS M.G.'S BEEN ARMED?
DA, MAJOR!
I AM MERELY FLYING WITH THE FALCONS AS AN OBSERVER. . . TO MAKE SURE THAT YOUR COMRADES DO THEIR DUTY FOR THE MOTHERLAND!
HE. . . HE IS CRAZY! HIS LUST FOR REVENGE HAS TURNED HIM INTO A DANGEROUS LUNATIC. . . !
LIKE ALL THE AIR-DIVISION COMMISSARS, KRASKIN IS A FULLY-TRAINED PILOT!
AND NOW HE HAS BECOME A MAD-MAN! HE IS COMING FOR YOU, JOHNNY RED. . . !
Meanwhile, as the Falcons headed North-West towards the Barents Sea. . .
HELL! TRUST YOUR LOUSY RUSSIAN CLIMATE TO PROVIDE US WITH A SNOW-STORM, ALEX!
DA! IT WILL BE ALMOST IMPOSSIBLE TO LINK UP WITH THE SHTURMO-VIKS IN THIS WEATHER. . .
Sure enough. . .
WE'RE TOO LATE, ALL RIGHT. . . LOOK AT THAT! YOUR BOMBER BOYS HAVE STARTED WITHOUT US!

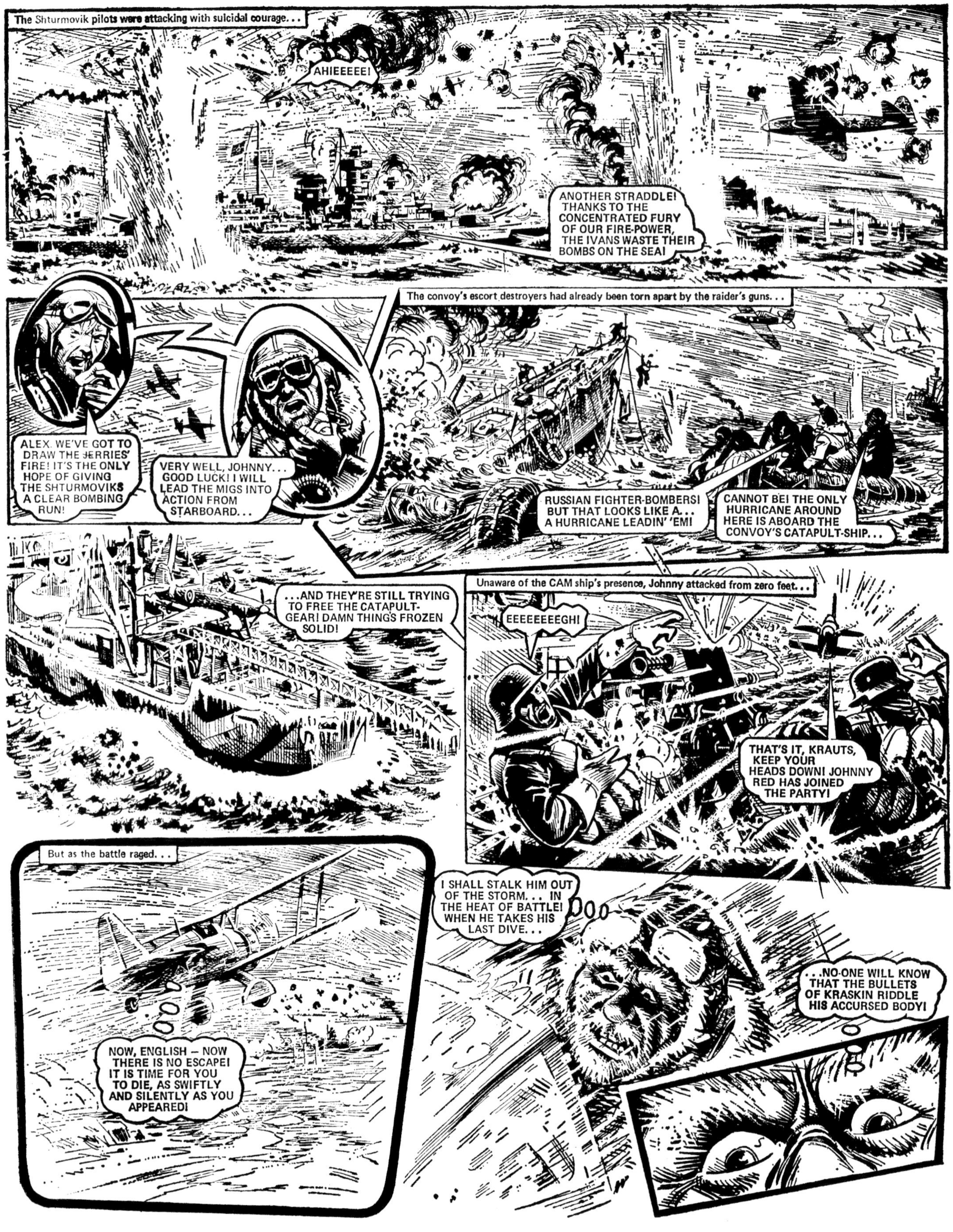
The Shturmovik pilots were attacking with suicidal courage...
AHIEEEEE!
ANOTHER STRADDLE! THANKS TO THE CONCENTRATED FURY OF OUR FIRE-POWER, THE IVANS WASTE THEIR BOMBS ON THE SEA!
ALEX. WE'VE GOT TO DRAW THE JERRIES' FIRE! IT'S THE ONLY HOPE OF GIVING THE SHTURMOVIKS A CLEAR BOMBING RUN!
VERY WELL, JOHNNY... GOOD LUCK! I WILL LEAD THE MIGS INTO ACTION FROM STARBOARD...
The convoy's escort destroyers had already been torn apart by the raider's guns...
RUSSIAN FIGHTER-BOMBERS! BUT THAT LOOKS LIKE A... A HURRICANE LEADIN' 'EM!
CANNOT BE! THE ONLY HURRICANE AROUND HERE IS ABOARD THE CONVOY'S CATAPULT-SHIP...
...AND THEY'RE STILL TRYING TO FREE THE CATAPULT-GEAR! DAMN THINGS FROZEN SOLID!
Unaware of the CAM ship's presence, Johnny attacked from zero feet...
EEEEEEEEGH!
THAT'S IT, KRAUTS, KEEP YOUR HEADS DOWN! JOHNNY RED HAS JOINED THE PARTY!
But as the battle raged...
NOW, ENGLISH – NOW THERE IS NO ESCAPE! IT IS TIME FOR YOU TO DIE, AS SWIFTLY AND SILENTLY AS YOU APPEARED!
I SHALL STALK HIM OUT OF THE STORM... IN THE HEAT OF BATTLE! WHEN HE TAKES HIS LAST DIVE...
...NO-ONE WILL KNOW THAT THE BULLETS OF KRASKIN RIDDLE HIS ACCURSED BODY!

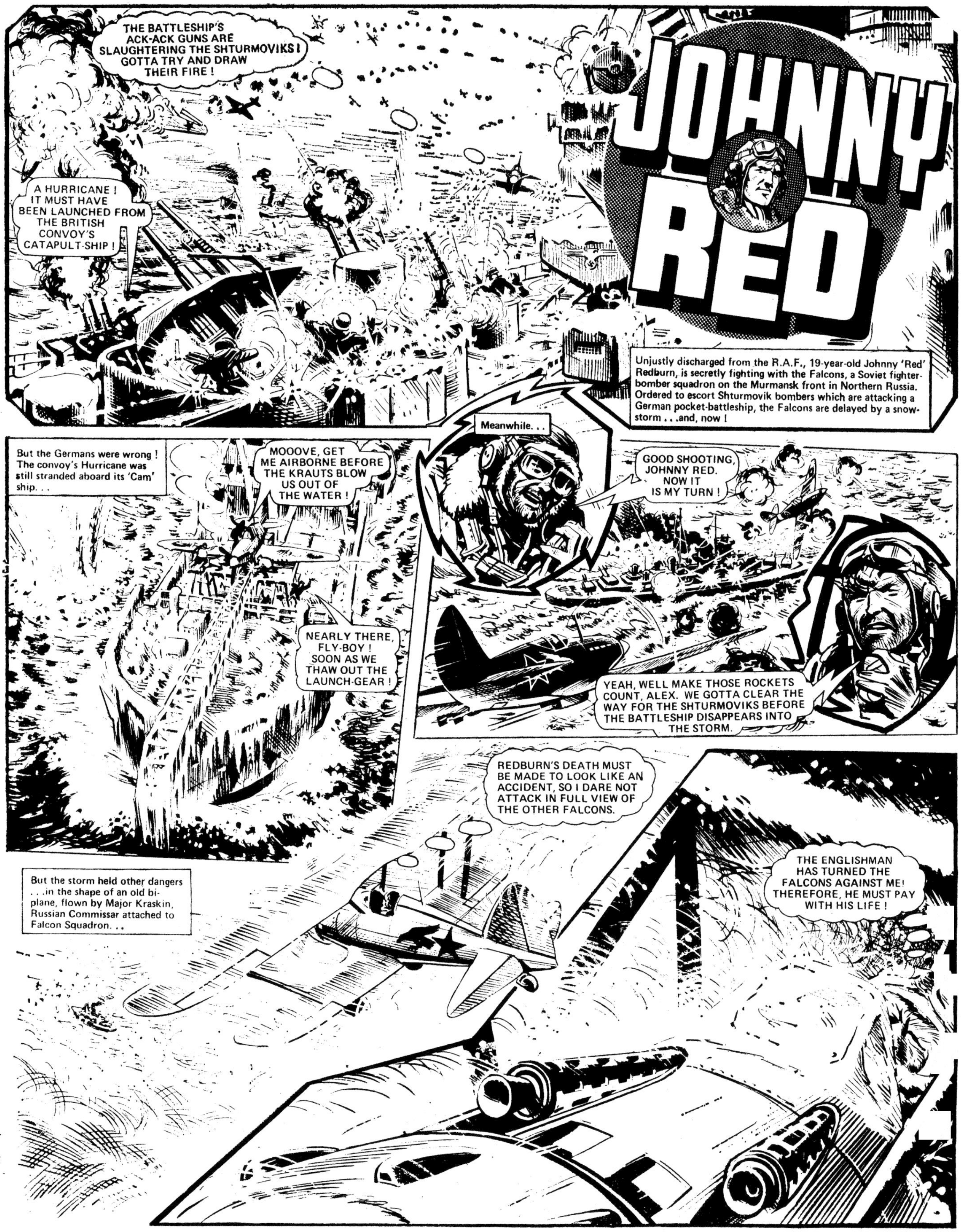
THE BATTLESHIP'S ACK-ACK GUNS ARE SLAUGHTERING THE SHTURMOVIKS! GOTTA TRY AND DRAW THEIR FIRE!
JOHNNY RED
A HURRICANE! IT MUST HAVE BEEN LAUNCHED FROM THE BRITISH CONVOY'S CATAPULT-SHIP!
Unjustly discharged from the R.A.F., 19-year-old Johnny 'Red' Redburn, is secretly fighting with the Falcons, a Soviet fighter-bomber squadron on the Murmansk front in Northern Russia. Ordered to escort Shturmovik bombers which are attacking a German pocket-battleship, the Falcons are delayed by a snow-storm . . . and, now!
But the Germans were wrong! The convoy's Hurricane was still stranded aboard its 'Cam' ship. . .
MOOOVE, GET ME AIRBORNE BEFORE THE KRAUTS BLOW US OUT OF THE WATER!
NEARLY THERE, FLY-BOY! SOON AS WE THAW OUT THE LAUNCH-GEAR!
Meanwhile. . .
GOOD SHOOTING, JOHNNY RED. NOW IT IS MY TURN!
YEAH, WELL MAKE THOSE ROCKETS COUNT, ALEX. WE GOTTA CLEAR THE WAY FOR THE SHTURMOVIKS BEFORE THE BATTLESHIP DISAPPEARS INTO THE STORM.
But the storm held other dangers . . . in the shape of an old bi-plane, flown by Major Kraskin, Russian Commissar attached to Falcon Squadron. . .
REDBURN'S DEATH MUST BE MADE TO LOOK LIKE AN ACCIDENT, SO I DARE NOT ATTACK IN FULL VIEW OF THE OTHER FALCONS.
THE ENGLISHMAN HAS TURNED THE FALCONS AGAINST ME! THEREFORE, HE MUST PAY WITH HIS LIFE!

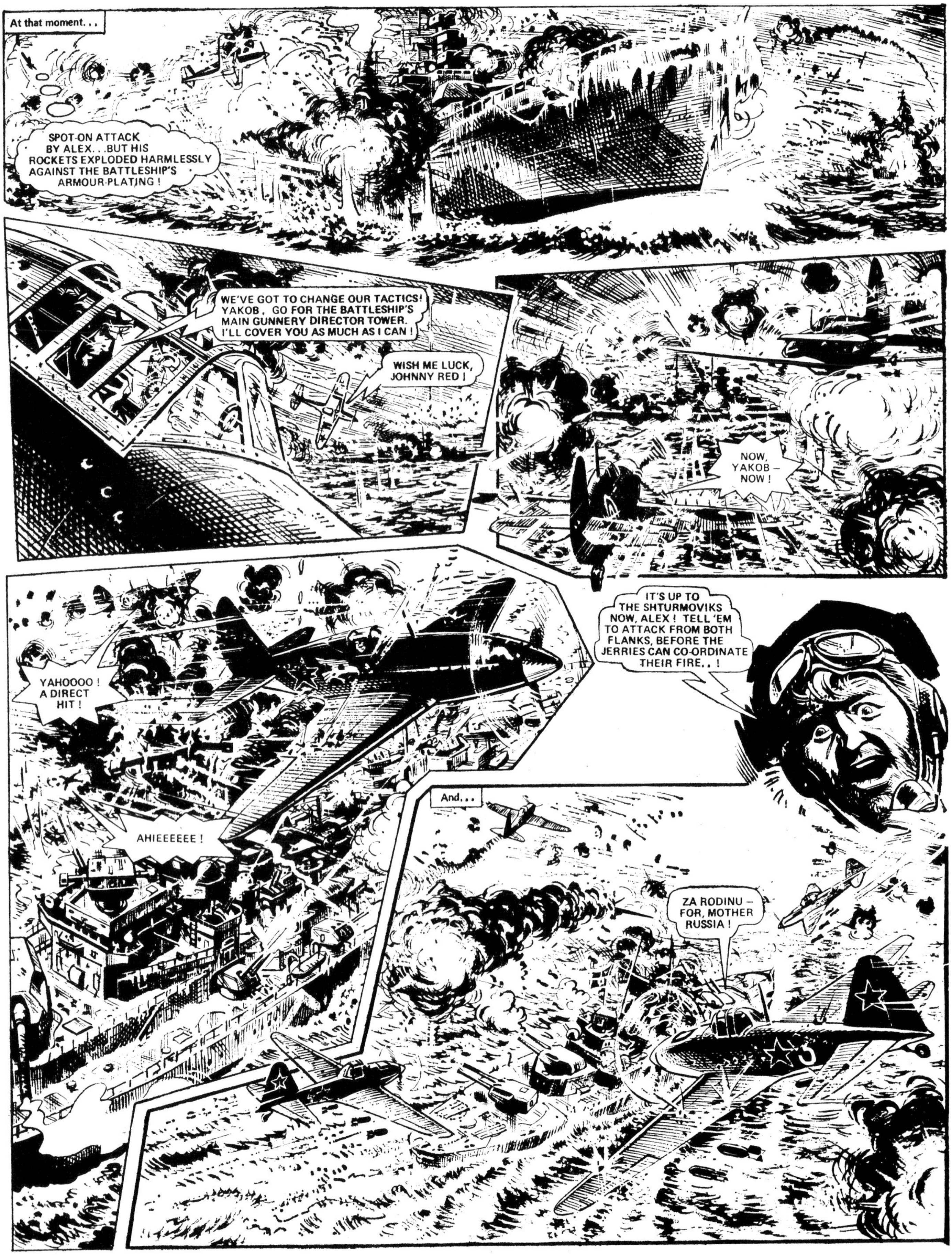
At that moment. . .
SPOT-ON ATTACK BY ALEX. . .BUT HIS ROCKETS EXPLODED HARMLESSLY AGAINST THE BATTLESHIP'S ARMOUR-PLATING !
WE'VE GOT TO CHANGE OUR TACTICS! YAKOB, GO FOR THE BATTLESHIP'S MAIN GUNNERY DIRECTOR TOWER. I'LL COVER YOU AS MUCH AS I CAN !
WISH ME LUCK, JOHNNY RED !
NOW, YAKOB – NOW !
YAHOOOO ! A DIRECT HIT !
AHIEEEEEE !
IT'S UP TO THE SHTURMOVIKS NOW, ALEX ! TELL 'EM TO ATTACK FROM BOTH FLANKS, BEFORE THE JERRIES CAN CO-ORDINATE THEIR FIRE. . !
And. . .
ZA RODINU – FOR, MOTHER RUSSIA !

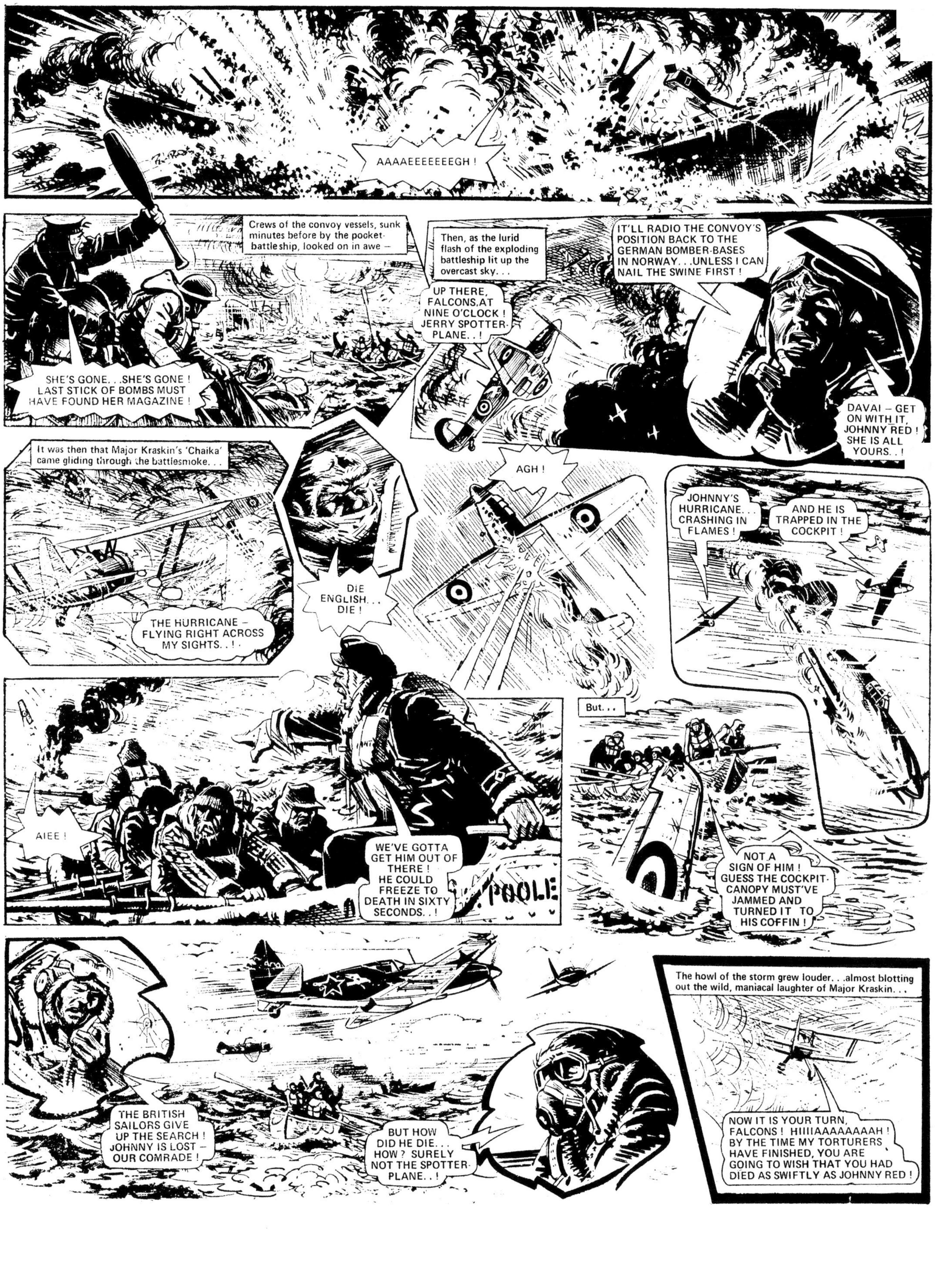

AAAAEEEEEEEGH !
Crews of the convoy vessels, sunk minutes before by the pocket-battleship, looked on in awe –
SHE'S GONE. . .SHE'S GONE ! LAST STICK OF BOMBS MUST HAVE FOUND HER MAGAZINE !
Then, as the lurid flash of the exploding battleship lit up the overcast sky. . .
UP THERE, FALCONS, AT NINE O'CLOCK ! JERRY SPOTTER-PLANE. . !
IT'LL RADIO THE CONVOY'S POSITION BACK TO THE GERMAN BOMBER-BASES IN NORWAY. . .UNLESS I CAN NAIL THE SWINE FIRST !
DAVAI – GET ON WITH IT, JOHNNY RED ! SHE IS ALL YOURS. . !
It was then that Major Kraskin's 'Chaika' came gliding through the battlesmoke. . .
THE HURRICANE – FLYING RIGHT ACROSS MY SIGHTS. . ! .
DIE ENGLISH. . . DIE !
AGH !
JOHNNY'S HURRICANE. . CRASHING IN FLAMES !
AND HE IS TRAPPED IN THE COCKPIT !
AIEE !
WE'VE GOTTA GET HIM OUT OF THERE ! HE COULD FREEZE TO DEATH IN SIXTY SECONDS. . !
POOLE
But. . .
NOT A SIGN OF HIM ! GUESS THE COCKPIT-CANOPY MUST'VE JAMMED AND TURNED IT TO HIS COFFIN !
THE BRITISH SAILORS GIVE UP THE SEARCH ! JOHNNY IS LOST – OUR COMRADE !
BUT HOW DID HE DIE. . . HOW ? SURELY NOT THE SPOTTER-PLANE. . !
The howl of the storm grew louder. . .almost blotting out the wild, maniacal laughter of Major Kraskin. . .
NOW IT IS YOUR TURN, FALCONS ! HIIIIAAAAAAAAH ! BY THE TIME MY TORTURERS HAVE FINISHED, YOU ARE GOING TO WISH THAT YOU HAD DIED AS SWIFTLY AS JOHNNY RED !

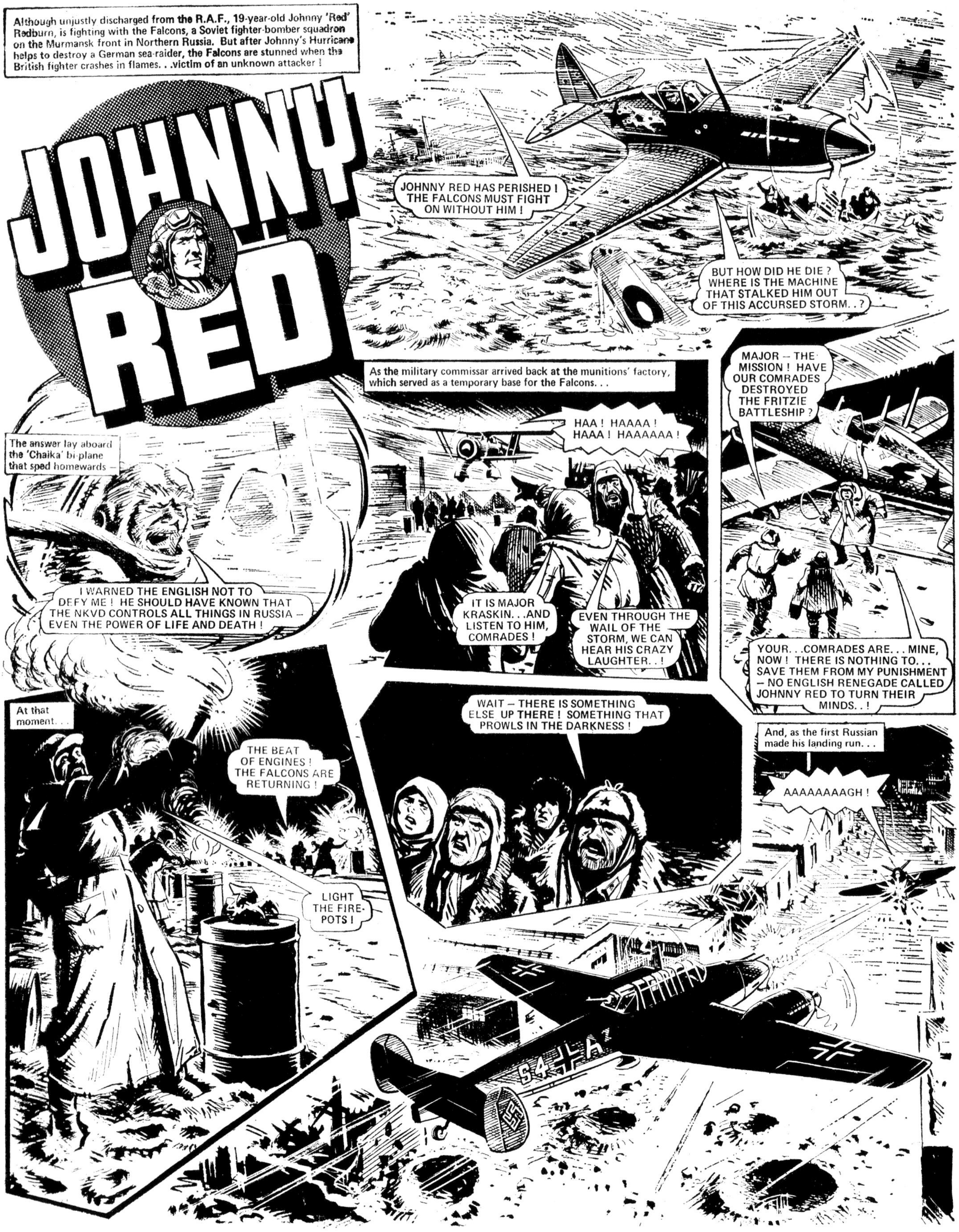
Although unjustly discharged from the R.A.F., 19-year-old Johnny 'Red' Redburn, is fighting with the Falcons, a Soviet fighter-bomber squadron on the Murmansk front in Northern Russia. But after Johnny's Hurricane helps to destroy a German sea-raider, the Falcons are stunned when the British fighter crashes in flames. . .victim of an unknown attacker !
JOHNNY RED
JOHNNY RED HAS PERISHED ! THE FALCONS MUST FIGHT ON WITHOUT HIM !
BUT HOW DID HE DIE ? WHERE IS THE MACHINE THAT STALKED HIM OUT OF THIS ACCURSED STORM. . ?
The answer lay aboard the 'Chaika' bi-plane that sped homewards –
I WARNED THE ENGLISH NOT TO DEFY ME ! HE SHOULD HAVE KNOWN THAT THE NKVD CONTROLS ALL THINGS IN RUSSIA – EVEN THE POWER OF LIFE AND DEATH !
As the military commissar arrived back at the munitions' factory, which served as a temporary base for the Falcons. . .
HAA ! HAAAA ! HAAA ! HAAAAAA !
IT IS MAJOR KRASKIN. . .AND LISTEN TO HIM, COMRADES !
EVEN THROUGH THE WAIL OF THE STORM, WE CAN HEAR HIS CRAZY LAUGHTER. . !
MAJOR – THE MISSION ! HAVE OUR COMRADES DESTROYED THE FRITZIE BATTLESHIP ?
YOUR. . .COMRADES ARE. . . MINE, NOW ! THERE IS NOTHING TO. . . SAVE THEM FROM MY PUNISHMENT – NO ENGLISH RENEGADE CALLED JOHNNY RED TO TURN THEIR MINDS. . !
At that moment. . .
THE BEAT OF ENGINES ! THE FALCONS ARE RETURNING !
LIGHT THE FIRE-POTS !
WAIT – THERE IS SOMETHING ELSE UP THERE ! SOMETHING THAT PROWLS IN THE DARKNESS !
And, as the first Russian made his landing run. . .
AAAAAAAAGH !

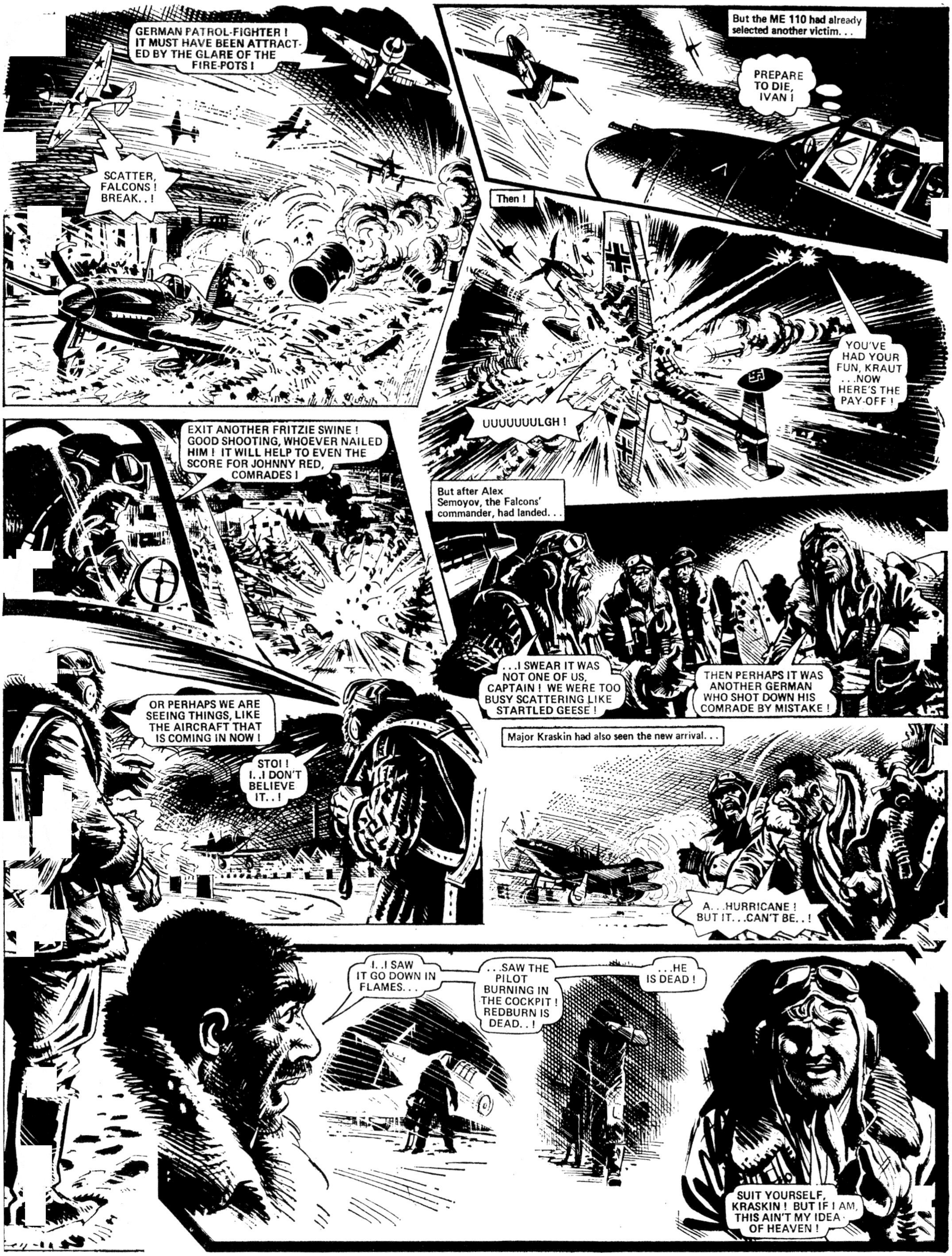
GERMAN PATROL-FIGHTER ! IT MUST HAVE BEEN ATTRACTED BY THE GLARE OF THE FIRE-POTS !
SCATTER, FALCONS ! BREAK. . !
But the ME 110 had already selected another victim. . .
PREPARE TO DIE, IVAN !
Then !
YOU'VE HAD YOUR FUN, KRAUT . . .NOW HERE'S THE PAY-OFF !
UUUUUUULGH !
EXIT ANOTHER FRITZIE SWINE ! GOOD SHOOTING, WHOEVER NAILED HIM ! IT WILL HELP TO EVEN THE SCORE FOR JOHNNY RED, COMRADES !
But after Alex Semoyov, the Falcons' commander, had landed. . .
. . .I SWEAR IT WAS NOT ONE OF US, CAPTAIN ! WE WERE TOO BUSY SCATTERING LIKE STARTLED GEESE !
THEN PERHAPS IT WAS ANOTHER GERMAN WHO SHOT DOWN HIS COMRADE BY MISTAKE !
OR PERHAPS WE ARE SEEING THINGS, LIKE THE AIRCRAFT THAT IS COMING IN NOW !
STOI ! I. .I DON'T BELIEVE IT. . !
Major Kraskin had also seen the new arrival. . .
A. . .HURRICANE ! BUT IT. . .CAN'T BE. . !
I. .I SAW IT GO DOWN IN FLAMES. . .
. . .SAW THE PILOT BURNING IN THE COCKPIT ! REDBURN IS DEAD. . !
. . .HE IS DEAD !
SUIT YOURSELF, KRASKIN ! BUT IF I AM, THIS AIN'T MY IDEA OF HEAVEN !

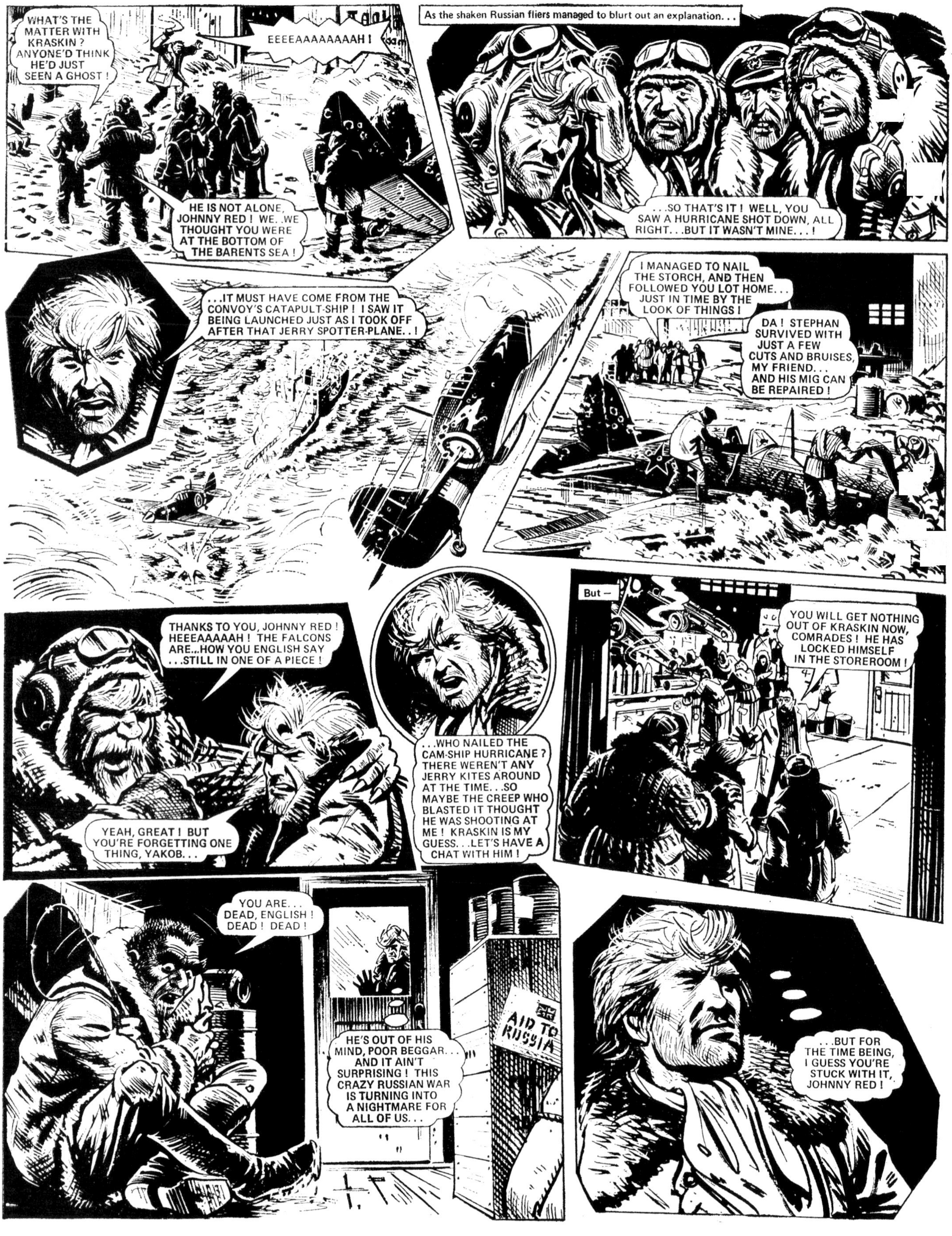

WHAT'S THE MATTER WITH KRASKIN? ANYONE'D THINK HE'D JUST SEEN A GHOST!
EEEEAAAAAAAAAH!
HE IS NOT ALONE, JOHNNY RED! WE..WE THOUGHT YOU WERE AT THE BOTTOM OF THE BARENTS SEA!
As the shaken Russian fliers managed to blurt out an explanation...
...SO THAT'S IT! WELL, YOU SAW A HURRICANE SHOT DOWN, ALL RIGHT...BUT IT WASN'T MINE...!
...IT MUST HAVE COME FROM THE CONVOY'S CATAPULT-SHIP! I SAW IT BEING LAUNCHED JUST AS I TOOK OFF AFTER THAT JERRY SPOTTER-PLANE..!
I MANAGED TO NAIL THE STORCH, AND THEN FOLLOWED YOU LOT HOME... JUST IN TIME BY THE LOOK OF THINGS!
DA! STEPHAN SURVIVED WITH JUST A FEW CUTS AND BRUISES, MY FRIEND... AND HIS MIG CAN BE REPAIRED!
THANKS TO YOU, JOHNNY RED! HEEEAAAAAH! THE FALCONS ARE...HOW YOU ENGLISH SAY ...STILL IN ONE OF A PIECE!
YEAH, GREAT! BUT YOU'RE FORGETTING ONE THING, YAKOB...
...WHO NAILED THE CAM-SHIP HURRICANE? THERE WEREN'T ANY JERRY KITES AROUND AT THE TIME...SO MAYBE THE CREEP WHO BLASTED IT THOUGHT HE WAS SHOOTING AT ME! KRASKIN IS MY GUESS...LET'S HAVE A CHAT WITH HIM!
But –
YOU WILL GET NOTHING OUT OF KRASKIN NOW, COMRADES! HE HAS LOCKED HIMSELF IN THE STOREROOM!
YOU ARE... DEAD, ENGLISH! DEAD! DEAD!
HE'S OUT OF HIS MIND, POOR BEGGAR... AND IT AIN'T SURPRISING! THIS CRAZY RUSSIAN WAR IS TURNING INTO A NIGHTMARE FOR ALL OF US...
AID TO RUSSIA
...BUT FOR THE TIME BEING, I GUESS YOU'RE STUCK WITH IT, JOHNNY RED!

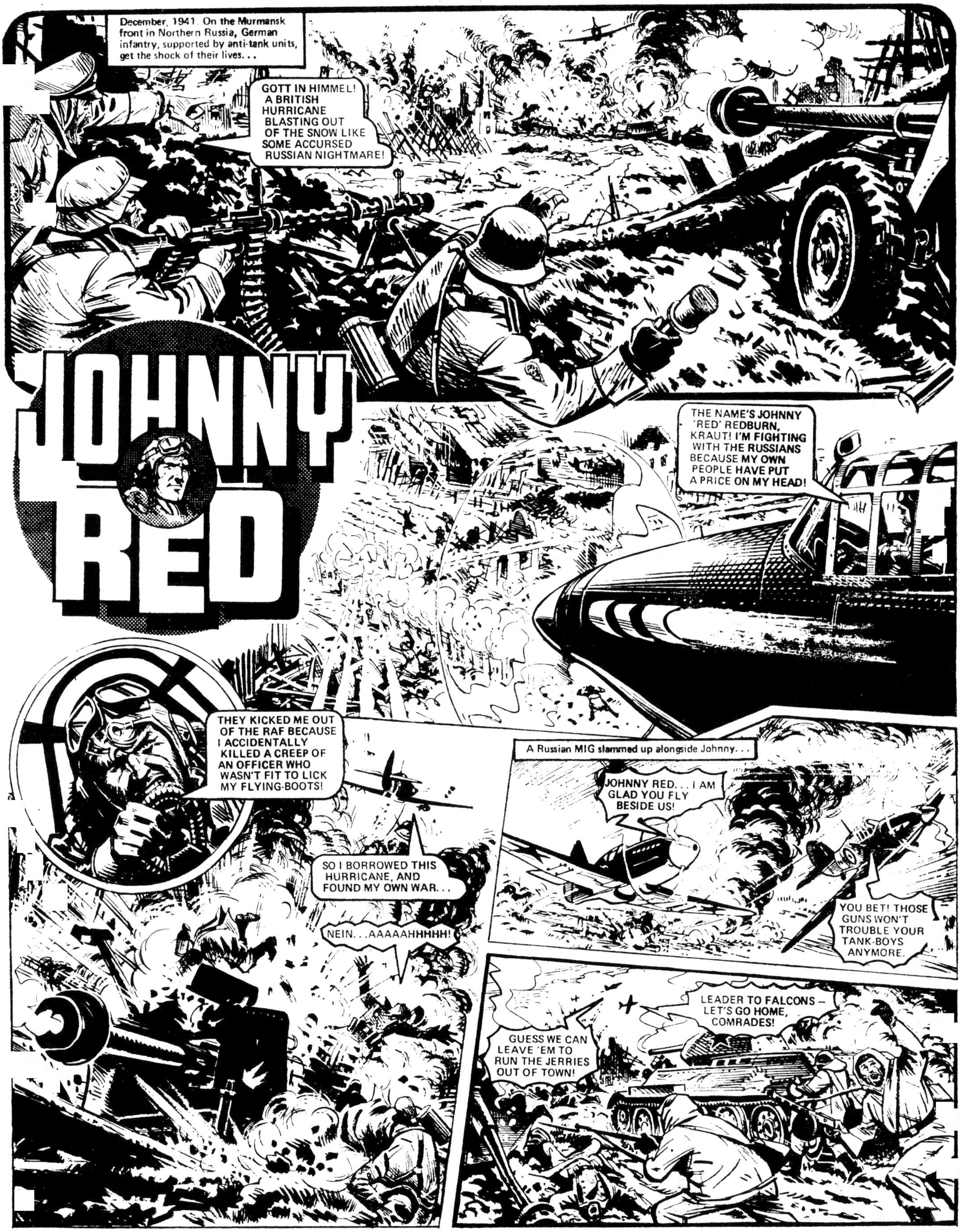
December, 1941. On the Murmansk front in Northern Russia, German infantry, supported by anti-tank units, get the shock of their lives...
GOTT IN HIMMEL! A BRITISH HURRICANE BLASTING OUT OF THE SNOW LIKE SOME ACCURSED RUSSIAN NIGHTMARE!
JOHNNY RED
THE NAME'S JOHNNY 'RED' REDBURN, KRAUT! I'M FIGHTING WITH THE RUSSIANS BECAUSE MY OWN PEOPLE HAVE PUT A PRICE ON MY HEAD!
THEY KICKED ME OUT OF THE RAF BECAUSE I ACCIDENTALLY KILLED A CREEP OF AN OFFICER WHO WASN'T FIT TO LICK MY FLYING-BOOTS!
SO I BORROWED THIS HURRICANE, AND FOUND MY OWN WAR...
NEIN...AAAAAHHHHH!
A Russian MIG slammed up alongside Johnny...
JOHNNY RED... I AM GLAD YOU FLY BESIDE US!
YOU BET! THOSE GUNS WON'T TROUBLE YOUR TANK-BOYS ANYMORE.
LEADER TO FALCONS – LET'S GO HOME, COMRADES!
GUESS WE CAN LEAVE 'EM TO RUN THE JERRIES OUT OF TOWN!

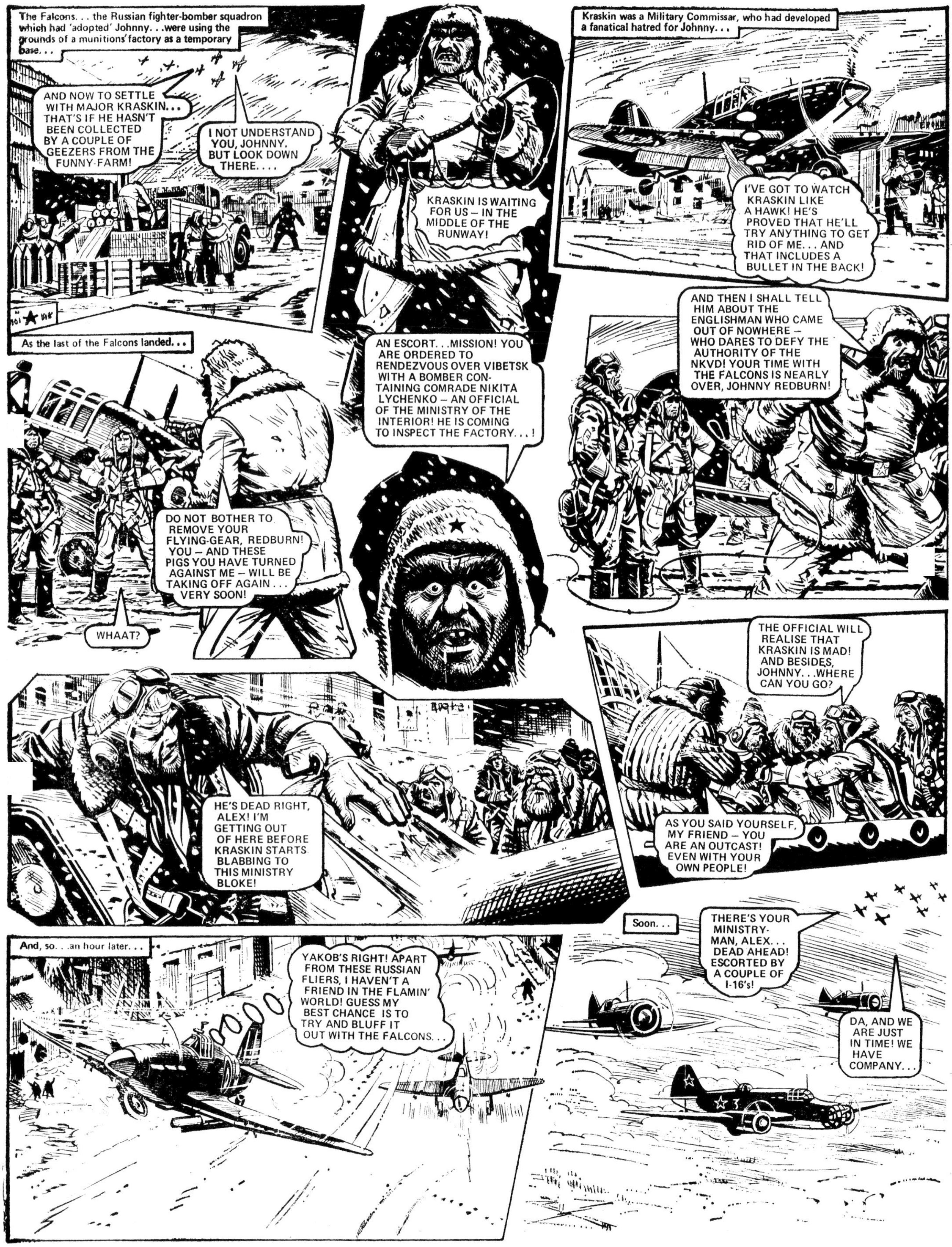

The Falcons. . . the Russian fighter-bomber squadron which had 'adopted' Johnny. . .were using the grounds of a munitions' factory as a temporary base. . .
AND NOW TO SETTLE WITH MAJOR KRASKIN. . . THAT'S IF HE HASN'T BEEN COLLECTED BY A COUPLE OF GEEZERS FROM THE FUNNY-FARM!
I NOT UNDERSTAND YOU, JOHNNY, BUT LOOK DOWN THERE. . . .
KRASKIN IS WAITING FOR US – IN THE MIDDLE OF THE RUNWAY!
Kraskin was a Military Commissar, who had developed a fanatical hatred for Johnny. . .
I'VE GOT TO WATCH KRASKIN LIKE A HAWK! HE'S PROVED THAT HE'LL TRY ANYTHING TO GET RID OF ME. . . AND THAT INCLUDES A BULLET IN THE BACK!
As the last of the Falcons landed. . .
DO NOT BOTHER TO REMOVE YOUR FLYING-GEAR, REDBURN! YOU – AND THESE PIGS YOU HAVE TURNED AGAINST ME – WILL BE TAKING OFF AGAIN . . . VERY SOON!
WHAAT?
AN ESCORT. . .MISSION! YOU ARE ORDERED TO RENDEZVOUS OVER VIBETSK WITH A BOMBER CONTAINING COMRADE NIKITA LYCHENKO – AN OFFICIAL OF THE MINISTRY OF THE INTERIOR! HE IS COMING TO INSPECT THE FACTORY. . . !
AND THEN I SHALL TELL HIM ABOUT THE ENGLISHMAN WHO CAME OUT OF NOWHERE – WHO DARES TO DEFY THE AUTHORITY OF THE NKVD! YOUR TIME WITH THE FALCONS IS NEARLY OVER, JOHNNY REDBURN!
HE'S DEAD RIGHT, ALEX! I'M GETTING OUT OF HERE BEFORE KRASKIN STARTS BLABBING TO THIS MINISTRY BLOKE!
THE OFFICIAL WILL REALISE THAT KRASKIN IS MAD! AND BESIDES, JOHNNY. . .WHERE CAN YOU GO?
AS YOU SAID YOURSELF, MY FRIEND – YOU ARE AN OUTCAST! EVEN WITH YOUR OWN PEOPLE!
And, so. . .an hour later. . .
YAKOB'S RIGHT! APART FROM THESE RUSSIAN FLIERS, I HAVEN'T A FRIEND IN THE FLAMIN' WORLD! GUESS MY BEST CHANCE IS TO TRY AND BLUFF IT OUT WITH THE FALCONS. . .
Soon. . .
THERE'S YOUR MINISTRY-MAN, ALEX. . . DEAD AHEAD! ESCORTED BY A COUPLE OF I-16's!
DA, AND WE ARE JUST IN TIME! WE HAVE COMPANY. . .

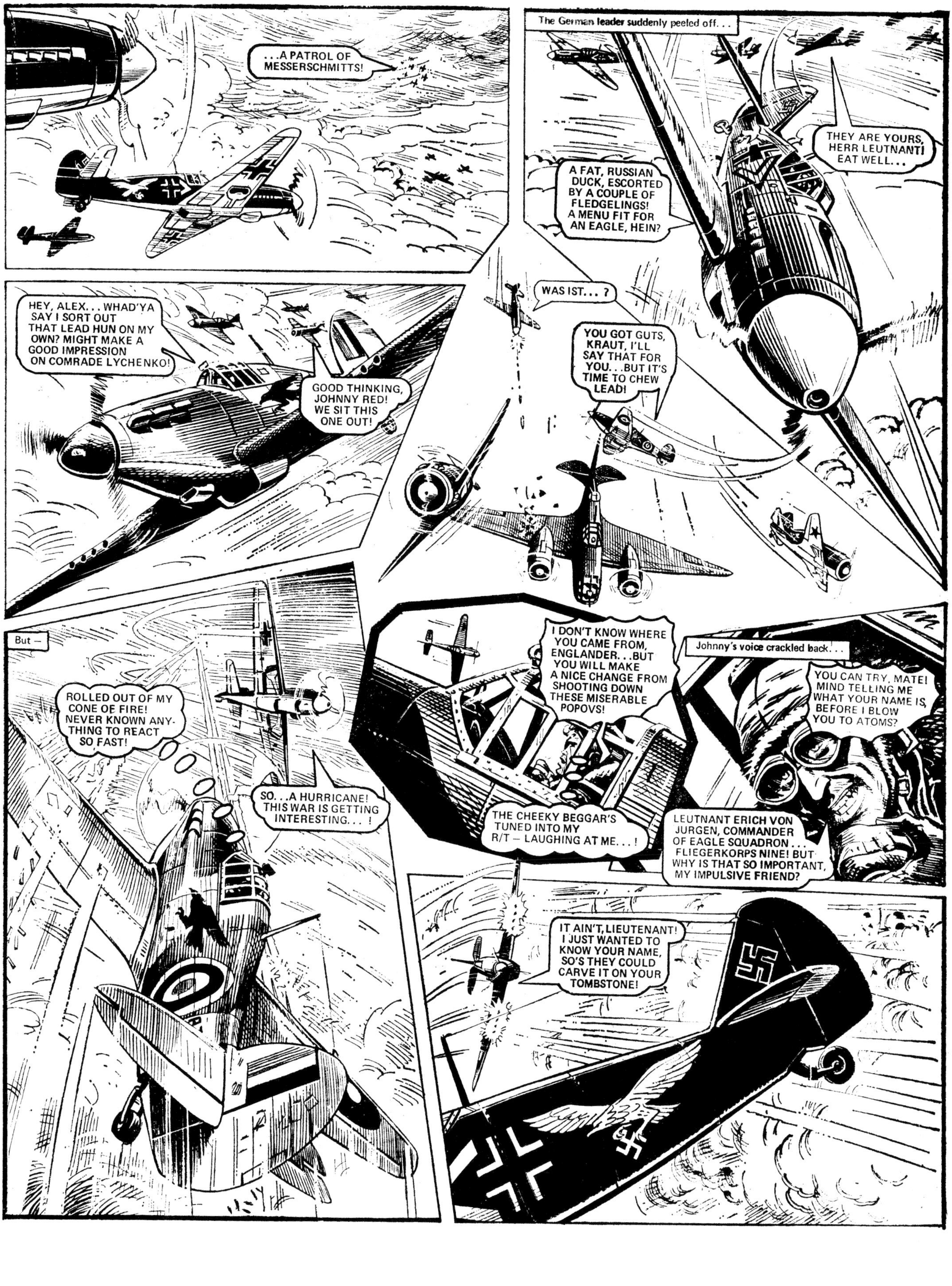
...A PATROL OF MESSERSCHMITTS!
The German leader suddenly peeled off...
A FAT, RUSSIAN DUCK, ESCORTED BY A COUPLE OF FLEDGELINGS! A MENU FIT FOR AN EAGLE, HEIN?
THEY ARE YOURS, HERR LEUTNANT! EAT WELL...
HEY, ALEX... WHAD'YA SAY I SORT OUT THAT LEAD HUN ON MY OWN? MIGHT MAKE A GOOD IMPRESSION ON COMRADE LYCHENKO!
GOOD THINKING, JOHNNY RED! WE SIT THIS ONE OUT!
WAS IST... ?
YOU GOT GUTS, KRAUT, I'LL SAY THAT FOR YOU... BUT IT'S TIME TO CHEW LEAD!
But —
ROLLED OUT OF MY CONE OF FIRE! NEVER KNOWN ANY-THING TO REACT SO FAST!
SO... A HURRICANE! THIS WAR IS GETTING INTERESTING... !
I DON'T KNOW WHERE YOU CAME FROM, ENGLANDER... BUT YOU WILL MAKE A NICE CHANGE FROM SHOOTING DOWN THESE MISERABLE POPOVS!
THE CHEEKY BEGGAR'S TUNED INTO MY R/T – LAUGHING AT ME... !
Johnny's voice crackled back...
YOU CAN TRY, MATE! MIND TELLING ME WHAT YOUR NAME IS, BEFORE I BLOW YOU TO ATOMS?
LEUTNANT ERICH VON JURGEN, COMMANDER OF EAGLE SQUADRON... FLIEGERKORPS NINE! BUT WHY IS THAT SO IMPORTANT, MY IMPULSIVE FRIEND?
IT AIN'T, LIEUTENANT! I JUST WANTED TO KNOW YOUR NAME, SO'S THEY COULD CARVE IT ON YOUR TOMBSTONE!

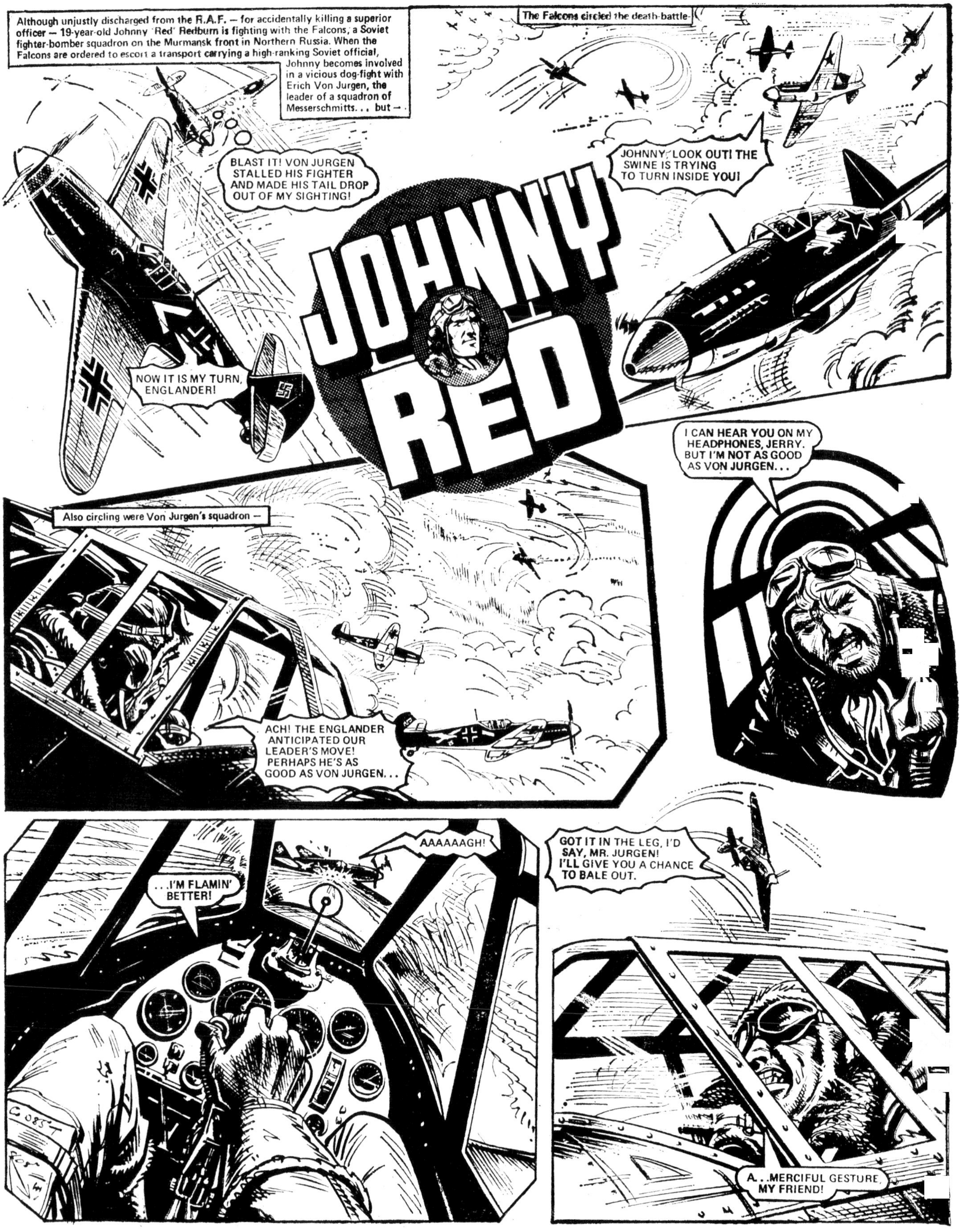
Although unjustly discharged from the R.A.F. — for accidentally killing a superior officer — 19-year-old Johnny 'Red' Redburn is fighting with the Falcons, a Soviet fighter-bomber squadron on the Murmansk front in Northern Russia. When the Falcons are ordered to escort a transport carrying a high-ranking Soviet official, Johnny becomes involved in a vicious dog-fight with Erich Von Jurgen, the leader of a squadron of Messerschmitts. . . but —
The Falcons circled the death-battle—
JOHNNY RED
BLAST IT! VON JURGEN STALLED HIS FIGHTER AND MADE HIS TAIL DROP OUT OF MY SIGHTING!
JOHNNY, LOOK OUT! THE SWINE IS TRYING TO TURN INSIDE YOU!
NOW IT IS MY TURN, ENGLANDER!
I CAN HEAR YOU ON MY HEADPHONES, JERRY. BUT I'M NOT AS GOOD AS VON JURGEN. . .
Also circling were Von Jurgen's squadron —
ACH! THE ENGLANDER ANTICIPATED OUR LEADER'S MOVE! PERHAPS HE'S AS GOOD AS VON JURGEN. . .
. . .I'M FLAMIN' BETTER!
AAAAAAGH!
GOT IT IN THE LEG, I'D SAY, MR. JURGEN! I'LL GIVE YOU A CHANCE TO BALE OUT.
A. . .MERCIFUL GESTURE, MY FRIEND!

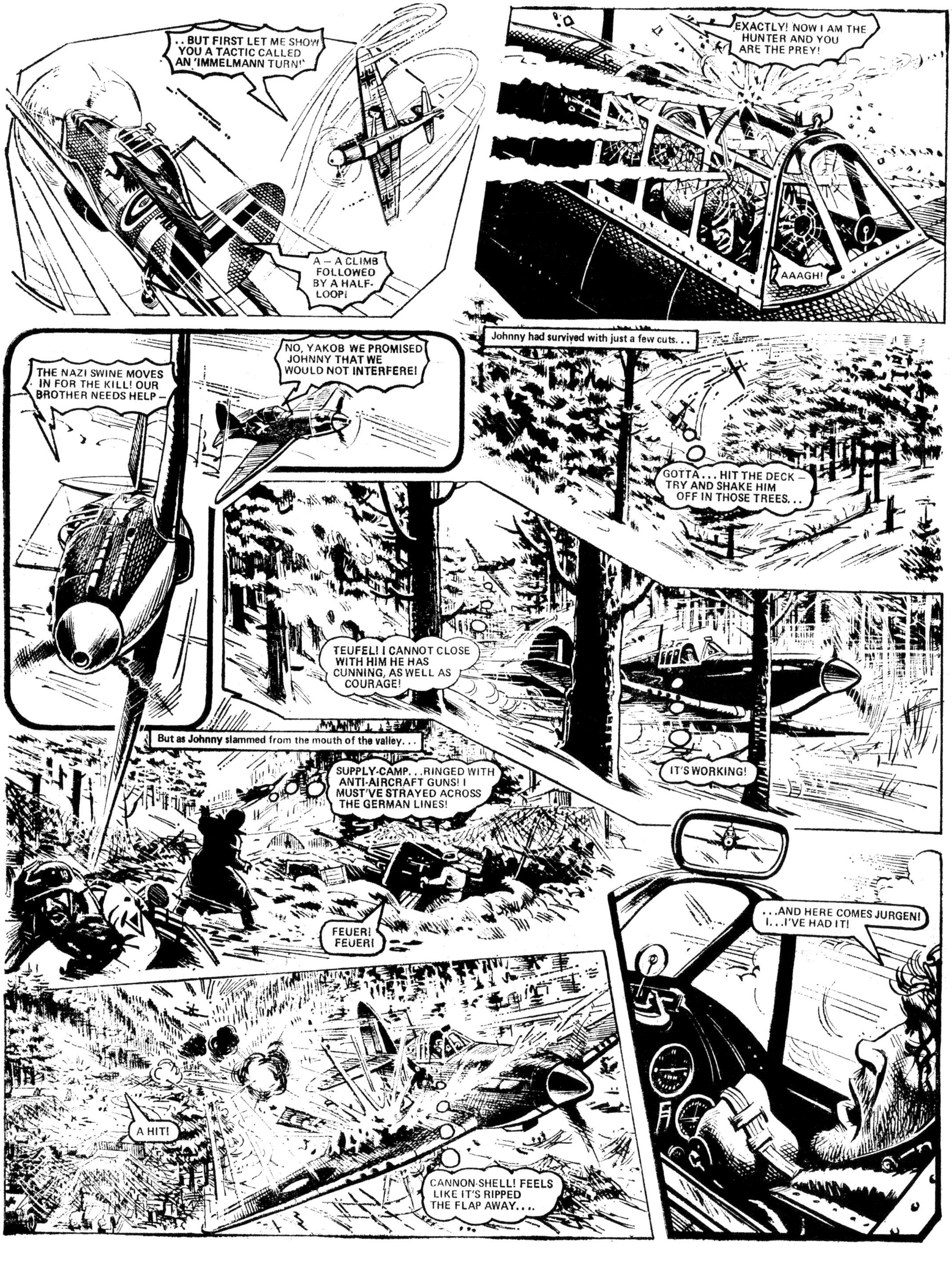

..BUT FIRST LET ME SHOW YOU A TACTIC CALLED AN 'IMMELMANN TURN!'
A – A CLIMB FOLLOWED BY A HALF-LOOP!
EXACTLY! NOW I AM THE HUNTER AND YOU ARE THE PREY!
AAAGH!
THE NAZI SWINE MOVES IN FOR THE KILL! OUR BROTHER NEEDS HELP –
NO, YAKOB WE PROMISED JOHNNY THAT WE WOULD NOT INTERFERE!
Johnny had survived with just a few cuts...
GOTTA... HIT THE DECK – TRY AND SHAKE HIM OFF IN THOSE TREES...
TEUFEL! I CANNOT CLOSE WITH HIM HE HAS CUNNING, AS WELL AS COURAGE!
IT'S WORKING!
But as Johnny slammed from the mouth of the valley...
SUPPLY-CAMP...RINGED WITH ANTI-AIRCRAFT GUNS! I MUST'VE STRAYED ACROSS THE GERMAN LINES!
FEUER! FEUER!
A HIT!
CANNON-SHELL! FEELS LIKE IT'S RIPPED THE FLAP AWAY....
...AND HERE COMES JURGEN! I...I'VE HAD IT!

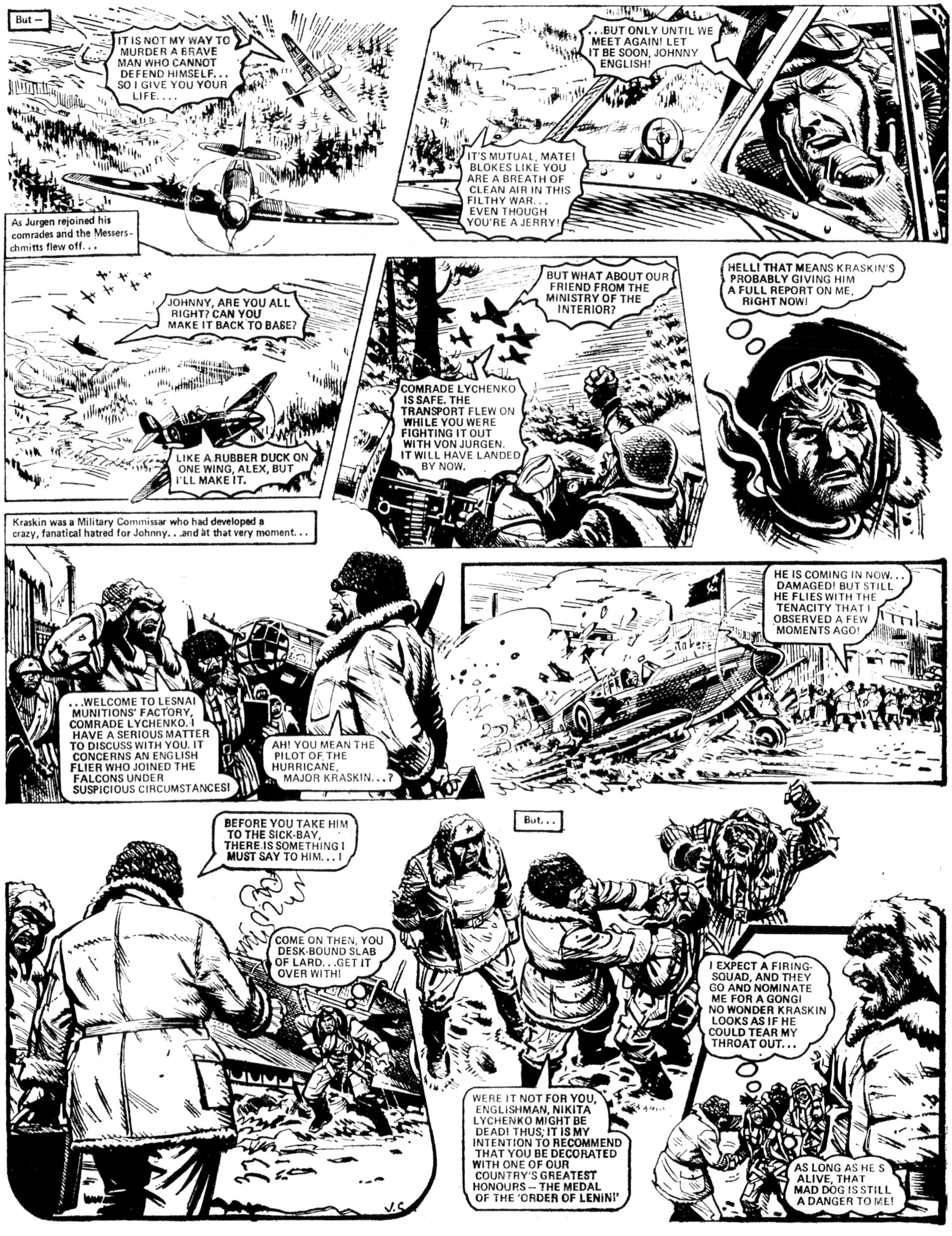
But –
IT IS NOT MY WAY TO MURDER A BRAVE MAN WHO CANNOT DEFEND HIMSELF... SO I GIVE YOU YOUR LIFE....
...BUT ONLY UNTIL WE MEET AGAIN! LET IT BE SOON, JOHNNY ENGLISH!
IT'S MUTUAL, MATE! BLOKES LIKE YOU ARE A BREATH OF CLEAN AIR IN THIS FILTHY WAR... EVEN THOUGH YOU'RE A JERRY!
As Jurgen rejoined his comrades and the Messers-chmitts flew off...
JOHNNY, ARE YOU ALL RIGHT? CAN YOU MAKE IT BACK TO BASE?
LIKE A RUBBER DUCK ON ONE WING, ALEX, BUT I'LL MAKE IT.
BUT WHAT ABOUT OUR FRIEND FROM THE MINISTRY OF THE INTERIOR?
COMRADE LYCHENKO IS SAFE. THE TRANSPORT FLEW ON WHILE YOU WERE FIGHTING IT OUT WITH VON JURGEN. IT WILL HAVE LANDED BY NOW.
HELL! THAT MEANS KRASKIN'S PROBABLY GIVING HIM A FULL REPORT ON ME, RIGHT NOW!
Kraskin was a Military Commissar who had developed a crazy, fanatical hatred for Johnny... and at that very moment...
...WELCOME TO LESNAI MUNITIONS' FACTORY, COMRADE LYCHENKO. I HAVE A SERIOUS MATTER TO DISCUSS WITH YOU. IT CONCERNS AN ENGLISH FLIER WHO JOINED THE FALCONS UNDER SUSPICIOUS CIRCUMSTANCES!
AH! YOU MEAN THE PILOT OF THE HURRICANE, MAJOR KRASKIN...?
HE IS COMING IN NOW... DAMAGED! BUT STILL HE FLIES WITH THE TENACITY THAT I OBSERVED A FEW MOMENTS AGO!
BEFORE YOU TAKE HIM TO THE SICK-BAY, THERE IS SOMETHING I MUST SAY TO HIM...!
COME ON THEN, YOU DESK-BOUND SLAB OF LARD... GET IT OVER WITH!
But...
WERE IT NOT FOR YOU, ENGLISHMAN, NIKITA LYCHENKO MIGHT BE DEAD! THUS, IT IS MY INTENTION TO RECOMMEND THAT YOU BE DECORATED WITH ONE OF OUR COUNTRY'S GREATEST HONOURS – THE MEDAL OF THE 'ORDER OF LENIN!'
I EXPECT A FIRING-SQUAD, AND THEY GO AND NOMINATE ME FOR A GONG! NO WONDER KRASKIN LOOKS AS IF HE COULD TEAR MY THROAT OUT...
AS LONG AS HE'S ALIVE, THAT MAD DOG IS STILL A DANGER TO ME!
V.C

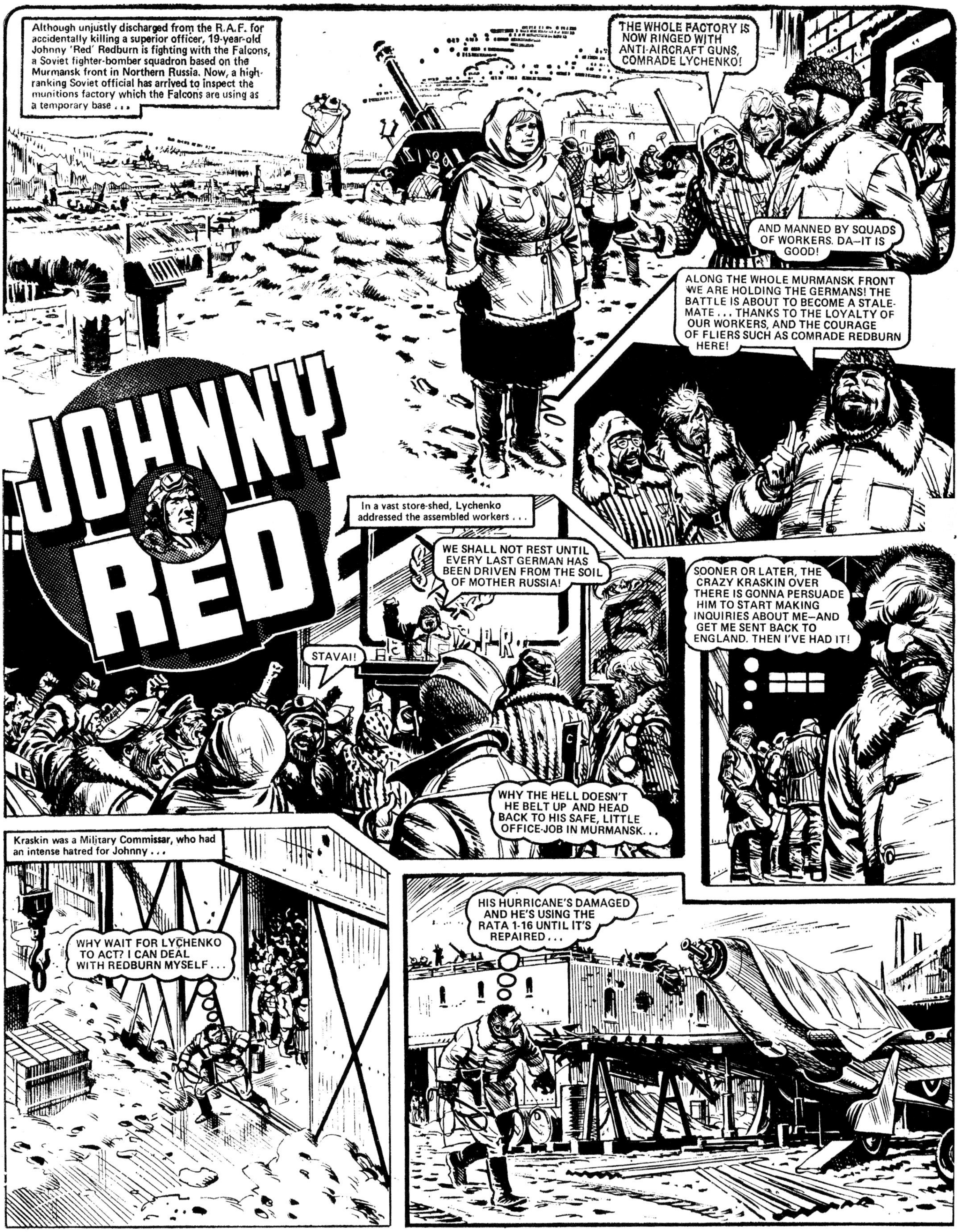

Although unjustly discharged from the R.A.F. for accidentally killing a superior officer, 19-year-old Johnny 'Red' Redburn is fighting with the Falcons, a Soviet fighter-bomber squadron based on the Murmansk front in Northern Russia. Now, a high-ranking Soviet official has arrived to inspect the munitions factory which the Falcons are using as a temporary base . . .
THE WHOLE FACTORY IS NOW RINGED WITH ANTI-AIRCRAFT GUNS, COMRADE LYCHENKO!
AND MANNED BY SQUADS OF WORKERS. DA—IT IS GOOD!
JOHNNY RED
ALONG THE WHOLE MURMANSK FRONT WE ARE HOLDING THE GERMANS! THE BATTLE IS ABOUT TO BECOME A STALE-MATE . . . THANKS TO THE LOYALTY OF OUR WORKERS, AND THE COURAGE OF FLIERS SUCH AS COMRADE REDBURN HERE!
In a vast store-shed, Lychenko addressed the assembled workers . . .
WE SHALL NOT REST UNTIL EVERY LAST GERMAN HAS BEEN DRIVEN FROM THE SOIL OF MOTHER RUSSIA!
STAVAI!
WHY THE HELL DOESN'T HE BELT UP AND HEAD BACK TO HIS SAFE, LITTLE OFFICE-JOB IN MURMANSK . . .
SOONER OR LATER, THE CRAZY KRASKIN OVER THERE IS GONNA PERSUADE HIM TO START MAKING INQUIRIES ABOUT ME—AND GET ME SENT BACK TO ENGLAND. THEN I'VE HAD IT!
Kraskin was a Military Commissar, who had an intense hatred for Johnny . . .
WHY WAIT FOR LYCHENKO TO ACT? I CAN DEAL WITH REDBURN MYSELF . . .
HIS HURRICANE'S DAMAGED AND HE'S USING THE RATA 1-16 UNTIL IT'S REPAIRED . . .

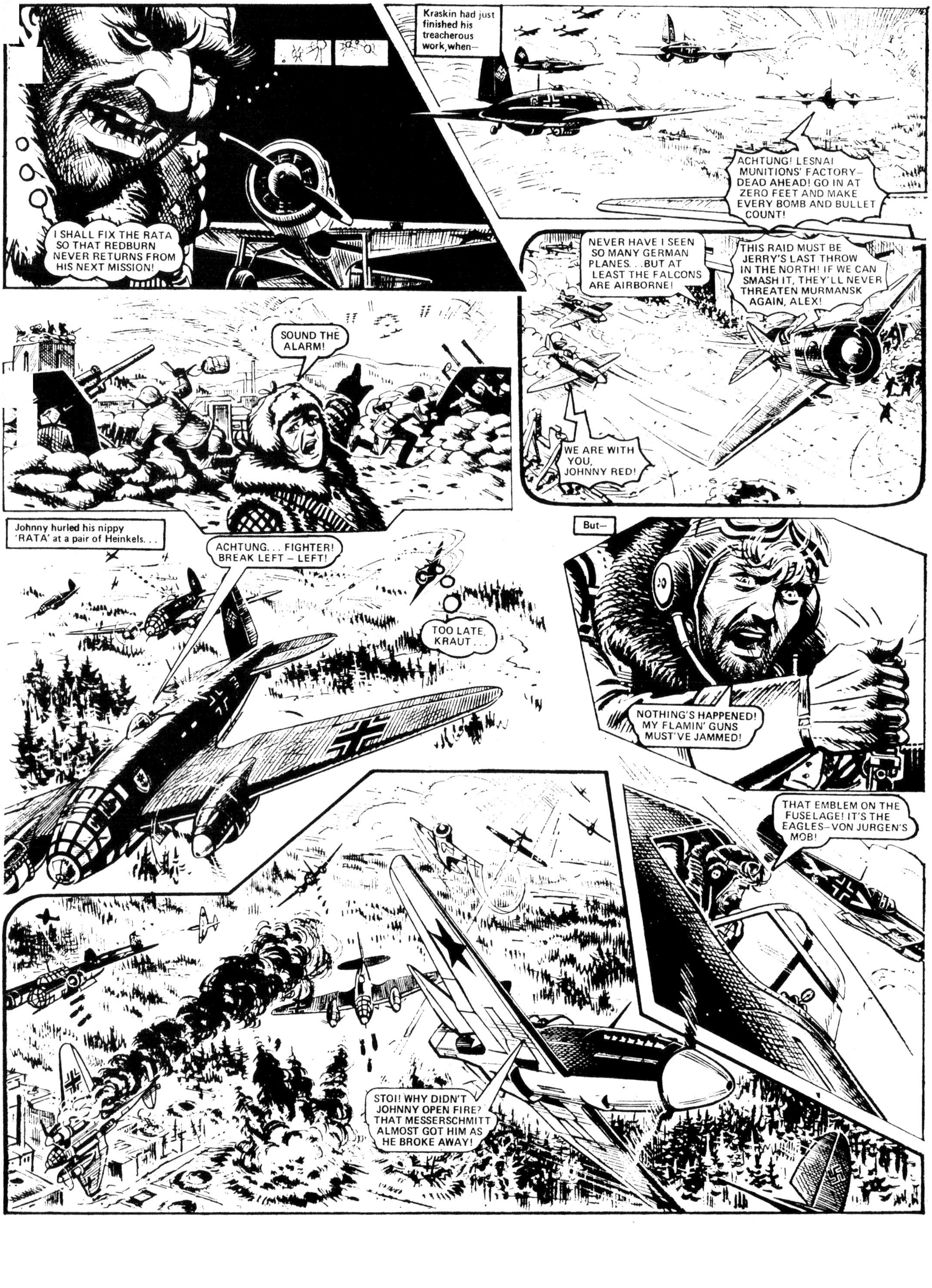
I SHALL FIX THE RATA SO THAT REDBURN NEVER RETURNS FROM HIS NEXT MISSION!
Kraskin had just finished his treacherous work, when—
ACHTUNG! LESNAI MUNITIONS' FACTORY— DEAD AHEAD! GO IN AT ZERO FEET AND MAKE EVERY BOMB AND BULLET COUNT!
SOUND THE ALARM!
NEVER HAVE I SEEN SO MANY GERMAN PLANES. . .BUT AT LEAST THE FALCONS ARE AIRBORNE!
THIS RAID MUST BE JERRY'S LAST THROW IN THE NORTH! IF WE CAN SMASH IT, THEY'LL NEVER THREATEN MURMANSK AGAIN, ALEX!
WE ARE WITH YOU, JOHNNY RED!
Johnny hurled his nippy 'RATA' at a pair of Heinkels. . .
ACHTUNG. . . FIGHTER! BREAK LEFT – LEFT!
TOO LATE, KRAUT. . .
But—
NOTHING'S HAPPENED! MY FLAMIN' GUNS MUST'VE JAMMED!
THAT EMBLEM ON THE FUSELAGE! IT'S THE EAGLES–VON JURGEN'S MOB!
STOI! WHY DIDN'T JOHNNY OPEN FIRE? THAT MESSERSCHMITT ALMOST GOT HIM AS HE BROKE AWAY!

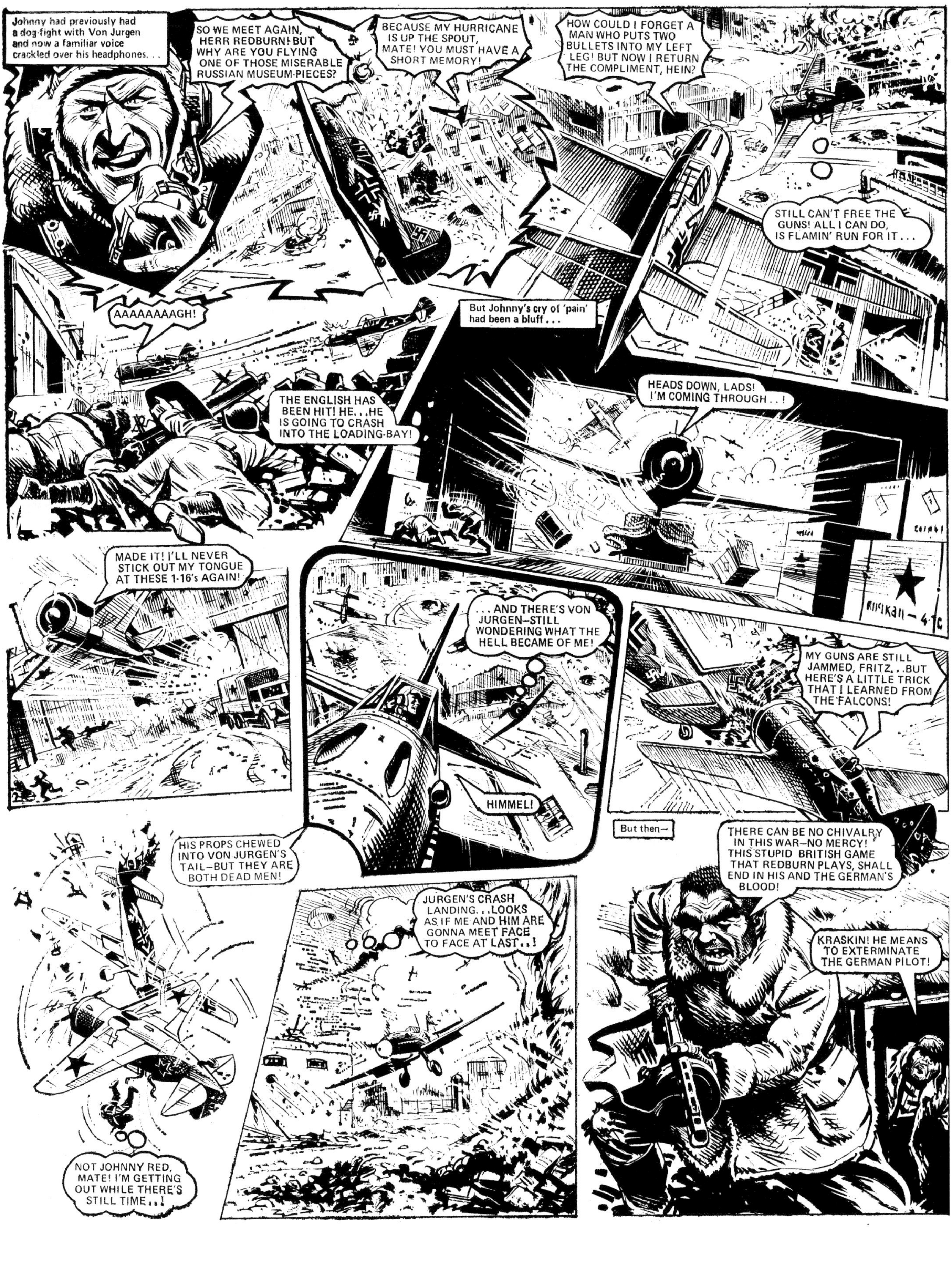
Johnny had previously had a dog-fight with Von Jurgen and now a familiar voice crackled over his headphones. . .
SO WE MEET AGAIN, HERR REDBURN! BUT WHY ARE YOU FLYING ONE OF THOSE MISERABLE RUSSIAN MUSEUM-PIECES?
BECAUSE MY HURRICANE IS UP THE SPOUT, MATE! YOU MUST HAVE A SHORT MEMORY!
HOW COULD I FORGET A MAN WHO PUTS TWO BULLETS INTO MY LEFT LEG! BUT NOW I RETURN THE COMPLIMENT, HEIN?
STILL CAN'T FREE THE GUNS! ALL I CAN DO, IS FLAMIN' RUN FOR IT . . .
AAAAAAAAGH!
THE ENGLISH HAS BEEN HIT! HE. . .HE IS GOING TO CRASH INTO THE LOADING-BAY!
But Johnny's cry of 'pain' had been a bluff . . .
HEADS DOWN, LADS! I'M COMING THROUGH . . !
MADE IT! I'LL NEVER STICK OUT MY TONGUE AT THESE 1-16's AGAIN!
. . . AND THERE'S VON JURGEN—STILL WONDERING WHAT THE HELL BECAME OF ME!
HIMMEL!
MY GUNS ARE STILL JAMMED, FRITZ. . .BUT HERE'S A LITTLE TRICK THAT I LEARNED FROM THE FALCONS!
HIS PROPS CHEWED INTO VON JURGEN'S TAIL—BUT THEY ARE BOTH DEAD MEN!
NOT JOHNNY RED, MATE! I'M GETTING OUT WHILE THERE'S STILL TIME . . !
JURGEN'S CRASH LANDING. . .LOOKS AS IF ME AND HIM ARE GONNA MEET FACE TO FACE AT LAST . . !
But then—
THERE CAN BE NO CHIVALRY IN THIS WAR—NO MERCY! THIS STUPID BRITISH GAME THAT REDBURN PLAYS, SHALL END IN HIS AND THE GERMAN'S BLOOD!
KRASKIN! HE MEANS TO EXTERMINATE THE GERMAN PILOT!

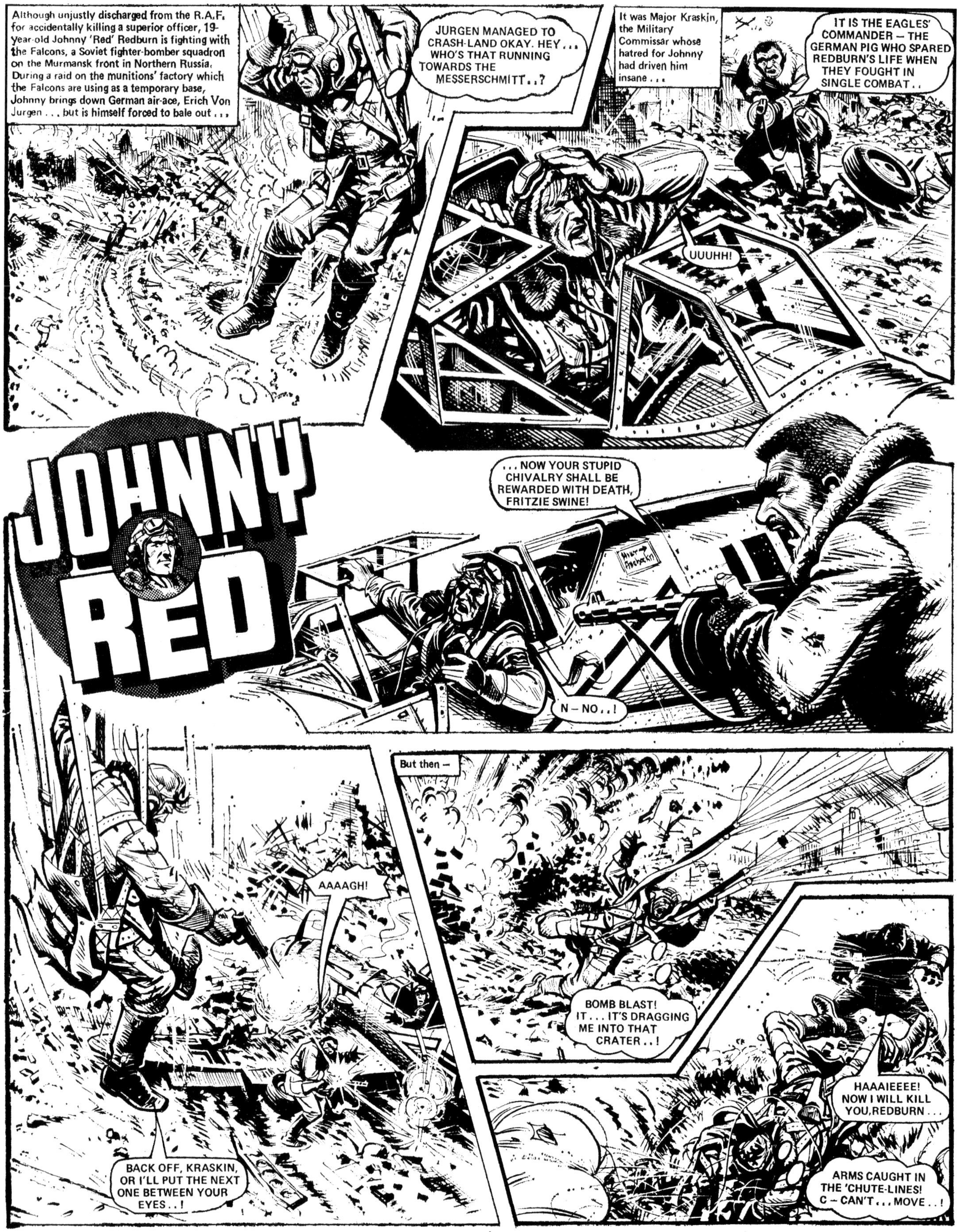
Although unjustly discharged from the R.A.F. for accidentally killing a superior officer, 19-year-old Johnny 'Red' Redburn is fighting with the Falcons, a Soviet fighter-bomber squadron on the Murmansk front in Northern Russia. During a raid on the munitions' factory which the Falcons are using as a temporary base, Johnny brings down German air-ace, Erich Von Jurgen . . . but is himself forced to bale out . . .
JURGEN MANAGED TO CRASH-LAND OKAY. HEY . . . WHO'S THAT RUNNING TOWARDS THE MESSERSCHMITT . . ?
UUUHH!
It was Major Kraskin, the Military Commissar whose hatred for Johnny had driven him insane . . .
IT IS THE EAGLES' COMMANDER — THE GERMAN PIG WHO SPARED REDBURN'S LIFE WHEN THEY FOUGHT IN SINGLE COMBAT . .
JOHNNY RED
. . . NOW YOUR STUPID CHIVALRY SHALL BE REWARDED WITH DEATH, FRITZIE SWINE!
N – NO . . !
AAAAGH!
BACK OFF, KRASKIN, OR I'LL PUT THE NEXT ONE BETWEEN YOUR EYES . . !
But then –
BOMB BLAST! IT . . . IT'S DRAGGING ME INTO THAT CRATER . . !
HAAAIEEEE! NOW I WILL KILL YOU, REDBURN . . .
ARMS CAUGHT IN THE 'CHUTE-LINES! C – CAN'T . . . MOVE . . !

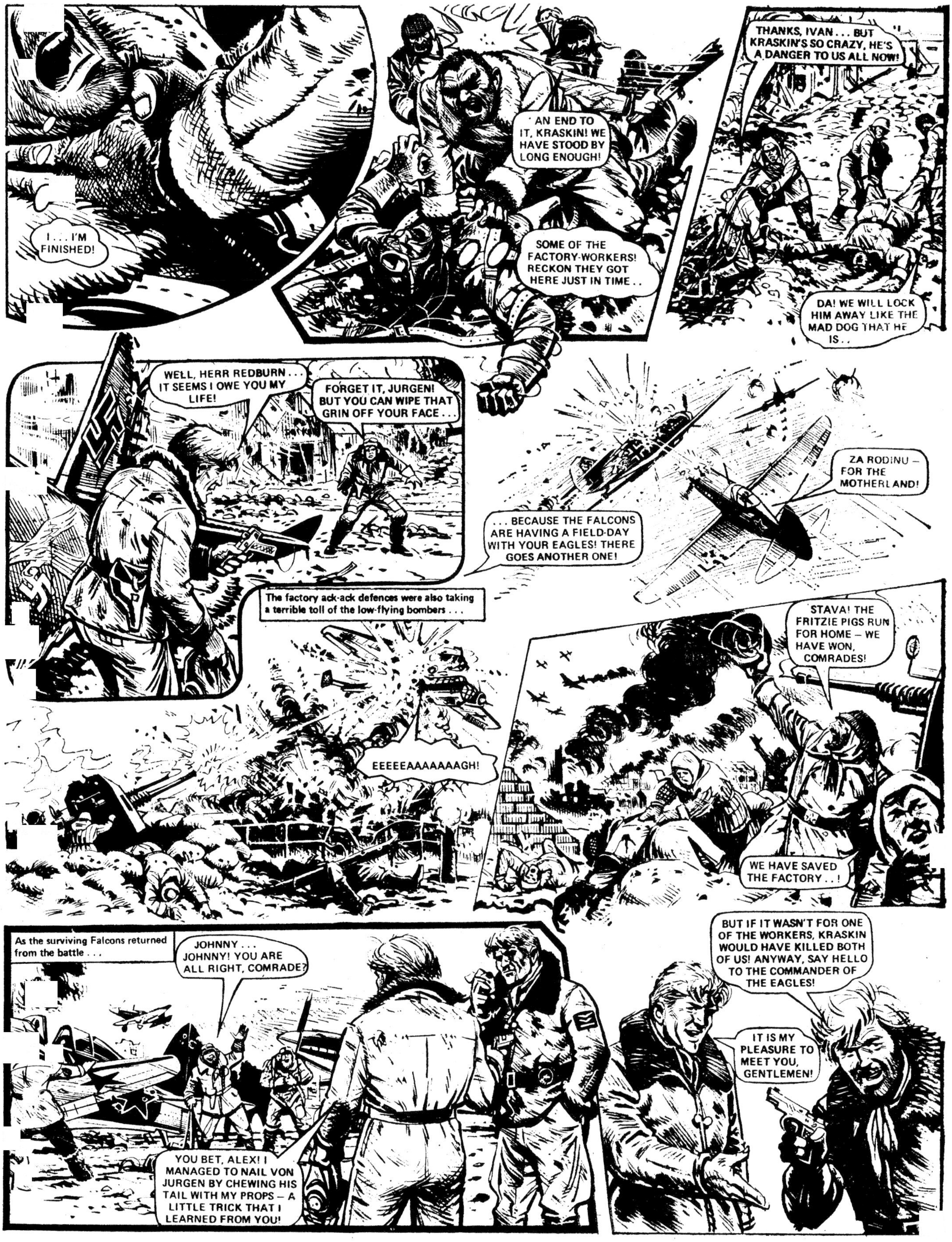
I . . . I'M FINISHED!
AN END TO IT, KRASKIN! WE HAVE STOOD BY LONG ENOUGH!
SOME OF THE FACTORY-WORKERS! RECKON THEY GOT HERE JUST IN TIME . .
THANKS, IVAN . . . BUT KRASKIN'S SO CRAZY, HE'S A DANGER TO US ALL NOW!
DA! WE WILL LOCK HIM AWAY LIKE THE MAD DOG THAT HE IS . .
WELL, HERR REDBURN . . . IT SEEMS I OWE YOU MY LIFE!
FORGET IT, JURGEN! BUT YOU CAN WIPE THAT GRIN OFF YOUR FACE . . .
. . . BECAUSE THE FALCONS ARE HAVING A FIELD-DAY WITH YOUR EAGLES! THERE GOES ANOTHER ONE!
ZA RODINU – FOR THE MOTHERLAND!
The factory ack-ack defences were also taking a terrible toll of the low-flying bombers . . .
EEEEEAAAAAAAGH!
STAVA! THE FRITZIE PIGS RUN FOR HOME – WE HAVE WON, COMRADES!
WE HAVE SAVED THE FACTORY . . !
As the surviving Falcons returned from the battle . . .
JOHNNY . . . JOHNNY! YOU ARE ALL RIGHT, COMRADE?
YOU BET, ALEX! I MANAGED TO NAIL VON JURGEN BY CHEWING HIS TAIL WITH MY PROPS – A LITTLE TRICK THAT I LEARNED FROM YOU!
BUT IF IT WASN'T FOR ONE OF THE WORKERS, KRASKIN WOULD HAVE KILLED BOTH OF US! ANYWAY, SAY HELLO TO THE COMMANDER OF THE EAGLES!
IT IS MY PLEASURE TO MEET YOU, GENTLEMEN!

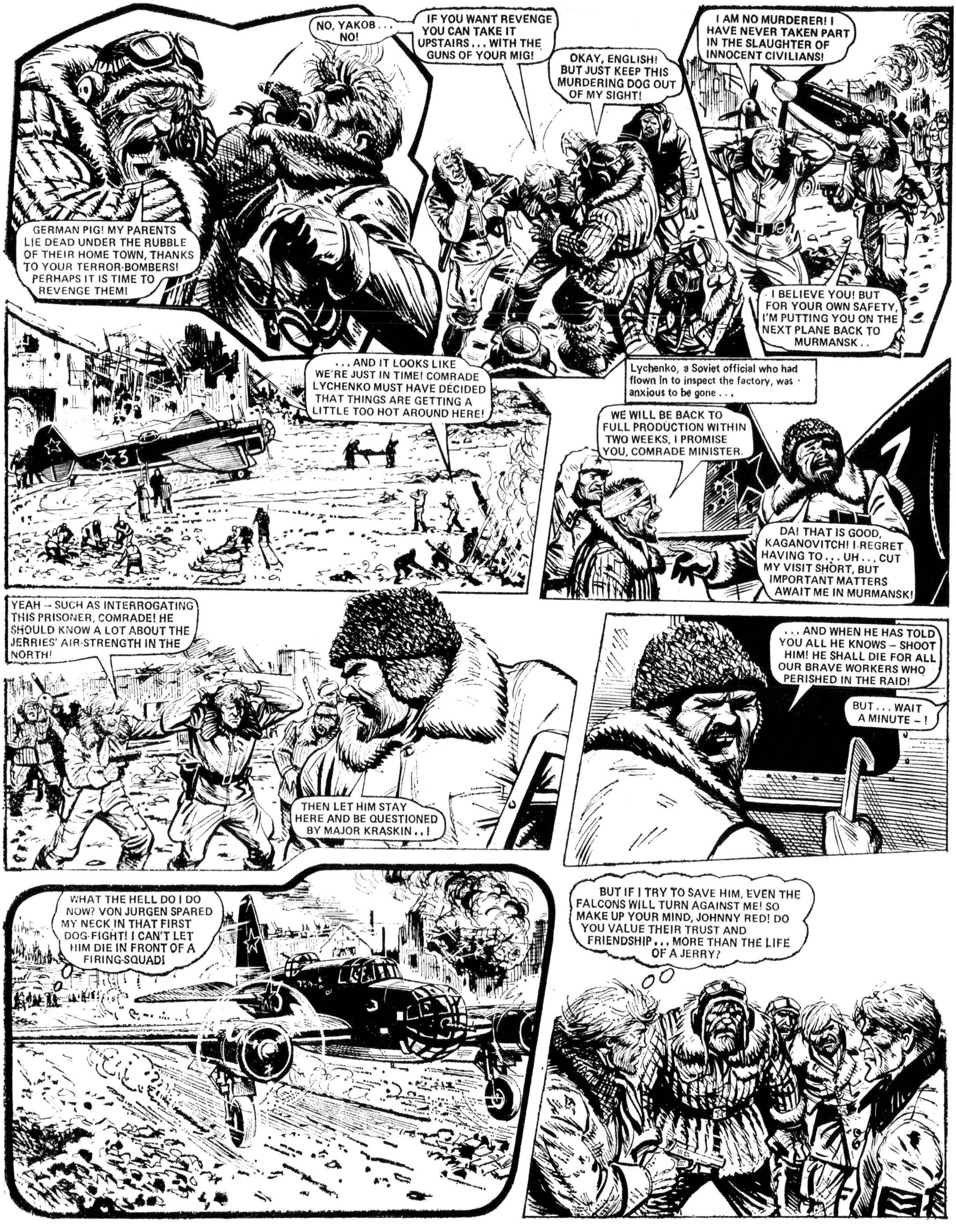
NO, YAKOB . . . NO!
IF YOU WANT REVENGE YOU CAN TAKE IT UPSTAIRS . . . WITH THE GUNS OF YOUR MIG!
GERMAN PIG! MY PARENTS LIE DEAD UNDER THE RUBBLE OF THEIR HOME TOWN, THANKS TO YOUR TERROR-BOMBERS! PERHAPS IT IS TIME TO REVENGE THEM!
OKAY, ENGLISH! BUT JUST KEEP THIS MURDERING DOG OUT OF MY SIGHT!
I AM NO MURDERER! I HAVE NEVER TAKEN PART IN THE SLAUGHTER OF INNOCENT CIVILIANS!
I BELIEVE YOU! BUT FOR YOUR OWN SAFETY, I'M PUTTING YOU ON THE NEXT PLANE BACK TO MURMANSK . .
. . . AND IT LOOKS LIKE WE'RE JUST IN TIME! COMRADE LYCHENKO MUST HAVE DECIDED THAT THINGS ARE GETTING A LITTLE TOO HOT AROUND HERE!
Lychenko, a Soviet official who had flown in to inspect the factory, was anxious to be gone . . .
WE WILL BE BACK TO FULL PRODUCTION WITHIN TWO WEEKS, I PROMISE YOU, COMRADE MINISTER.
DA! THAT IS GOOD, KAGANOVITCH! I REGRET HAVING TO . . . UH . . . CUT MY VISIT SHORT, BUT IMPORTANT MATTERS AWAIT ME IN MURMANSK!
YEAH – SUCH AS INTERROGATING THIS PRISONER, COMRADE! HE SHOULD KNOW A LOT ABOUT THE JERRIES' AIR-STRENGTH IN THE NORTH!
THEN LET HIM STAY HERE AND BE QUESTIONED BY MAJOR KRASKIN . . !
. . . AND WHEN HE HAS TOLD YOU ALL HE KNOWS – SHOOT HIM! HE SHALL DIE FOR ALL OUR BRAVE WORKERS WHO PERISHED IN THE RAID!
BUT . . . WAIT A MINUTE – !
WHAT THE HELL DO I DO NOW? VON JURGEN SPARED MY NECK IN THAT FIRST DOG-FIGHT! I CAN'T LET HIM DIE IN FRONT OF A FIRING-SQUAD!
BUT IF I TRY TO SAVE HIM, EVEN THE FALCONS WILL TURN AGAINST ME! SO MAKE UP YOUR MIND, JOHNNY RED! DO YOU VALUE THEIR TRUST AND FRIENDSHIP . . . MORE THAN THE LIFE OF A JERRY?

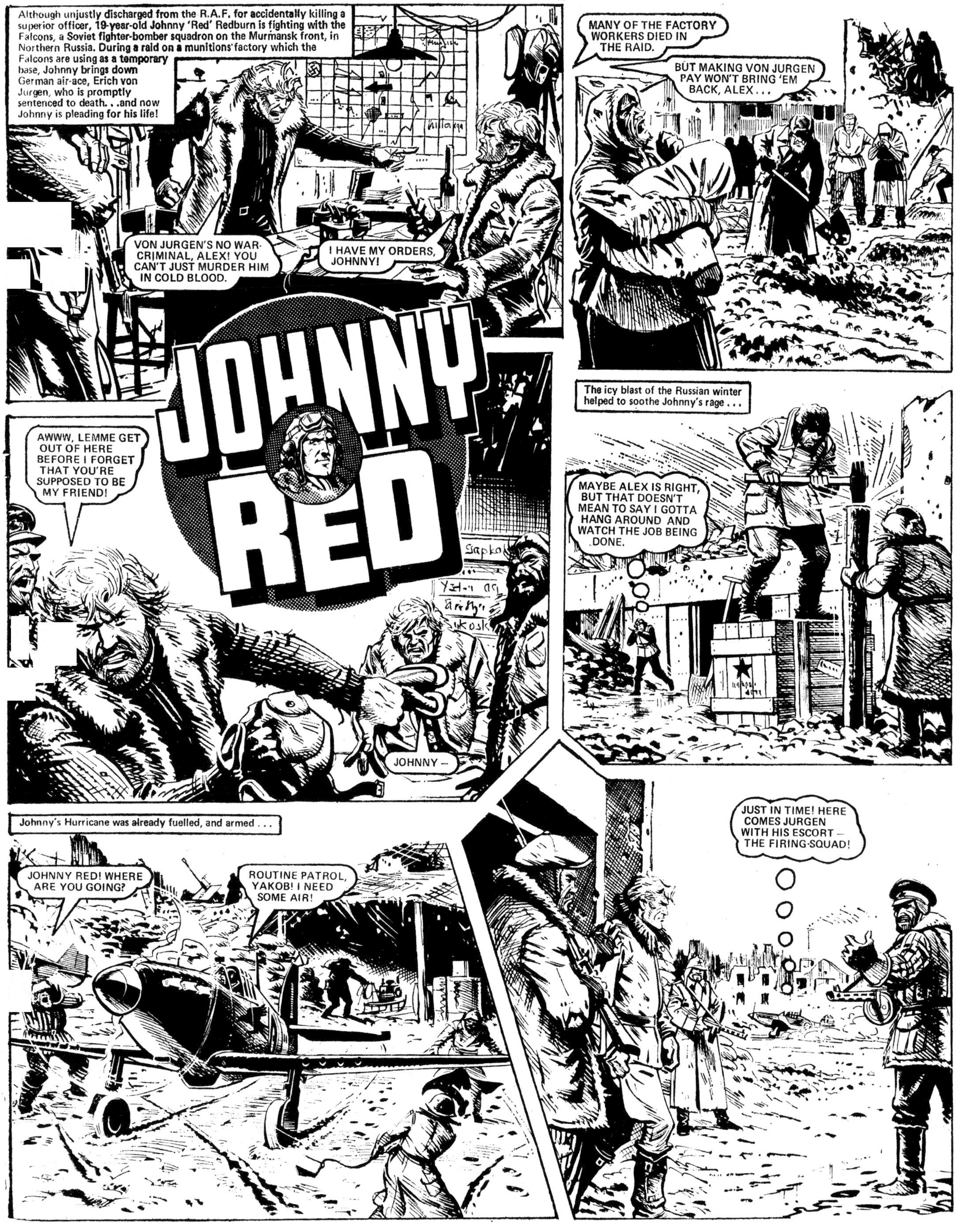
Although unjustly discharged from the R.A.F. for accidentally killing a superior officer, 19-year-old Johnny 'Red' Redburn is fighting with the Falcons, a Soviet fighter-bomber squadron on the Murmansk front, in Northern Russia. During a raid on a munitions factory which the Falcons are using as a temporary base, Johnny brings down German air-ace, Erich von Jurgen, who is promptly sentenced to death. . .and now Johnny is pleading for his life!
VON JURGEN'S NO WAR-CRIMINAL, ALEX! YOU CAN'T JUST MURDER HIM IN COLD BLOOD.
I HAVE MY ORDERS, JOHNNY!
MANY OF THE FACTORY WORKERS DIED IN THE RAID.
BUT MAKING VON JURGEN PAY WON'T BRING 'EM BACK, ALEX . . .
JOHNNY RED
AWWW, LEMME GET OUT OF HERE BEFORE I FORGET THAT YOU'RE SUPPOSED TO BE MY FRIEND!
JOHNNY –
The icy blast of the Russian winter helped to soothe Johnny's rage . . .
MAYBE ALEX IS RIGHT, BUT THAT DOESN'T MEAN TO SAY I GOTTA HANG AROUND AND WATCH THE JOB BEING DONE.
Johnny's Hurricane was already fuelled, and armed . . .
JOHNNY RED! WHERE ARE YOU GOING?
ROUTINE PATROL, YAKOB! I NEED SOME AIR!
JUST IN TIME! HERE COMES JURGEN WITH HIS ESCORT – THE FIRING-SQUAD!

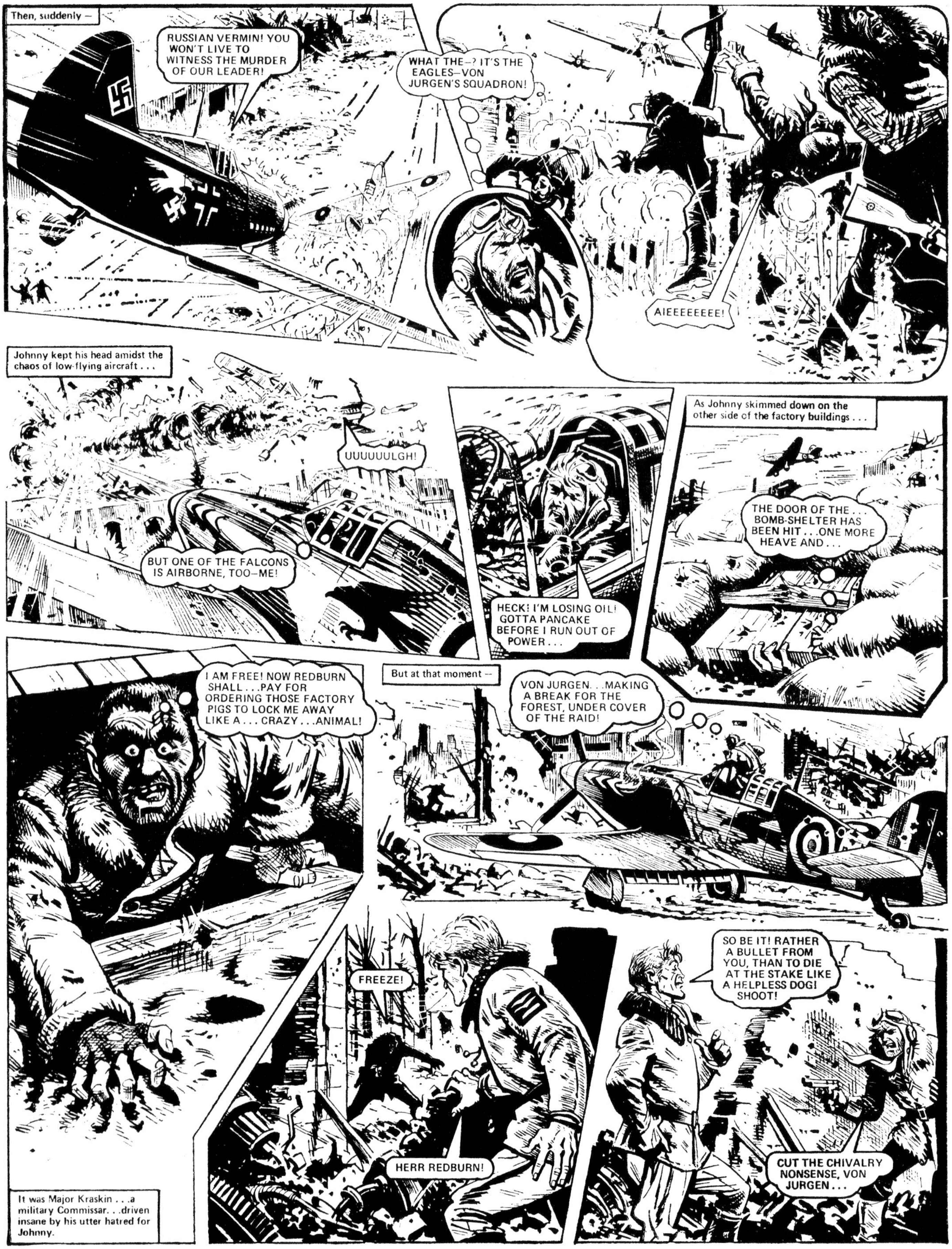
Then, suddenly –
RUSSIAN VERMIN! YOU WON'T LIVE TO WITNESS THE MURDER OF OUR LEADER!
WHAT THE–? IT'S THE EAGLES–VON JURGEN'S SQUADRON!
AIEEEEEEEE!
Johnny kept his head amidst the chaos of low-flying aircraft . . .
UUUUUULGH!
BUT ONE OF THE FALCONS IS AIRBORNE, TOO–ME!
HECK! I'M LOSING OIL! GOTTA PANCAKE BEFORE I RUN OUT OF POWER . . .
As Johnny skimmed down on the other side of the factory buildings . . .
THE DOOR OF THE . . BOMB-SHELTER HAS BEEN HIT . . . ONE MORE HEAVE AND . . .
I AM FREE! NOW REDBURN SHALL . . . PAY FOR ORDERING THOSE FACTORY PIGS TO LOCK ME AWAY LIKE A . . . CRAZY . . . ANIMAL!
It was Major Kraskin . . .a military Commissar. . .driven insane by his utter hatred for Johnny.
But at that moment –
VON JURGEN. . .MAKING A BREAK FOR THE FOREST, UNDER COVER OF THE RAID!
FREEZE!
HERR REDBURN!
SO BE IT! RATHER A BULLET FROM YOU, THAN TO DIE AT THE STAKE LIKE A HELPLESS DOG! SHOOT!
CUT THE CHIVALRY NONSENSE, VON JURGEN . . .

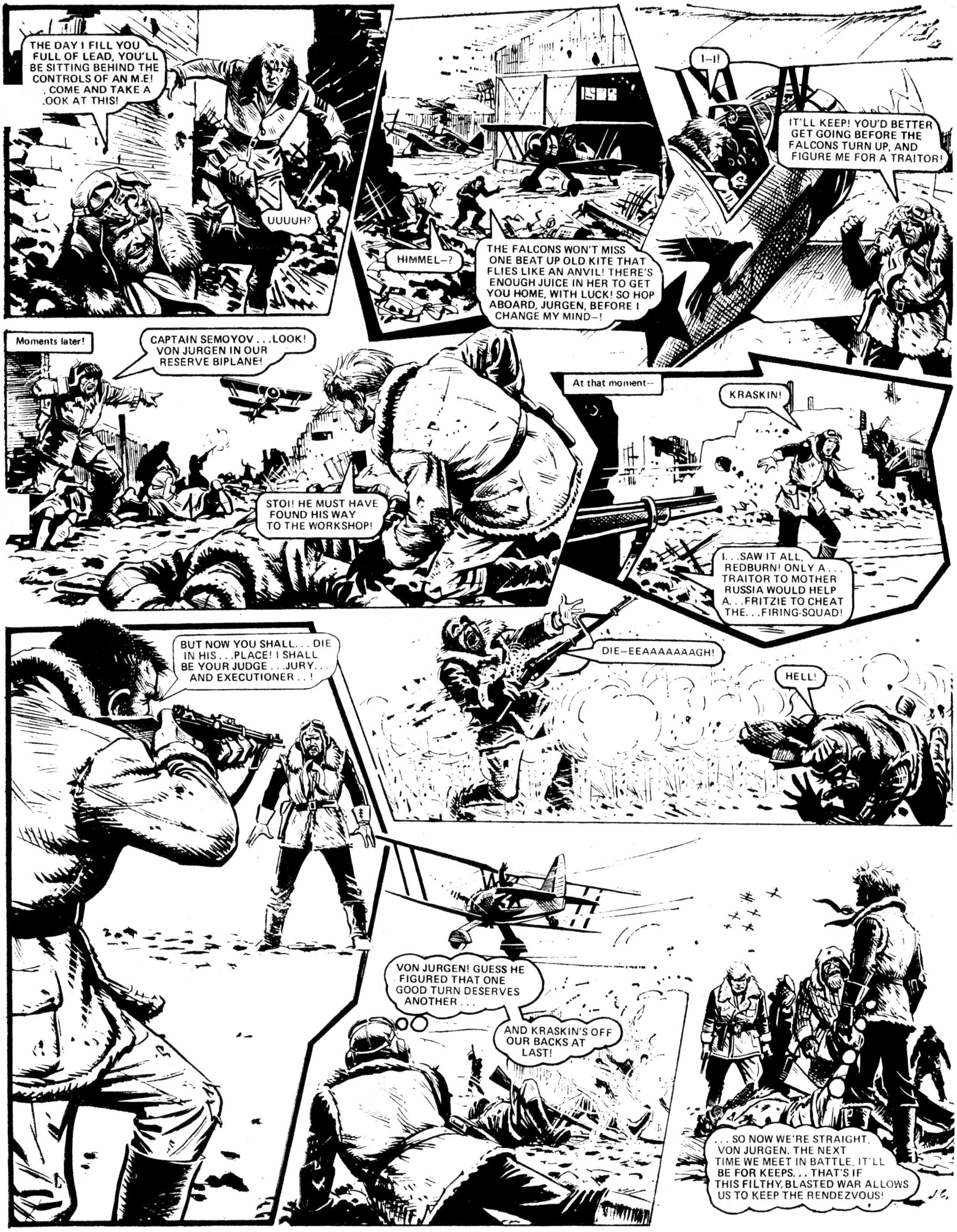
THE DAY I FILL YOU FULL OF LEAD, YOU'LL BE SITTING BEHIND THE CONTROLS OF AN M.E! , COME AND TAKE A OOK AT THIS!
UUUUH?
HIMMEL–?
THE FALCONS WON'T MISS ONE BEAT UP OLD KITE THAT FLIES LIKE AN ANVIL! THERE'S ENOUGH JUICE IN HER TO GET YOU HOME, WITH LUCK! SO HOP ABOARD, JURGEN, BEFORE I CHANGE MY MIND–!
I–I!
IT'LL KEEP! YOU'D BETTER GET GOING BEFORE THE FALCONS TURN UP, AND FIGURE ME FOR A TRAITOR!
Moments later!
CAPTAIN SEMOYOV . . . LOOK! VON JURGEN IN OUR RESERVE BIPLANE!
STOI! HE MUST HAVE FOUND HIS WAY TO THE WORKSHOP!
At that moment–
KRASKIN!
I . . . SAW IT ALL, REDBURN! ONLY A . . . TRAITOR TO MOTHER RUSSIA WOULD HELP A . . . FRITZIE TO CHEAT THE . . . FIRING-SQUAD!
BUT NOW YOU SHALL . . . DIE IN HIS . . . PLACE! I SHALL BE YOUR JUDGE . . . JURY . . . AND EXECUTIONER . . !
DIE–EEAAAAAAAGH!
HELL!
VON JURGEN! GUESS HE FIGURED THAT ONE GOOD TURN DESERVES ANOTHER . . .
AND KRASKIN'S OFF OUR BACKS AT LAST!
. . . SO NOW WE'RE STRAIGHT, VON JURGEN. THE NEXT TIME WE MEET IN BATTLE, IT'LL BE FOR KEEPS . . . THAT'S IF THIS FILTHY, BLASTED WAR ALLOWS US TO KEEP THE RENDEZVOUS!
J.C.

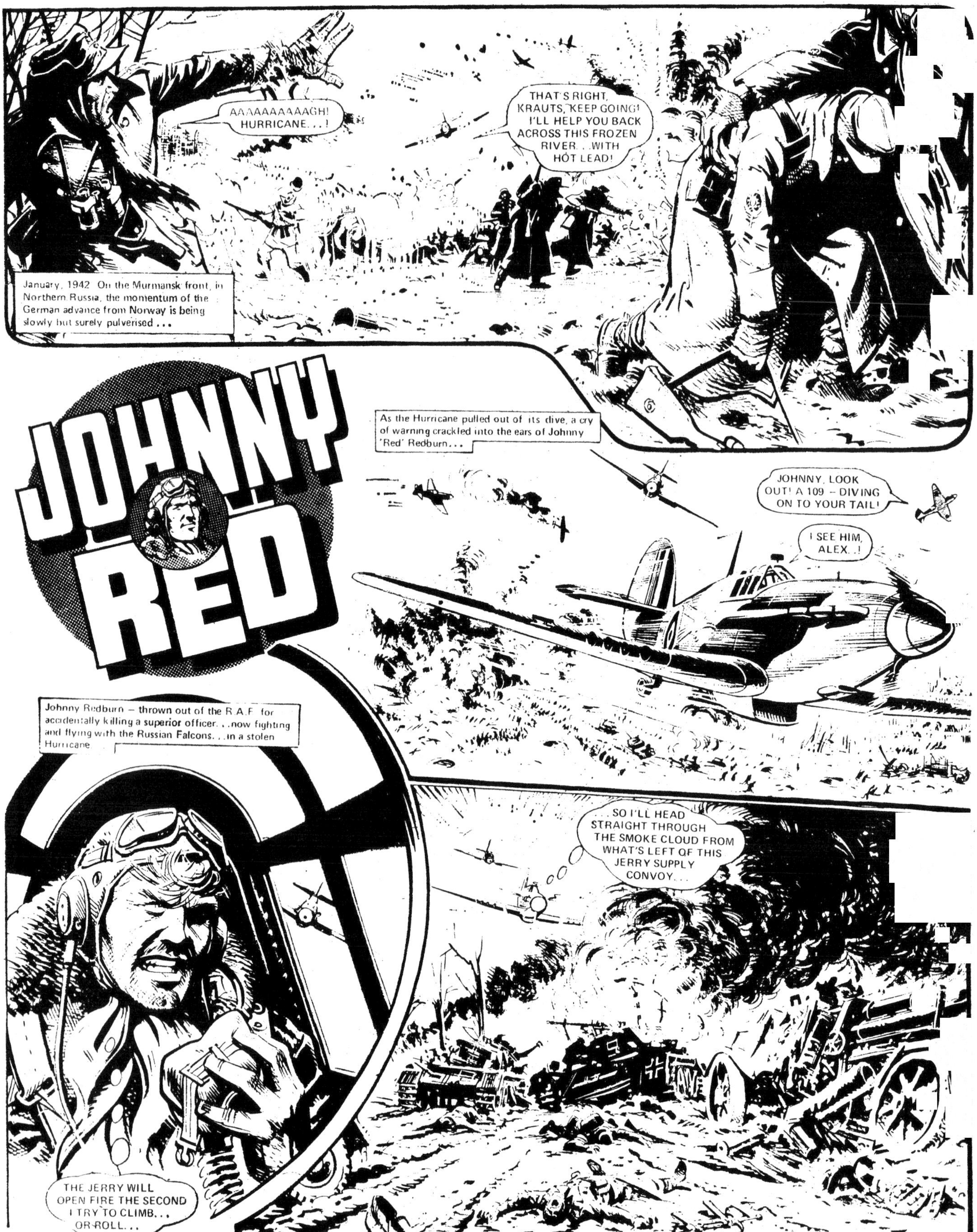

January, 1942. On the Murmansk front, in Northern Russia, the momentum of the German advance from Norway is being slowly but surely pulverised ...
AAAAAAAAAAGH! HURRICANE...!
THAT'S RIGHT, KRAUTS, KEEP GOING! I'LL HELP YOU BACK ACROSS THIS FROZEN RIVER...WITH HOT LEAD!
JOHNNY RED
As the Hurricane pulled out of its dive, a cry of warning crackled into the ears of Johnny 'Red' Redburn...
JOHNNY, LOOK OUT! A 109 – DIVING ON TO YOUR TAIL!
I SEE HIM, ALEX..!
Johnny Redburn – thrown out of the R.A.F. for accidentally killing a superior officer...now fighting and flying with the Russian Falcons...in a stolen Hurricane.
THE JERRY WILL OPEN FIRE THE SECOND I TRY TO CLIMB... OR ROLL...
...SO I'LL HEAD STRAIGHT THROUGH THE SMOKE CLOUD FROM WHAT'S LEFT OF THIS JERRY SUPPLY CONVOY...

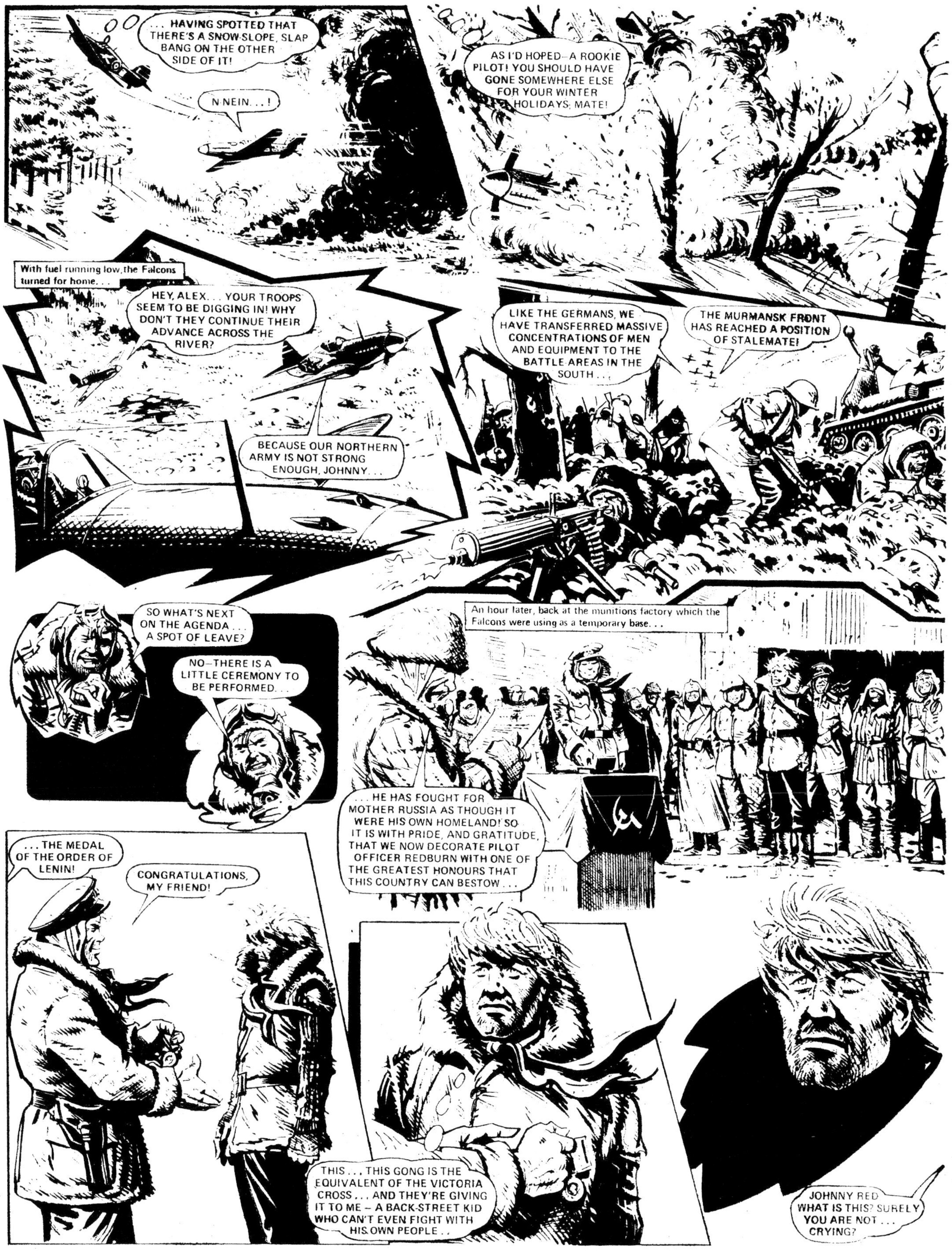

... HAVING SPOTTED THAT THERE'S A SNOW-SLOPE, SLAP BANG ON THE OTHER SIDE OF IT!
N-NEIN...!
AS I'D HOPED—A ROOKIE PILOT! YOU SHOULD HAVE GONE SOMEWHERE ELSE FOR YOUR WINTER HOLIDAYS, MATE!
With fuel running low, the Falcons turned for home...
HEY, ALEX... YOUR TROOPS SEEM TO BE DIGGING IN! WHY DON'T THEY CONTINUE THEIR ADVANCE ACROSS THE RIVER?
BECAUSE OUR NORTHERN ARMY IS NOT STRONG ENOUGH, JOHNNY...
LIKE THE GERMANS, WE HAVE TRANSFERRED MASSIVE CONCENTRATIONS OF MEN AND EQUIPMENT TO THE BATTLE AREAS IN THE SOUTH...
THE MURMANSK FRONT HAS REACHED A POSITION OF STALEMATE!
SO WHAT'S NEXT ON THE AGENDA... A SPOT OF LEAVE?
NO—THERE IS A LITTLE CEREMONY TO BE PERFORMED...
An hour later, back at the munitions factory which the Falcons were using as a temporary base...
... HE HAS FOUGHT FOR MOTHER RUSSIA AS THOUGH IT WERE HIS OWN HOMELAND! SO IT IS WITH PRIDE, AND GRATITUDE, THAT WE NOW DECORATE PILOT OFFICER REDBURN WITH ONE OF THE GREATEST HONOURS THAT THIS COUNTRY CAN BESTOW...
... THE MEDAL OF THE ORDER OF LENIN!
CONGRATULATIONS, MY FRIEND!
THIS... THIS GONG IS THE EQUIVALENT OF THE VICTORIA CROSS... AND THEY'RE GIVING IT TO ME – A BACK-STREET KID WHO CAN'T EVEN FIGHT WITH HIS OWN PEOPLE...
JOHNNY RED WHAT IS THIS? SURELY YOU ARE NOT... CRYING?

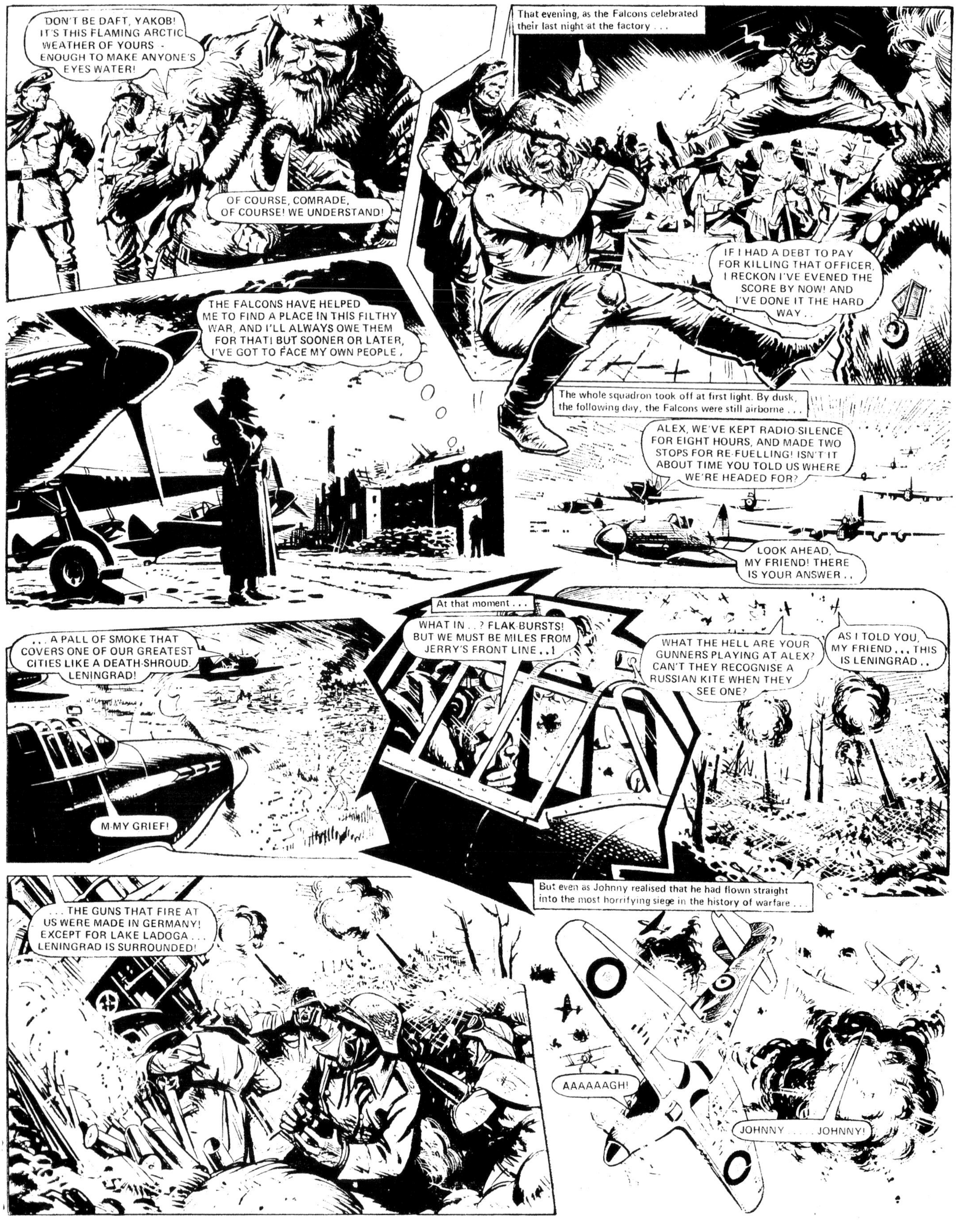
DON'T BE DAFT, YAKOB! IT'S THIS FLAMING ARCTIC WEATHER OF YOURS - ENOUGH TO MAKE ANYONE'S EYES WATER!
OF COURSE, COMRADE, OF COURSE! WE UNDERSTAND!
That evening, as the Falcons celebrated their last night at the factory . . .
IF I HAD A DEBT TO PAY FOR KILLING THAT OFFICER, I RECKON I'VE EVENED THE SCORE BY NOW! AND I'VE DONE IT THE HARD WAY . .
THE FALCONS HAVE HELPED ME TO FIND A PLACE IN THIS FILTHY WAR, AND I'LL ALWAYS OWE THEM FOR THAT! BUT SOONER OR LATER, I'VE GOT TO FACE MY OWN PEOPLE . .
The whole squadron took off at first light. By dusk, the following day, the Falcons were still airborne . . .
ALEX, WE'VE KEPT RADIO SILENCE FOR EIGHT HOURS, AND MADE TWO STOPS FOR RE-FUELLING! ISN'T IT ABOUT TIME YOU TOLD US WHERE WE'RE HEADED FOR?
LOOK AHEAD, MY FRIEND! THERE IS YOUR ANSWER . .
. . . A PALL OF SMOKE THAT COVERS ONE OF OUR GREATEST CITIES LIKE A DEATH-SHROUD. LENINGRAD!
M-MY GRIEF!
At that moment . . .
WHAT IN . . ? FLAK BURSTS! BUT WE MUST BE MILES FROM JERRY'S FRONT LINE . . !
WHAT THE HELL ARE YOUR GUNNERS PLAYING AT ALEX? CAN'T THEY RECOGNISE A RUSSIAN KITE WHEN THEY SEE ONE?
AS I TOLD YOU, MY FRIEND . . . THIS IS LENINGRAD . .
. . . THE GUNS THAT FIRE AT US WERE MADE IN GERMANY! EXCEPT FOR LAKE LADOGA . . . LENINGRAD IS SURROUNDED!
But even as Johnny realised that he had flown straight into the most horrifying siege in the history of warfare . . .
AAAAAAGH!
JOHNNY . . . . JOHNNY!

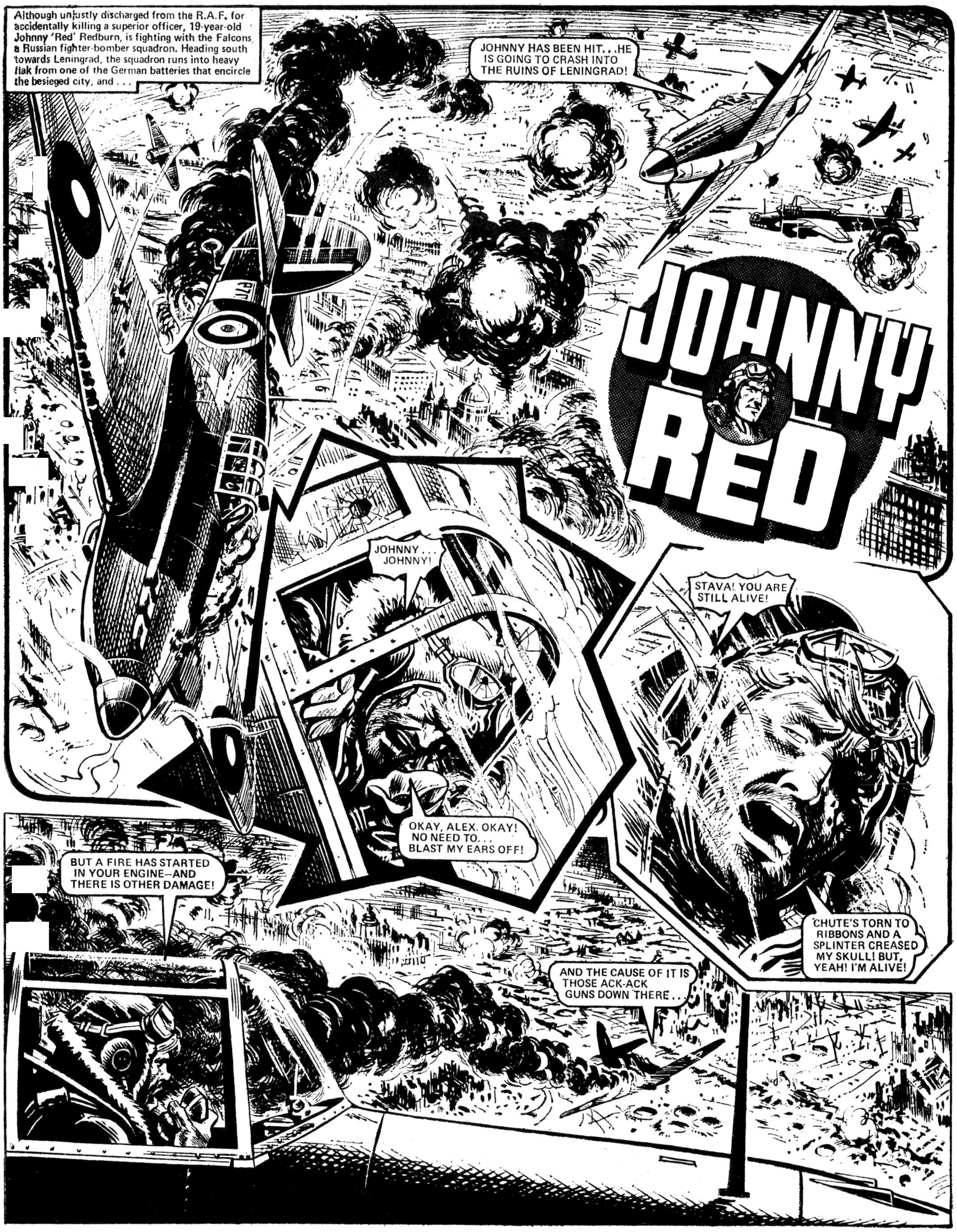
Although unjustly discharged from the R.A.F. for accidentally killing a superior officer, 19-year-old Johnny 'Red' Redburn, is fighting with the Falcons a Russian fighter-bomber squadron. Heading south towards Leningrad, the squadron runs into heavy flak from one of the German batteries that encircle the besieged city, and . . .
JOHNNY HAS BEEN HIT. . HE IS GOING TO CRASH INTO THE RUINS OF LENINGRAD!
JOHNNY RED
JOHNNY. . JOHNNY!
OKAY, ALEX. OKAY! NO NEED TO. . . BLAST MY EARS OFF!
STAVA! YOU ARE STILL ALIVE!
'CHUTE'S TORN TO RIBBONS AND A SPLINTER CREASED MY SKULL! BUT, YEAH! I'M ALIVE!
BUT A FIRE HAS STARTED IN YOUR ENGINE—AND THERE IS OTHER DAMAGE!
AND THE CAUSE OF IT IS THOSE ACK-ACK GUNS DOWN THERE . .

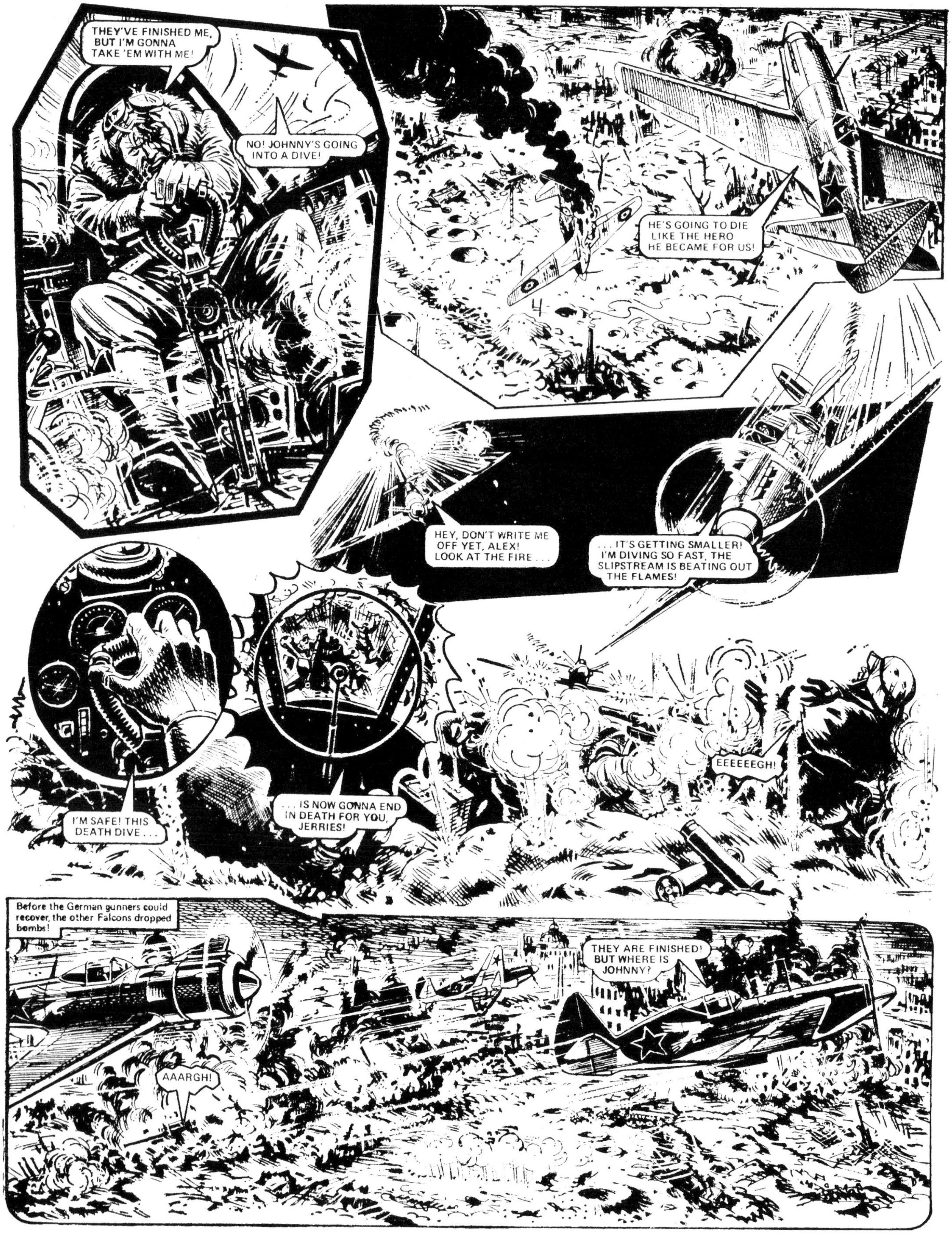

THEY'VE FINISHED ME, BUT I'M GONNA TAKE 'EM WITH ME!
NO! JOHNNY'S GOING INTO A DIVE!
HE'S GOING TO DIE LIKE THE HERO HE BECAME FOR US!
HEY, DON'T WRITE ME OFF YET, ALEX! LOOK AT THE FIRE . . .
. . . IT'S GETTING SMALLER! I'M DIVING SO FAST, THE SLIPSTREAM IS BEATING OUT THE FLAMES!
I'M SAFE! THIS DEATH DIVE . . .
. . . IS NOW GONNA END IN DEATH FOR YOU, JERRIES!
EEEEEEGH!
Before the German gunners could recover, the other Falcons dropped bombs!
THEY ARE FINISHED! BUT WHERE IS JOHNNY?
AAARGH!

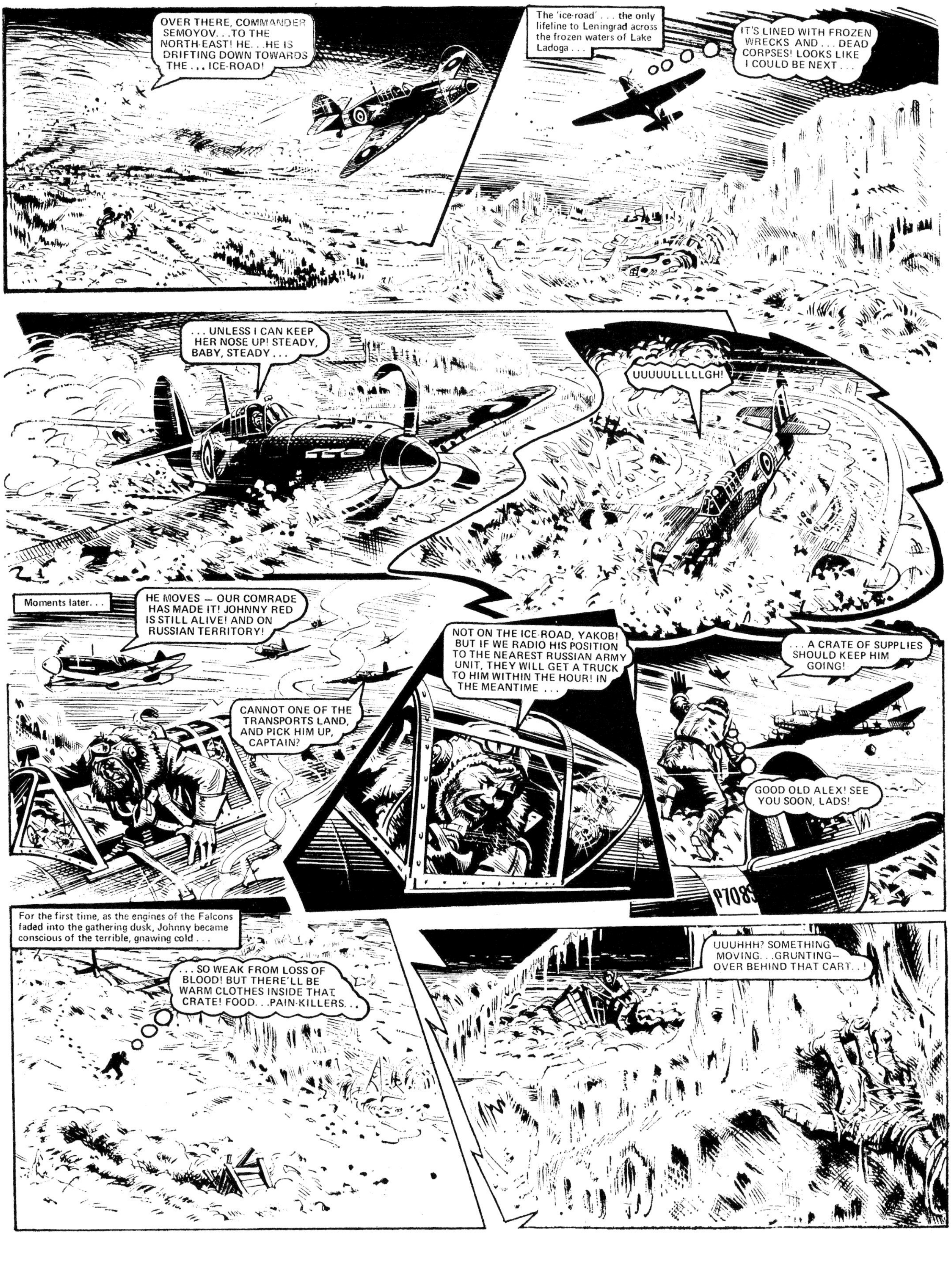
OVER THERE, COMMANDER SEMOYOV. . .TO THE NORTH-EAST! HE. . .HE IS DRIFTING DOWN TOWARDS THE . . . ICE-ROAD!
The 'ice-road' . . . the only lifeline to Leningrad across the frozen waters of Lake Ladoga . . .
IT'S LINED WITH FROZEN WRECKS AND . . . DEAD CORPSES! LOOKS LIKE I COULD BE NEXT . . .
. . . UNLESS I CAN KEEP HER NOSE UP! STEADY, BABY, STEADY . . .
UUUUULLLLLGH!
Moments later. . .
HE MOVES – OUR COMRADE HAS MADE IT! JOHNNY RED IS STILL ALIVE! AND ON RUSSIAN TERRITORY!
CANNOT ONE OF THE TRANSPORTS LAND, AND PICK HIM UP, CAPTAIN?
NOT ON THE ICE-ROAD, YAKOB! BUT IF WE RADIO HIS POSITION TO THE NEAREST RUSSIAN ARMY UNIT, THEY WILL GET A TRUCK TO HIM WITHIN THE HOUR! IN THE MEANTIME . . .
. . . A CRATE OF SUPPLIES SHOULD KEEP HIM GOING!
GOOD OLD ALEX! SEE YOU SOON, LADS!
P708
For the first time, as the engines of the Falcons faded into the gathering dusk, Johnny became conscious of the terrible, gnawing cold . . .
. . . SO WEAK FROM LOSS OF BLOOD! BUT THERE'LL BE WARM CLOTHES INSIDE THAT CRATE! FOOD. . .PAIN-KILLERS. . .
UUUHHH? SOMETHING MOVING. . .GRUNTING– OVER BEHIND THAT CART. . . !

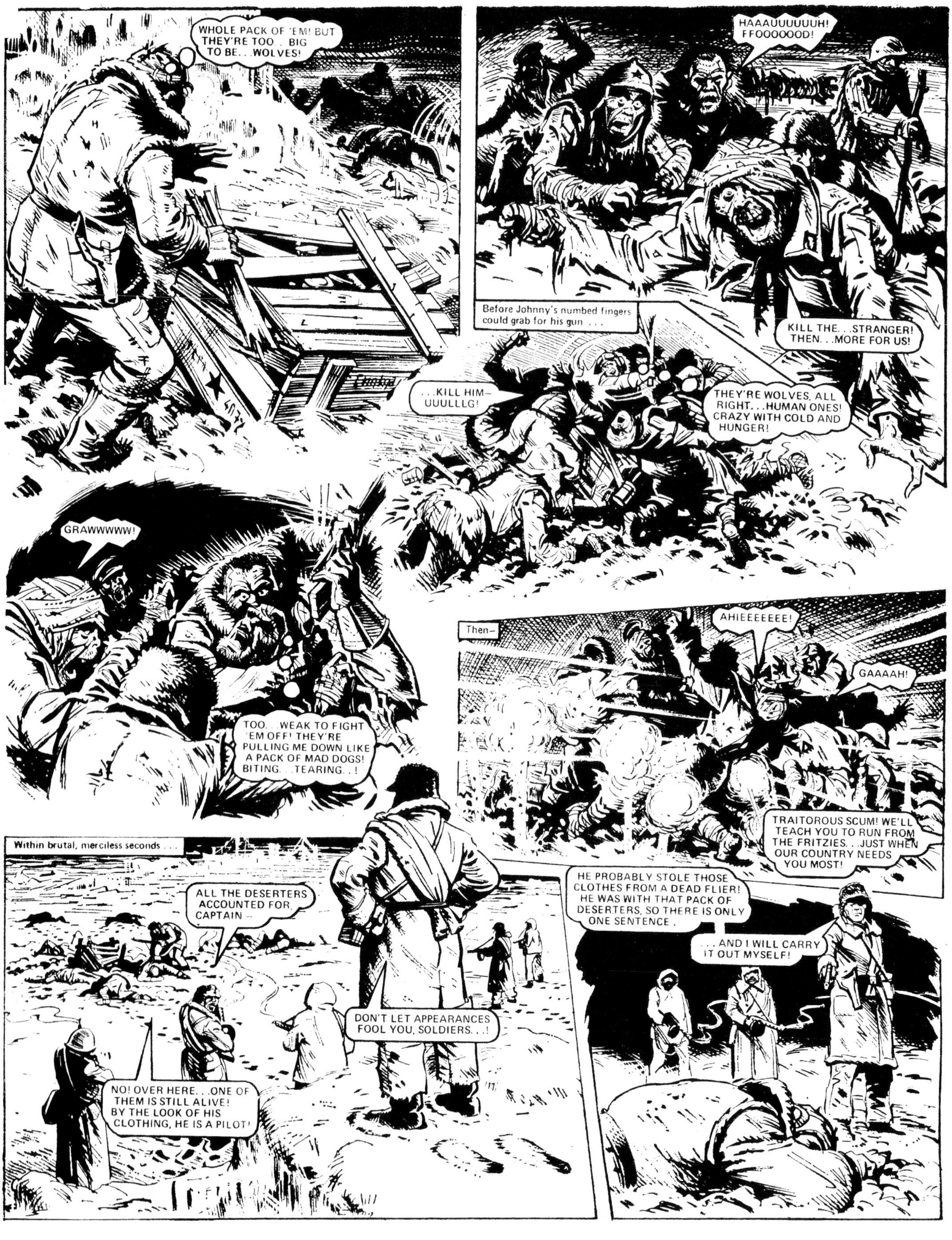
WHOLE PACK OF 'EM! BUT THEY'RE TOO.. BIG TO BE...WOLVES!
HAAAUUUUUUH! FFOOOOOOD!
Before Johnny's numbed fingers could grab for his gun...
KILL THE...STRANGER! THEN...MORE FOR US!
...KILL HIM– UUULLLG!
THEY'RE WOLVES, ALL RIGHT...HUMAN ONES! CRAZY WITH COLD AND HUNGER!
GRAWWWWW!
TOO...WEAK TO FIGHT 'EM OFF! THEY'RE PULLING ME DOWN LIKE A PACK OF MAD DOGS! BITING...TEARING..!
Then–
AHIEEEEEEE!
GAAAAH!
TRAITOROUS SCUM! WE'LL TEACH YOU TO RUN FROM THE FRITZIES...JUST WHEN OUR COUNTRY NEEDS YOU MOST!
Within brutal, merciless seconds...
ALL THE DESERTERS ACCOUNTED FOR, CAPTAIN –
NO! OVER HERE...ONE OF THEM IS STILL ALIVE! BY THE LOOK OF HIS CLOTHING, HE IS A PILOT!
DON'T LET APPEARANCES FOOL YOU, SOLDIERS...!
HE PROBABLY STOLE THOSE CLOTHES FROM A DEAD FLIER! HE WAS WITH THAT PACK OF DESERTERS, SO THERE IS ONLY ONE SENTENCE.
...AND I WILL CARRY IT OUT MYSELF!

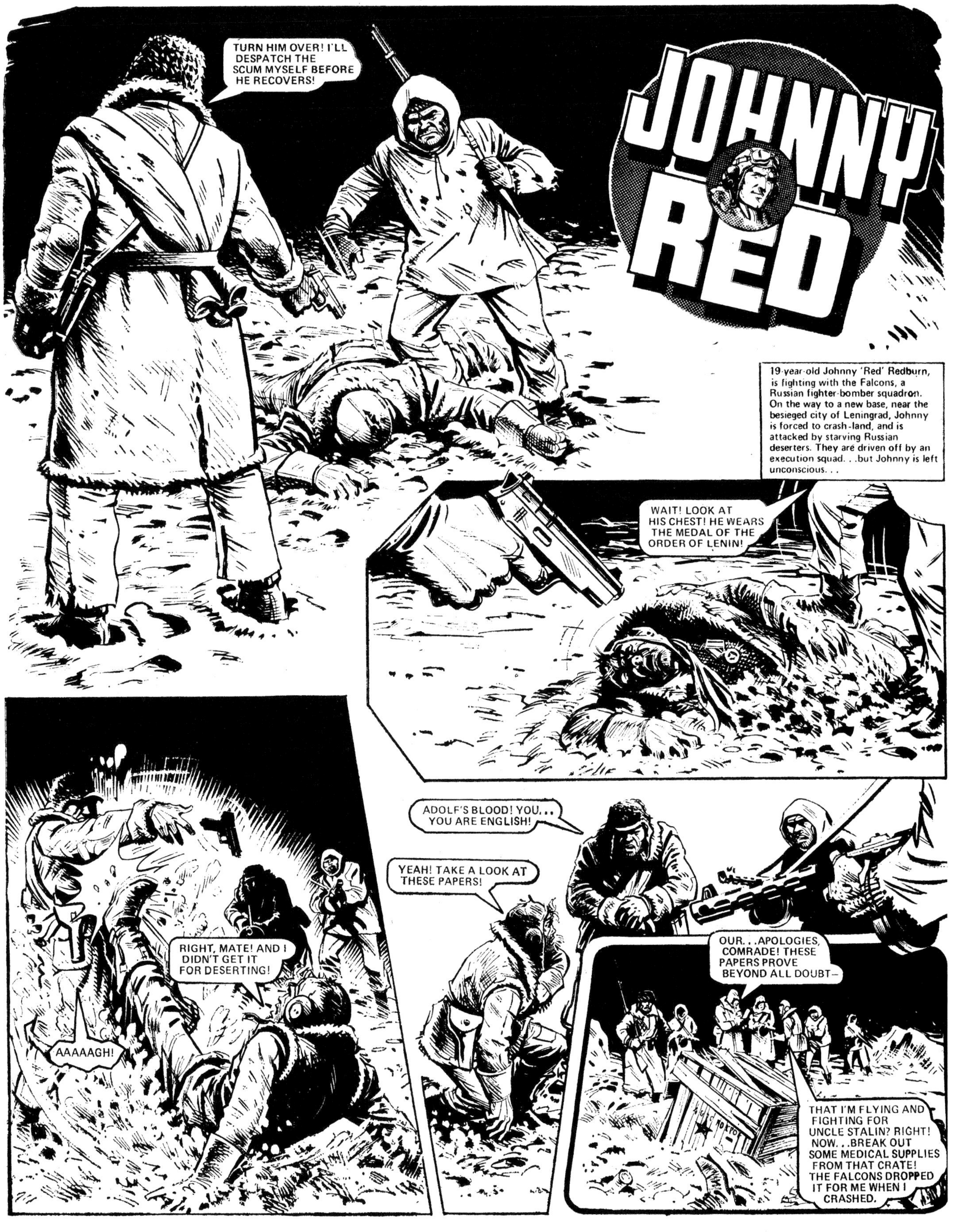
TURN HIM OVER! I'LL DESPATCH THE SCUM MYSELF BEFORE HE RECOVERS!
JOHNNY RED
19-year-old Johnny 'Red' Redburn, is fighting with the Falcons, a Russian fighter-bomber squadron. On the way to a new base, near the besieged city of Leningrad, Johnny is forced to crash-land, and is attacked by starving Russian deserters. They are driven off by an execution squad. . .but Johnny is left unconscious. . .
WAIT! LOOK AT HIS CHEST! HE WEARS THE MEDAL OF THE ORDER OF LENIN!
RIGHT, MATE! AND I DIDN'T GET IT FOR DESERTING!
AAAAAGH!
ADOLF'S BLOOD! YOU. . YOU ARE ENGLISH!
YEAH! TAKE A LOOK AT THESE PAPERS!
OUR. . .APOLOGIES, COMRADE! THESE PAPERS PROVE BEYOND ALL DOUBT—
THAT I'M FLYING AND FIGHTING FOR UNCLE STALIN? RIGHT! NOW. . .BREAK OUT SOME MEDICAL SUPPLIES FROM THAT CRATE! THE FALCONS DROPPED IT FOR ME WHEN I CRASHED.

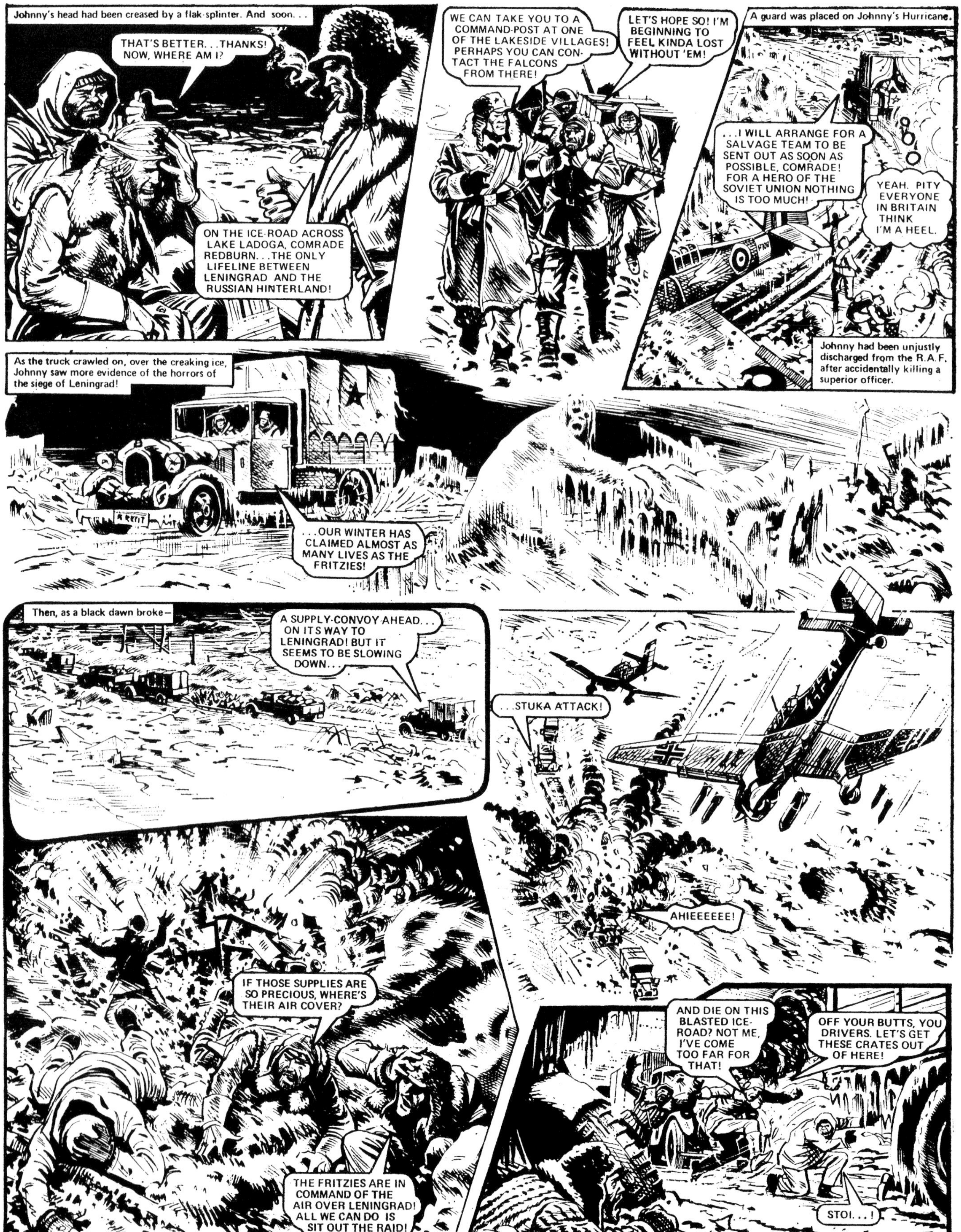

Johnny's head had been creased by a flak-splinter. And soon. . .
THAT'S BETTER. . .THANKS! NOW, WHERE AM I?
ON THE ICE-ROAD ACROSS LAKE LADOGA, COMRADE REDBURN. . .THE ONLY LIFELINE BETWEEN LENINGRAD AND THE RUSSIAN HINTERLAND!
WE CAN TAKE YOU TO A COMMAND-POST AT ONE OF THE LAKESIDE VILLAGES! PERHAPS YOU CAN CONTACT THE FALCONS FROM THERE!
LET'S HOPE SO! I'M BEGINNING TO FEEL KINDA LOST WITHOUT 'EM!
A guard was placed on Johnny's Hurricane.
. . .I WILL ARRANGE FOR A SALVAGE TEAM TO BE SENT OUT AS SOON AS POSSIBLE, COMRADE! FOR A HERO OF THE SOVIET UNION NOTHING IS TOO MUCH!
YEAH. PITY EVERYONE IN BRITAIN THINK I'M A HEEL.
Johnny had been unjustly discharged from the R.A.F. after accidentally killing a superior officer.
As the truck crawled on, over the creaking ice, Johnny saw more evidence of the horrors of the siege of Leningrad!
. . .OUR WINTER HAS CLAIMED ALMOST AS MANY LIVES AS THE FRITZIES!
Then, as a black dawn broke—
A SUPPLY-CONVOY AHEAD. . . ON ITS WAY TO LENINGRAD! BUT IT SEEMS TO BE SLOWING DOWN. . .
. . .STUKA ATTACK!
AHIEEEEEE!
IF THOSE SUPPLIES ARE SO PRECIOUS, WHERE'S THEIR AIR COVER?
THE FRITZIES ARE IN COMMAND OF THE AIR OVER LENINGRAD! ALL WE CAN DO IS SIT OUT THE RAID!
AND DIE ON THIS BLASTED ICE-ROAD? NOT ME, I'VE COME TOO FAR FOR THAT!
OFF YOUR BUTTS, YOU DRIVERS. LET'S GET THESE CRATES OUT OF HERE!
STOI. . .!

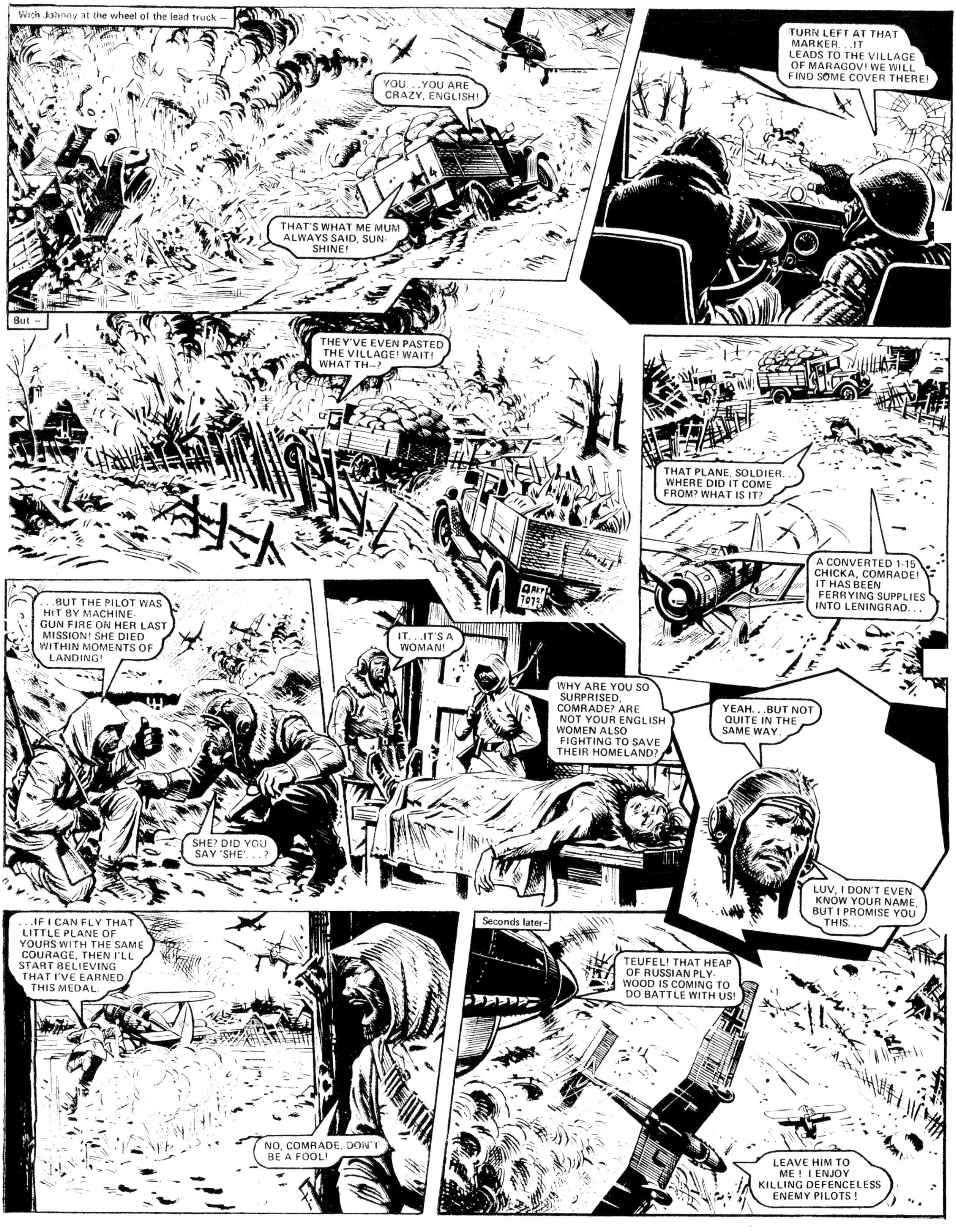
With Johnny at the wheel of the lead truck –
YOU. . .YOU ARE CRAZY, ENGLISH!
THAT'S WHAT ME MUM ALWAYS SAID, SUN-SHINE!
TURN LEFT AT THAT MARKER. . .IT LEADS TO THE VILLAGE OF MARAGOV! WE WILL FIND SOME COVER THERE!
But –
THEY'VE EVEN PASTED THE VILLAGE! WAIT! WHAT TH–?
THAT PLANE, SOLDIER. . . WHERE DID IT COME FROM? WHAT IS IT?
A CONVERTED 1-15 CHICKA, COMRADE! IT HAS BEEN FERRYING SUPPLIES INTO LENINGRAD. . .
. . .BUT THE PILOT WAS HIT BY MACHINE-GUN FIRE ON HER LAST MISSION! SHE DIED WITHIN MOMENTS OF LANDING!
SHE? DID YOU SAY 'SHE'. . .?
IT. . .IT'S A WOMAN!
WHY ARE YOU SO SURPRISED, COMRADE? ARE NOT YOUR ENGLISH WOMEN ALSO FIGHTING TO SAVE THEIR HOMELAND?
YEAH. . .BUT NOT QUITE IN THE SAME WAY.
LUV, I DON'T EVEN KNOW YOUR NAME, BUT I PROMISE YOU THIS. . .
. . .IF I CAN FLY THAT LITTLE PLANE OF YOURS WITH THE SAME COURAGE, THEN I'LL START BELIEVING THAT I'VE EARNED THIS MEDAL.
NO, COMRADE, DON'T BE A FOOL!
Seconds later–
TEUFEL! THAT HEAP OF RUSSIAN PLY-WOOD IS COMING TO DO BATTLE WITH US!
LEAVE HIM TO ME ! I ENJOY KILLING DEFENCELESS ENEMY PILOTS !

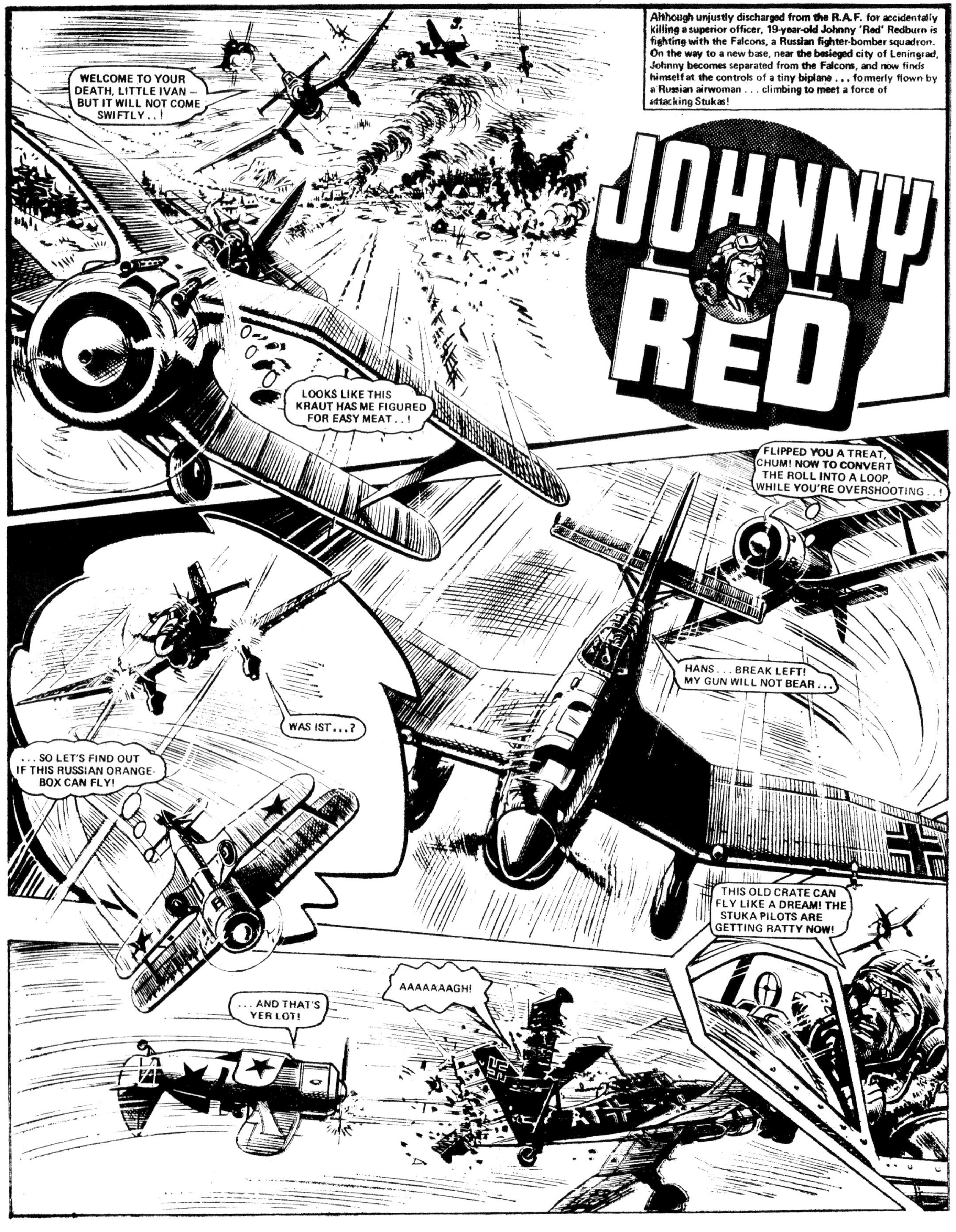
Although unjustly discharged from the R.A.F. for accidentally killing a superior officer, 19-year-old Johnny 'Red' Redburn is fighting with the Falcons, a Russian fighter-bomber squadron. On the way to a new base, near the besieged city of Leningrad, Johnny becomes separated from the Falcons, and now finds himself at the controls of a tiny biplane . . . formerly flown by a Russian airwoman . . . climbing to meet a force of attacking Stukas!
JOHNNY RED
WELCOME TO YOUR DEATH, LITTLE IVAN – BUT IT WILL NOT COME SWIFTLY . . !
LOOKS LIKE THIS KRAUT HAS ME FIGURED FOR EASY MEAT . . !
FLIPPED YOU A TREAT, CHUM! NOW TO CONVERT THE ROLL INTO A LOOP, WHILE YOU'RE OVERSHOOTING . . !
HANS . . . BREAK LEFT! MY GUN WILL NOT BEAR . . .
WAS IST . . . ?
. . . SO LET'S FIND OUT IF THIS RUSSIAN ORANGE-BOX CAN FLY!
THIS OLD CRATE CAN FLY LIKE A DREAM! THE STUKA PILOTS ARE GETTING RATTY NOW!
AAAAAAAGH!
. . . AND THAT'S YER LOT!

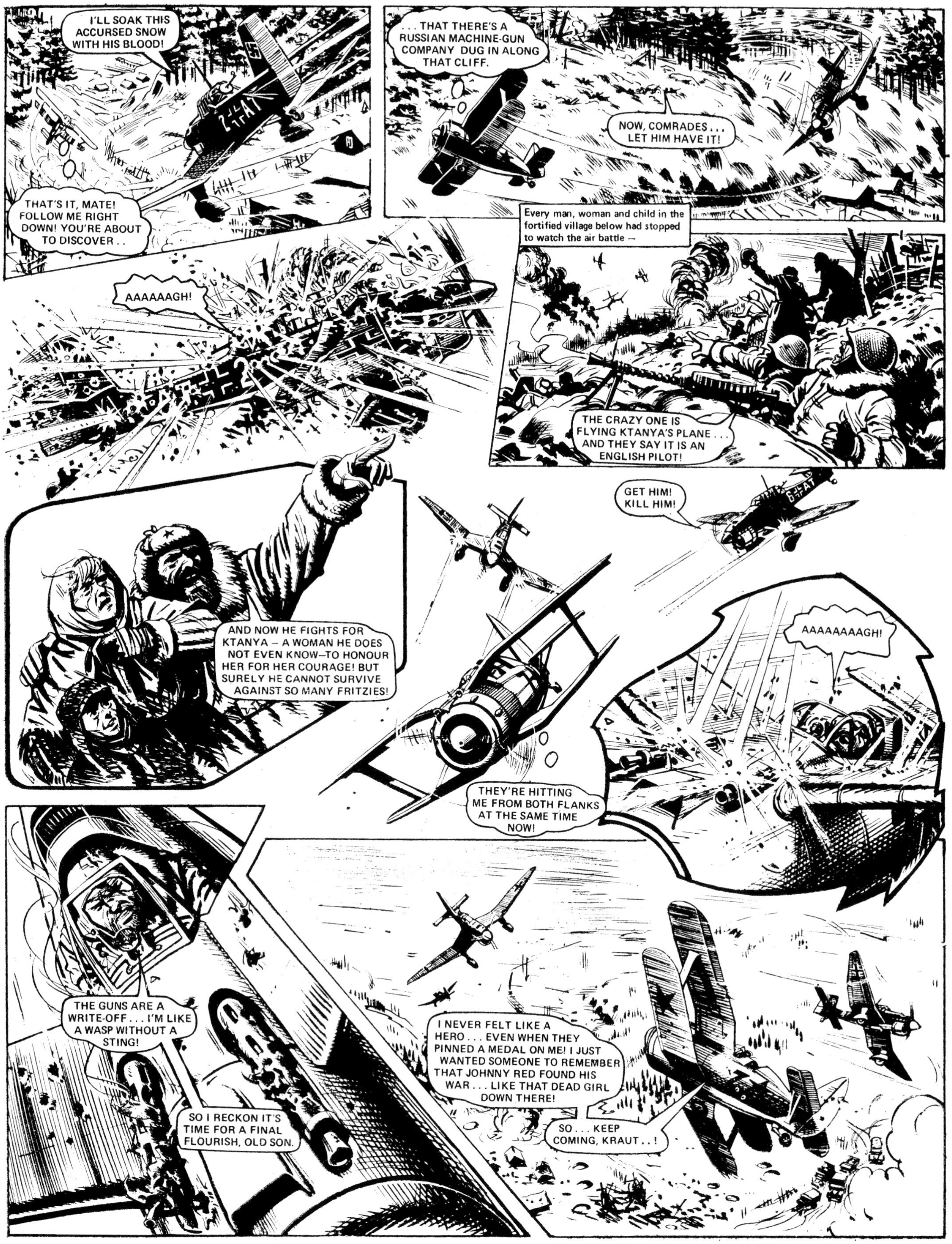
I'LL SOAK THIS ACCURSED SNOW WITH HIS BLOOD!
THAT'S IT, MATE! FOLLOW ME RIGHT DOWN! YOU'RE ABOUT TO DISCOVER . .
. . . THAT THERE'S A RUSSIAN MACHINE-GUN COMPANY DUG IN ALONG THAT CLIFF.
NOW, COMRADES . . . LET HIM HAVE IT!
AAAAAAGH!
Every man, woman and child in the fortified village below had stopped to watch the air battle –
THE CRAZY ONE IS FLYING KTANYA'S PLANE . . . AND THEY SAY IT IS AN ENGLISH PILOT!
AND NOW HE FIGHTS FOR KTANYA – A WOMAN HE DOES NOT EVEN KNOW–TO HONOUR HER FOR HER COURAGE! BUT SURELY HE CANNOT SURVIVE AGAINST SO MANY FRITZIES!
GET HIM! KILL HIM!
THEY'RE HITTING ME FROM BOTH FLANKS AT THE SAME TIME NOW!
AAAAAAAAGH!
THE GUNS ARE A WRITE-OFF . . . I'M LIKE A WASP WITHOUT A STING!
SO I RECKON IT'S TIME FOR A FINAL FLOURISH, OLD SON.
I NEVER FELT LIKE A HERO . . . EVEN WHEN THEY PINNED A MEDAL ON ME! I JUST WANTED SOMEONE TO REMEMBER THAT JOHNNY RED FOUND HIS WAR . . . LIKE THAT DEAD GIRL DOWN THERE!
SO . . . KEEP COMING, KRAUT . . !

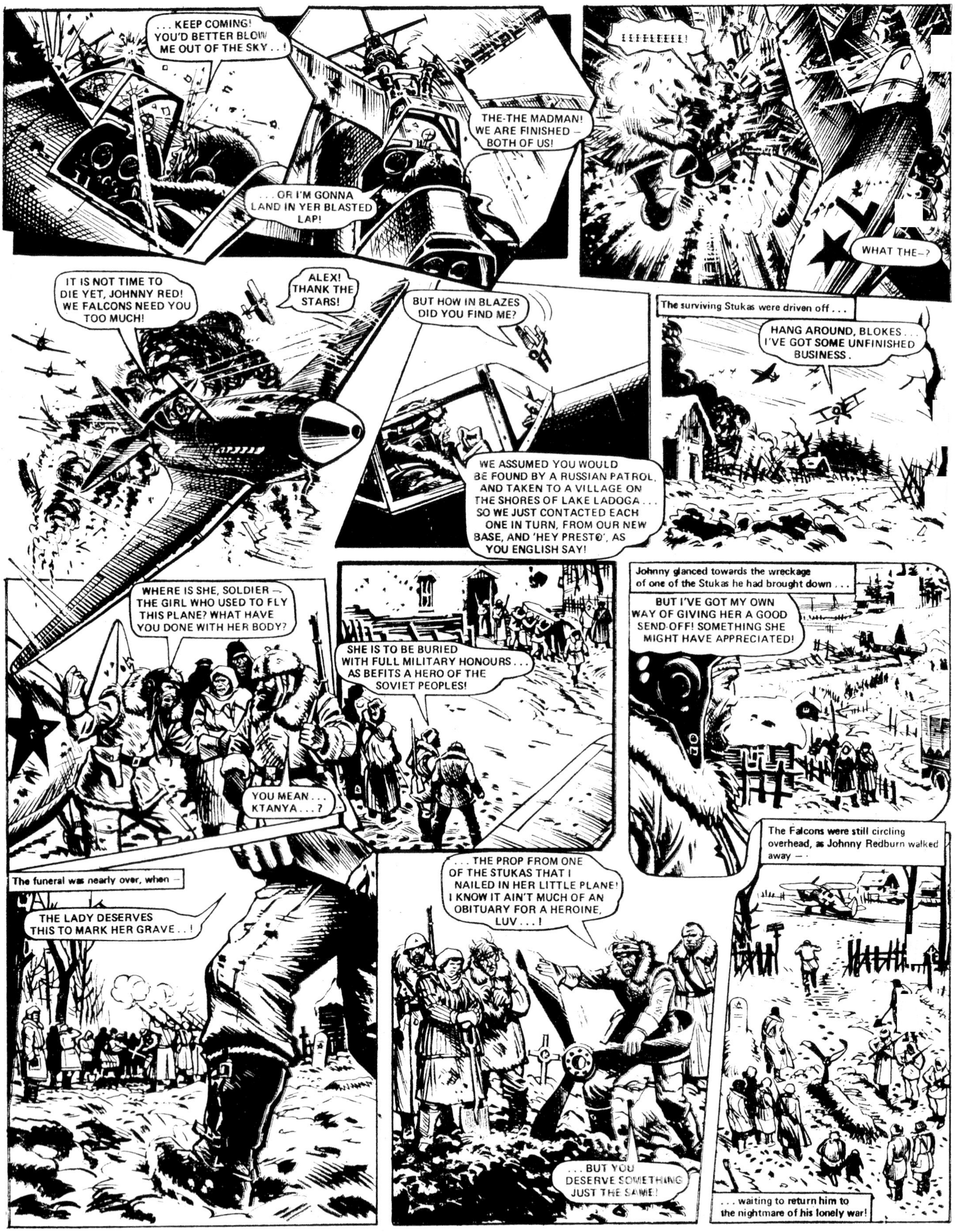

. . . KEEP COMING! YOU'D BETTER BLOW ME OUT OF THE SKY . . !
. . . OR I'M GONNA LAND IN YER BLASTED LAP!
THE-THE MADMAN! WE ARE FINISHED — BOTH OF US!
EEEEEEEEE!
WHAT THE–?
IT IS NOT TIME TO DIE YET, JOHNNY RED! WE FALCONS NEED YOU TOO MUCH!
ALEX! THANK THE STARS!
BUT HOW IN BLAZES DID YOU FIND ME?
WE ASSUMED YOU WOULD BE FOUND BY A RUSSIAN PATROL, AND TAKEN TO A VILLAGE ON THE SHORES OF LAKE LADOGA . . . SO WE JUST CONTACTED EACH ONE IN TURN, FROM OUR NEW BASE, AND 'HEY PRESTO', AS YOU ENGLISH SAY!
The surviving Stukas were driven off . . .
HANG AROUND, BLOKES . . . I'VE GOT SOME UNFINISHED BUSINESS.
WHERE IS SHE, SOLDIER — THE GIRL WHO USED TO FLY THIS PLANE? WHAT HAVE YOU DONE WITH HER BODY?
YOU MEAN . . . KTANYA . . .?
SHE IS TO BE BURIED WITH FULL MILITARY HONOURS . . . AS BEFITS A HERO OF THE SOVIET PEOPLES!
Johnny glanced towards the wreckage of one of the Stukas he had brought down . . .
BUT I'VE GOT MY OWN WAY OF GIVING HER A GOOD SEND-OFF! SOMETHING SHE MIGHT HAVE APPRECIATED!
The funeral was nearly over, when —
THE LADY DESERVES THIS TO MARK HER GRAVE . . !
. . . THE PROP FROM ONE OF THE STUKAS THAT I NAILED IN HER LITTLE PLANE! I KNOW IT AIN'T MUCH OF AN OBITUARY FOR A HEROINE, LUV . . . !
. . . BUT YOU DESERVE SOMETHING JUST THE SAME!
The Falcons were still circling overhead, as Johnny Redburn walked away —
. . . waiting to return him to the nightmare of his lonely war!

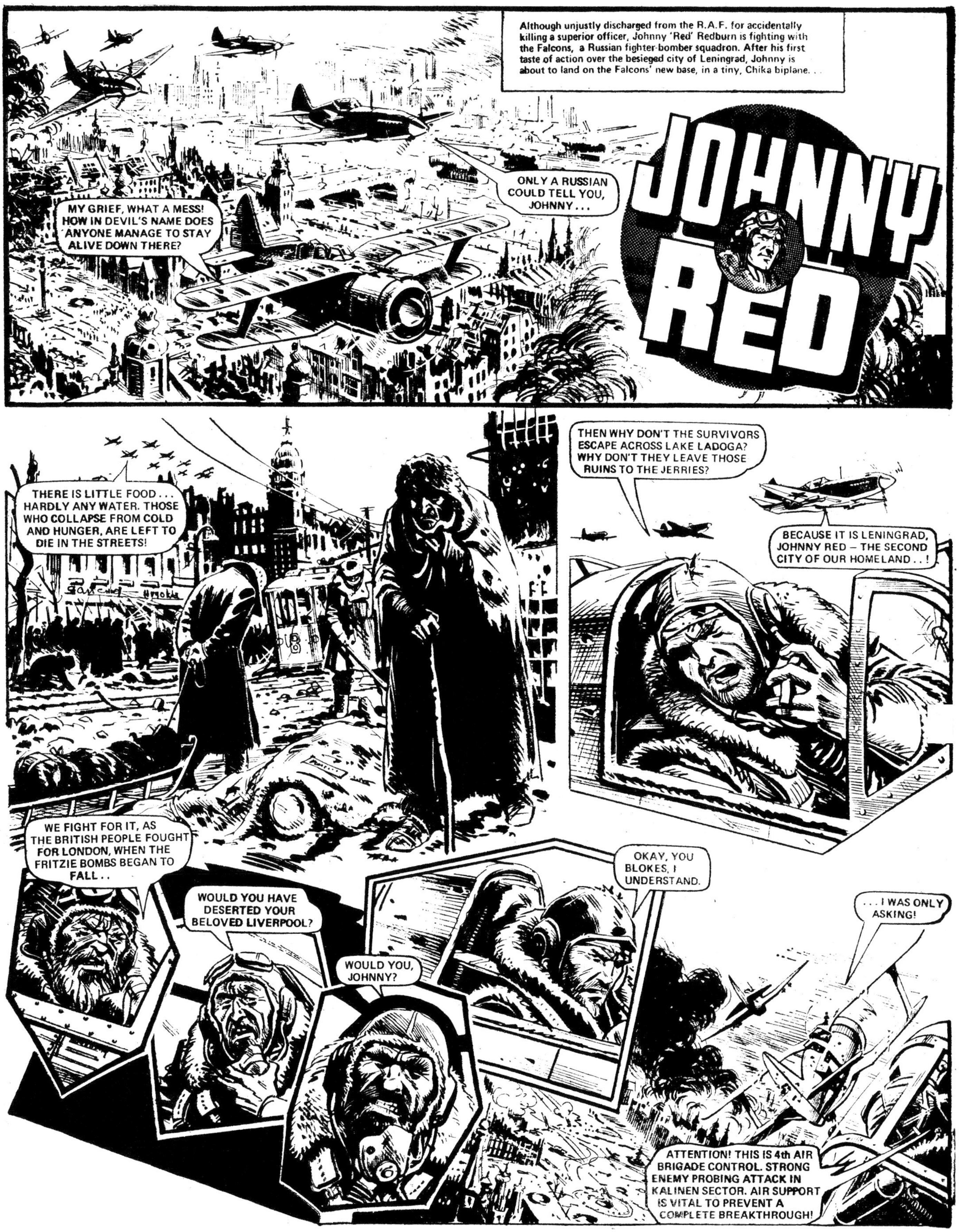
Although unjustly discharged from the R.A.F. for accidentally killing a superior officer, Johnny 'Red' Redburn is fighting with the Falcons, a Russian fighter-bomber squadron. After his first taste of action over the besieged city of Leningrad, Johnny is about to land on the Falcons' new base, in a tiny, Chika biplane. .
JOHNNY RED
MY GRIEF, WHAT A MESS! HOW IN DEVIL'S NAME DOES ANYONE MANAGE TO STAY ALIVE DOWN THERE?
ONLY A RUSSIAN COULD TELL YOU, JOHNNY . . .
THERE IS LITTLE FOOD . . . HARDLY ANY WATER. THOSE WHO COLLAPSE FROM COLD AND HUNGER, ARE LEFT TO DIE IN THE STREETS!
THEN WHY DON'T THE SURVIVORS ESCAPE ACROSS LAKE LADOGA? WHY DON'T THEY LEAVE THOSE RUINS TO THE JERRIES?
BECAUSE IT IS LENINGRAD, JOHNNY RED – THE SECOND CITY OF OUR HOMELAND . . !
WE FIGHT FOR IT, AS THE BRITISH PEOPLE FOUGHT FOR LONDON, WHEN THE FRITZIE BOMBS BEGAN TO FALL . .
WOULD YOU HAVE DESERTED YOUR BELOVED LIVERPOOL?
WOULD YOU, JOHNNY?
OKAY, YOU BLOKES, I UNDERSTAND.
. . . I WAS ONLY ASKING!
ATTENTION! THIS IS 4th AIR BRIGADE CONTROL. STRONG ENEMY PROBING ATTACK IN KALINEN SECTOR. AIR SUPPORT IS VITAL TO PREVENT A COMPLETE BREAKTHROUGH!

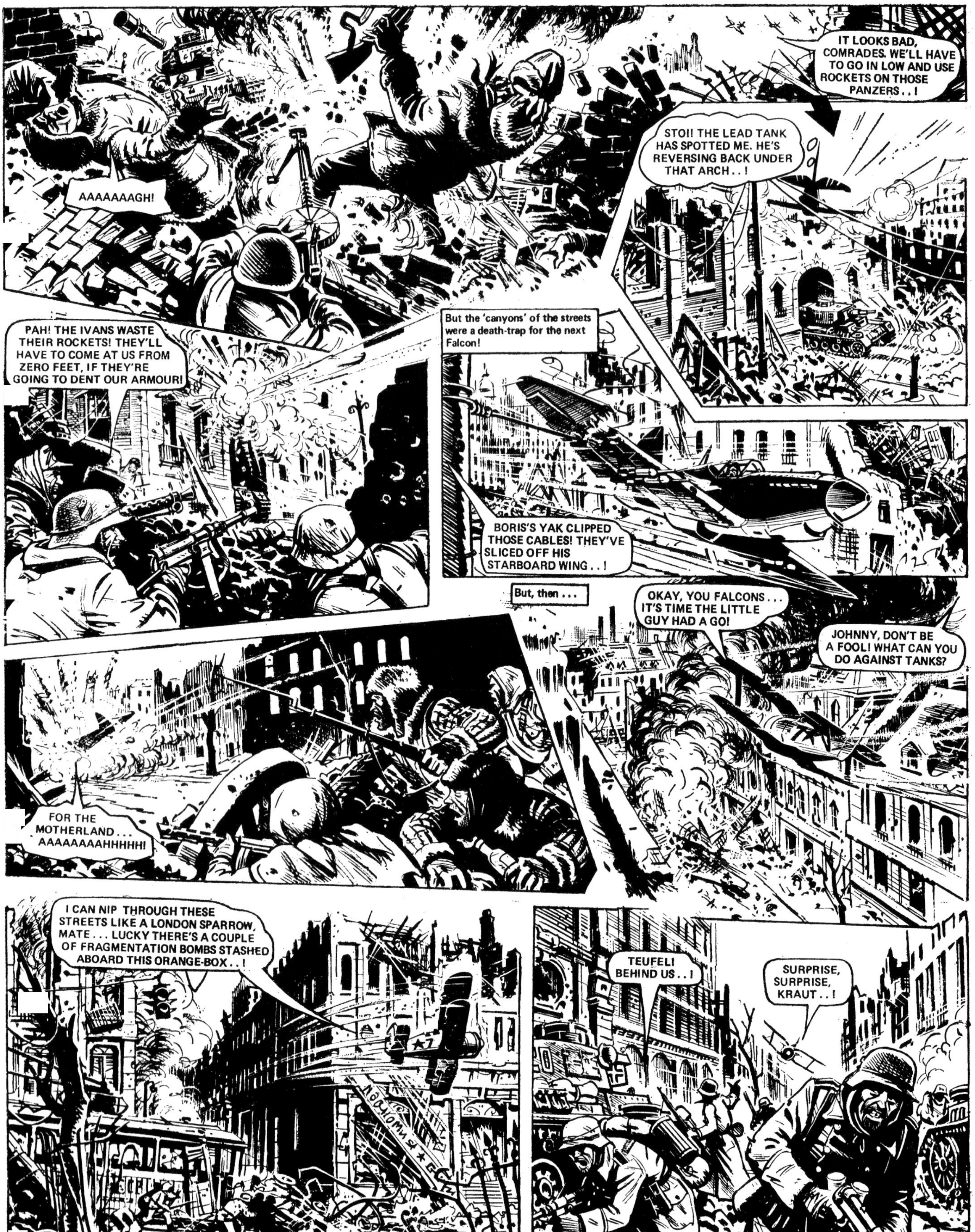
IT LOOKS BAD, COMRADES. WE'LL HAVE TO GO IN LOW AND USE ROCKETS ON THOSE PANZERS . . !
AAAAAAAGH!
STOI! THE LEAD TANK HAS SPOTTED ME. HE'S REVERSING BACK UNDER THAT ARCH . . !
PAH! THE IVANS WASTE THEIR ROCKETS! THEY'LL HAVE TO COME AT US FROM ZERO FEET, IF THEY'RE GOING TO DENT OUR ARMOUR!
But the 'canyons' of the streets were a death-trap for the next Falcon!
BORIS'S YAK CLIPPED THOSE CABLES! THEY'VE SLICED OFF HIS STARBOARD WING . . !
FOR THE MOTHERLAND . . . AAAAAAAAHHHHH!
But, then . . .
OKAY, YOU FALCONS . . . IT'S TIME THE LITTLE GUY HAD A GO!
JOHNNY, DON'T BE A FOOL! WHAT CAN YOU DO AGAINST TANKS?
I CAN NIP THROUGH THESE STREETS LIKE A LONDON SPARROW, MATE . . . LUCKY THERE'S A COUPLE OF FRAGMENTATION BOMBS STASHED ABOARD THIS ORANGE-BOX . . !
TEUFEL! BEHIND US . . !
SURPRISE, SURPRISE, KRAUT . . !

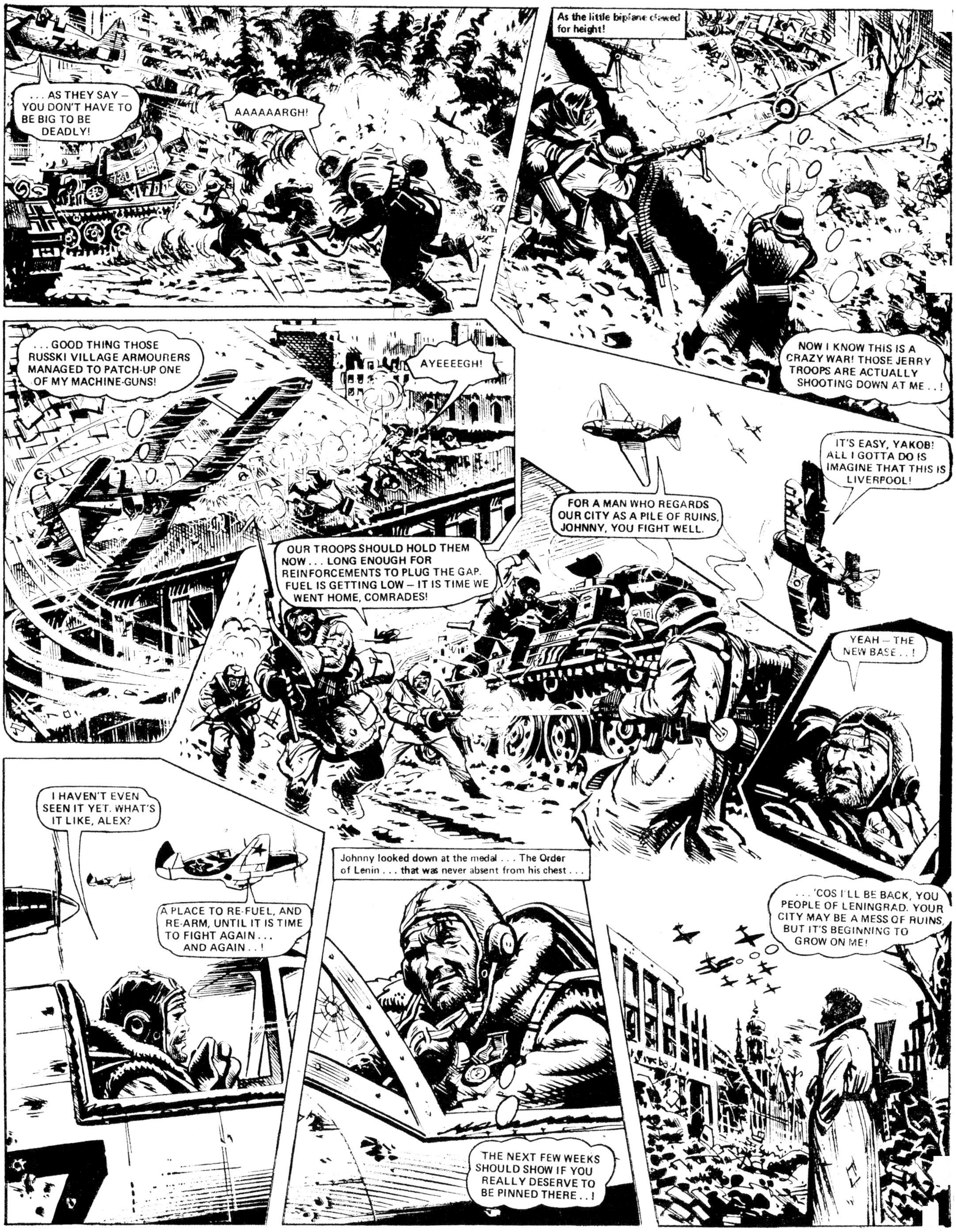

. . . AS THEY SAY – YOU DON'T HAVE TO BE BIG TO BE DEADLY!
AAAAAARGH!
As the little biplane clawed for height!
NOW I KNOW THIS IS A CRAZY WAR! THOSE JERRY TROOPS ARE ACTUALLY SHOOTING DOWN AT ME . . !
. . . GOOD THING THOSE RUSSKI VILLAGE ARMOURERS MANAGED TO PATCH-UP ONE OF MY MACHINE-GUNS!
AYEEEEGH!
IT'S EASY, YAKOB! ALL I GOTTA DO IS IMAGINE THAT THIS IS LIVERPOOL!
FOR A MAN WHO REGARDS OUR CITY AS A PILE OF RUINS, JOHNNY, YOU FIGHT WELL.
OUR TROOPS SHOULD HOLD THEM NOW . . . LONG ENOUGH FOR REINFORCEMENTS TO PLUG THE GAP. FUEL IS GETTING LOW – IT IS TIME WE WENT HOME, COMRADES!
YEAH – THE NEW BASE . . !
I HAVEN'T EVEN SEEN IT YET. WHAT'S IT LIKE, ALEX?
A PLACE TO RE-FUEL, AND RE-ARM, UNTIL IT IS TIME TO FIGHT AGAIN . . . AND AGAIN . . !
Johnny looked down at the medal . . . The Order of Lenin . . . that was never absent from his chest . . .
THE NEXT FEW WEEKS SHOULD SHOW IF YOU REALLY DESERVE TO BE PINNED THERE . . !
. . . 'COS I'LL BE BACK, YOU PEOPLE OF LENINGRAD. YOUR CITY MAY BE A MESS OF RUINS, BUT IT'S BEGINNING TO GROW ON ME!

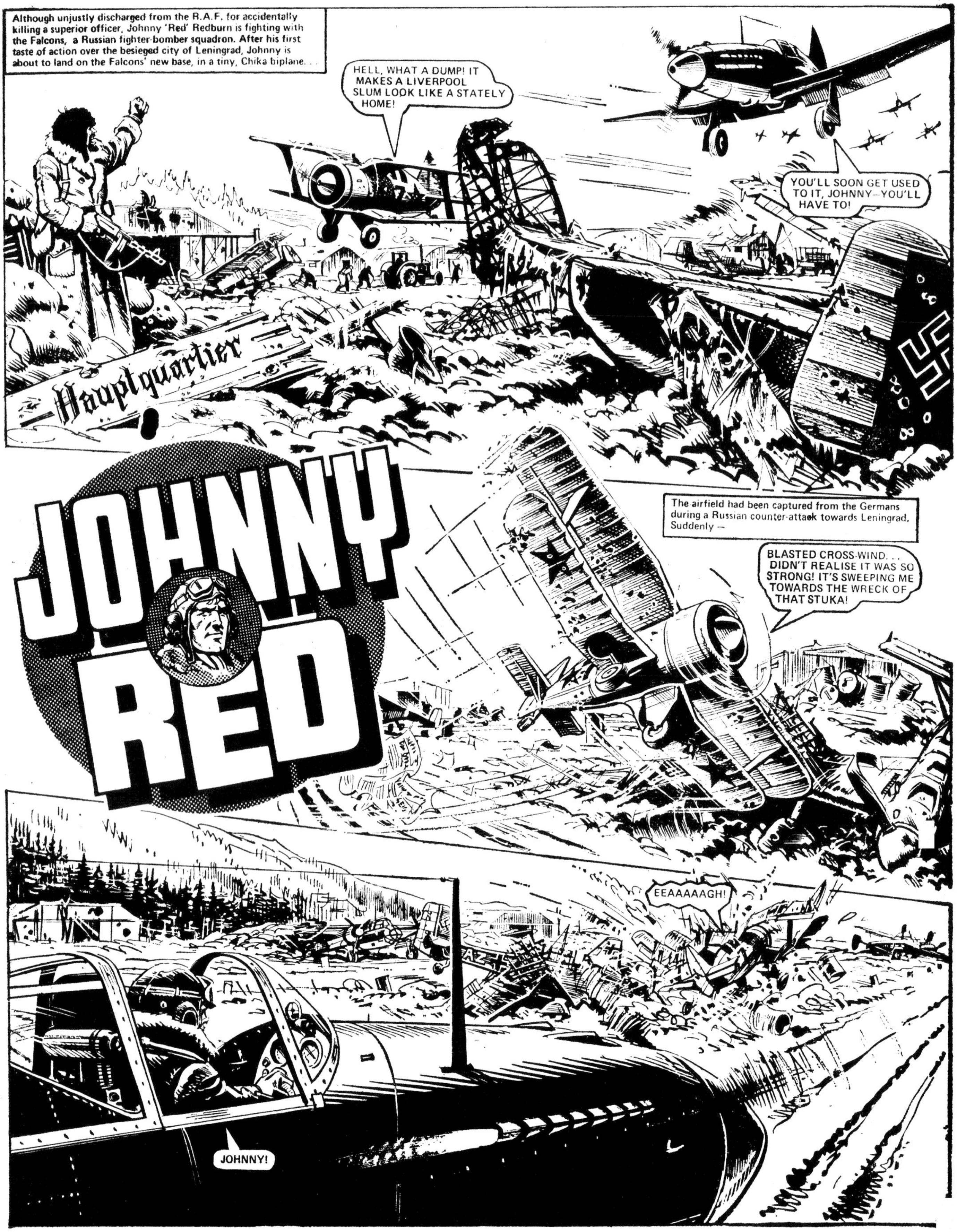
Although unjustly discharged from the R.A.F. for accidentally killing a superior officer, Johnny 'Red' Redburn is fighting with the Falcons, a Russian fighter-bomber squadron. After his first taste of action over the besieged city of Leningrad, Johnny is about to land on the Falcons' new base, in a tiny, Chika biplane. . .
HELL, WHAT A DUMP! IT MAKES A LIVERPOOL SLUM LOOK LIKE A STATELY HOME!
YOU'LL SOON GET USED TO IT, JOHNNY–YOU'LL HAVE TO!
Hauptquartier
JOHNNY RED
The airfield had been captured from the Germans during a Russian counter-attack towards Leningrad. Suddenly –
BLASTED CROSS-WIND. . . DIDN'T REALISE IT WAS SO STRONG! IT'S SWEEPING ME TOWARDS THE WRECK OF THAT STUKA!
EEAAAAAGH!
JOHNNY!

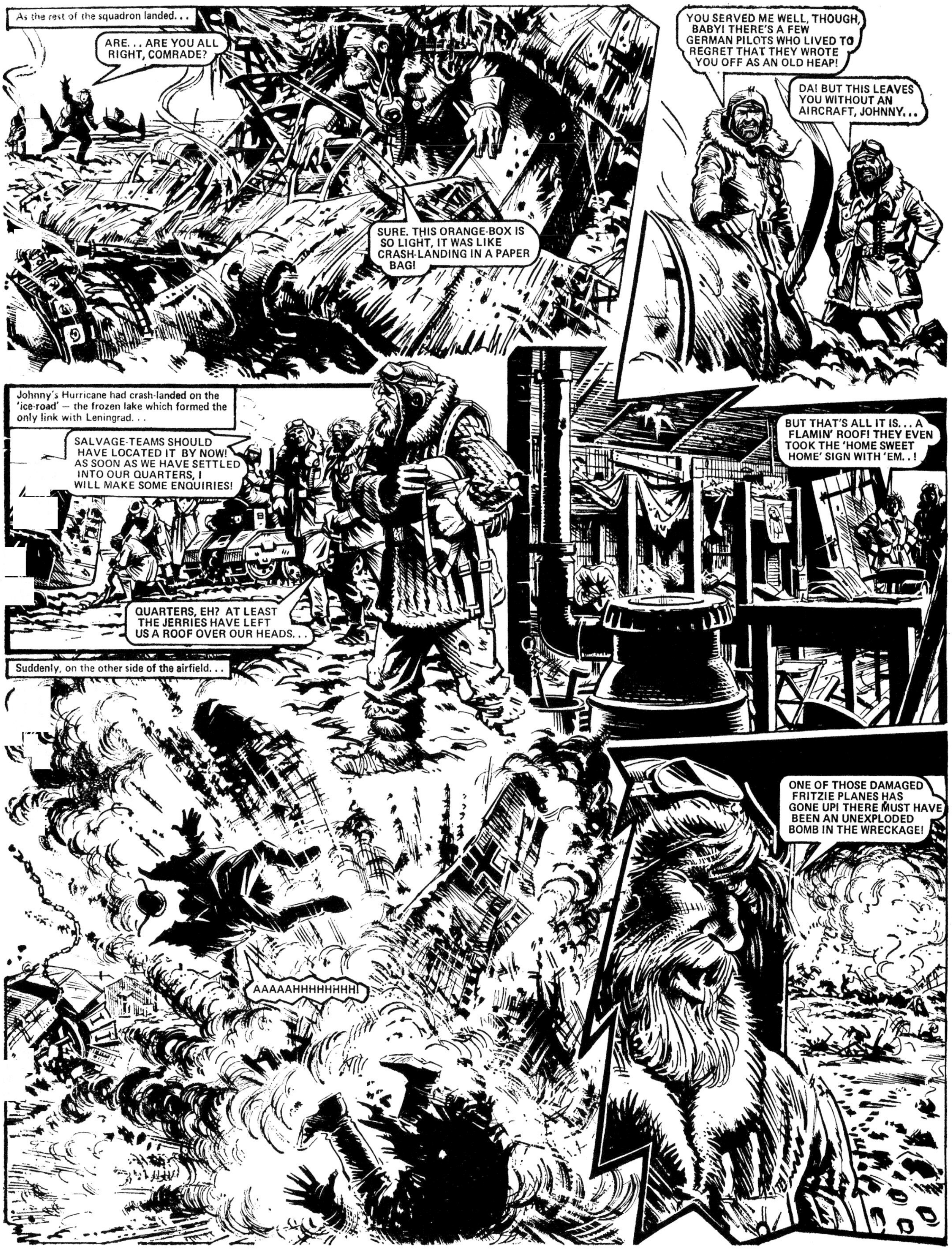
As the rest of the squadron landed...
ARE... ARE YOU ALL RIGHT, COMRADE?
SURE. THIS ORANGE-BOX IS SO LIGHT, IT WAS LIKE CRASH-LANDING IN A PAPER BAG!
YOU SERVED ME WELL, THOUGH, BABY! THERE'S A FEW GERMAN PILOTS WHO LIVED TO REGRET THAT THEY WROTE YOU OFF AS AN OLD HEAP!
DA! BUT THIS LEAVES YOU WITHOUT AN AIRCRAFT, JOHNNY...
Johnny's Hurricane had crash-landed on the 'ice-road' — the frozen lake which formed the only link with Leningrad...
SALVAGE-TEAMS SHOULD HAVE LOCATED IT BY NOW! AS SOON AS WE HAVE SETTLED INTO OUR QUARTERS, I WILL MAKE SOME ENQUIRIES!
QUARTERS, EH? AT LEAST THE JERRIES HAVE LEFT US A ROOF OVER OUR HEADS...
BUT THAT'S ALL IT IS... A FLAMIN' ROOF! THEY EVEN TOOK THE 'HOME SWEET HOME' SIGN WITH 'EM..!
Suddenly, on the other side of the airfield...
AAAAAHHHHHHHH!
ONE OF THOSE DAMAGED FRITZIE PLANES HAS GONE UP! THERE MUST HAVE BEEN AN UNEXPLODED BOMB IN THE WRECKAGE!

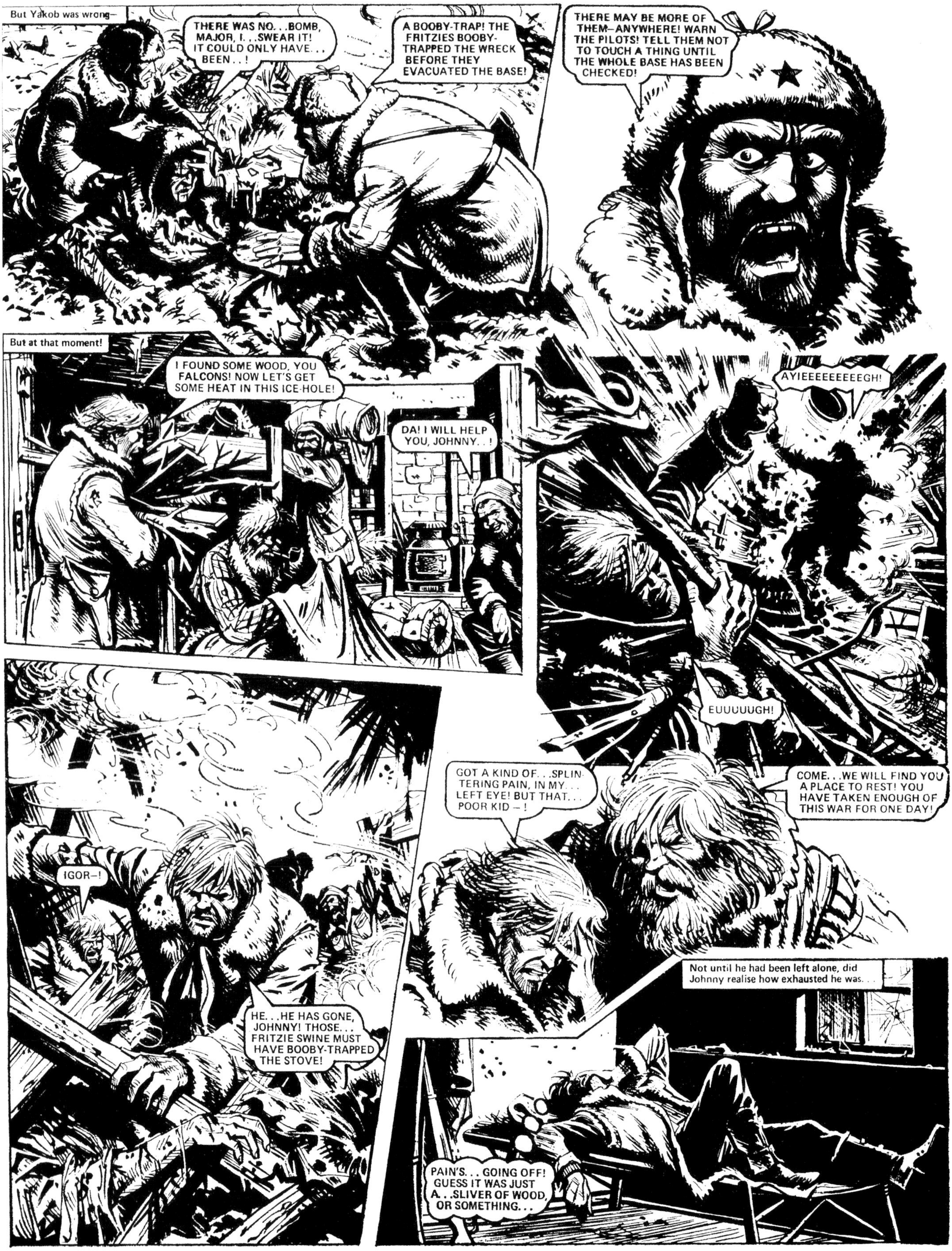

But Yakob was wrong—
THERE WAS NO. . .BOMB, MAJOR, I. . .SWEAR IT! IT COULD ONLY HAVE. . . BEEN. . !
A BOOBY-TRAP! THE FRITZIES BOOBY-TRAPPED THE WRECK BEFORE THEY EVACUATED THE BASE!
THERE MAY BE MORE OF THEM—ANYWHERE! WARN THE PILOTS! TELL THEM NOT TO TOUCH A THING UNTIL THE WHOLE BASE HAS BEEN CHECKED!
But at that moment!
I FOUND SOME WOOD, YOU FALCONS! NOW LET'S GET SOME HEAT IN THIS ICE-HOLE!
DA! I WILL HELP YOU, JOHNNY. . !
AYIEEEEEEEEEGH!
EUUUUUGH!
IGOR—!
HE. . .HE HAS GONE, JOHNNY! THOSE. . . FRITZIE SWINE MUST HAVE BOOBY-TRAPPED THE STOVE!
GOT A KIND OF. . .SPLINTERING PAIN, IN MY. . . LEFT EYE! BUT THAT. . . POOR KID—!
COME. . .WE WILL FIND YOU A PLACE TO REST! YOU HAVE TAKEN ENOUGH OF THIS WAR FOR ONE DAY!
Not until he had been left alone, did Johnny realise how exhausted he was. . .
PAIN'S. . . GOING OFF! GUESS IT WAS JUST A. . SLIVER OF WOOD, OR SOMETHING. . .

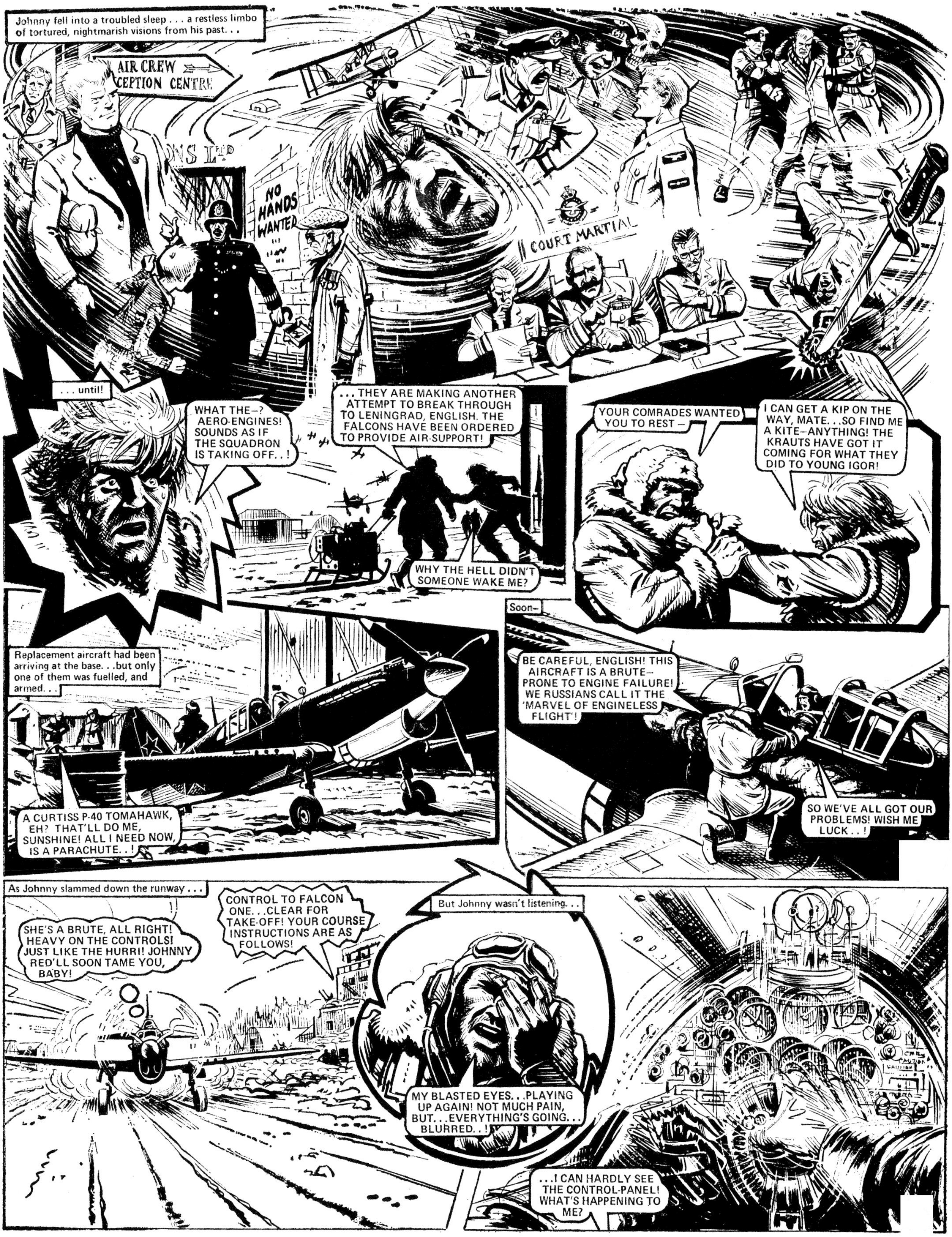

Johnny fell into a troubled sleep . . . a restless limbo of tortured, nightmarish visions from his past. . .
AIR CREW
CEPTION CENTRE
NO HANDS WANTED
COURT MARTIAL
. . . until!
WHAT THE–? AERO-ENGINES! SOUNDS AS IF THE SQUADRON IS TAKING OFF. . !
. . . THEY ARE MAKING ANOTHER ATTEMPT TO BREAK THROUGH TO LENINGRAD, ENGLISH. THE FALCONS HAVE BEEN ORDERED TO PROVIDE AIR-SUPPORT!
WHY THE HELL DIDN'T SOMEONE WAKE ME?
YOUR COMRADES WANTED YOU TO REST –
I CAN GET A KIP ON THE WAY, MATE. . .SO FIND ME A KITE–ANYTHING! THE KRAUTS HAVE GOT IT COMING FOR WHAT THEY DID TO YOUNG IGOR!
Replacement aircraft had been arriving at the base. . .but only one of them was fuelled, and armed. .
A CURTISS P-40 TOMAHAWK, EH? THAT'LL DO ME, SUNSHINE! ALL I NEED NOW, IS A PARACHUTE. . !
Soon–
BE CAREFUL, ENGLISH! THIS AIRCRAFT IS A BRUTE– PRONE TO ENGINE FAILURE! WE RUSSIANS CALL IT THE 'MARVEL OF ENGINELESS FLIGHT'!
SO WE'VE ALL GOT OUR PROBLEMS! WISH ME LUCK . . !
As Johnny slammed down the runway . . .
SHE'S A BRUTE, ALL RIGHT! HEAVY ON THE CONTROLS! JUST LIKE THE HURRI! JOHNNY RED'LL SOON TAME YOU, BABY!
CONTROL TO FALCON ONE. . .CLEAR FOR TAKE-OFF! YOUR COURSE INSTRUCTIONS ARE AS FOLLOWS!
But Johnny wasn't listening. . .
MY BLASTED EYES. . PLAYING UP AGAIN! NOT MUCH PAIN, BUT. . . EVERYTHING'S GOING. . . BLURRED. . !
. . . I CAN HARDLY SEE THE CONTROL-PANEL! WHAT'S HAPPENING TO ME?

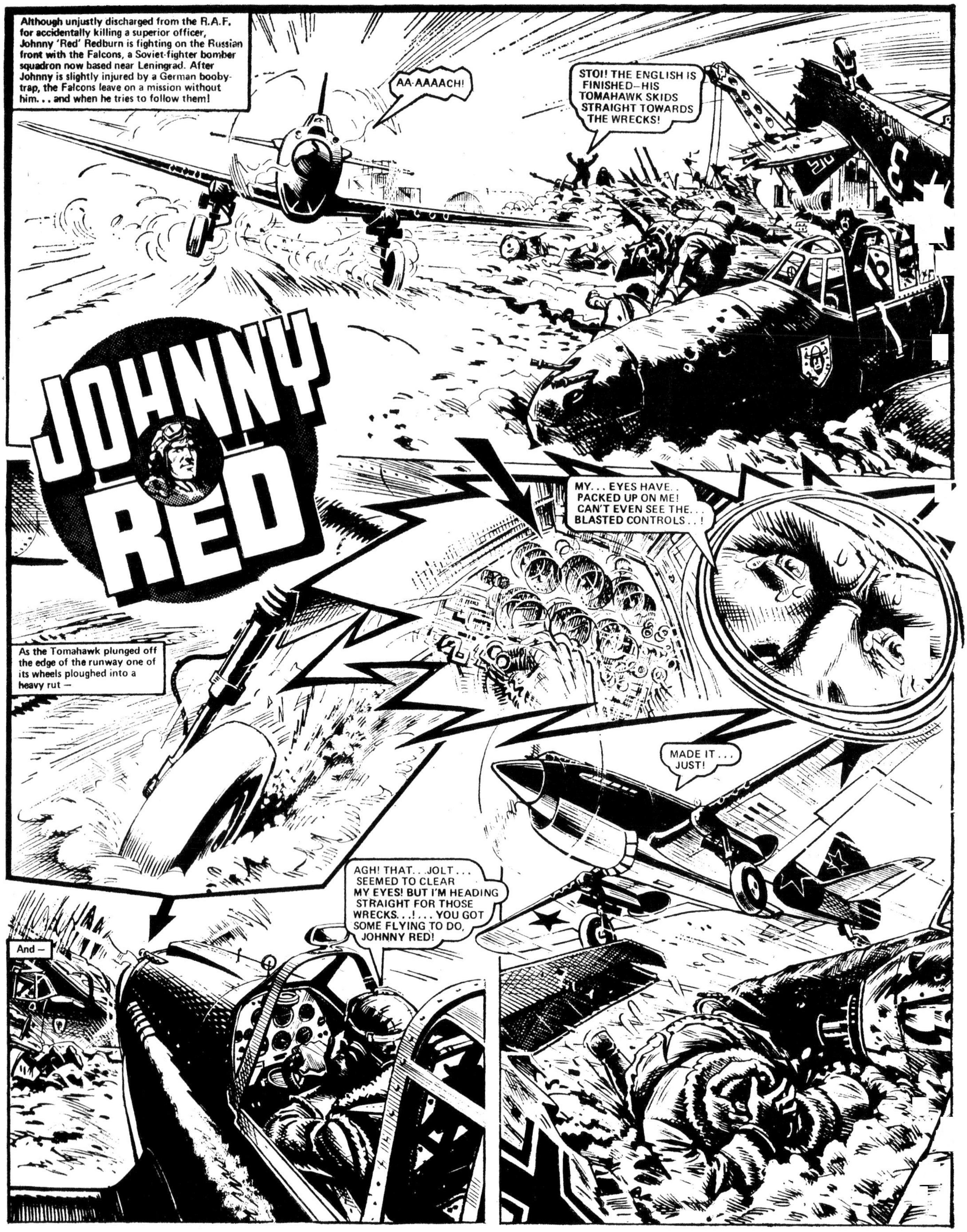
Although unjustly discharged from the R.A.F. for accidentally killing a superior officer, Johnny 'Red' Redburn is fighting on the Russian front with the Falcons, a Soviet-fighter bomber squadron now based near Leningrad. After Johnny is slightly injured by a German booby-trap, the Falcons leave on a mission without him. . . and when he tries to follow them!
AA-AAAACH!
STOI! THE ENGLISH IS FINISHED—HIS TOMAHAWK SKIDS STRAIGHT TOWARDS THE WRECKS!
JOHNNY RED
MY. . . EYES HAVE. . PACKED UP ON ME! CAN'T EVEN SEE THE. . . BLASTED CONTROLS. . !
As the Tomahawk plunged off the edge of the runway one of its wheels ploughed into a heavy rut —
AGH! THAT. . JOLT. . . SEEMED TO CLEAR MY EYES! BUT I'M HEADING STRAIGHT FOR THOSE WRECKS. . .! . . . YOU GOT SOME FLYING TO DO, JOHNNY RED!
MADE IT. . . JUST!
And —

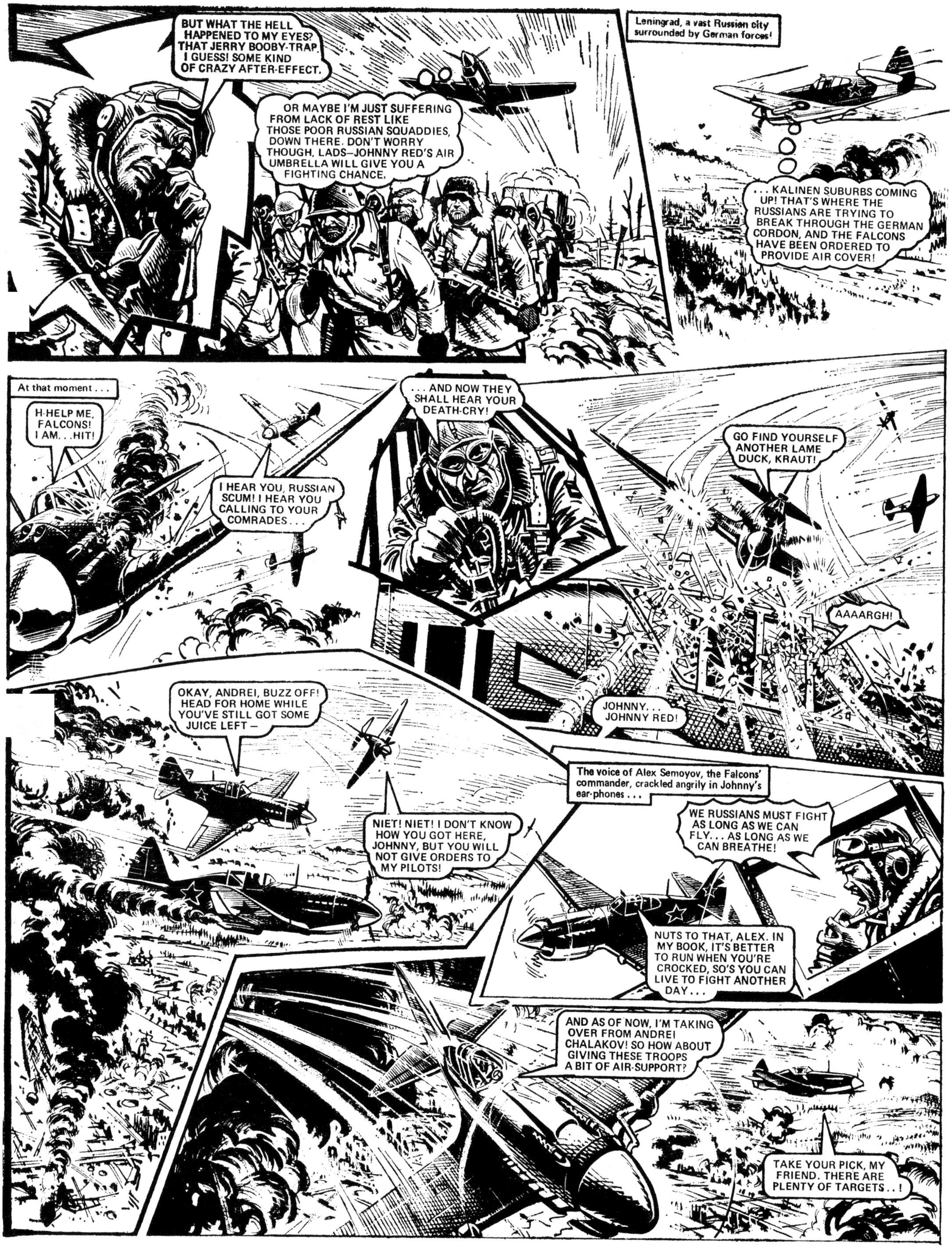

BUT WHAT THE HELL HAPPENED TO MY EYES? THAT JERRY BOOBY-TRAP, I GUESS! SOME KIND OF CRAZY AFTER-EFFECT.
OR MAYBE I'M JUST SUFFERING FROM LACK OF REST LIKE THOSE POOR RUSSIAN SQUADDIES, DOWN THERE. DON'T WORRY THOUGH, LADS—JOHNNY RED'S AIR UMBRELLA WILL GIVE YOU A FIGHTING CHANCE.
Leningrad, a vast Russian city surrounded by German forces!
. . . KALINEN SUBURBS COMING UP! THAT'S WHERE THE RUSSIANS ARE TRYING TO BREAK THROUGH THE GERMAN CORDON, AND THE FALCONS HAVE BEEN ORDERED TO PROVIDE AIR COVER!
At that moment . . .
H-HELP ME, FALCONS! I AM. . .HIT!
I HEAR YOU, RUSSIAN SCUM! I HEAR YOU CALLING TO YOUR COMRADES . . .
. . . AND NOW THEY SHALL HEAR YOUR DEATH-CRY!
GO FIND YOURSELF ANOTHER LAME DUCK, KRAUT!
AAAARGH!
JOHNNY. . . JOHNNY RED!
OKAY, ANDREI, BUZZ OFF! HEAD FOR HOME WHILE YOU'VE STILL GOT SOME JUICE LEFT –
NIET! NIET! I DON'T KNOW HOW YOU GOT HERE, JOHNNY, BUT YOU WILL NOT GIVE ORDERS TO MY PILOTS!
The voice of Alex Semoyov, the Falcons' commander, crackled angrily in Johnny's ear-phones . . .
WE RUSSIANS MUST FIGHT AS LONG AS WE CAN FLY. . . AS LONG AS WE CAN BREATHE!
NUTS TO THAT, ALEX. IN MY BOOK, IT'S BETTER TO RUN WHEN YOU'RE CROCKED, SO'S YOU CAN LIVE TO FIGHT ANOTHER DAY . . .
AND AS OF NOW, I'M TAKING OVER FROM ANDREI CHALAKOV! SO HOW ABOUT GIVING THESE TROOPS A BIT OF AIR-SUPPORT?
TAKE YOUR PICK, MY FRIEND. THERE ARE PLENTY OF TARGETS . . !

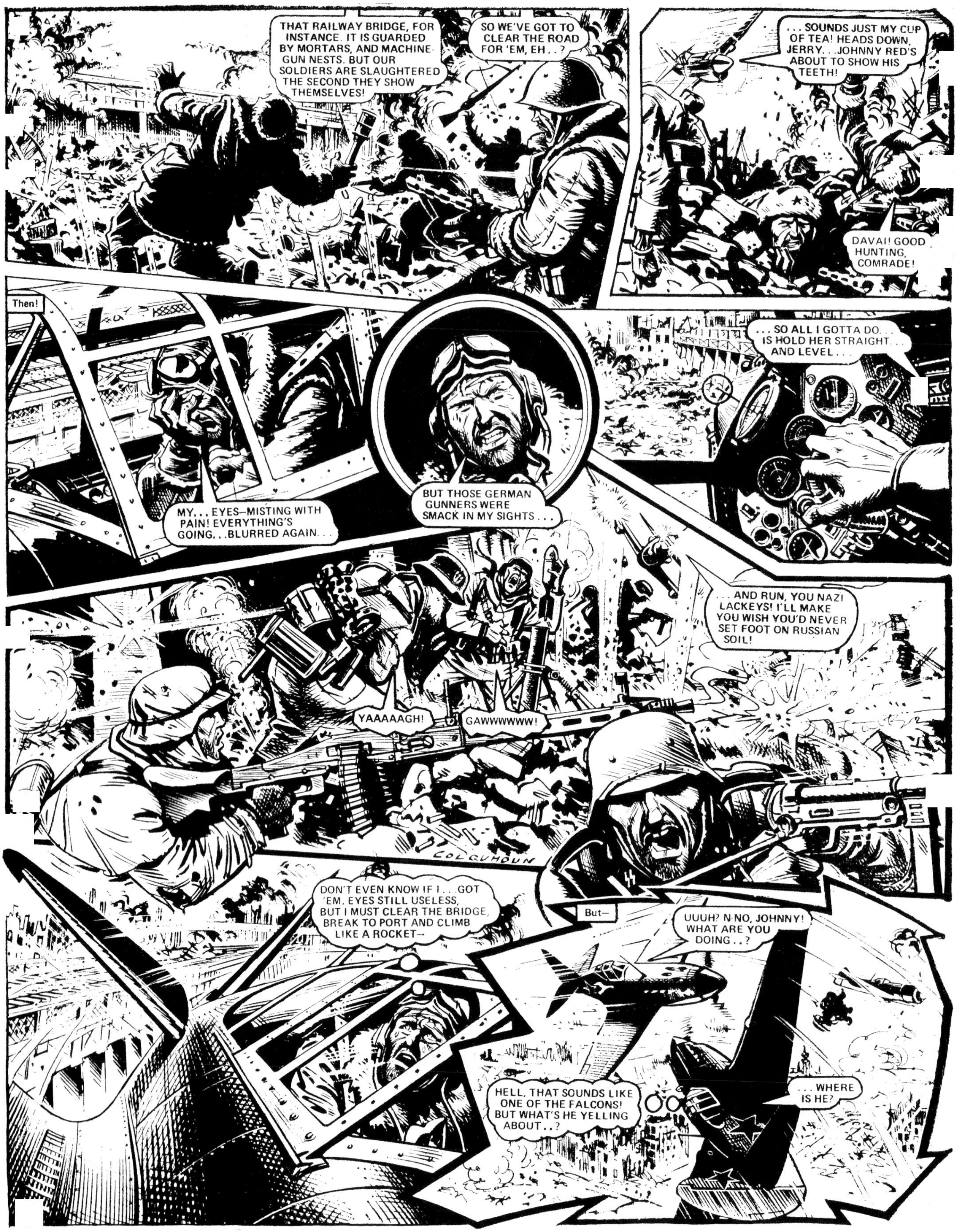

THAT RAILWAY BRIDGE, FOR INSTANCE. IT IS GUARDED BY MORTARS, AND MACHINE-GUN NESTS. BUT OUR SOLDIERS ARE SLAUGHTERED THE SECOND THEY SHOW THEMSELVES!
SO WE'VE GOT TO CLEAR THE ROAD FOR 'EM, EH..?
. . . SOUNDS JUST MY CUP OF TEA! HEADS DOWN, JERRY. . . JOHNNY RED'S ABOUT TO SHOW HIS TEETH!
DAVAI! GOOD HUNTING, COMRADE!
Then!
MY. . . EYES–MISTING WITH PAIN! EVERYTHING'S GOING. . . BLURRED AGAIN. . .
BUT THOSE GERMAN GUNNERS WERE SMACK IN MY SIGHTS . . .
. . . SO ALL I GOTTA DO. . . IS HOLD HER STRAIGHT. . . AND LEVEL . . .
. . . AND RUN, YOU NAZI LACKEYS! I'LL MAKE YOU WISH YOU'D NEVER SET FOOT ON RUSSIAN SOIL!
YAAAAAGH!
GAWWWWWW!
COLQUHOUN
DON'T EVEN KNOW IF I . . . GOT 'EM. EYES STILL USELESS, BUT I MUST CLEAR THE BRIDGE, BREAK TO PORT AND CLIMB LIKE A ROCKET–
But–
UUUH? N-NO, JOHNNY! WHAT ARE YOU DOING . . ?
HELL, THAT SOUNDS LIKE ONE OF THE FALCONS! BUT WHAT'S HE YELLING ABOUT . . ?
. . . WHERE IS HE?

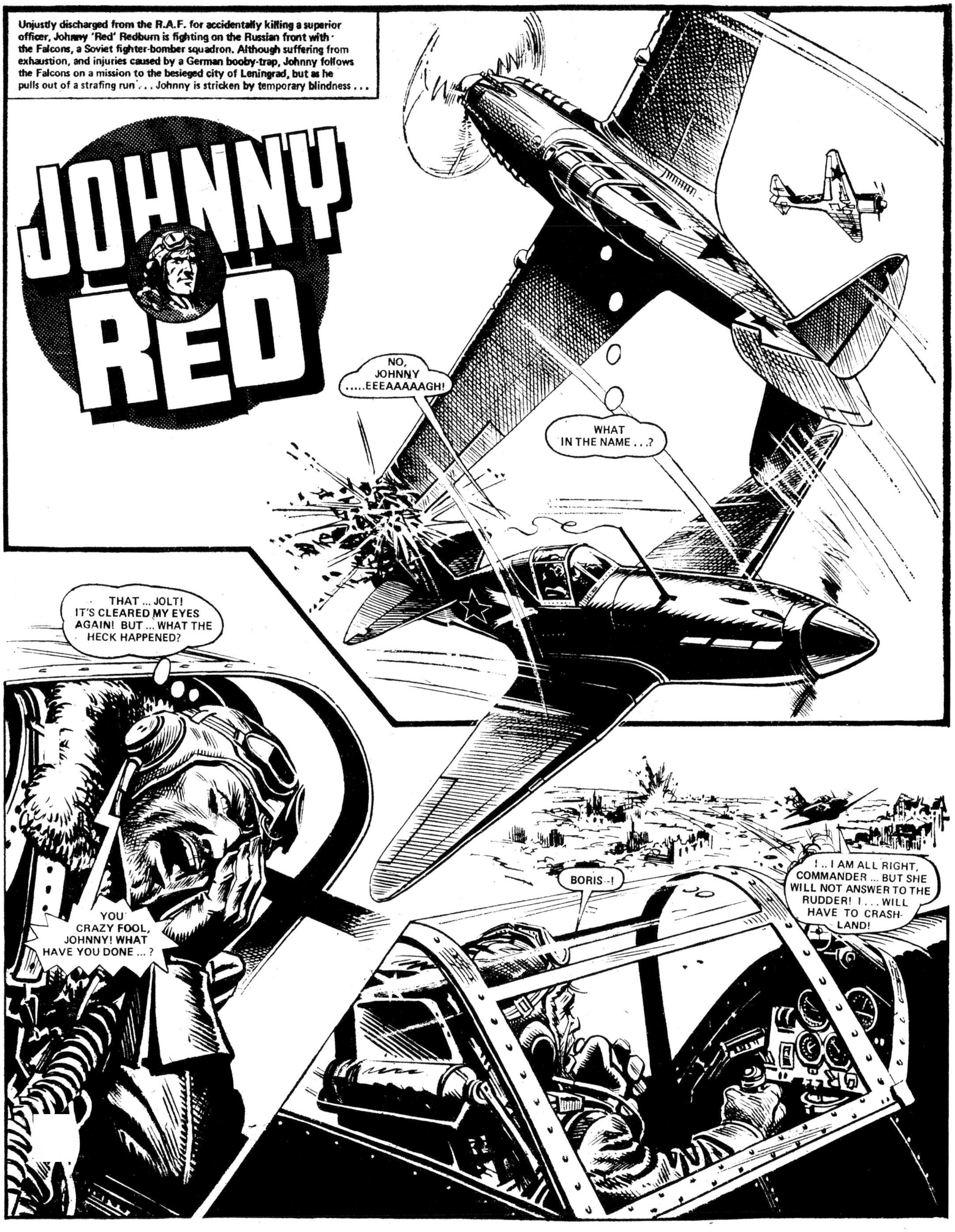

Unjustly discharged from the R.A.F. for accidentally killing a superior officer, Johnny 'Red' Redburn is fighting on the Russian front with the Falcons, a Soviet fighter-bomber squadron. Although suffering from exhaustion, and injuries caused by a German booby-trap, Johnny follows the Falcons on a mission to the besieged city of Leningrad, but as he pulls out of a strafing run . . . Johnny is stricken by temporary blindness . . .
JOHNNY RED
NO, JOHNNY .....EEEAAAAAAGH!
WHAT IN THE NAME . . .?
THAT ... JOLT! IT'S CLEARED MY EYES AGAIN! BUT ... WHAT THE HECK HAPPENED?
YOU CRAZY FOOL, JOHNNY! WHAT HAVE YOU DONE ... ?
BORIS--!
I .. I AM ALL RIGHT, COMMANDER ... BUT SHE WILL NOT ANSWER TO THE RUDDER! I . . . WILL HAVE TO CRASH-LAND!

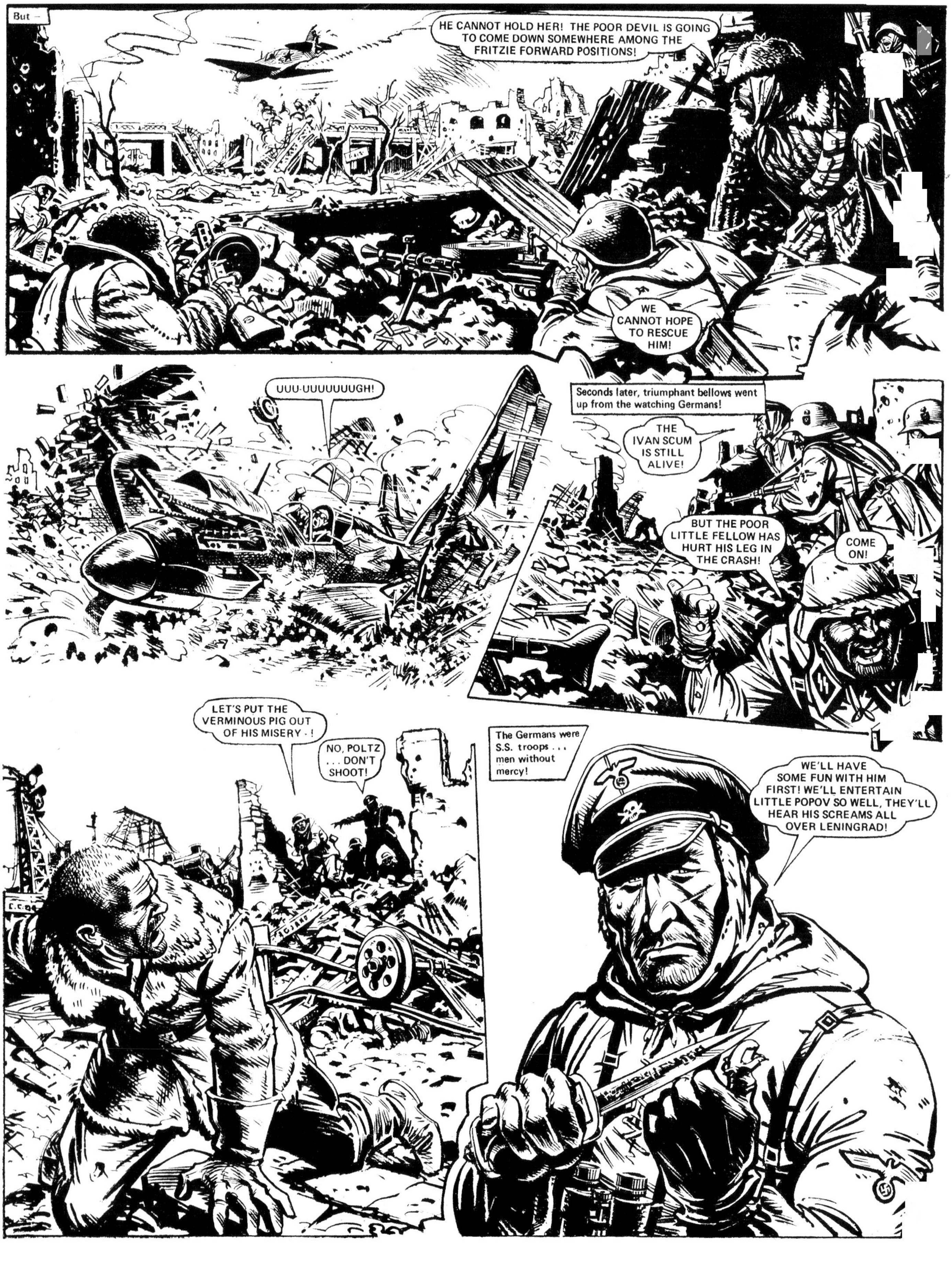

But —
HE CANNOT HOLD HER! THE POOR DEVIL IS GOING TO COME DOWN SOMEWHERE AMONG THE FRITZIE FORWARD POSITIONS!
WE CANNOT HOPE TO RESCUE HIM!
UUU-UUUUUUUGH!
Seconds later, triumphant bellows went up from the watching Germans!
THE IVAN SCUM IS STILL ALIVE!
BUT THE POOR LITTLE FELLOW HAS HURT HIS LEG IN THE CRASH!
COME ON!
LET'S PUT THE VERMINOUS PIG OUT OF HIS MISERY - !
NO, POLTZ . . . DON'T SHOOT!
The Germans were S.S. troops . . . men without mercy!
WE'LL HAVE SOME FUN WITH HIM FIRST! WE'LL ENTERTAIN LITTLE POPOV SO WELL, THEY'LL HEAR HIS SCREAMS ALL OVER LENINGRAD!

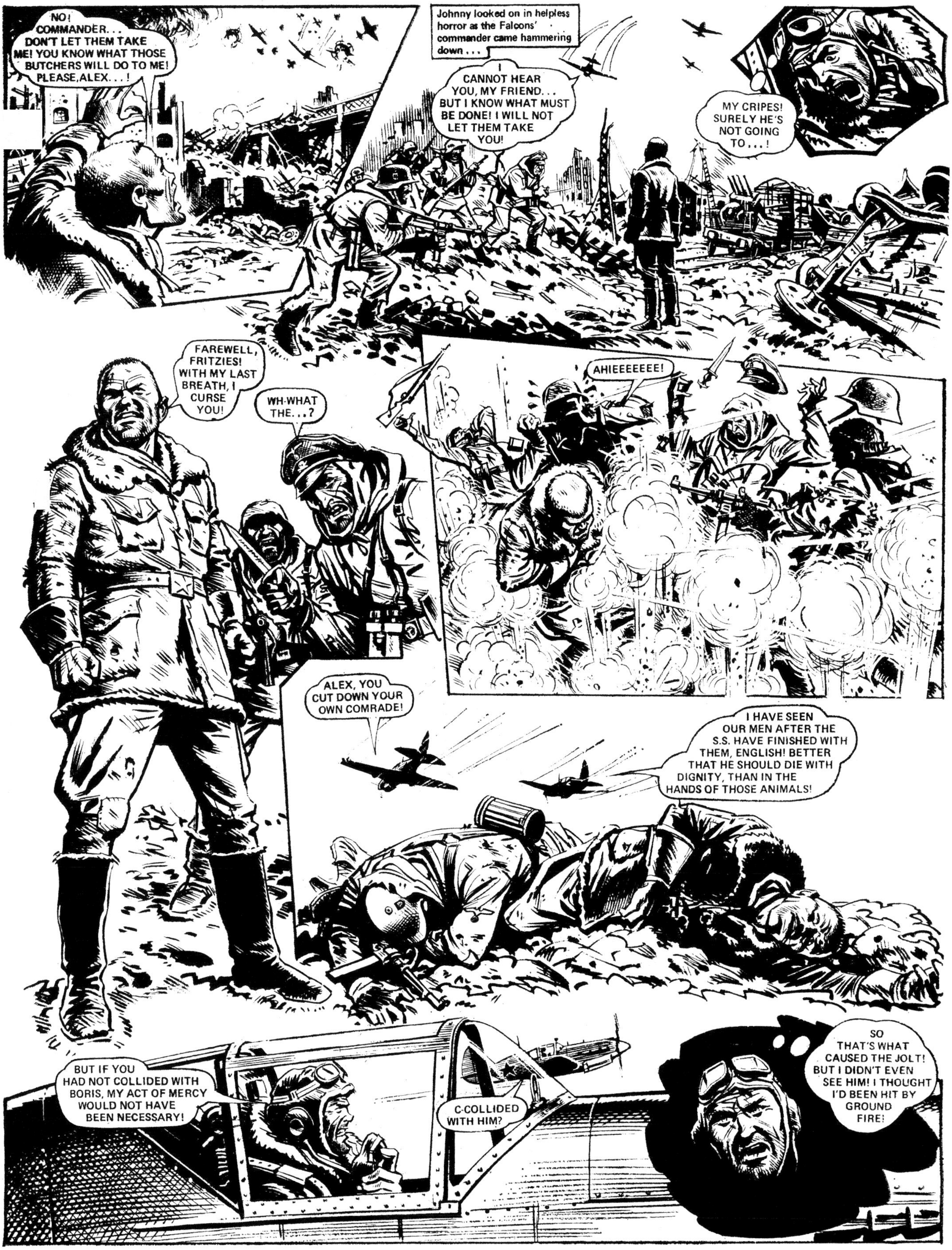
NO! COMMANDER... DON'T LET THEM TAKE ME! YOU KNOW WHAT THOSE BUTCHERS WILL DO TO ME! PLEASE, ALEX...!
Johnny looked on in helpless horror as the Falcons' commander came hammering down...
I CANNOT HEAR YOU, MY FRIEND... BUT I KNOW WHAT MUST BE DONE! I WILL NOT LET THEM TAKE YOU!
MY CRIPES! SURELY HE'S NOT GOING TO...!
FAREWELL, FRITZIES! WITH MY LAST BREATH, I CURSE YOU!
WH-WHAT THE...?
AHIEEEEEEE!
ALEX, YOU CUT DOWN YOUR OWN COMRADE!
I HAVE SEEN OUR MEN AFTER THE S.S. HAVE FINISHED WITH THEM, ENGLISH! BETTER THAT HE SHOULD DIE WITH DIGNITY, THAN IN THE HANDS OF THOSE ANIMALS!
BUT IF YOU HAD NOT COLLIDED WITH BORIS, MY ACT OF MERCY WOULD NOT HAVE BEEN NECESSARY!
C-COLLIDED WITH HIM?
SO THAT'S WHAT CAUSED THE JOLT! BUT I DIDN'T EVEN SEE HIM! I THOUGHT I'D BEEN HIT BY GROUND FIRE!

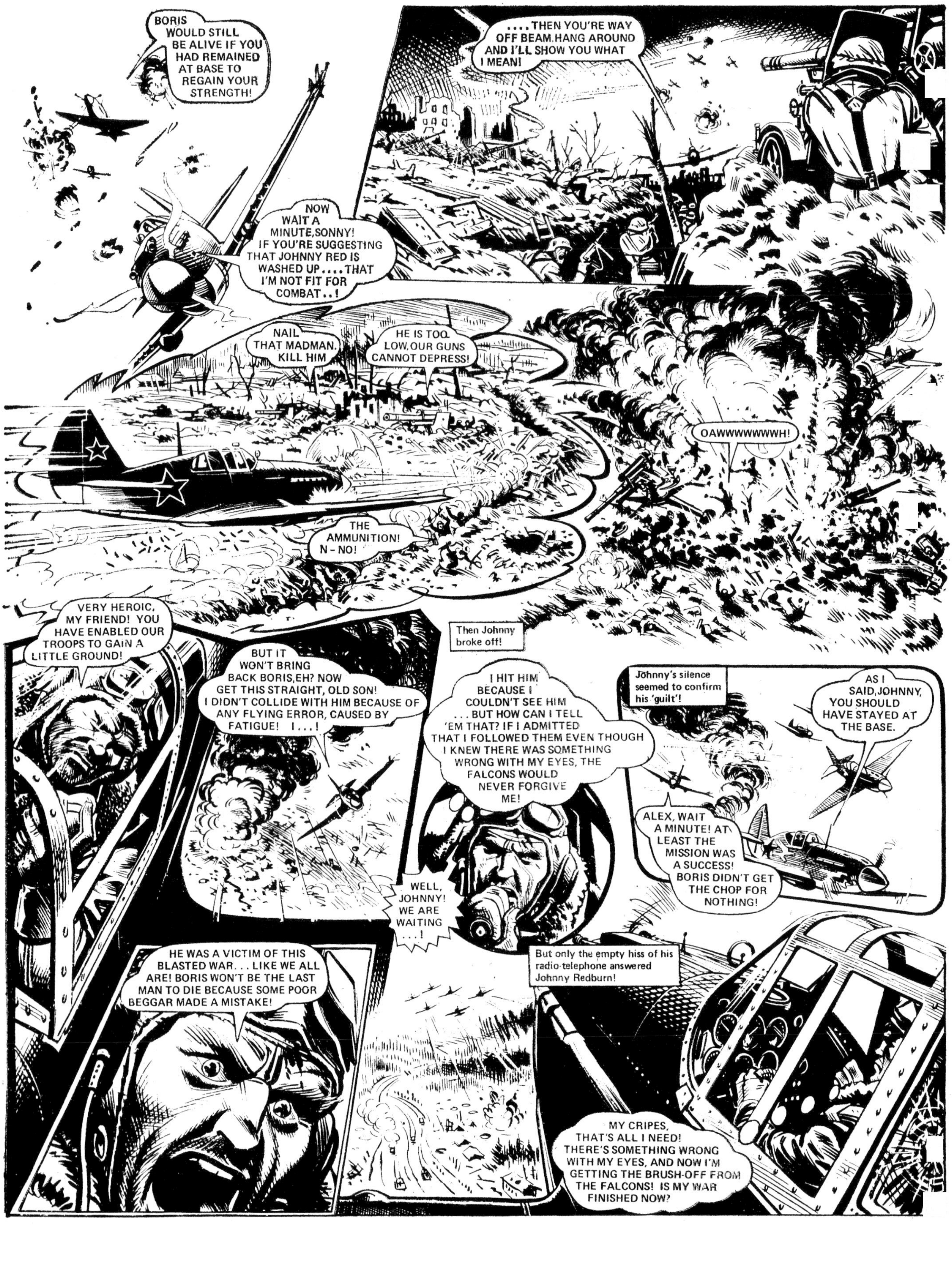

BORIS WOULD STILL BE ALIVE IF YOU HAD REMAINED AT BASE TO REGAIN YOUR STRENGTH!
....THEN YOU'RE WAY OFF BEAM. HANG AROUND AND I'LL SHOW YOU WHAT I MEAN!
NOW WAIT A MINUTE, SONNY! IF YOU'RE SUGGESTING THAT JOHNNY RED IS WASHED UP.... THAT I'M NOT FIT FOR COMBAT..!
NAIL THAT MADMAN. KILL HIM
HE IS TOO LOW, OUR GUNS CANNOT DEPRESS!
OAWWWWWWWH!
THE AMMUNITION! N-NO!
VERY HEROIC, MY FRIEND! YOU HAVE ENABLED OUR TROOPS TO GAIN A LITTLE GROUND!
Then Johnny broke off!
BUT IT WON'T BRING BACK BORIS, EH? NOW GET THIS STRAIGHT, OLD SON! I DIDN'T COLLIDE WITH HIM BECAUSE OF ANY FLYING ERROR, CAUSED BY FATIGUE! I...!
I HIT HIM BECAUSE I COULDN'T SEE HIM ... BUT HOW CAN I TELL 'EM THAT? IF I ADMITTED THAT I FOLLOWED THEM EVEN THOUGH I KNEW THERE WAS SOMETHING WRONG WITH MY EYES, THE FALCONS WOULD NEVER FORGIVE ME!
WELL, JOHNNY! WE ARE WAITING ...!
Johnny's silence seemed to confirm his 'guilt'!
AS I SAID, JOHNNY, YOU SHOULD HAVE STAYED AT THE BASE.
ALEX, WAIT A MINUTE! AT LEAST THE MISSION WAS A SUCCESS! BORIS DIDN'T GET THE CHOP FOR NOTHING!
HE WAS A VICTIM OF THIS BLASTED WAR... LIKE WE ALL ARE! BORIS WON'T BE THE LAST MAN TO DIE BECAUSE SOME POOR BEGGAR MADE A MISTAKE!
But only the empty hiss of his radio-telephone answered Johnny Redburn!
MY CRIPES, THAT'S ALL I NEED! THERE'S SOMETHING WRONG WITH MY EYES, AND NOW I'M GETTING THE BRUSH-OFF FROM THE FALCONS! IS MY WAR FINISHED NOW?

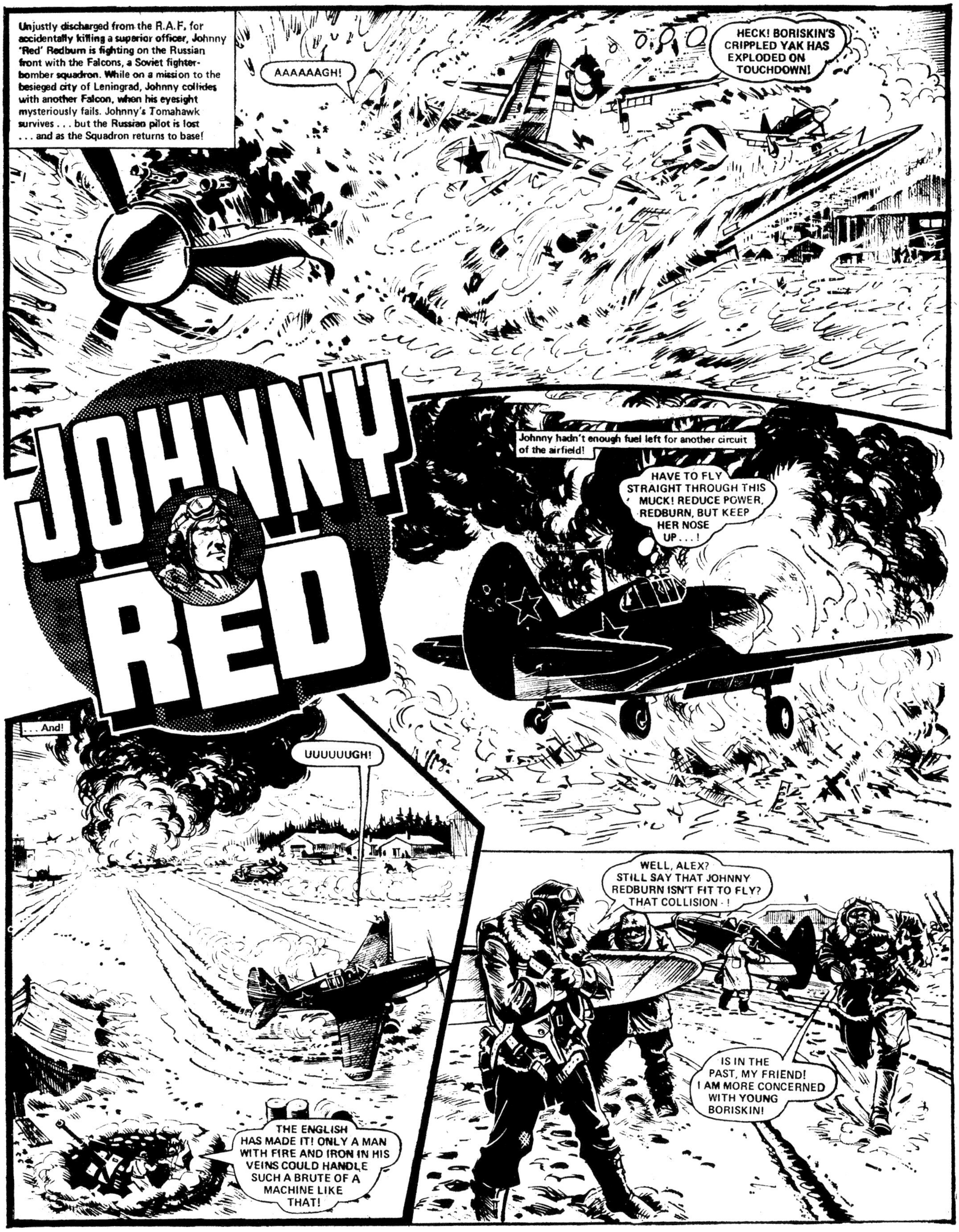
Unjustly discharged from the R.A.F. for accidentally killing a superior officer, Johnny 'Red' Redburn is fighting on the Russian front with the Falcons, a Soviet fighter-bomber squadron. While on a mission to the besieged city of Leningrad, Johnny collides with another Falcon, when his eyesight mysteriously fails. Johnny's Tomahawk survives . . . but the Russian pilot is lost . . . and as the Squadron returns to base!
AAAAAAGH!
HECK! BORISKIN'S CRIPPLED YAK HAS EXPLODED ON TOUCHDOWN!
JOHNNY RED
Johnny hadn't enough fuel left for another circuit of the airfield!
HAVE TO FLY STRAIGHT THROUGH THIS MUCK! REDUCE POWER, REDBURN, BUT KEEP HER NOSE UP . . . !
. . . And!
UUUUUUGH!
THE ENGLISH HAS MADE IT! ONLY A MAN WITH FIRE AND IRON IN HIS VEINS COULD HANDLE SUCH A BRUTE OF A MACHINE LIKE THAT!
WELL, ALEX? STILL SAY THAT JOHNNY REDBURN ISN'T FIT TO FLY? THAT COLLISION - !
IS IN THE PAST, MY FRIEND! I AM MORE CONCERNED WITH YOUNG BORISKIN!

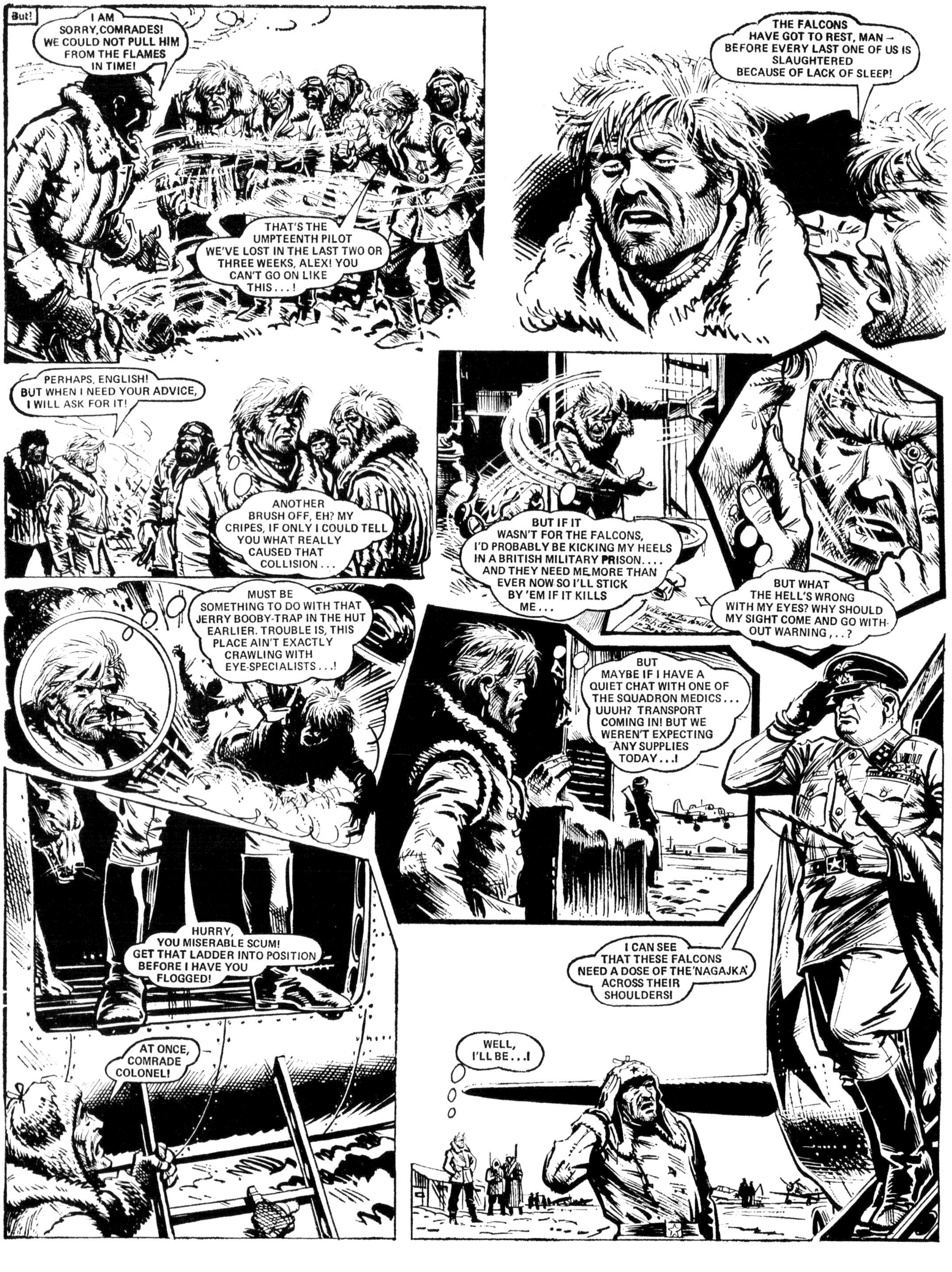
But!
I AM SORRY, COMRADES! WE COULD NOT PULL HIM FROM THE FLAMES IN TIME!
THAT'S THE UMPTEENTH PILOT WE'VE LOST IN THE LAST TWO OR THREE WEEKS, ALEX! YOU CAN'T GO ON LIKE THIS...!
THE FALCONS HAVE GOT TO REST, MAN – BEFORE EVERY LAST ONE OF US IS SLAUGHTERED BECAUSE OF LACK OF SLEEP!
PERHAPS, ENGLISH! BUT WHEN I NEED YOUR ADVICE, I WILL ASK FOR IT!
ANOTHER BRUSH OFF, EH? MY CRIPES, IF ONLY I COULD TELL YOU WHAT REALLY CAUSED THAT COLLISION...
BUT IF IT WASN'T FOR THE FALCONS, I'D PROBABLY BE KICKING MY HEELS IN A BRITISH MILITARY PRISON.... AND THEY NEED ME MORE THAN EVER NOW SO I'LL STICK BY 'EM IF IT KILLS ME...
BUT WHAT THE HELL'S WRONG WITH MY EYES? WHY SHOULD MY SIGHT COME AND GO WITHOUT WARNING,..?
MUST BE SOMETHING TO DO WITH THAT JERRY BOOBY-TRAP IN THE HUT EARLIER. TROUBLE IS, THIS PLACE AIN'T EXACTLY CRAWLING WITH EYE-SPECIALISTS...!
BUT MAYBE IF I HAVE A QUIET CHAT WITH ONE OF THE SQUADRON MEDICS... UUUH? TRANSPORT COMING IN! BUT WE WEREN'T EXPECTING ANY SUPPLIES TODAY...!
HURRY, YOU MISERABLE SCUM! GET THAT LADDER INTO POSITION BEFORE I HAVE YOU FLOGGED!
AT ONCE, COMRADE COLONEL!
I CAN SEE THAT THESE FALCONS NEED A DOSE OF THE 'NAGAJKA' ACROSS THEIR SHOULDERS!
WELL, I'LL BE...!

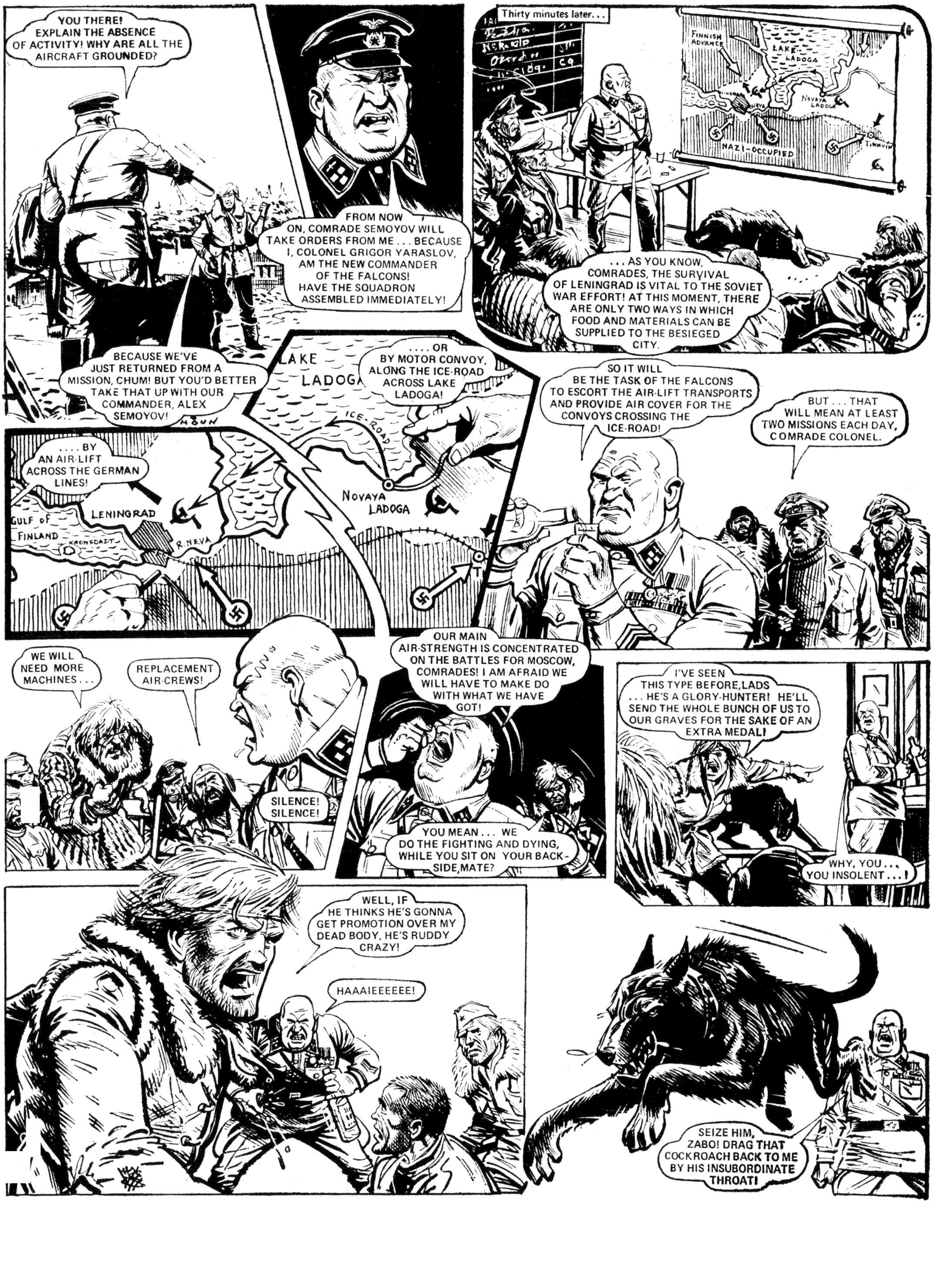
YOU THERE! EXPLAIN THE ABSENCE OF ACTIVITY! WHY ARE ALL THE AIRCRAFT GROUNDED?
BECAUSE WE'VE JUST RETURNED FROM A MISSION, CHUM! BUT YOU'D BETTER TAKE THAT UP WITH OUR COMMANDER, ALEX SEMOYOV!
FROM NOW ON, COMRADE SEMOYOV WILL TAKE ORDERS FROM ME . . . BECAUSE I, COLONEL GRIGOR YARASLOV, AM THE NEW COMMANDER OF THE FALCONS! HAVE THE SQUADRON ASSEMBLED IMMEDIATELY!
Thirty minutes later. . .
FINNISH ADVANCE
LAKE LADOGA
NEVA
NOVAYA LADOGA
NAZI-OCCUPIED
TIKHVIN
. . . AS YOU KNOW, COMRADES, THE SURVIVAL OF LENINGRAD IS VITAL TO THE SOVIET WAR EFFORT! AT THIS MOMENT, THERE ARE ONLY TWO WAYS IN WHICH FOOD AND MATERIALS CAN BE SUPPLIED TO THE BESIEGED CITY.
. . . . BY AN AIR-LIFT ACROSS THE GERMAN LINES!
GULF OF FINLAND
KRONSDADT
LENINGRAD
R. NEVA
LAKE LADOGA
ICE-ROAD
NOVAYA LADOGA
. . . . OR BY MOTOR CONVOY, ALONG THE ICE-ROAD ACROSS LAKE LADOGA!
SO IT WILL BE THE TASK OF THE FALCONS TO ESCORT THE AIR-LIFT TRANSPORTS AND PROVIDE AIR COVER FOR THE CONVOYS CROSSING THE ICE-ROAD!
BUT . . . THAT WILL MEAN AT LEAST TWO MISSIONS EACH DAY, COMRADE COLONEL.
WE WILL NEED MORE MACHINES . . .
REPLACEMENT AIR-CREWS!
SILENCE! SILENCE!
OUR MAIN AIR-STRENGTH IS CONCENTRATED ON THE BATTLES FOR MOSCOW, COMRADES! I AM AFRAID WE WILL HAVE TO MAKE DO WITH WHAT WE HAVE GOT!
YOU MEAN . . . WE DO THE FIGHTING AND DYING, WHILE YOU SIT ON YOUR BACK-SIDE, MATE?
I'VE SEEN THIS TYPE BEFORE, LADS . . . HE'S A GLORY-HUNTER! HE'LL SEND THE WHOLE BUNCH OF US TO OUR GRAVES FOR THE SAKE OF AN EXTRA MEDAL!
WHY, YOU . . . YOU INSOLENT . . . !
WELL, IF HE THINKS HE'S GONNA GET PROMOTION OVER MY DEAD BODY, HE'S RUDDY CRAZY!
HAAAIEEEEEE!
SEIZE HIM, ZABO! DRAG THAT COCKROACH BACK TO ME BY HIS INSUBORDINATE THROAT!

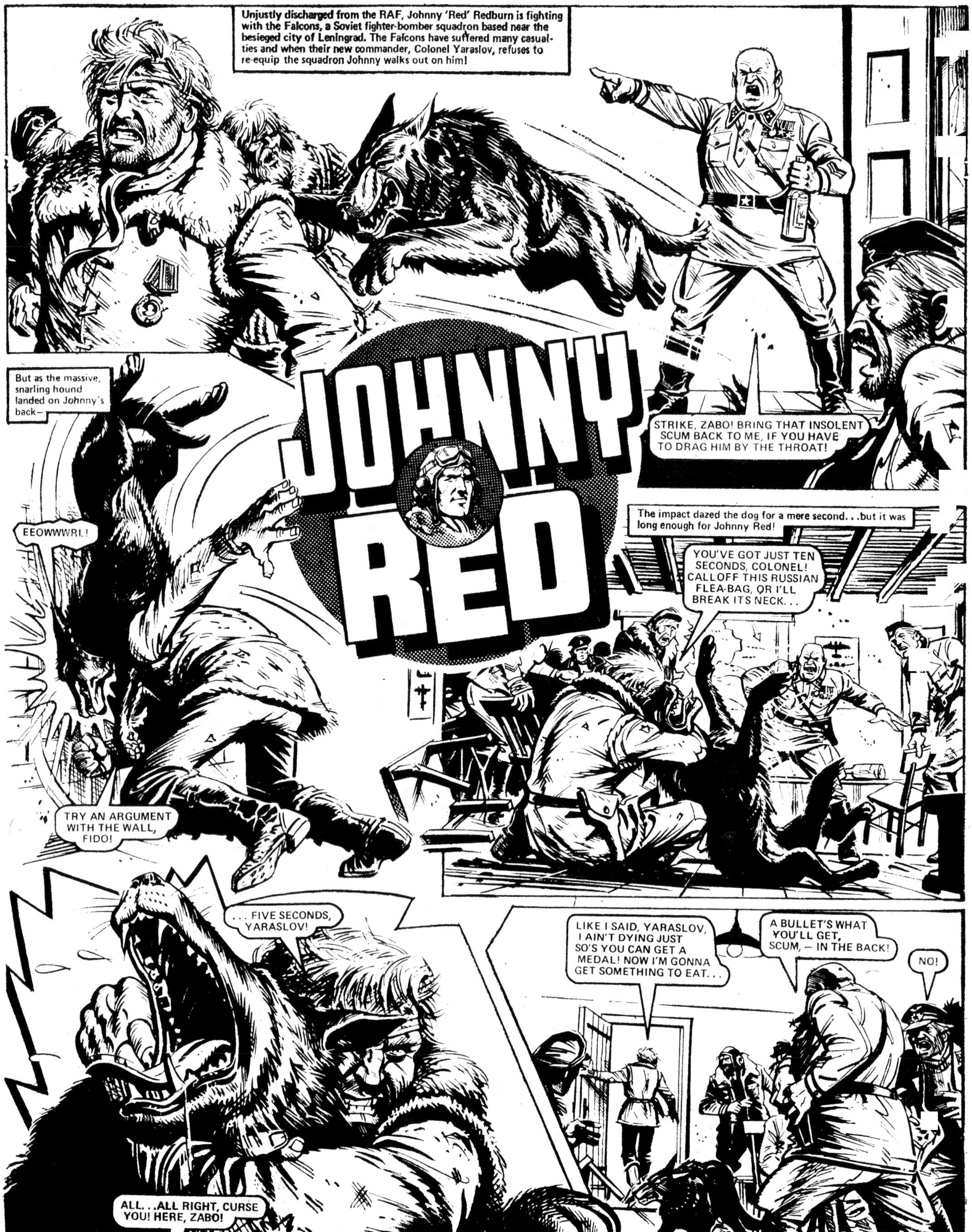
Unjustly discharged from the RAF, Johnny 'Red' Redburn is fighting with the Falcons, a Soviet fighter-bomber squadron based near the besieged city of Leningrad. The Falcons have suffered many casualties and when their new commander, Colonel Yaraslov, refuses to re-equip the squadron Johnny walks out on him!
JOHNNY RED
STRIKE, ZABO! BRING THAT INSOLENT SCUM BACK TO ME, IF YOU HAVE TO DRAG HIM BY THE THROAT!
But as the massive, snarling hound landed on Johnny's back–
EEOWWWRL!
TRY AN ARGUMENT WITH THE WALL, FIDO!
The impact dazed the dog for a mere second. . .but it was long enough for Johnny Red!
YOU'VE GOT JUST TEN SECONDS, COLONEL! CALL OFF THIS RUSSIAN FLEA-BAG, OR I'LL BREAK ITS NECK. . .
. . . FIVE SECONDS, YARASLOV!
ALL. . .ALL RIGHT, CURSE YOU! HERE, ZABO!
LIKE I SAID, YARASLOV, I AIN'T DYING JUST SO'S YOU CAN GET A MEDAL! NOW I'M GONNA GET SOMETHING TO EAT. . .
A BULLET'S WHAT YOU'LL GET, SCUM, – IN THE BACK!
NO!

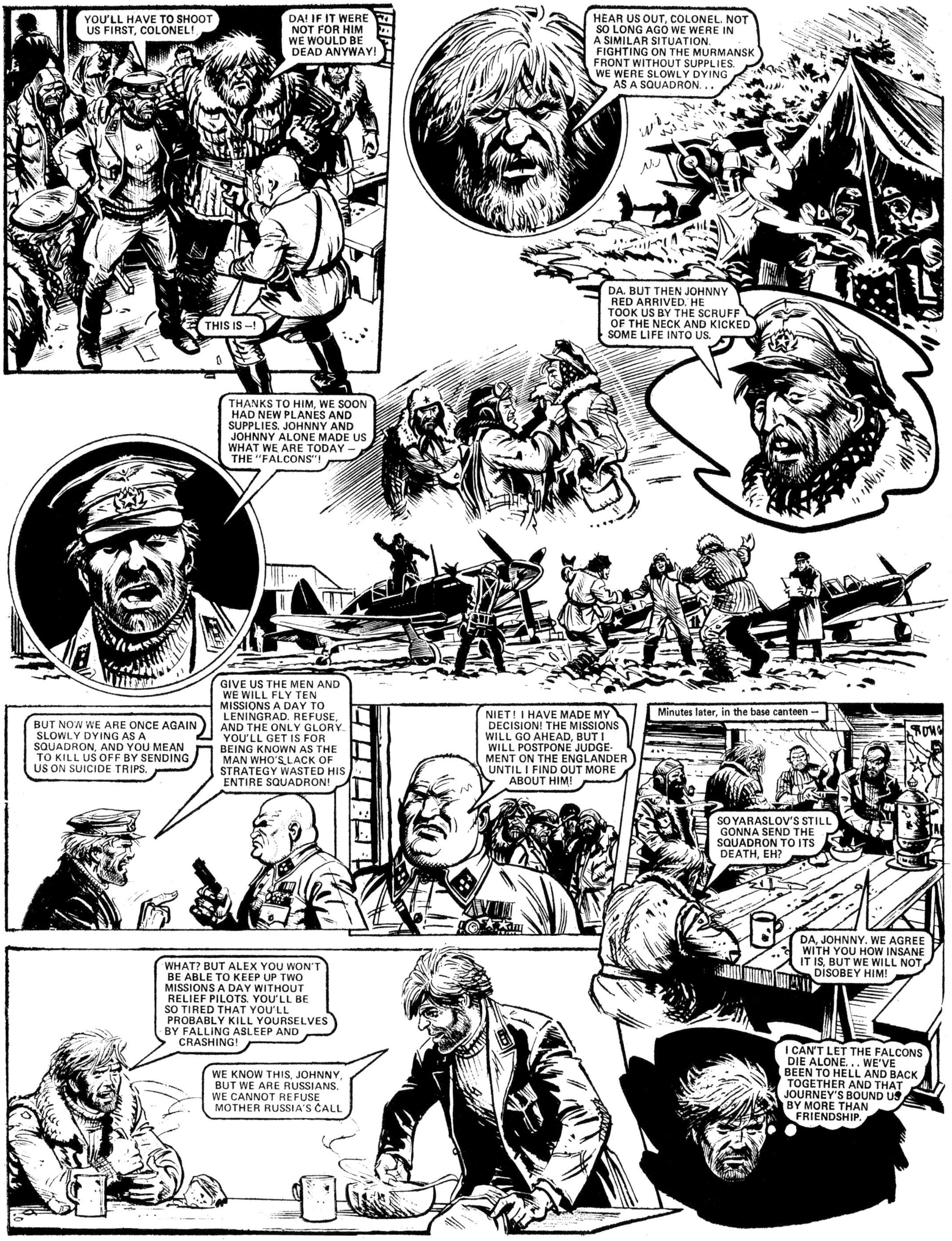
YOU'LL HAVE TO SHOOT US FIRST, COLONEL!
DA! IF IT WERE NOT FOR HIM WE WOULD BE DEAD ANYWAY!
THIS IS —!
HEAR US OUT, COLONEL. NOT SO LONG AGO WE WERE IN A SIMILAR SITUATION. FIGHTING ON THE MURMANSK FRONT WITHOUT SUPPLIES. WE WERE SLOWLY DYING AS A SQUADRON. . .
DA. BUT THEN JOHNNY RED ARRIVED. HE TOOK US BY THE SCRUFF OF THE NECK AND KICKED SOME LIFE INTO US.
THANKS TO HIM, WE SOON HAD NEW PLANES AND SUPPLIES. JOHNNY AND JOHNNY ALONE MADE US WHAT WE ARE TODAY — THE "FALCONS"!
BUT NOW WE ARE ONCE AGAIN SLOWLY DYING AS A SQUADRON, AND YOU MEAN TO KILL US OFF BY SENDING US ON SUICIDE TRIPS.
GIVE US THE MEN AND WE WILL FLY TEN MISSIONS A DAY TO LENINGRAD. REFUSE, AND THE ONLY GLORY YOU'LL GET IS FOR BEING KNOWN AS THE MAN WHO'S LACK OF STRATEGY WASTED HIS ENTIRE SQUADRON!
NIET! I HAVE MADE MY DECISION! THE MISSIONS WILL GO AHEAD, BUT I WILL POSTPONE JUDGEMENT ON THE ENGLANDER UNTIL I FIND OUT MORE ABOUT HIM!
Minutes later, in the base canteen —
SO YARASLOV'S STILL GONNA SEND THE SQUADRON TO ITS DEATH, EH?
DA, JOHNNY. WE AGREE WITH YOU HOW INSANE IT IS, BUT WE WILL NOT DISOBEY HIM!
WHAT? BUT ALEX YOU WON'T BE ABLE TO KEEP UP TWO MISSIONS A DAY WITHOUT RELIEF PILOTS. YOU'LL BE SO TIRED THAT YOU'LL PROBABLY KILL YOURSELVES BY FALLING ASLEEP AND CRASHING!
WE KNOW THIS, JOHNNY, BUT WE ARE RUSSIANS. WE CANNOT REFUSE MOTHER RUSSIA'S CALL
I CAN'T LET THE FALCONS DIE ALONE. . . WE'VE BEEN TO HELL AND BACK TOGETHER AND THAT JOURNEY'S BOUND US BY MORE THAN FRIENDSHIP.

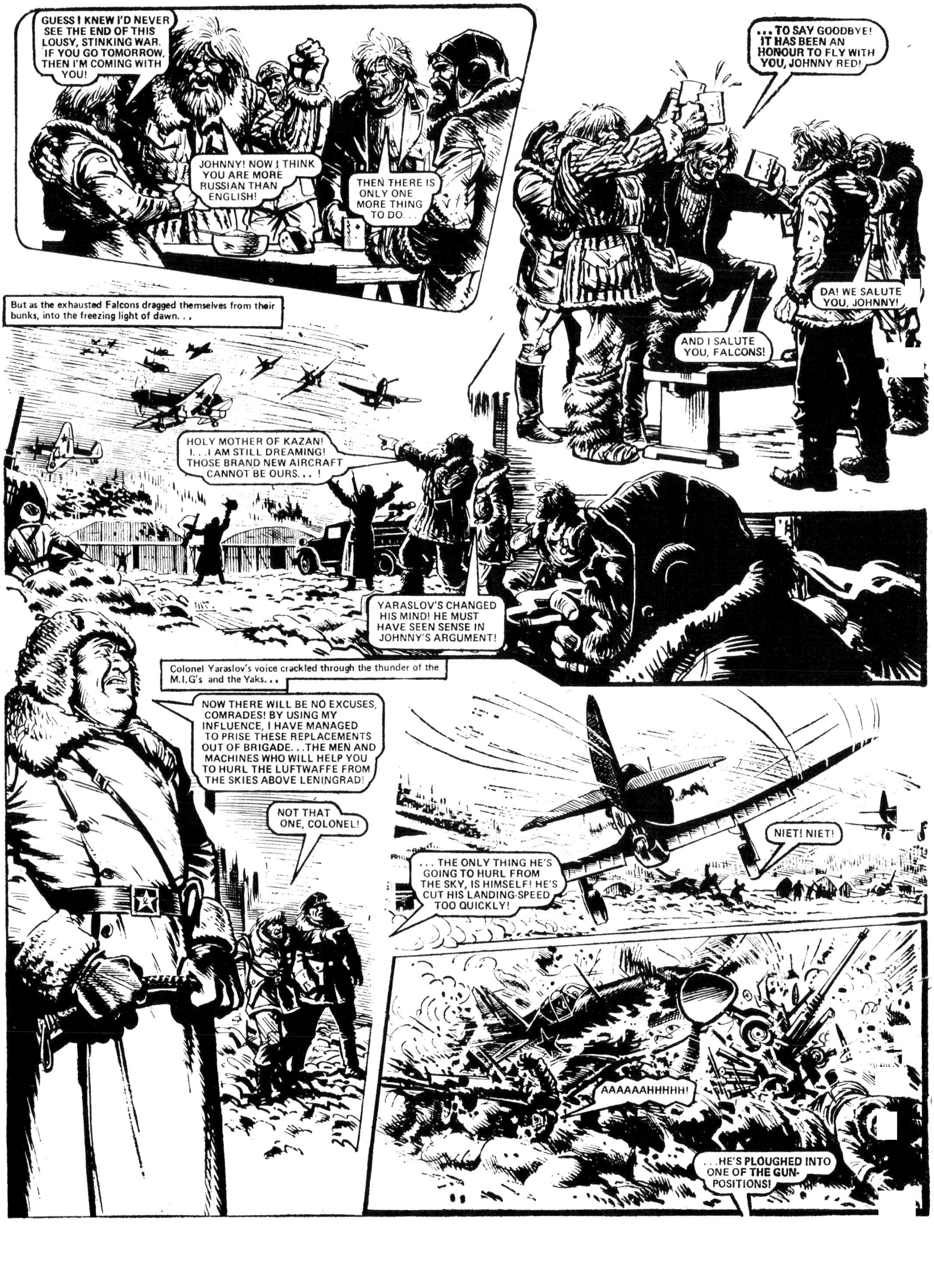

GUESS I KNEW I'D NEVER SEE THE END OF THIS LOUSY, STINKING WAR. IF YOU GO TOMORROW, THEN I'M COMING WITH YOU!
JOHNNY! NOW I THINK YOU ARE MORE RUSSIAN THAN ENGLISH!
THEN THERE IS ONLY ONE MORE THING TO DO. . .
. . . TO SAY GOODBYE! IT HAS BEEN AN HONOUR TO FLY WITH YOU, JOHNNY RED!
DA! WE SALUTE YOU, JOHNNY!
AND I SALUTE YOU, FALCONS!
But as the exhausted Falcons dragged themselves from their bunks, into the freezing light of dawn. . .
HOLY MOTHER OF KAZAN! I. . . I AM STILL DREAMING! THOSE BRAND NEW AIRCRAFT CANNOT BE OURS. . . !
YARASLOV'S CHANGED HIS MIND! HE MUST HAVE SEEN SENSE IN JOHNNY'S ARGUMENT!
Colonel Yaraslov's voice crackled through the thunder of the M.I.G's and the Yaks. . .
NOW THERE WILL BE NO EXCUSES, COMRADES! BY USING MY INFLUENCE, I HAVE MANAGED TO PRISE THESE REPLACEMENTS OUT OF BRIGADE. . . THE MEN AND MACHINES WHO WILL HELP YOU TO HURL THE LUFTWAFFE FROM THE SKIES ABOVE LENINGRAD!
NOT THAT ONE, COLONEL!
. . . THE ONLY THING HE'S GOING TO HURL FROM THE SKY, IS HIMSELF! HE'S CUT HIS LANDING-SPEED TOO QUICKLY!
NIET! NIET!
AAAAAAHHHHH!
. . . HE'S PLOUGHED INTO ONE OF THE GUN-POSITIONS!

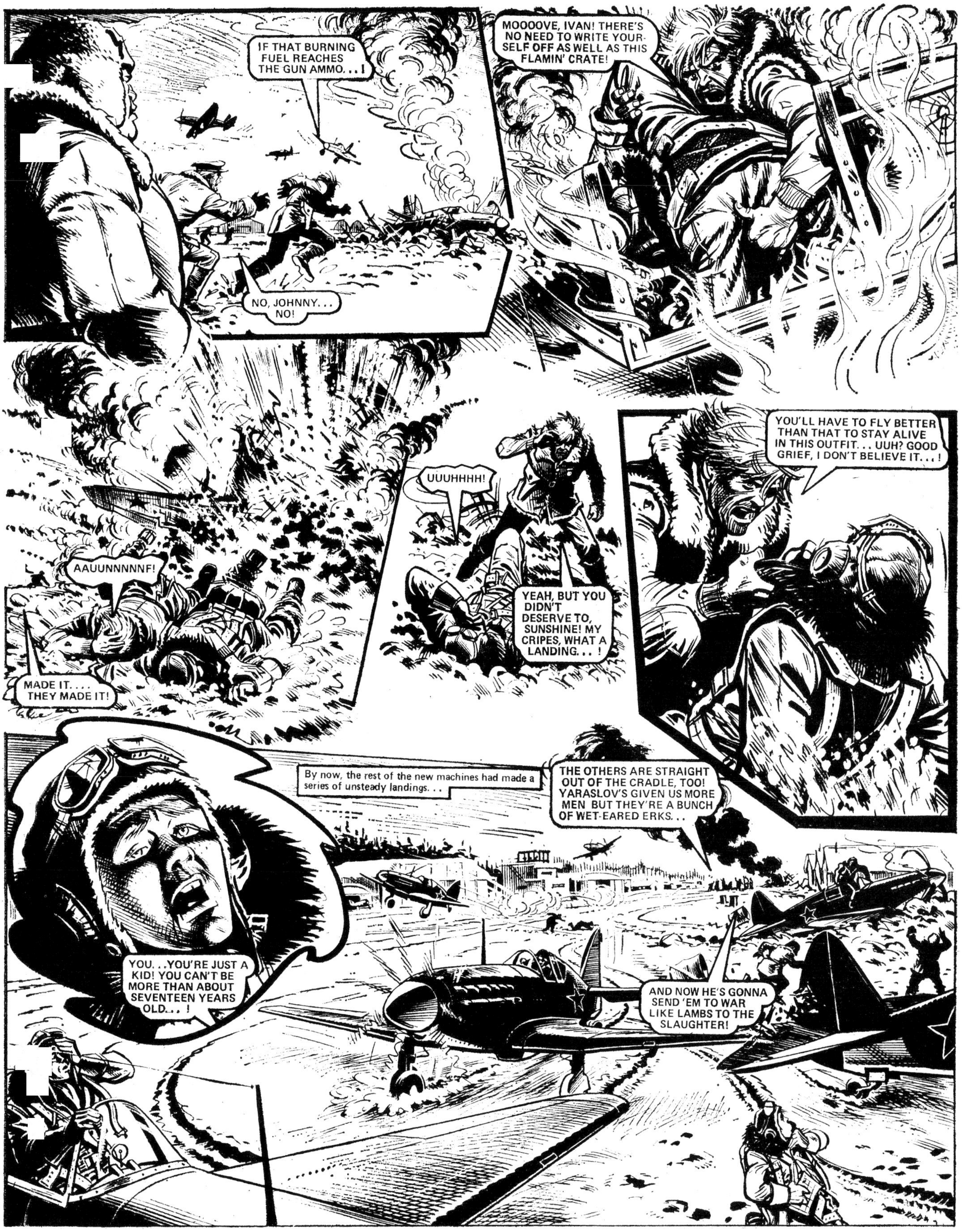

IF THAT BURNING FUEL REACHES THE GUN AMMO. . . !
NO, JOHNNY. . . NO!
MOOOOVE, IVAN! THERE'S NO NEED TO WRITE YOURSELF OFF AS WELL AS THIS FLAMIN' CRATE!
AAUUNNNNNF!
MADE IT. . . . THEY MADE IT!
UUUHHHH!
YEAH, BUT YOU DIDN'T DESERVE TO, SUNSHINE! MY CRIPES, WHAT A LANDING. . . !
YOU'LL HAVE TO FLY BETTER THAN THAT TO STAY ALIVE IN THIS OUTFIT. . . UUH? GOOD GRIEF, I DON'T BELIEVE IT. . . !
By now, the rest of the new machines had made a series of unsteady landings. . .
THE OTHERS ARE STRAIGHT OUT OF THE CRADLE, TOO! YARASLOV'S GIVEN US MORE MEN BUT THEY'RE A BUNCH OF WET-EARED ERKS. . .
YOU. . .YOU'RE JUST A KID! YOU CAN'T BE MORE THAN ABOUT SEVENTEEN YEARS OLD. . . !
AND NOW HE'S GONNA SEND 'EM TO WAR LIKE LAMBS TO THE SLAUGHTER!

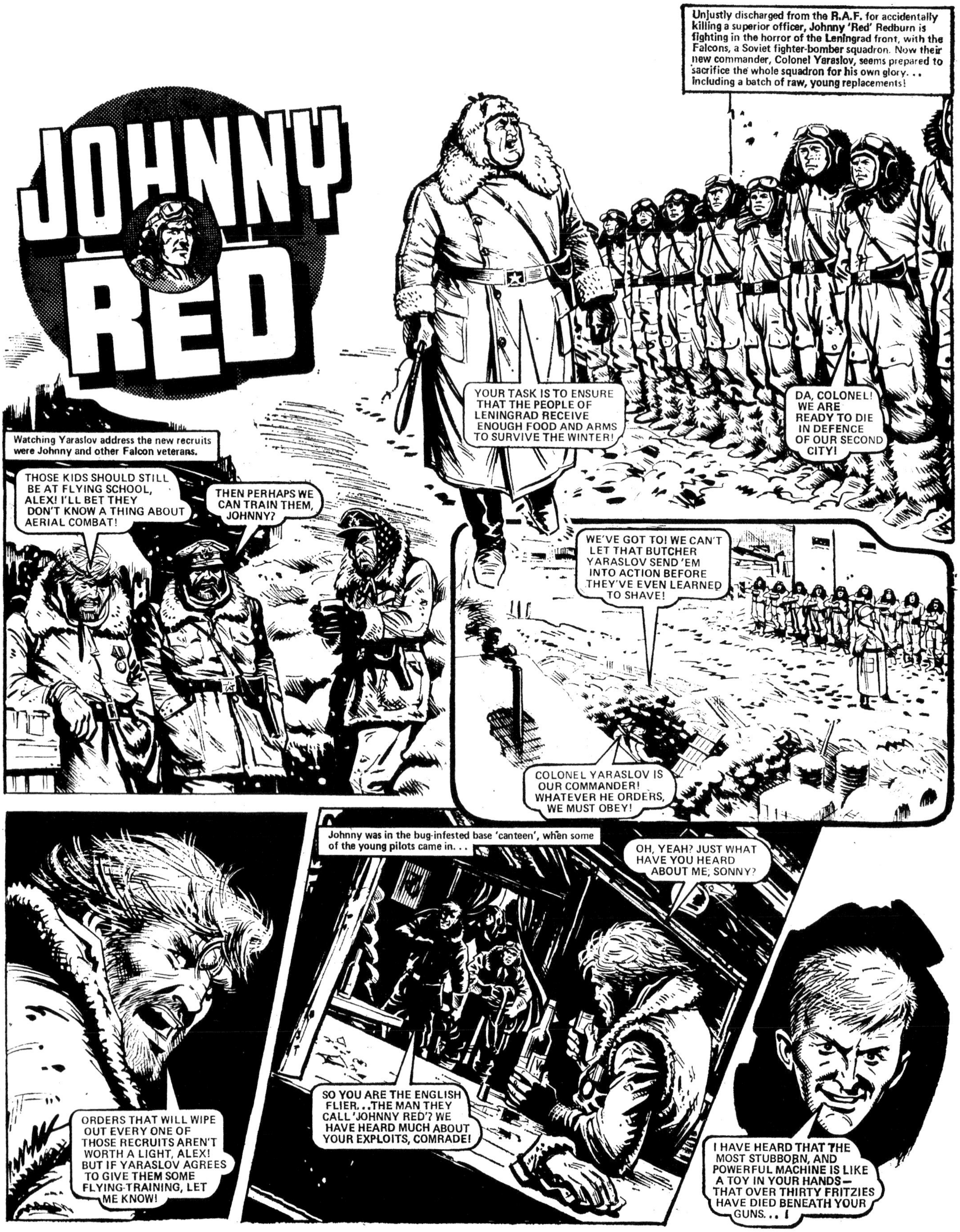
JOHNNY RED
Unjustly discharged from the R.A.F. for accidentally killing a superior officer, Johnny 'Red' Redburn is fighting in the horror of the Leningrad front, with the Falcons, a Soviet fighter-bomber squadron. Now their new commander, Colonel Yaraslov, seems prepared to sacrifice the whole squadron for his own glory. . . Including a batch of raw, young replacements!
YOUR TASK IS TO ENSURE THAT THE PEOPLE OF LENINGRAD RECEIVE ENOUGH FOOD AND ARMS TO SURVIVE THE WINTER!
DA, COLONEL! WE ARE READY TO DIE IN DEFENCE OF OUR SECOND CITY!
Watching Yaraslov address the new recruits were Johnny and other Falcon veterans.
THOSE KIDS SHOULD STILL BE AT FLYING SCHOOL, ALEX! I'LL BET THEY DON'T KNOW A THING ABOUT AERIAL COMBAT!
THEN PERHAPS WE CAN TRAIN THEM, JOHNNY?
WE'VE GOT TO! WE CAN'T LET THAT BUTCHER YARASLOV SEND 'EM INTO ACTION BEFORE THEY'VE EVEN LEARNED TO SHAVE!
COLONEL YARASLOV IS OUR COMMANDER! WHATEVER HE ORDERS, WE MUST OBEY!
ORDERS THAT WILL WIPE OUT EVERY ONE OF THOSE RECRUITS AREN'T WORTH A LIGHT, ALEX! BUT IF YARASLOV AGREES TO GIVE THEM SOME FLYING-TRAINING, LET ME KNOW!
Johnny was in the bug-infested base 'canteen', when some of the young pilots came in. . .
SO YOU ARE THE ENGLISH FLIER. . .THE MAN THEY CALL 'JOHNNY RED'? WE HAVE HEARD MUCH ABOUT YOUR EXPLOITS, COMRADE!
OH, YEAH? JUST WHAT HAVE YOU HEARD ABOUT ME, SONNY?
I HAVE HEARD THAT THE MOST STUBBORN, AND POWERFUL MACHINE IS LIKE A TOY IN YOUR HANDS— THAT OVER THIRTY FRITZIES HAVE DIED BENEATH YOUR GUNS. . . !

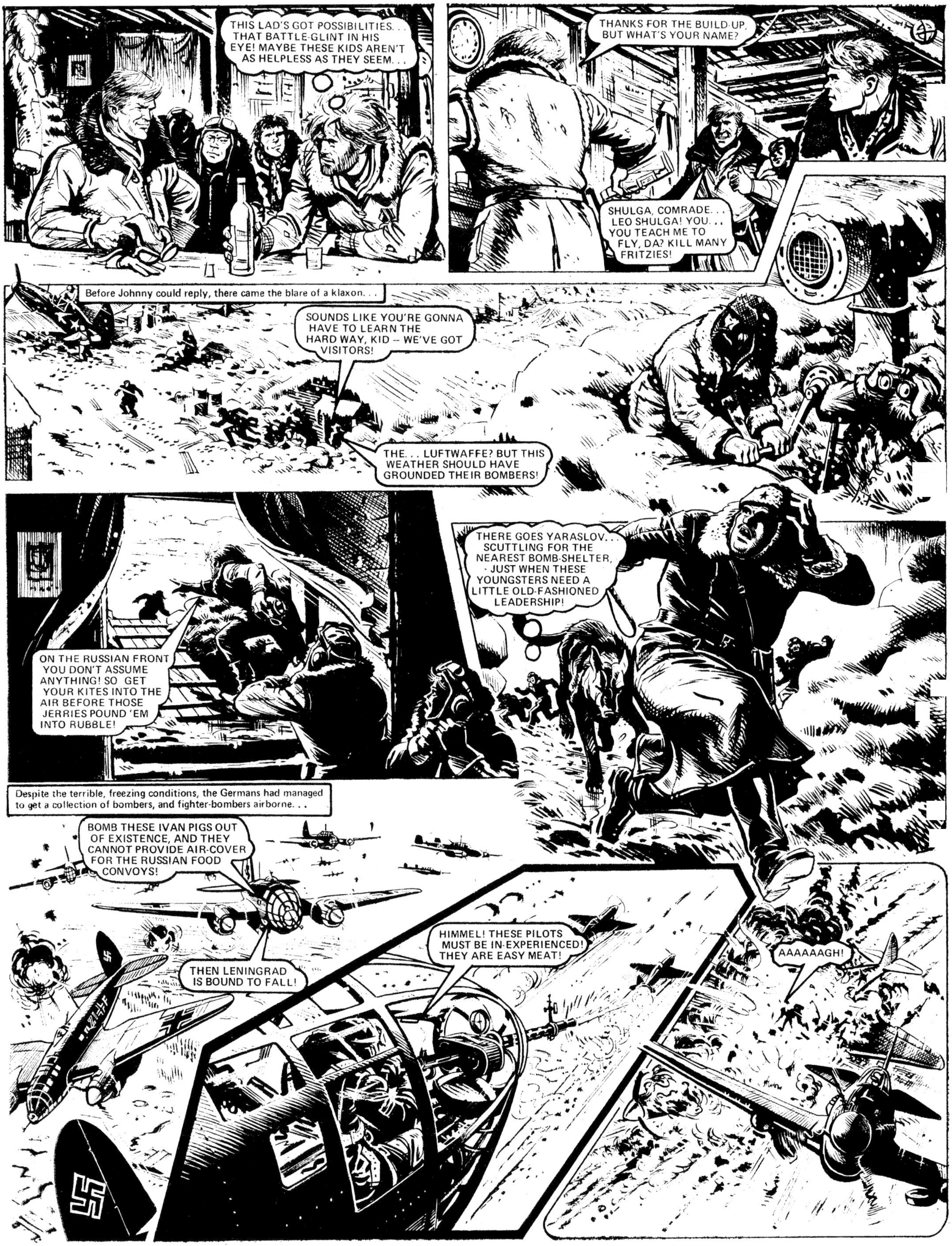
THIS LAD'S GOT POSSIBILITIES. . . THAT BATTLE-GLINT IN HIS EYE! MAYBE THESE KIDS AREN'T AS HELPLESS AS THEY SEEM. . .
THANKS FOR THE BUILD-UP, BUT WHAT'S YOUR NAME?
SHULGA, COMRADE. . . LEO SHULGA! YOU. . . YOU TEACH ME TO FLY, DA? KILL MANY FRITZIES!
Before Johnny could reply, there came the blare of a klaxon. . .
SOUNDS LIKE YOU'RE GONNA HAVE TO LEARN THE HARD WAY, KID -- WE'VE GOT VISITORS!
THE. . . LUFTWAFFE? BUT THIS WEATHER SHOULD HAVE GROUNDED THEIR BOMBERS!
ON THE RUSSIAN FRONT YOU DON'T ASSUME ANYTHING! SO GET YOUR KITES INTO THE AIR BEFORE THOSE JERRIES POUND 'EM INTO RUBBLE!
THERE GOES YARASLOV. . . SCUTTLING FOR THE NEAREST BOMB-SHELTER, · JUST WHEN THESE YOUNGSTERS NEED A LITTLE OLD-FASHIONED LEADERSHIP!
Despite the terrible, freezing conditions, the Germans had managed to get a collection of bombers, and fighter-bombers airborne. . .
BOMB THESE IVAN PIGS OUT OF EXISTENCE, AND THEY CANNOT PROVIDE AIR-COVER FOR THE RUSSIAN FOOD CONVOYS!
THEN LENINGRAD IS BOUND TO FALL!
HIMMEL! THESE PILOTS MUST BE IN-EXPERIENCED! THEY ARE EASY MEAT!
AAAAAAGH!

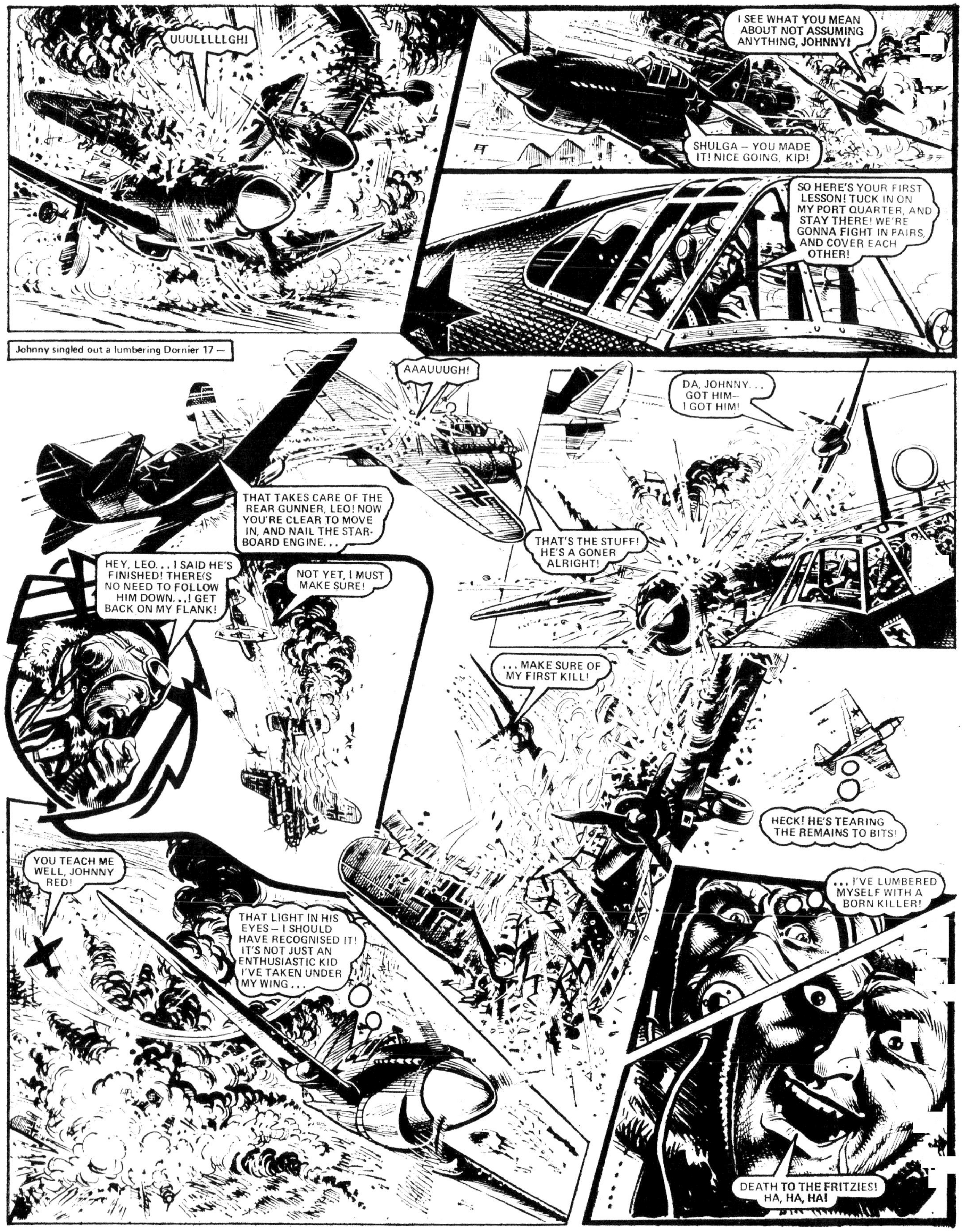
UUULLLLLGH!
I SEE WHAT YOU MEAN ABOUT NOT ASSUMING ANYTHING, JOHNNY!
SHULGA – YOU MADE IT! NICE GOING, KID!
SO HERE'S YOUR FIRST LESSON! TUCK IN ON MY PORT QUARTER, AND STAY THERE! WE'RE GONNA FIGHT IN PAIRS, AND COVER EACH OTHER!
Johnny singled out a lumbering Dornier 17 –
AAAUUUGH!
THAT TAKES CARE OF THE REAR GUNNER, LEO! NOW YOU'RE CLEAR TO MOVE IN, AND NAIL THE STARBOARD ENGINE...
DA, JOHNNY... GOT HIM– I GOT HIM!
THAT'S THE STUFF! HE'S A GONER ALRIGHT!
HEY, LEO... I SAID HE'S FINISHED! THERE'S NO NEED TO FOLLOW HIM DOWN...! GET BACK ON MY FLANK!
NOT YET, I MUST MAKE SURE!
...MAKE SURE OF MY FIRST KILL!
HECK! HE'S TEARING THE REMAINS TO BITS!
YOU TEACH ME WELL, JOHNNY RED!
THAT LIGHT IN HIS EYES – I SHOULD HAVE RECOGNISED IT! IT'S NOT JUST AN ENTHUSIASTIC KID I'VE TAKEN UNDER MY WING...
...I'VE LUMBERED MYSELF WITH A BORN KILLER!
DEATH TO THE FRITZIES! HA, HA, HA!

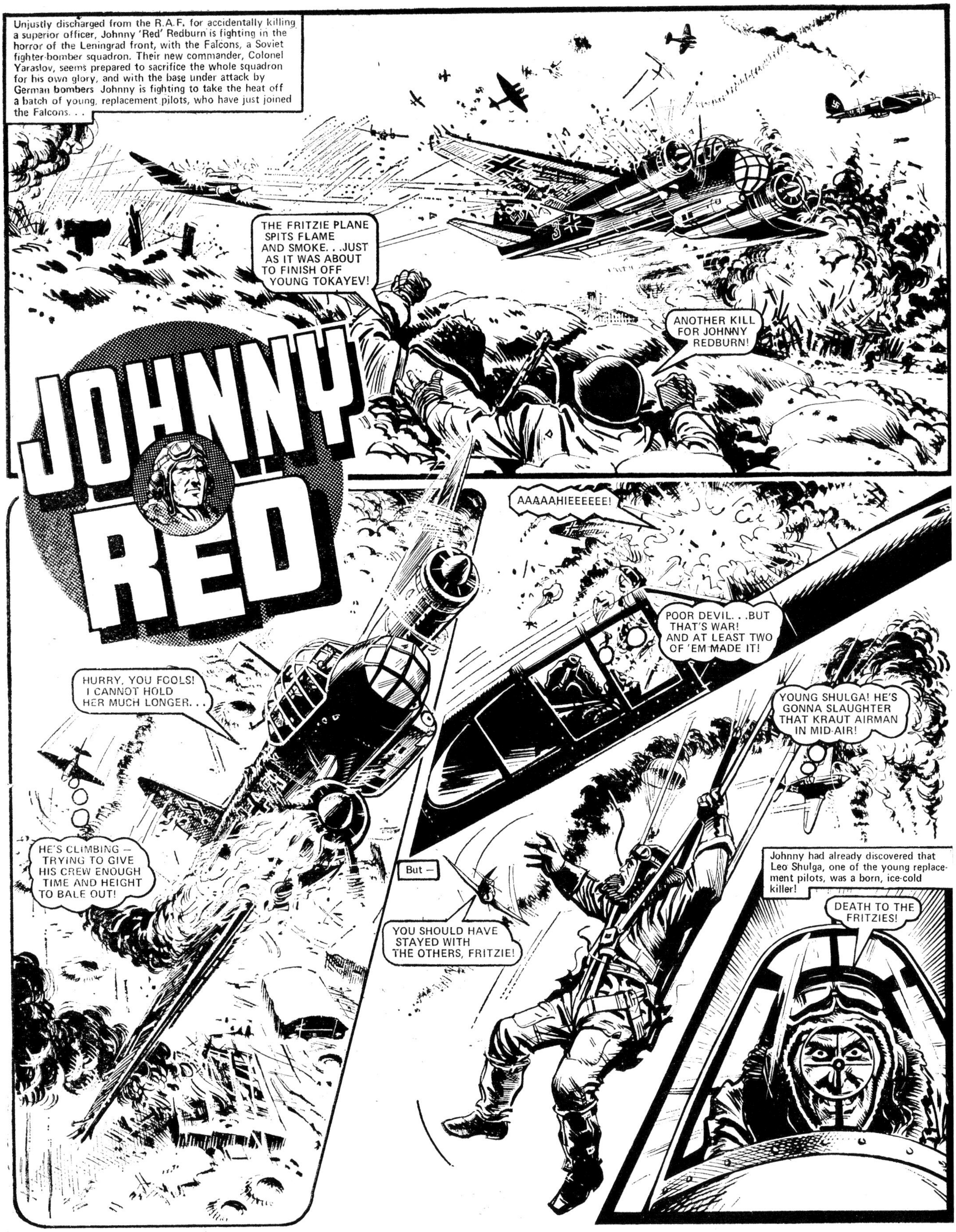
Unjustly discharged from the R.A.F. for accidentally killing a superior officer, Johnny 'Red' Redburn is fighting in the horror of the Leningrad front, with the Falcons, a Soviet fighter-bomber squadron. Their new commander, Colonel Yaraslov, seems prepared to sacrifice the whole squadron for his own glory, and with the base under attack by German bombers Johnny is fighting to take the heat off a batch of young, replacement pilots, who have just joined the Falcons. . .
THE FRITZIE PLANE SPITS FLAME AND SMOKE. . .JUST AS IT WAS ABOUT TO FINISH OFF YOUNG TOKAYEV!
ANOTHER KILL FOR JOHNNY REDBURN!
JOHNNY RED
HURRY, YOU FOOLS! I CANNOT HOLD HER MUCH LONGER. . .
HE'S CLIMBING — TRYING TO GIVE HIS CREW ENOUGH TIME AND HEIGHT TO BALE OUT!
AAAAAHIEEEEEE!
POOR DEVIL. . .BUT THAT'S WAR! AND AT LEAST TWO OF 'EM MADE IT!
YOUNG SHULGA! HE'S GONNA SLAUGHTER THAT KRAUT AIRMAN IN MID-AIR!
But —
YOU SHOULD HAVE STAYED WITH THE OTHERS, FRITZIE!
Johnny had already discovered that Leo Shulga, one of the young replacement pilots, was a born, ice-cold killer!
DEATH TO THE FRITZIES!

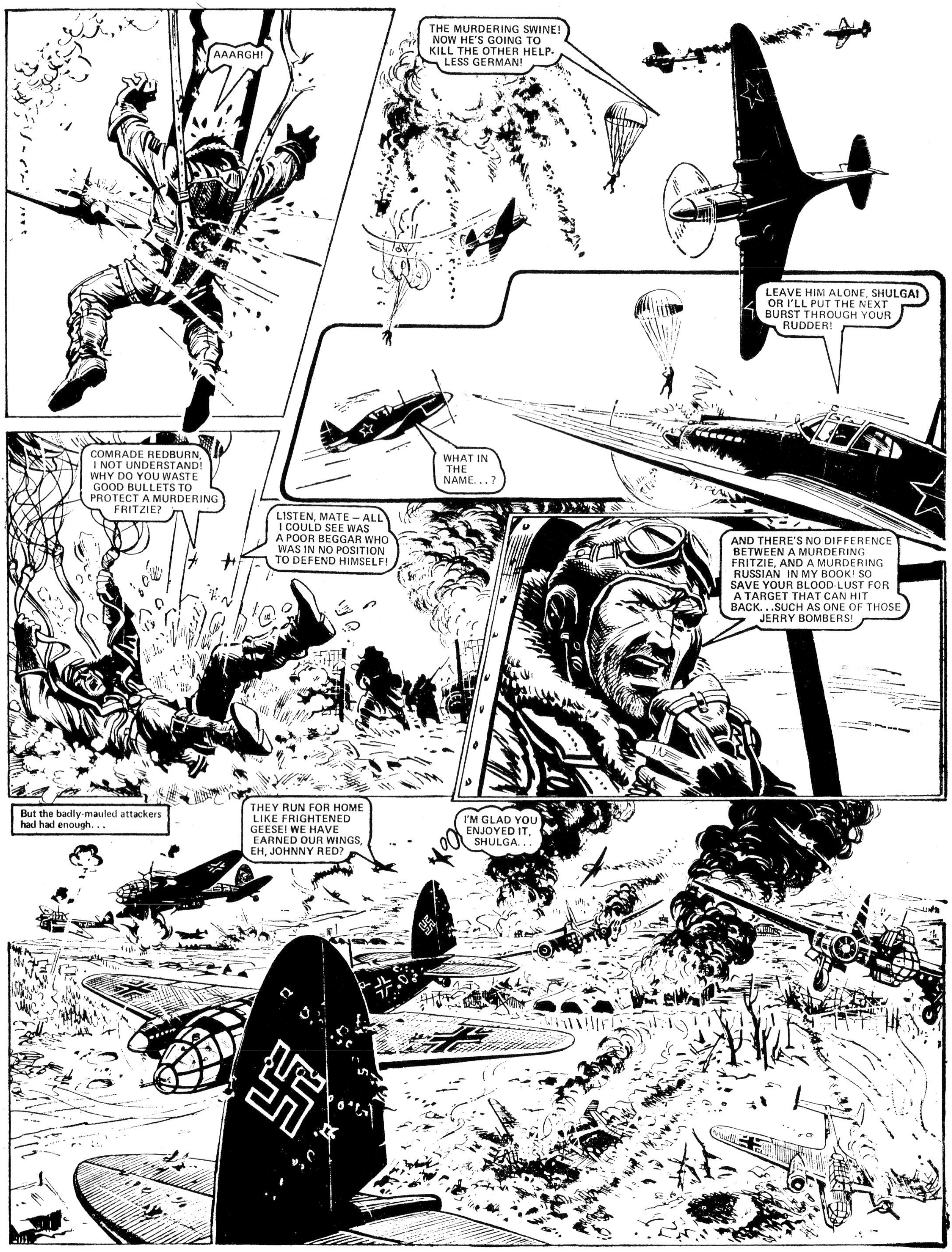
AAARGH!
THE MURDERING SWINE! NOW HE'S GOING TO KILL THE OTHER HELP-LESS GERMAN!
LEAVE HIM ALONE, SHULGA! OR I'LL PUT THE NEXT BURST THROUGH YOUR RUDDER!
WHAT IN THE NAME. . .?
COMRADE REDBURN, I NOT UNDERSTAND! WHY DO YOU WASTE GOOD BULLETS TO PROTECT A MURDERING FRITZIE?
LISTEN, MATE – ALL I COULD SEE WAS A POOR BEGGAR WHO WAS IN NO POSITION TO DEFEND HIMSELF!
AND THERE'S NO DIFFERENCE BETWEEN A MURDERING FRITZIE, AND A MURDERING RUSSIAN IN MY BOOK! SO SAVE YOUR BLOOD-LUST FOR A TARGET THAT CAN HIT BACK. . .SUCH AS ONE OF THOSE JERRY BOMBERS!
But the badly-mauled attackers had had enough. . .
THEY RUN FOR HOME LIKE FRIGHTENED GEESE! WE HAVE EARNED OUR WINGS, EH, JOHNNY RED?
I'M GLAD YOU ENJOYED IT, SHULGA. . .

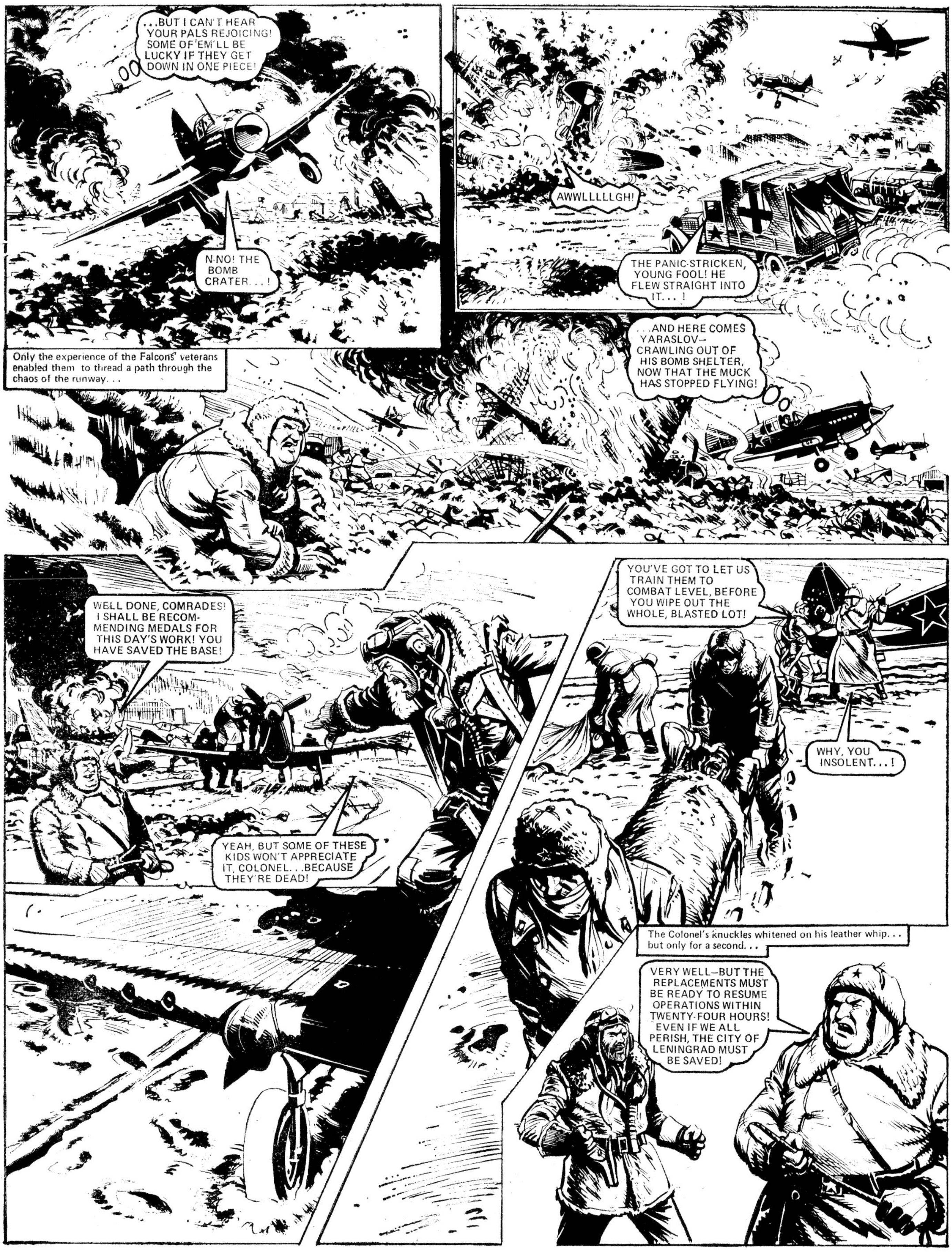

...BUT I CAN'T HEAR YOUR PALS REJOICING! SOME OF 'EM'LL BE LUCKY IF THEY GET DOWN IN ONE PIECE!
N-NO! THE BOMB CRATER...!
AWWLLLLLGH!
THE PANIC-STRICKEN, YOUNG FOOL! HE FLEW STRAIGHT INTO IT...!
Only the experience of the Falcons' veterans enabled them to thread a path through the chaos of the runway...
...AND HERE COMES YARASLOV— CRAWLING OUT OF HIS BOMB SHELTER, NOW THAT THE MUCK HAS STOPPED FLYING!
WELL DONE, COMRADES! I SHALL BE RECOMMENDING MEDALS FOR THIS DAY'S WORK! YOU HAVE SAVED THE BASE!
YEAH, BUT SOME OF THESE KIDS WON'T APPRECIATE IT, COLONEL...BECAUSE THEY'RE DEAD!
YOU'VE GOT TO LET US TRAIN THEM TO COMBAT LEVEL, BEFORE YOU WIPE OUT THE WHOLE, BLASTED LOT!
WHY, YOU INSOLENT...!
The Colonel's knuckles whitened on his leather whip... but only for a second...
VERY WELL—BUT THE REPLACEMENTS MUST BE READY TO RESUME OPERATIONS WITHIN TWENTY-FOUR HOURS! EVEN IF WE ALL PERISH, THE CITY OF LENINGRAD MUST BE SAVED!

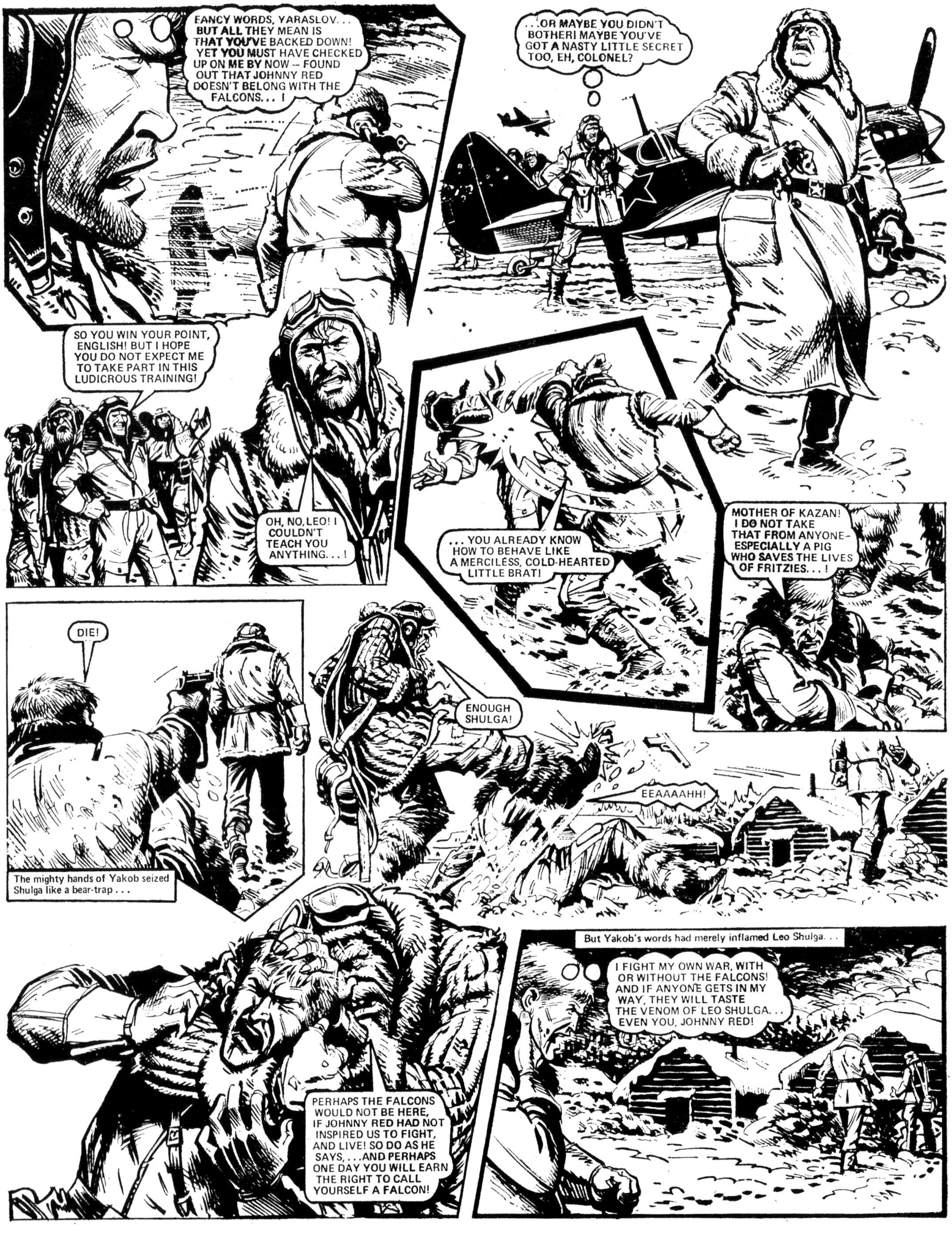
FANCY WORDS, YARASLOV. . . BUT ALL THEY MEAN IS THAT YOU'VE BACKED DOWN! YET YOU MUST HAVE CHECKED UP ON ME BY NOW -- FOUND OUT THAT JOHNNY RED DOESN'T BELONG WITH THE FALCONS. . . !
. . .OR MAYBE YOU DIDN'T BOTHER! MAYBE YOU'VE GOT A NASTY LITTLE SECRET TOO, EH, COLONEL?
SO YOU WIN YOUR POINT, ENGLISH! BUT I HOPE YOU DO NOT EXPECT ME TO TAKE PART IN THIS LUDICROUS TRAINING!
OH, NO, LEO! I COULDN'T TEACH YOU ANYTHING. . . !
. . . YOU ALREADY KNOW HOW TO BEHAVE LIKE A MERCILESS, COLD-HEARTED LITTLE BRAT!
MOTHER OF KAZAN! I DO NOT TAKE THAT FROM ANYONE-ESPECIALLY A PIG WHO SAVES THE LIVES OF FRITZIES. . . !
DIE!
ENOUGH SHULGA!
EEAAAAHH!
The mighty hands of Yakob seized Shulga like a bear-trap . . .
PERHAPS THE FALCONS WOULD NOT BE HERE, IF JOHNNY RED HAD NOT INSPIRED US TO FIGHT, AND LIVE! SO DO AS HE SAYS, . . .AND PERHAPS ONE DAY YOU WILL EARN THE RIGHT TO CALL YOURSELF A FALCON!
But Yakob's words had merely inflamed Leo Shulga. . .
I FIGHT MY OWN WAR, WITH OR WITHOUT THE FALCONS! AND IF ANYONE GETS IN MY WAY, THEY WILL TASTE THE VENOM OF LEO SHULGA. . . EVEN YOU, JOHNNY RED!

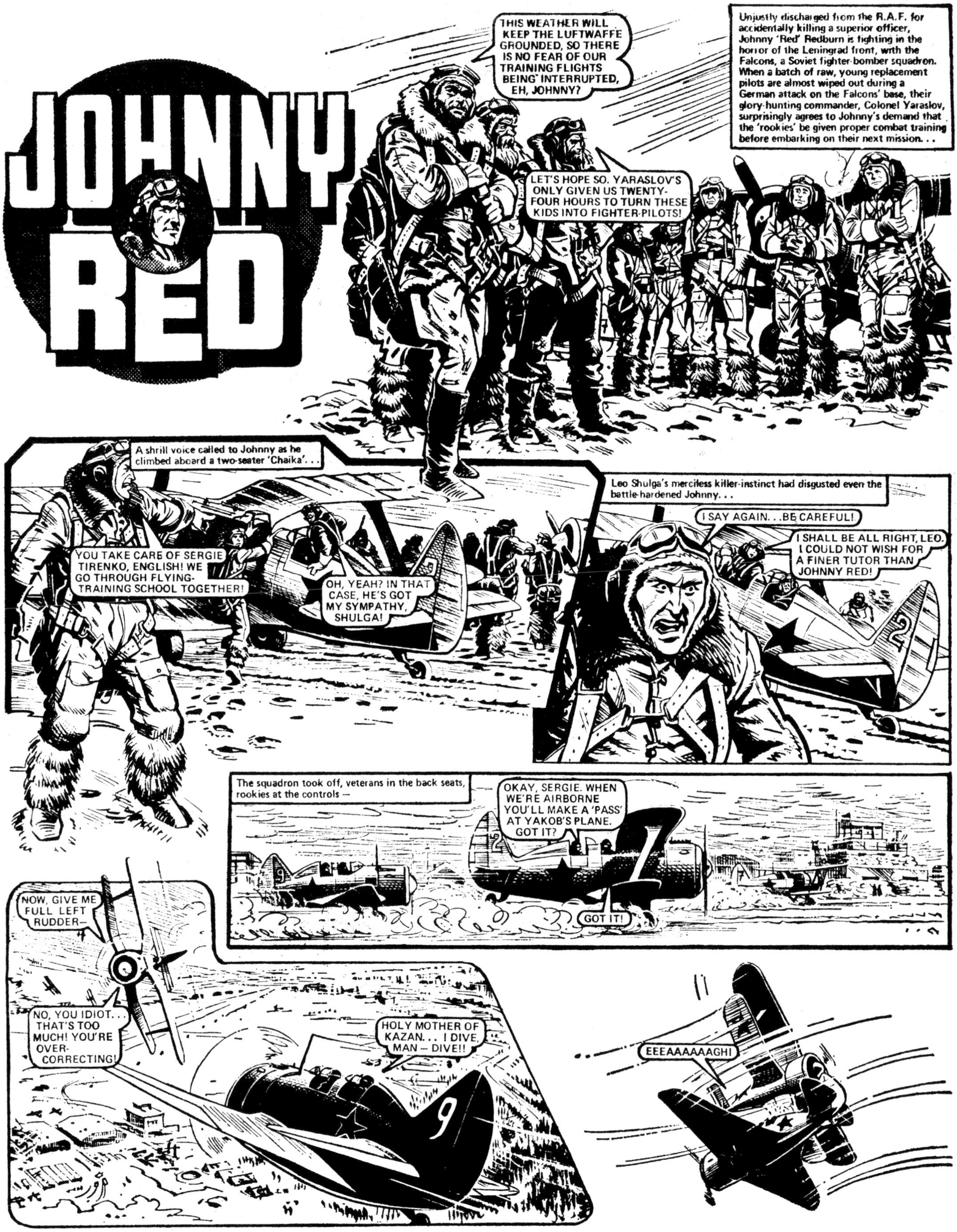
JOHNNY RED
Unjustly discharged from the R.A.F. for accidentally killing a superior officer, Johnny 'Red' Redburn is fighting in the horror of the Leningrad front, with the Falcons, a Soviet fighter-bomber squadron. When a batch of raw, young replacement pilots are almost wiped out during a German attack on the Falcons' base, their glory-hunting commander, Colonel Yaraslov, surprisingly agrees to Johnny's demand that the 'rookies' be given proper combat training before embarking on their next mission. . .
THIS WEATHER WILL KEEP THE LUFTWAFFE GROUNDED, SO THERE IS NO FEAR OF OUR TRAINING FLIGHTS BEING INTERRUPTED, EH, JOHNNY?
LET'S HOPE SO. YARASLOV'S ONLY GIVEN US TWENTY-FOUR HOURS TO TURN THESE KIDS INTO FIGHTER-PILOTS!
A shrill voice called to Johnny as he climbed aboard a two-seater 'Chaika'. . .
YOU TAKE CARE OF SERGIE TIRENKO, ENGLISH! WE GO THROUGH FLYING-TRAINING SCHOOL TOGETHER!
OH, YEAH? IN THAT CASE, HE'S GOT MY SYMPATHY, SHULGA!
Leo Shulga's merciless killer-instinct had disgusted even the battle-hardened Johnny. . .
I SAY AGAIN. . .BE CAREFUL!
I SHALL BE ALL RIGHT, LEO. I COULD NOT WISH FOR A FINER TUTOR THAN JOHNNY RED!
The squadron took off, veterans in the back seats, rookies at the controls —
OKAY, SERGIE. WHEN WE'RE AIRBORNE YOU'LL MAKE A 'PASS' AT YAKOB'S PLANE. GOT IT?
GOT IT!
NOW, GIVE ME FULL LEFT RUDDER—
NO, YOU IDIOT. . . THAT'S TOO MUCH! YOU'RE OVER-CORRECTING!
HOLY MOTHER OF KAZAN. . . I DIVE, MAN — DIVE!!
EEEAAAAAAGH!

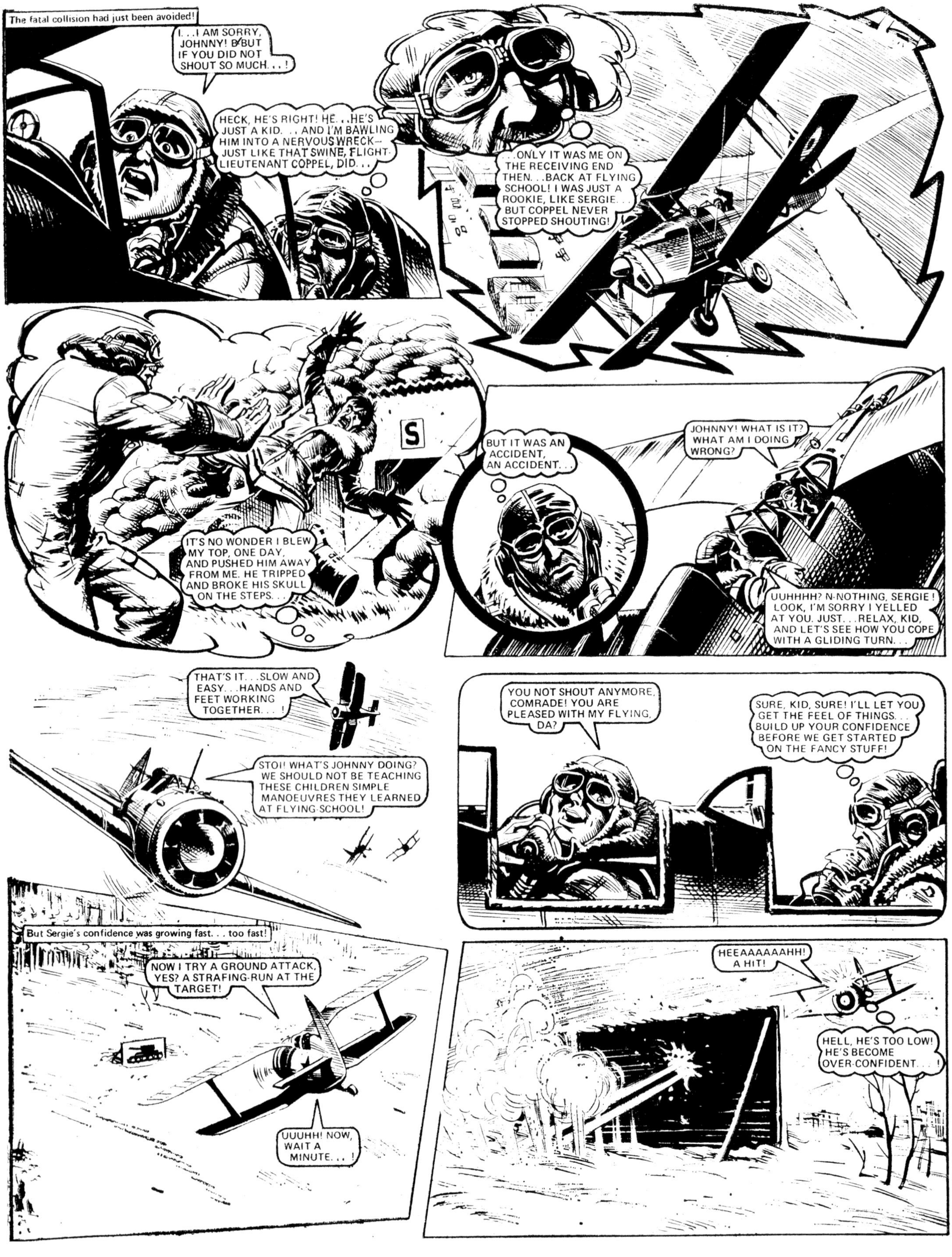

The fatal collision had just been avoided!
I. . . I AM SORRY, JOHNNY! B-BUT IF YOU DID NOT SHOUT SO MUCH. . . !
HECK, HE'S RIGHT! HE. . .HE'S JUST A KID. . . AND I'M BAWLING HIM INTO A NERVOUS WRECK— JUST LIKE THAT SWINE, FLIGHT-LIEUTENANT COPPEL, DID. . .
. . .ONLY IT WAS ME ON THE RECEIVING END THEN. . .BACK AT FLYING SCHOOL! I WAS JUST A ROOKIE, LIKE SERGIE. . . BUT COPPEL NEVER STOPPED SHOUTING!
S
IT'S NO WONDER I BLEW MY TOP, ONE DAY, AND PUSHED HIM AWAY FROM ME. HE TRIPPED AND BROKE HIS SKULL ON THE STEPS. . .
BUT IT WAS AN ACCIDENT, AN ACCIDENT. . .
JOHNNY! WHAT IS IT? WHAT AM I DOING WRONG?
UUHHHH? N-NOTHING, SERGIE! LOOK, I'M SORRY I YELLED AT YOU. JUST. . .RELAX, KID, AND LET'S SEE HOW YOU COPE WITH A GLIDING TURN. . .
THAT'S IT. . .SLOW AND EASY. . .HANDS AND FEET WORKING TOGETHER. . . !
STOI! WHAT'S JOHNNY DOING? WE SHOULD NOT BE TEACHING THESE CHILDREN SIMPLE MANOEUVRES THEY LEARNED AT FLYING-SCHOOL!
YOU NOT SHOUT ANYMORE, COMRADE! YOU ARE PLEASED WITH MY FLYING, DA?
SURE, KID, SURE! I'LL LET YOU GET THE FEEL OF THINGS. . . BUILD UP YOUR CONFIDENCE BEFORE WE GET STARTED ON THE FANCY STUFF!
But Sergie's confidence was growing fast. . . too fast!
NOW I TRY A GROUND ATTACK, YES? A STRAFING-RUN AT THE TARGET!
UUUHH! NOW, WAIT A MINUTE. . . !
HEEAAAAAAHH! A HIT!
HELL, HE'S TOO LOW! HE'S BECOME OVER-CONFIDENT. . . !

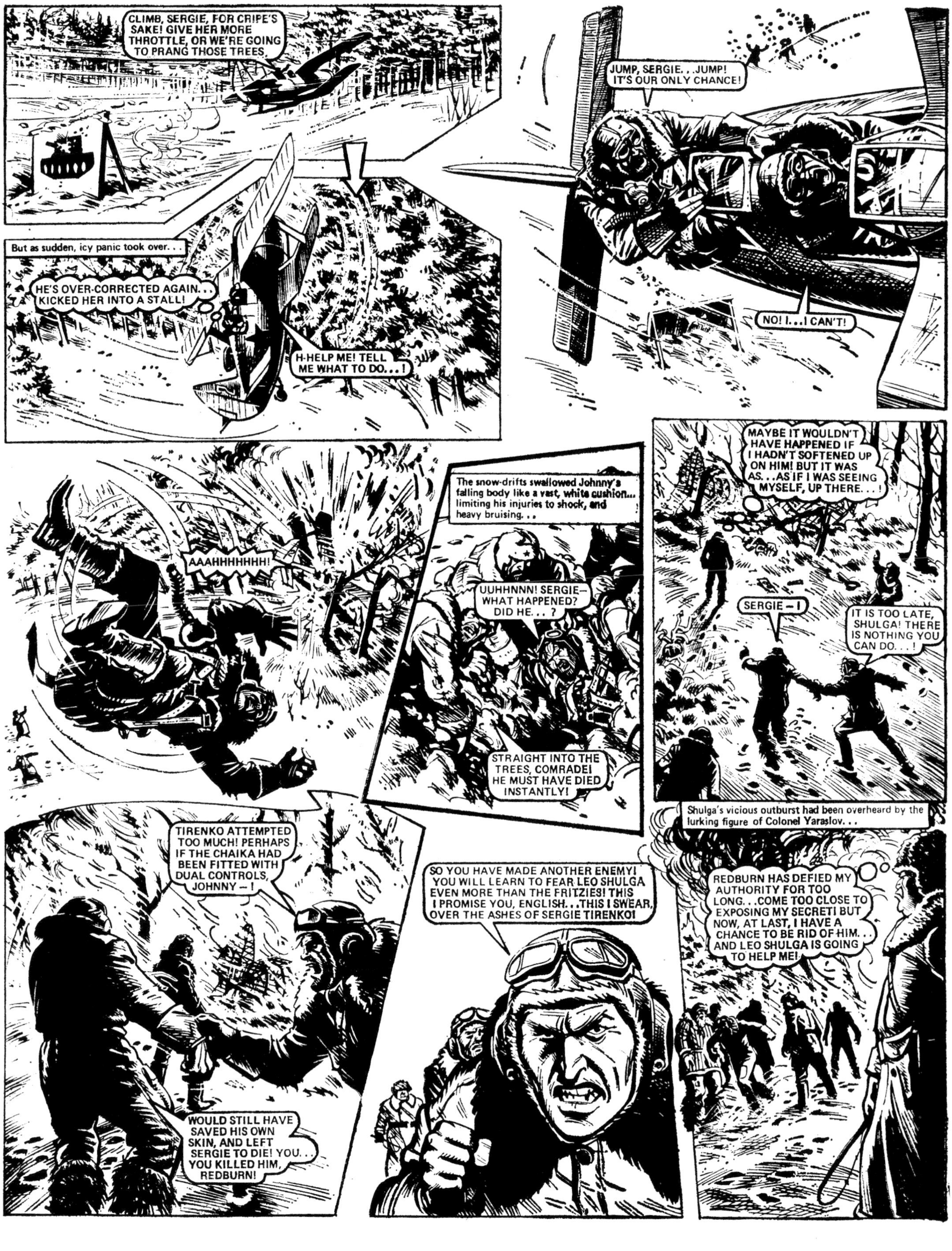
CLIMB, SERGIE, FOR CRIPE'S SAKE! GIVE HER MORE THROTTLE, OR WE'RE GOING TO PRANG THOSE TREES
But as sudden, icy panic took over...
HE'S OVER-CORRECTED AGAIN... KICKED HER INTO A STALL!
H-HELP ME! TELL ME WHAT TO DO...!
JUMP, SERGIE...JUMP! IT'S OUR ONLY CHANCE!
NO! I...I CAN'T!
AAAHHHHHHH!
The snow-drifts swallowed Johnny's falling body like a vast, white cushion... limiting his injuries to shock, and heavy bruising...
UUHHNNN! SERGIE— WHAT HAPPENED? DID HE...?
STRAIGHT INTO THE TREES, COMRADE! HE MUST HAVE DIED INSTANTLY!
MAYBE IT WOULDN'T HAVE HAPPENED IF I HADN'T SOFTENED UP ON HIM! BUT IT WAS AS...AS IF I WAS SEEING MYSELF, UP THERE...!
SERGIE—!
IT IS TOO LATE, SHULGA! THERE IS NOTHING YOU CAN DO...!
TIRENKO ATTEMPTED TOO MUCH! PERHAPS IF THE CHAIKA HAD BEEN FITTED WITH DUAL CONTROLS, JOHNNY—!
WOULD STILL HAVE SAVED HIS OWN SKIN, AND LEFT SERGIE TO DIE! YOU... YOU KILLED HIM, REDBURN!
SO YOU HAVE MADE ANOTHER ENEMY! YOU WILL LEARN TO FEAR LEO SHULGA EVEN MORE THAN THE FRITZIES! THIS I PROMISE YOU, ENGLISH...THIS I SWEAR, OVER THE ASHES OF SERGIE TIRENKO!
Shulga's vicious outburst had been overheard by the lurking figure of Colonel Yaraslov...
REDBURN HAS DEFIED MY AUTHORITY FOR TOO LONG...COME TOO CLOSE TO EXPOSING MY SECRET! BUT NOW, AT LAST, I HAVE A CHANCE TO BE RID OF HIM... AND LEO SHULGA IS GOING TO HELP ME!

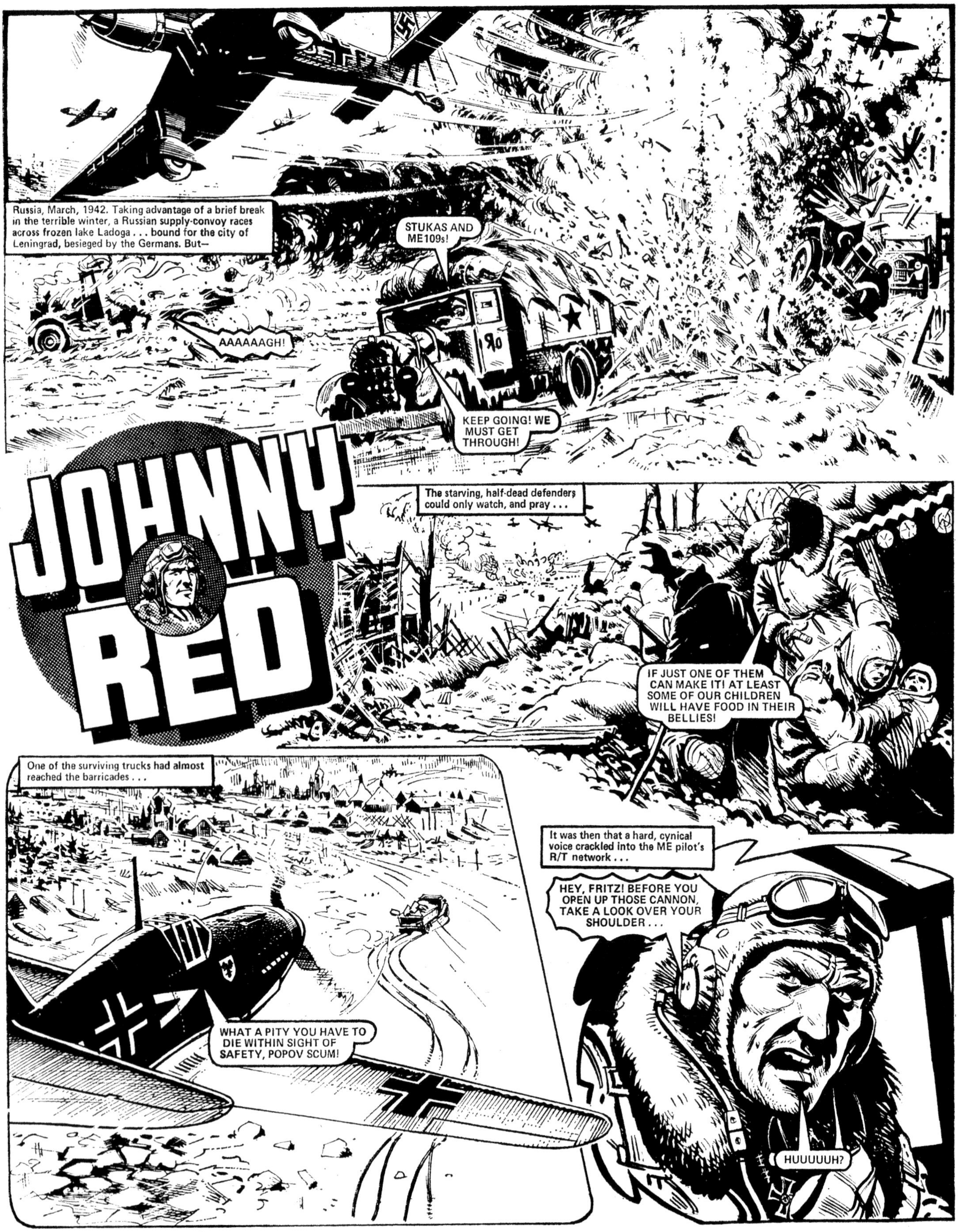

Russia, March, 1942. Taking advantage of a brief break in the terrible winter, a Russian supply-convoy races across frozen lake Ladoga . . . bound for the city of Leningrad, besieged by the Germans. But—
STUKAS AND ME109s!
AAAAAAGH!
KEEP GOING! WE MUST GET THROUGH!
JOHNNY RED
The starving, half-dead defenders could only watch, and pray . . .
IF JUST ONE OF THEM CAN MAKE IT! AT LEAST SOME OF OUR CHILDREN WILL HAVE FOOD IN THEIR BELLIES!
One of the surviving trucks had almost reached the barricades . . .
WHAT A PITY YOU HAVE TO DIE WITHIN SIGHT OF SAFETY, POPOV SCUM!
It was then that a hard, cynical voice crackled into the ME pilot's R/T network . . .
HEY, FRITZ! BEFORE YOU OPEN UP THOSE CANNON, TAKE A LOOK OVER YOUR SHOULDER . . .
HUUUUUH?

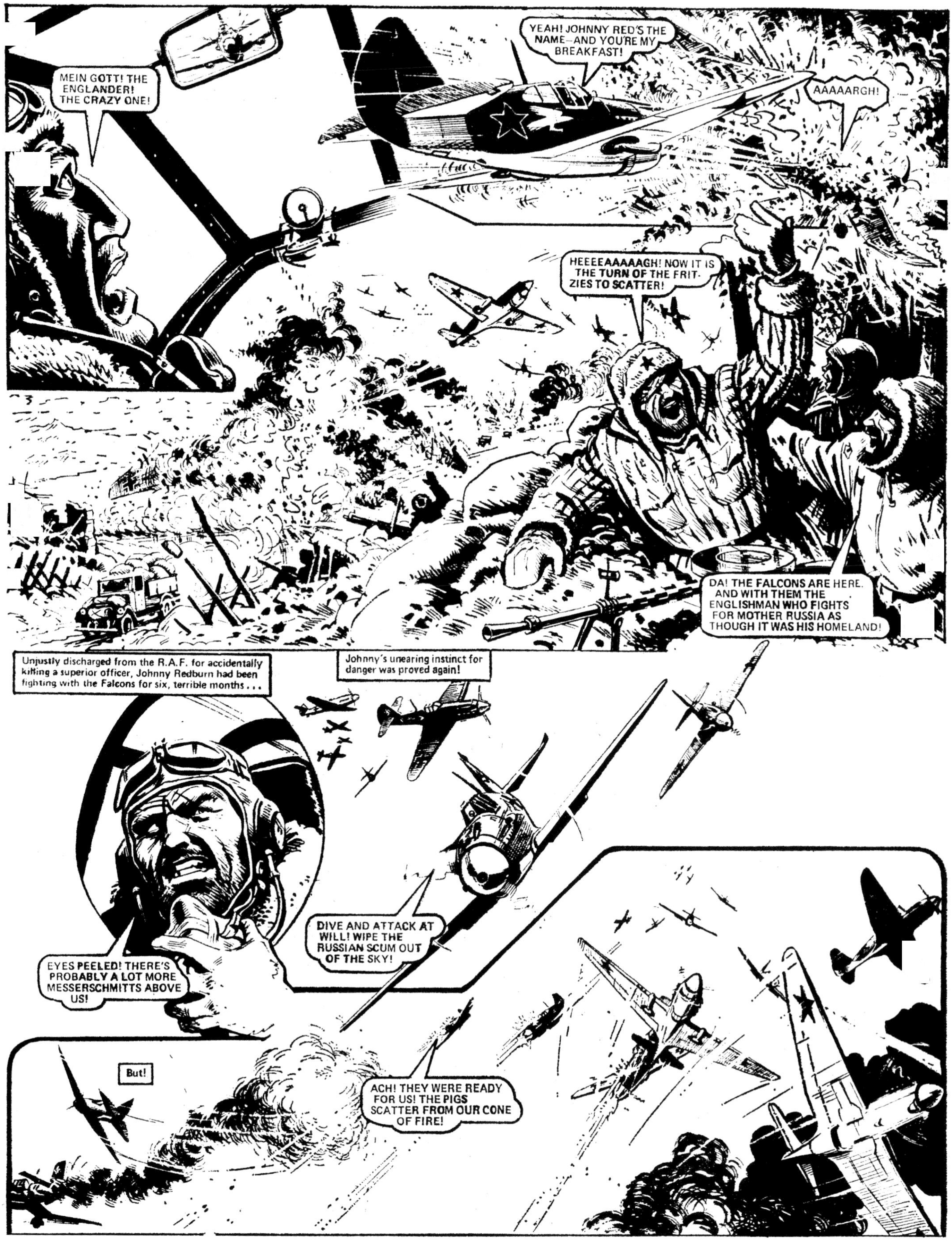
MEIN GOTT! THE ENGLANDER! THE CRAZY ONE!
YEAH! JOHNNY RED'S THE NAME—AND YOU'RE MY BREAKFAST!
AAAAARGH!
HEEEEAAAAAGH! NOW IT IS THE TURN OF THE FRIT-ZIES TO SCATTER!
DA! THE FALCONS ARE HERE. AND WITH THEM THE ENGLISHMAN WHO FIGHTS FOR MOTHER RUSSIA AS THOUGH IT WAS HIS HOMELAND!
Unjustly discharged from the R.A.F. for accidentally killing a superior officer, Johnny Redburn had been fighting with the Falcons for six, terrible months . . .
Johnny's unearing instinct for danger was proved again!
EYES PEELED! THERE'S PROBABLY A LOT MORE MESSERSCHMITTS ABOVE US!
DIVE AND ATTACK AT WILL! WIPE THE RUSSIAN SCUM OUT OF THE SKY!
But!
ACH! THEY WERE READY FOR US! THE PIGS SCATTER FROM OUR CONE OF FIRE!

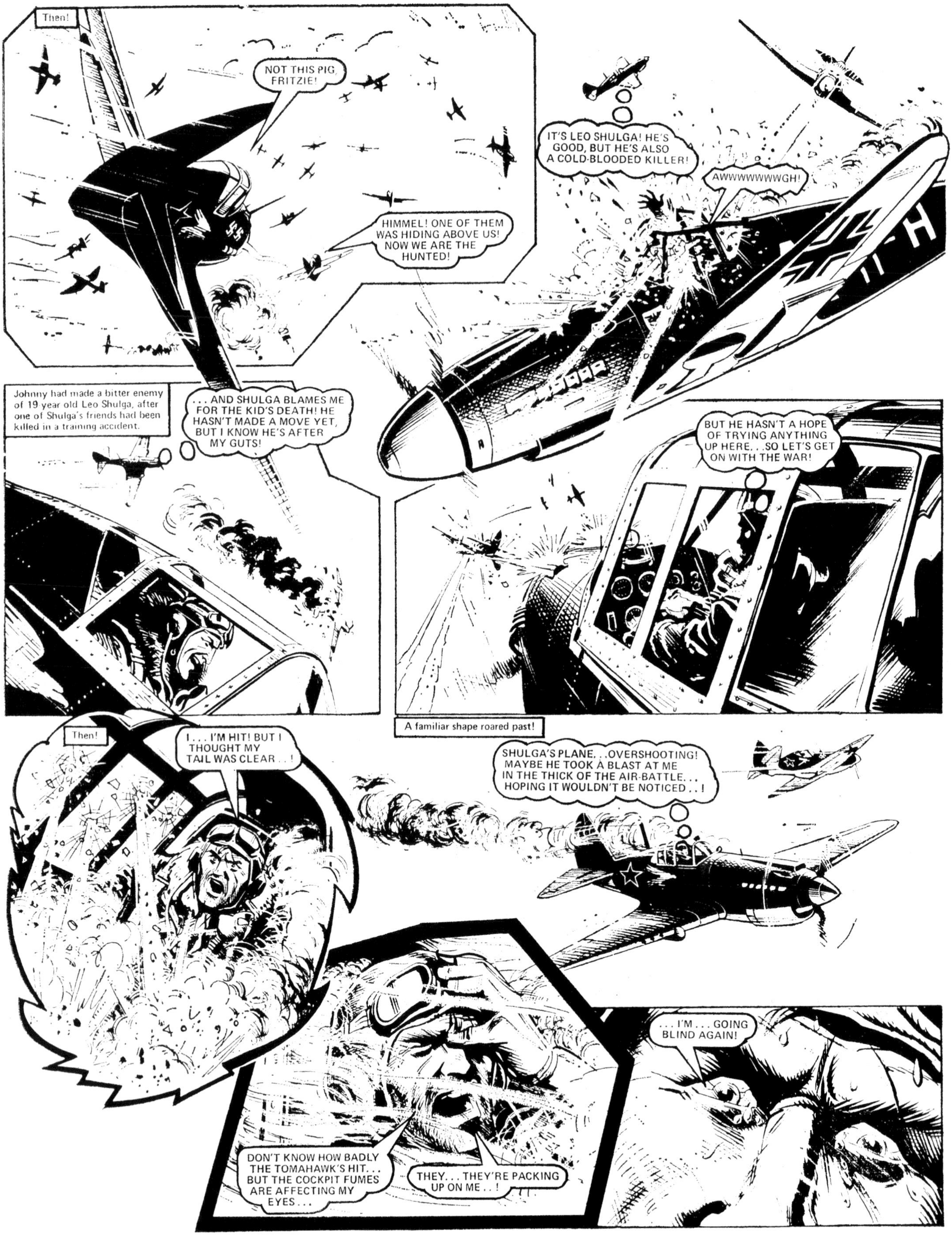
Then!
NOT THIS PIG, FRITZIE!
HIMMEL! ONE OF THEM WAS HIDING ABOVE US! NOW WE ARE THE HUNTED!
IT'S LEO SHULGA! HE'S GOOD, BUT HE'S ALSO A COLD-BLOODED KILLER!
AWWWWWWWGH!
Johnny had made a bitter enemy of 19 year old Leo Shulga, after one of Shulga's friends had been killed in a training accident.
. . . AND SHULGA BLAMES ME FOR THE KID'S DEATH! HE HASN'T MADE A MOVE YET, BUT I KNOW HE'S AFTER MY GUTS!
BUT HE HASN'T A HOPE OF TRYING ANYTHING UP HERE. . .SO LET'S GET ON WITH THE WAR!
Then!
I . . . I'M HIT! BUT I THOUGHT MY TAIL WAS CLEAR . . !
A familiar shape roared past!
SHULGA'S PLANE. . .OVERSHOOTING! MAYBE HE TOOK A BLAST AT ME IN THE THICK OF THE AIR-BATTLE. . . HOPING IT WOULDN'T BE NOTICED . . !
DON'T KNOW HOW BADLY THE TOMAHAWK'S HIT. . . BUT THE COCKPIT FUMES ARE AFFECTING MY EYES . . .
THEY. . . THEY'RE PACKING UP ON ME . . !
. . . I'M . . . GOING BLIND AGAIN!

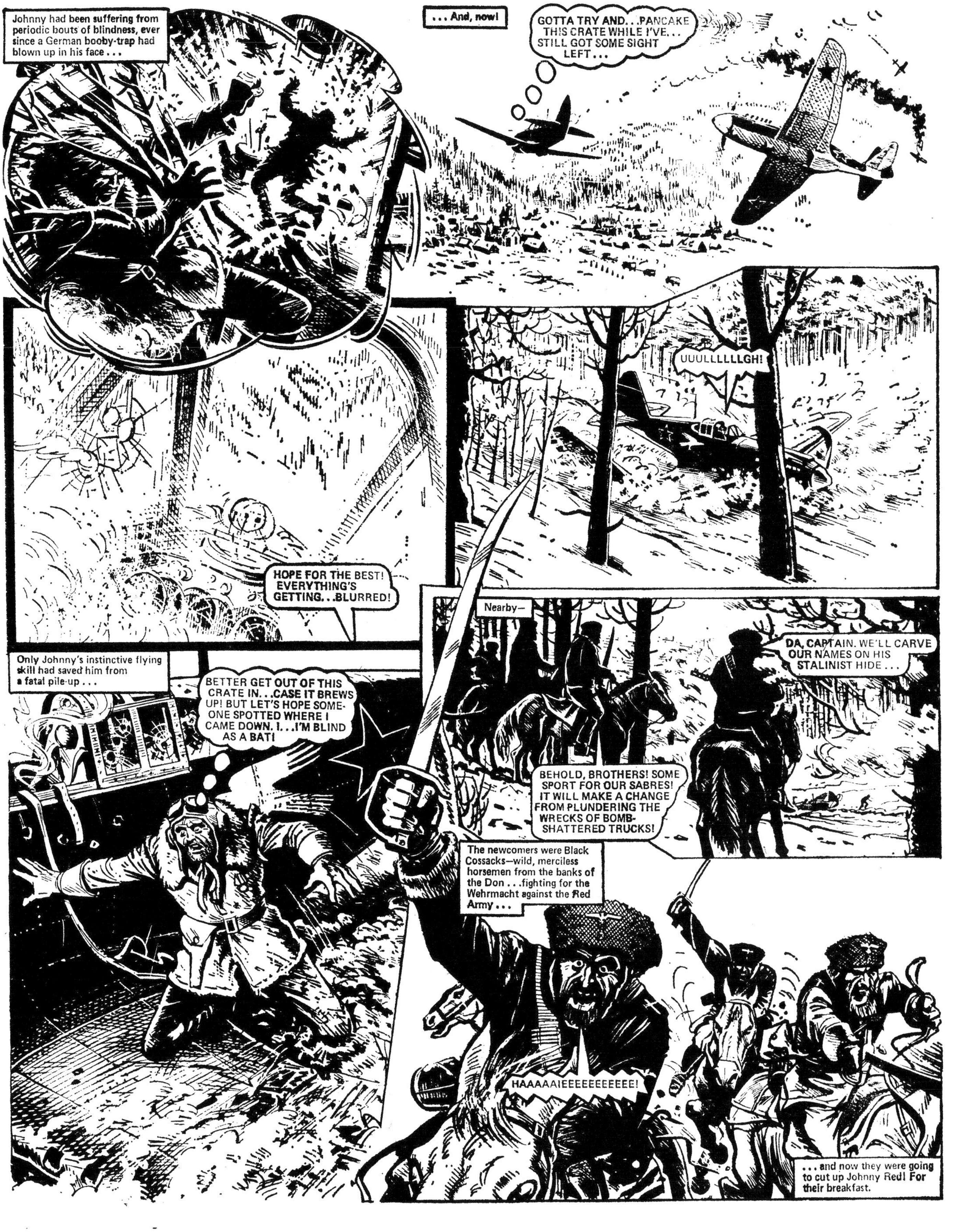

Johnny had been suffering from periodic bouts of blindness, ever since a German booby-trap had blown up in his face . . .
. . . And, now!
GOTTA TRY AND. . .PANCAKE THIS CRATE WHILE I'VE. . . STILL GOT SOME SIGHT LEFT . . .
HOPE FOR THE BEST! EVERYTHING'S GETTING. . .BLURRED!
UUULLLLLLGH!
Only Johnny's instinctive flying skill had saved him from a fatal pile-up . . .
BETTER GET OUT OF THIS CRATE IN. . .CASE IT BREWS UP! BUT LET'S HOPE SOME-ONE SPOTTED WHERE I CAME DOWN. I. . .I'M BLIND AS A BAT!
Nearby—
DA, CAPTAIN. WE'LL CARVE OUR NAMES ON HIS STALINIST HIDE . . .
BEHOLD, BROTHERS! SOME SPORT FOR OUR SABRES! IT WILL MAKE A CHANGE FROM PLUNDERING THE WRECKS OF BOMB-SHATTERED TRUCKS!
The newcomers were Black Cossacks—wild, merciless horsemen from the banks of the Don . . .fighting for the Wehrmacht against the Red Army . . .
HAAAAAIEEEEEEEEEEEE!
. . . and now they were going to cut up Johnny Red! For their breakfast.

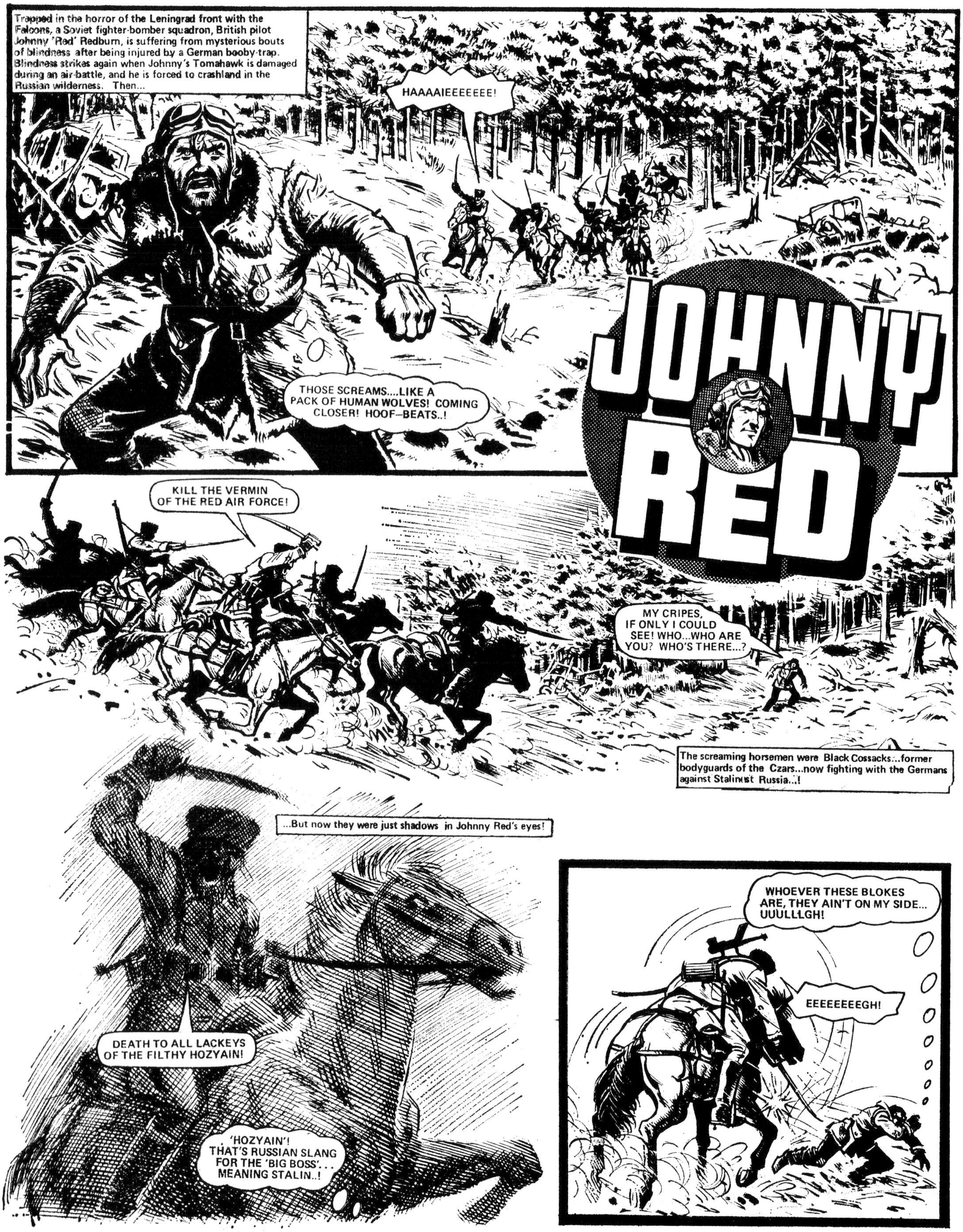
Trapped in the horror of the Leningrad front with the Falcons, a Soviet fighter-bomber squadron, British pilot Johnny 'Red' Redburn, is suffering from mysterious bouts of blindness after being injured by a German booby-trap. Blindness strikes again when Johnny's Tomahawk is damaged during an air-battle, and he is forced to crashland in the Russian wilderness. Then...
HAAAAIEEEEEEE!
THOSE SCREAMS....LIKE A PACK OF HUMAN WOLVES! COMING CLOSER! HOOF–BEATS..!
JOHNNY RED
KILL THE VERMIN OF THE RED AIR FORCE!
MY CRIPES, IF ONLY I COULD SEE! WHO...WHO ARE YOU? WHO'S THERE...?
The screaming horsemen were Black Cossacks...former bodyguards of the Czars...now fighting with the Germans against Stalinist Russia...!
...But now they were just shadows in Johnny Red's eyes!
DEATH TO ALL LACKEYS OF THE FILTHY HOZYAIN!
'HOZYAIN'! THAT'S RUSSIAN SLANG FOR THE 'BIG BOSS'... MEANING STALIN..!
WHOEVER THESE BLOKES ARE, THEY AIN'T ON MY SIDE... UUULLLGH!
EEEEEEEEGH!

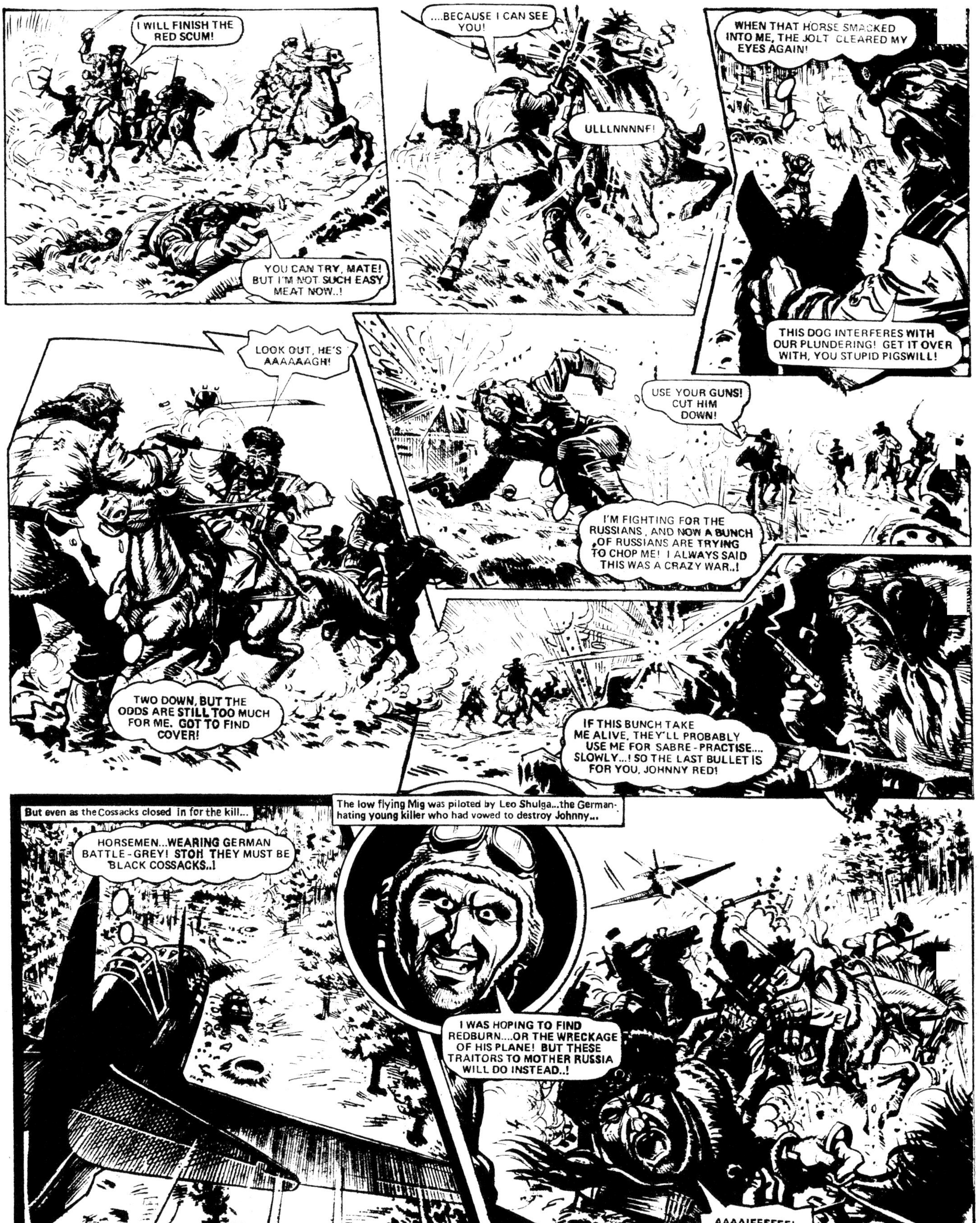
I WILL FINISH THE RED SCUM!
YOU CAN TRY, MATE! BUT I'M NOT SUCH EASY MEAT NOW..!
....BECAUSE I CAN SEE YOU!
ULLLNNNNF!
WHEN THAT HORSE SMACKED INTO ME, THE JOLT CLEARED MY EYES AGAIN!
THIS DOG INTERFERES WITH OUR PLUNDERING! GET IT OVER WITH, YOU STUPID PIGSWILL!
LOOK OUT, HE'S AAAAAAGH!
TWO DOWN, BUT THE ODDS ARE STILL TOO MUCH FOR ME. GOT TO FIND COVER!
USE YOUR GUNS! CUT HIM DOWN!
I'M FIGHTING FOR THE RUSSIANS, AND NOW A BUNCH OF RUSSIANS ARE TRYING TO CHOP ME! I ALWAYS SAID THIS WAS A CRAZY WAR..!
IF THIS BUNCH TAKE ME ALIVE, THEY'LL PROBABLY USE ME FOR SABRE-PRACTISE.... SLOWLY...! SO THE LAST BULLET IS FOR YOU, JOHNNY RED!
But even as the Cossacks closed in for the kill...
HORSEMEN...WEARING GERMAN BATTLE-GREY! STOH THEY MUST BE BLACK COSSACKS..!
The low flying Mig was piloted by Leo Shulga...the German-hating young killer who had vowed to destroy Johnny...
I WAS HOPING TO FIND REDBURN....OR THE WRECKAGE OF HIS PLANE! BUT THESE TRAITORS TO MOTHER RUSSIA WILL DO INSTEAD..!
AAAAIEEEEEE!

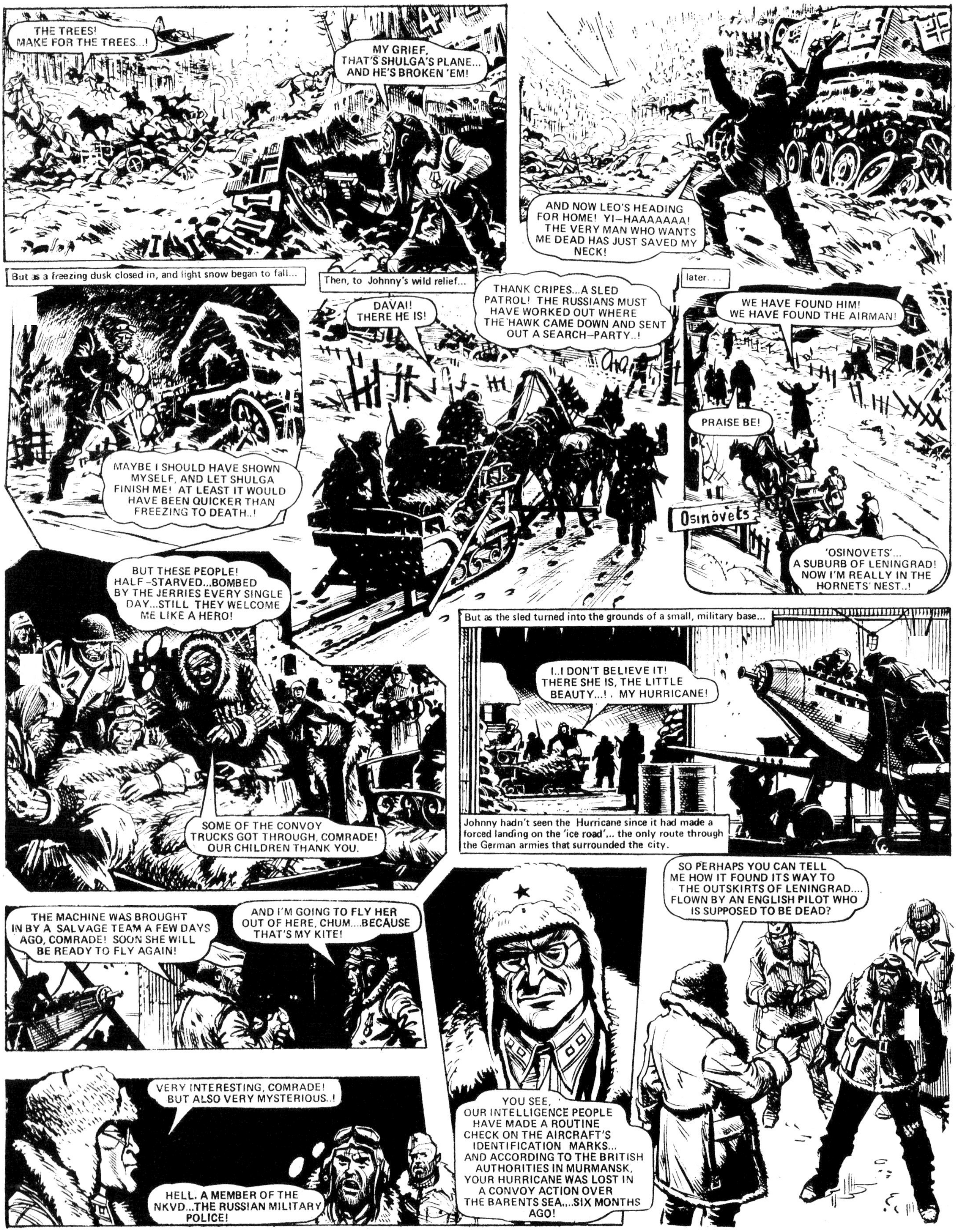
THE TREES! MAKE FOR THE TREES...!
MY GRIEF, THAT'S SHULGA'S PLANE... AND HE'S BROKEN 'EM!
AND NOW LEO'S HEADING FOR HOME! YI-HAAAAAAA! THE VERY MAN WHO WANTS ME DEAD HAS JUST SAVED MY NECK!
But as a freezing dusk closed in, and light snow began to fall...
MAYBE I SHOULD HAVE SHOWN MYSELF, AND LET SHULGA FINISH ME! AT LEAST IT WOULD HAVE BEEN QUICKER THAN FREEZING TO DEATH..!
Then, to Johnny's wild relief...
DAVAI! THERE HE IS!
THANK CRIPES...A SLED PATROL! THE RUSSIANS MUST HAVE WORKED OUT WHERE THE HAWK CAME DOWN AND SENT OUT A SEARCH-PARTY..!
later...
WE HAVE FOUND HIM! WE HAVE FOUND THE AIRMAN!
PRAISE BE!
Osinovets
'OSINOVETS'... A SUBURB OF LENINGRAD! NOW I'M REALLY IN THE HORNETS' NEST..!
BUT THESE PEOPLE! HALF-STARVED...BOMBED BY THE JERRIES EVERY SINGLE DAY...STILL THEY WELCOME ME LIKE A HERO!
SOME OF THE CONVOY TRUCKS GOT THROUGH, COMRADE! OUR CHILDREN THANK YOU.
But as the sled turned into the grounds of a small, military base...
I..I DON'T BELIEVE IT! THERE SHE IS, THE LITTLE BEAUTY...! MY HURRICANE!
Johnny hadn't seen the Hurricane since it had made a forced landing on the 'ice road'... the only route through the German armies that surrounded the city.
THE MACHINE WAS BROUGHT IN BY A SALVAGE TEAM A FEW DAYS AGO, COMRADE! SOON SHE WILL BE READY TO FLY AGAIN!
AND I'M GOING TO FLY HER OUT OF HERE, CHUM...BECAUSE THAT'S MY KITE!
SO PERHAPS YOU CAN TELL ME HOW IT FOUND ITS WAY TO THE OUTSKIRTS OF LENINGRAD.... FLOWN BY AN ENGLISH PILOT WHO IS SUPPOSED TO BE DEAD?
VERY INTERESTING, COMRADE! BUT ALSO VERY MYSTERIOUS..!
HELL, A MEMBER OF THE NKVD...THE RUSSIAN MILITARY POLICE!
YOU SEE, OUR INTELLIGENCE PEOPLE HAVE MADE A ROUTINE CHECK ON THE AIRCRAFT'S IDENTIFICATION MARKS... AND ACCORDING TO THE BRITISH AUTHORITIES IN MURMANSK, YOUR HURRICANE WAS LOST IN A CONVOY ACTION OVER THE BARENTS SEA,...SIX MONTHS AGO!

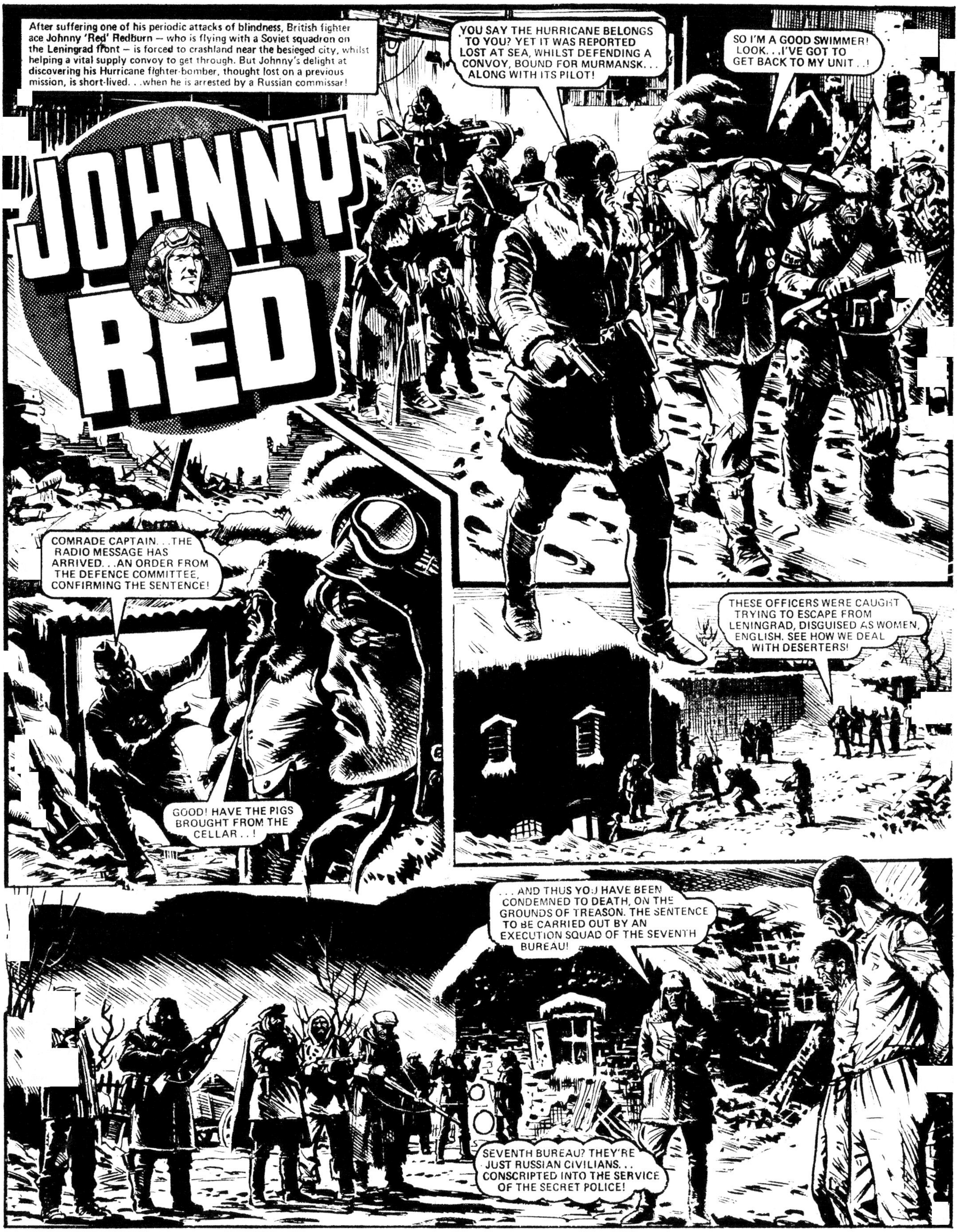
After suffering one of his periodic attacks of blindness, British fighter ace Johnny 'Red' Redburn — who is flying with a Soviet squadron on the Leningrad front — is forced to crashland near the besieged city, whilst helping a vital supply convoy to get through. But Johnny's delight at discovering his Hurricane fighter-bomber, thought lost on a previous mission, is short-lived. . .when he is arrested by a Russian commissar!
JOHNNY RED
YOU SAY THE HURRICANE BELONGS TO YOU? YET IT WAS REPORTED LOST AT SEA, WHILST DEFENDING A CONVOY, BOUND FOR MURMANSK. . . ALONG WITH ITS PILOT!
SO I'M A GOOD SWIMMER! LOOK. . .I'VE GOT TO GET BACK TO MY UNIT. .!
COMRADE CAPTAIN. . .THE RADIO MESSAGE HAS ARRIVED. . .AN ORDER FROM THE DEFENCE COMMITTEE, CONFIRMING THE SENTENCE!
GOOD! HAVE THE PIGS BROUGHT FROM THE CELLAR. .!
THESE OFFICERS WERE CAUGHT TRYING TO ESCAPE FROM LENINGRAD, DISGUISED AS WOMEN, ENGLISH. SEE HOW WE DEAL WITH DESERTERS!
. . .AND THUS YOU HAVE BEEN CONDEMNED TO DEATH, ON THE GROUNDS OF TREASON. THE SENTENCE TO BE CARRIED OUT BY AN EXECUTION SQUAD OF THE SEVENTH BUREAU!
SEVENTH BUREAU? THEY'RE JUST RUSSIAN CIVILIANS. . . CONSCRIPTED INTO THE SERVICE OF THE SECRET POLICE!

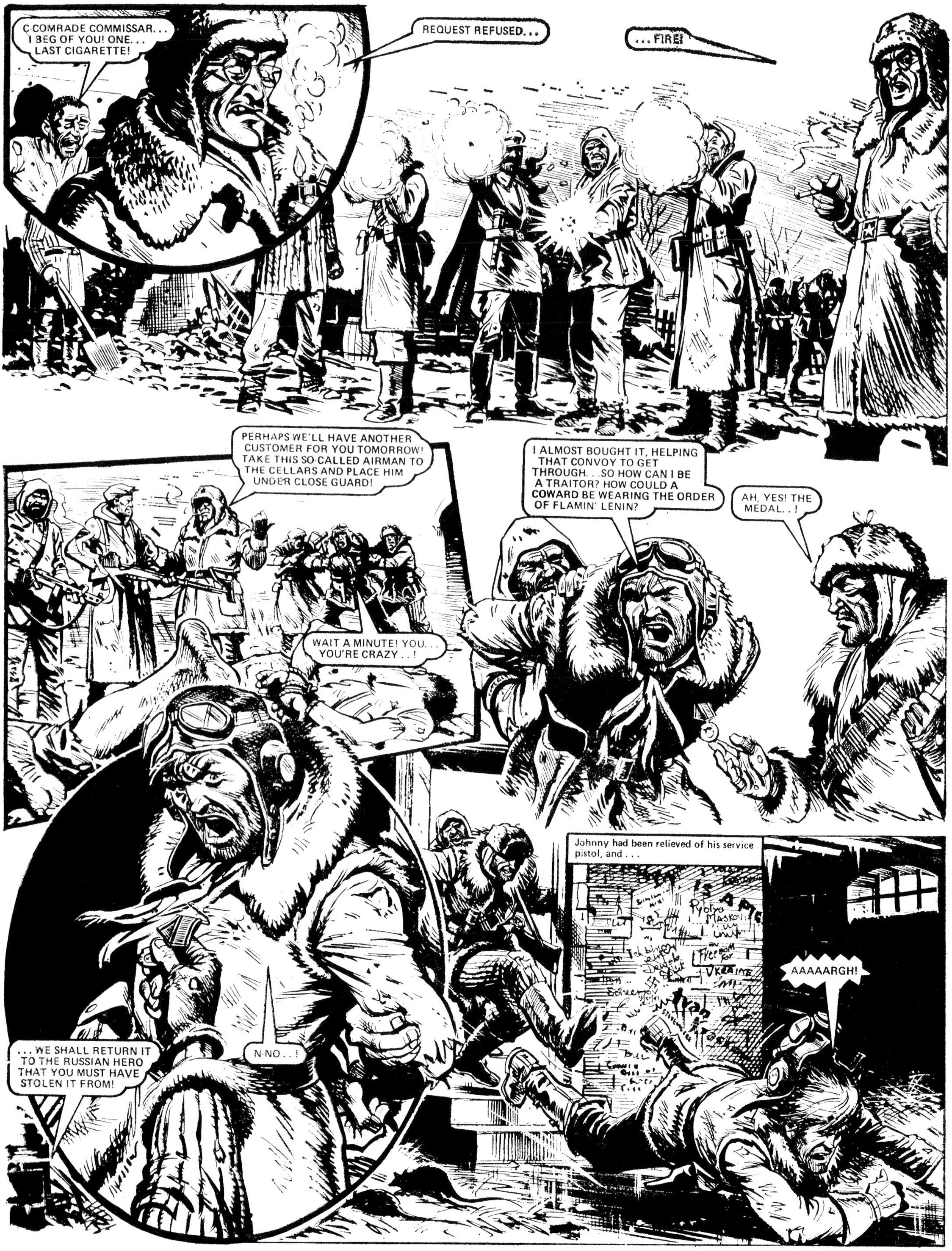
C-COMRADE COMMISSAR... I BEG OF YOU! ONE... LAST CIGARETTE!
REQUEST REFUSED...
...FIRE!
PERHAPS WE'LL HAVE ANOTHER CUSTOMER FOR YOU TOMORROW! TAKE THIS SO-CALLED AIRMAN TO THE CELLARS AND PLACE HIM UNDER CLOSE GUARD!
WAIT A MINUTE! YOU... YOU'RE CRAZY..!
I ALMOST BOUGHT IT, HELPING THAT CONVOY TO GET THROUGH...SO HOW CAN I BE A TRAITOR? HOW COULD A COWARD BE WEARING THE ORDER OF FLAMIN' LENIN?
AH, YES! THE MEDAL..!
...WE SHALL RETURN IT TO THE RUSSIAN HERO THAT YOU MUST HAVE STOLEN IT FROM!
N-NO..!
Johnny had been relieved of his service pistol, and...
AAAAARGH!

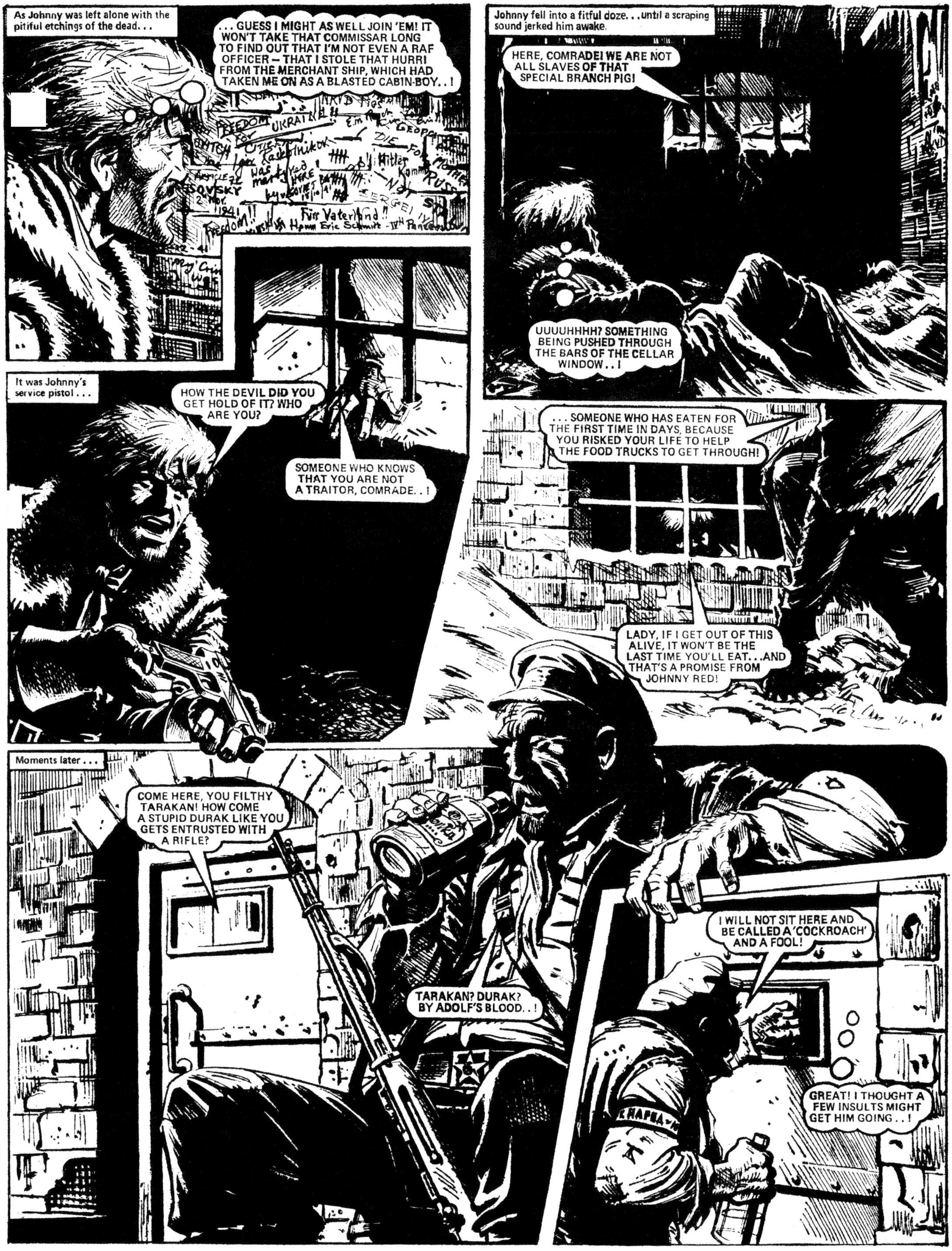
As Johnny was left alone with the pitiful etchings of the dead. . .
. . . GUESS I MIGHT AS WELL JOIN 'EM! IT WON'T TAKE THAT COMMISSAR LONG TO FIND OUT THAT I'M NOT EVEN A RAF OFFICER — THAT I STOLE THAT HURRI FROM THE MERCHANT SHIP, WHICH HAD TAKEN ME ON AS A BLASTED CABIN-BOY. . !
Johnny fell into a fitful doze. . . until a scraping sound jerked him awake.
HERE, COMRADE! WE ARE NOT ALL SLAVES OF THAT SPECIAL BRANCH PIG!
UUUUHHHH? SOMETHING BEING PUSHED THROUGH THE BARS OF THE CELLAR WINDOW . . !
It was Johnny's service pistol . . .
HOW THE DEVIL DID YOU GET HOLD OF IT? WHO ARE YOU?
SOMEONE WHO KNOWS THAT YOU ARE NOT A TRAITOR, COMRADE. . !
. . . SOMEONE WHO HAS EATEN FOR THE FIRST TIME IN DAYS, BECAUSE YOU RISKED YOUR LIFE TO HELP THE FOOD TRUCKS TO GET THROUGH!
LADY, IF I GET OUT OF THIS ALIVE, IT WON'T BE THE LAST TIME YOU'LL EAT. . . AND THAT'S A PROMISE FROM JOHNNY RED!
Moments later . . .
COME HERE, YOU FILTHY TARAKAN! HOW COME A STUPID DURAK LIKE YOU GETS ENTRUSTED WITH A RIFLE?
TARAKAN? DURAK? BY ADOLF'S BLOOD. . !
I WILL NOT SIT HERE AND BE CALLED A 'COCKROACH' AND A FOOL!
GREAT! I THOUGHT A FEW INSULTS MIGHT GET HIM GOING . . !

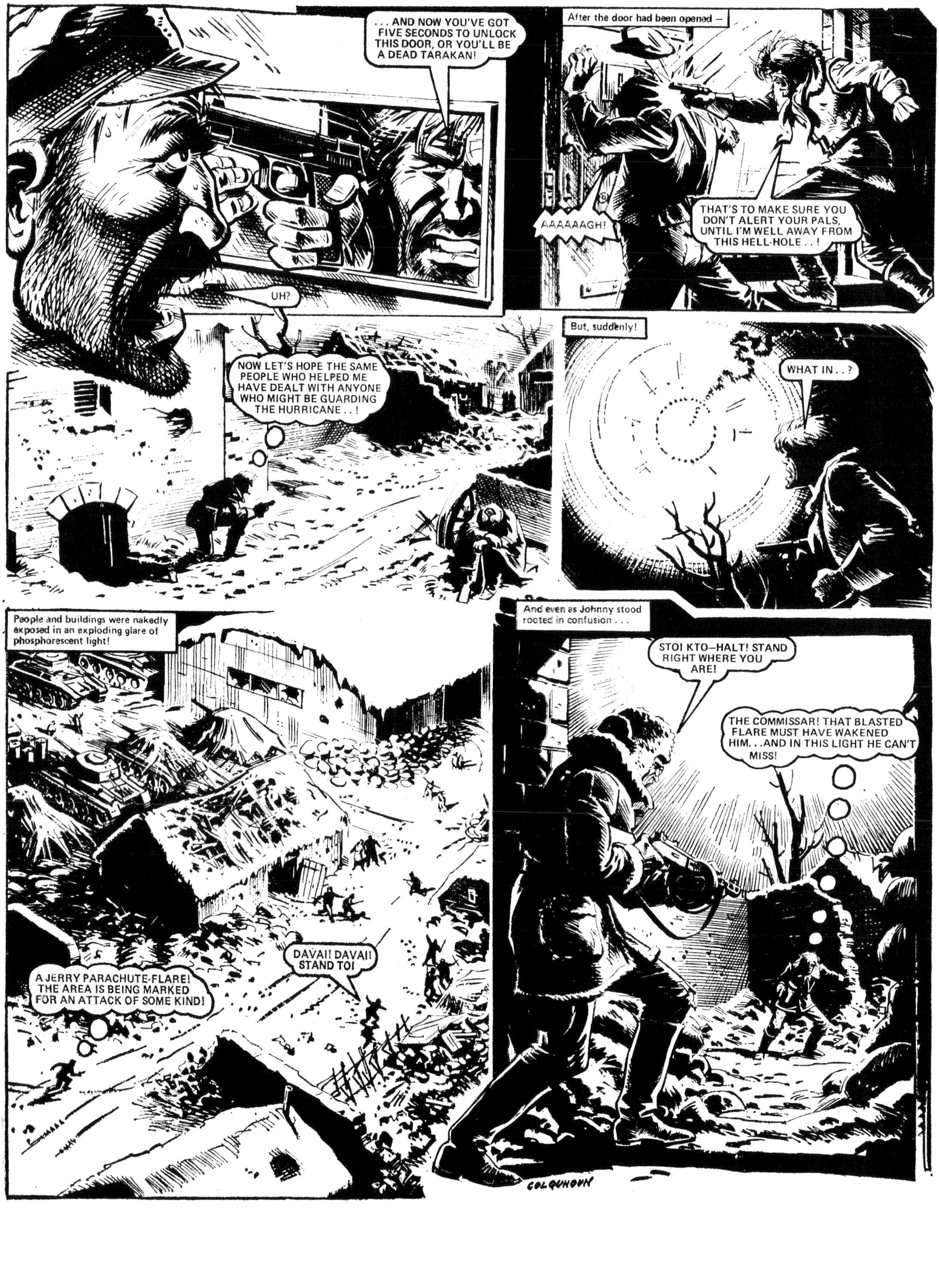

. . . AND NOW YOU'VE GOT FIVE SECONDS TO UNLOCK THIS DOOR, OR YOU'LL BE A DEAD TARAKAN!
UH?
After the door had been opened –
AAAAAAGH!
THAT'S TO MAKE SURE YOU DON'T ALERT YOUR PALS, UNTIL I'M WELL AWAY FROM THIS HELL-HOLE . . !
NOW LET'S HOPE THE SAME PEOPLE WHO HELPED ME HAVE DEALT WITH ANYONE WHO MIGHT BE GUARDING THE HURRICANE . . !
But, suddenly!
WHAT IN . . ?
People and buildings were nakedly exposed in an exploding glare of phosphorescent light!
A JERRY PARACHUTE-FLARE! THE AREA IS BEING MARKED FOR AN ATTACK OF SOME KIND!
DAVAI! DAVAI! STAND TO!
And even as Johnny stood rooted in confusion . . .
STOI KTO–HALT! STAND RIGHT WHERE YOU ARE!
THE COMMISSAR! THAT BLASTED FLARE MUST HAVE WAKENED HIM. . .AND IN THIS LIGHT HE CAN'T MISS!
COLQUHOUN

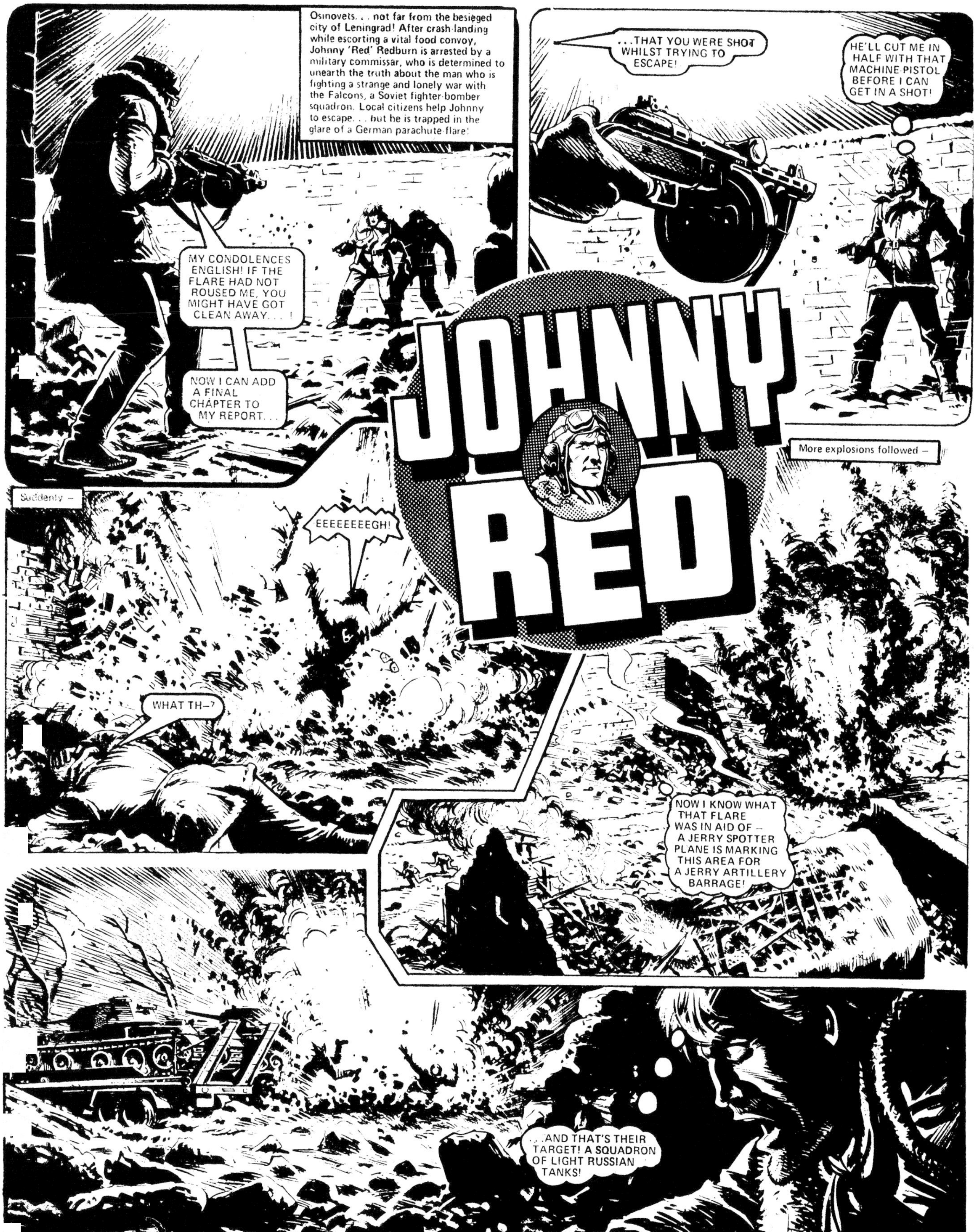

Osinovets. . . not far from the besieged city of Leningrad! After crash-landing while escorting a vital food convoy, Johnny 'Red' Redburn is arrested by a military commissar, who is determined to unearth the truth about the man who is fighting a strange and lonely war with the Falcons, a Soviet fighter-bomber squadron. Local citizens help Johnny to escape. . . but he is trapped in the glare of a German parachute flare!
MY CONDOLENCES ENGLISH! IF THE FLARE HAD NOT ROUSED ME, YOU MIGHT HAVE GOT CLEAN AWAY. . . !
NOW I CAN ADD A FINAL CHAPTER TO MY REPORT. . .
. . .THAT YOU WERE SHOT WHILST TRYING TO ESCAPE!
HE'LL CUT ME IN HALF WITH THAT MACHINE-PISTOL BEFORE I CAN GET IN A SHOT!
JOHNNY RED
Suddenly –
EEEEEEEEGH!
WHAT TH–?
More explosions followed –
NOW I KNOW WHAT THAT FLARE WAS IN AID OF – A JERRY SPOTTER PLANE IS MARKING THIS AREA FOR A JERRY ARTILLERY BARRAGE!
. . .AND THAT'S THEIR TARGET! A SQUADRON OF LIGHT RUSSIAN TANKS!

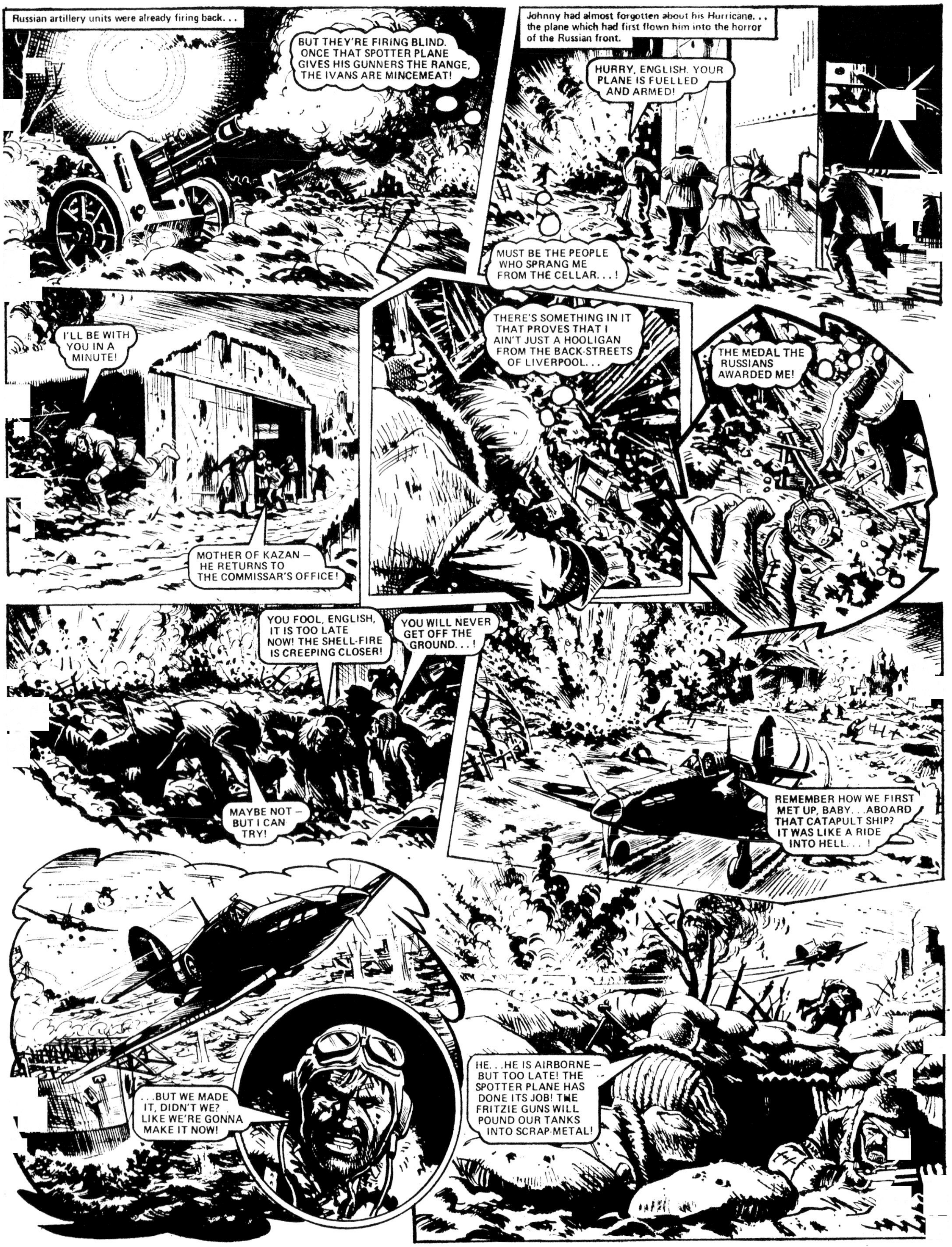

Russian artillery units were already firing back...
BUT THEY'RE FIRING BLIND. ONCE THAT SPOTTER PLANE GIVES HIS GUNNERS THE RANGE, THE IVANS ARE MINCEMEAT!
Johnny had almost forgotten about his Hurricane... the plane which had first flown him into the horror of the Russian front.
HURRY, ENGLISH. YOUR PLANE IS FUELLED AND ARMED!
MUST BE THE PEOPLE WHO SPRANG ME FROM THE CELLAR...!
I'LL BE WITH YOU IN A MINUTE!
MOTHER OF KAZAN — HE RETURNS TO THE COMMISSAR'S OFFICE!
THERE'S SOMETHING IN IT THAT PROVES THAT I AIN'T JUST A HOOLIGAN FROM THE BACK-STREETS OF LIVERPOOL...
THE MEDAL THE RUSSIANS AWARDED ME!
YOU FOOL, ENGLISH, IT IS TOO LATE NOW! THE SHELL-FIRE IS CREEPING CLOSER!
YOU WILL NEVER GET OFF THE GROUND...!
MAYBE NOT — BUT I CAN TRY!
REMEMBER HOW WE FIRST MET UP, BABY...ABOARD THAT CATAPULT SHIP? IT WAS LIKE A RIDE INTO HELL...!
...BUT WE MADE IT, DIDN'T WE? LIKE WE'RE GONNA MAKE IT NOW!
HE...HE IS AIRBORNE — BUT TOO LATE! THE SPOTTER PLANE HAS DONE ITS JOB! THE FRITZIE GUNS WILL POUND OUR TANKS INTO SCRAP-METAL!

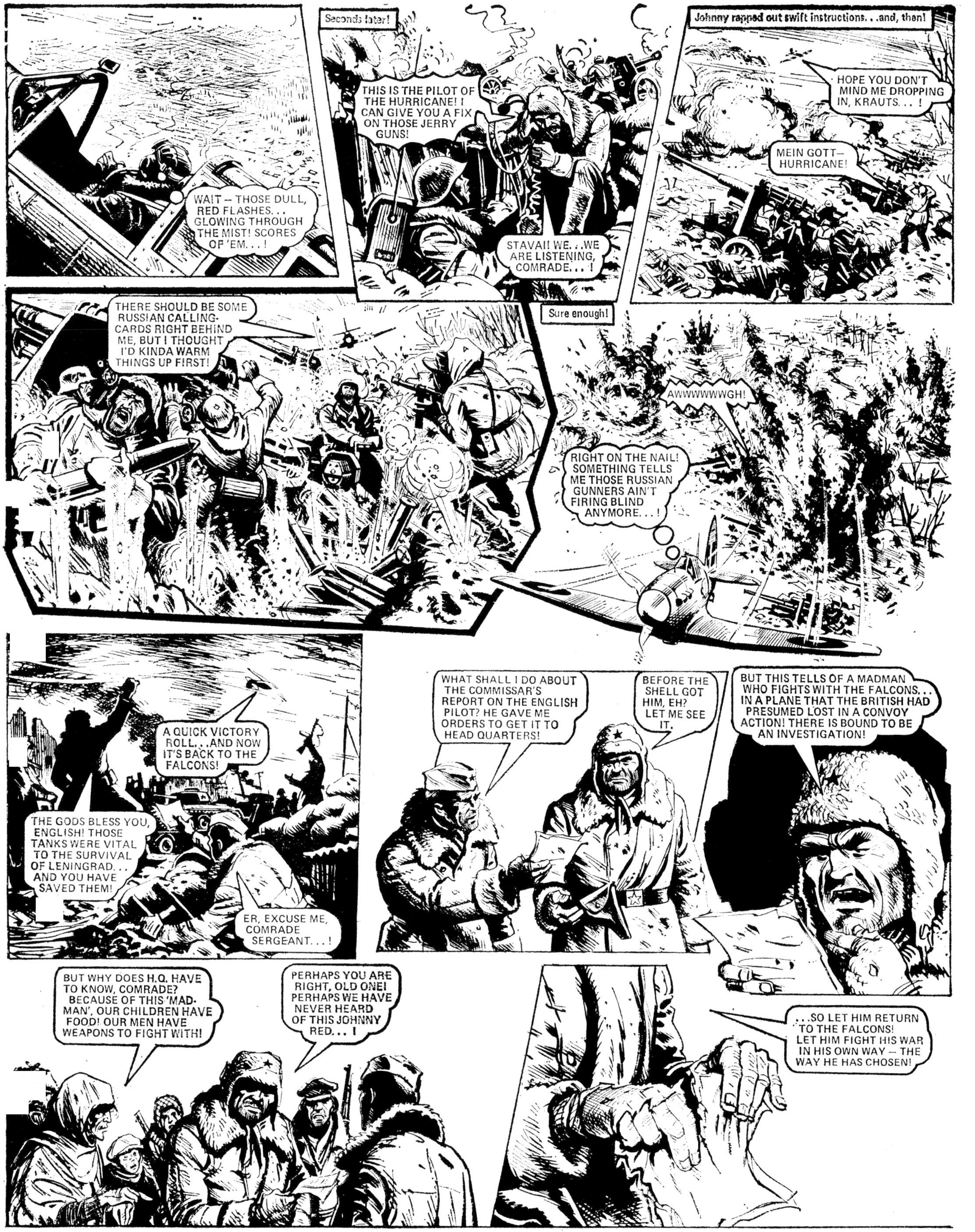

WAIT — THOSE DULL, RED FLASHES. . . GLOWING THROUGH THE MIST! SCORES OF 'EM. . . !
Seconds later!
THIS IS THE PILOT OF THE HURRICANE! I CAN GIVE YOU A FIX ON THOSE JERRY GUNS!
STAVAI! WE. . .WE ARE LISTENING, COMRADE. . . !
Johnny rapped out swift instructions. . .and, then!
HOPE YOU DON'T MIND ME DROPPING IN, KRAUTS. . . !
MEIN GOTT— HURRICANE!
THERE SHOULD BE SOME RUSSIAN CALLING-CARDS RIGHT BEHIND ME, BUT I THOUGHT I'D KINDA WARM THINGS UP FIRST!
Sure enough!
AWWWWWWGH!
RIGHT ON THE NAIL! SOMETHING TELLS ME THOSE RUSSIAN GUNNERS AIN'T FIRING BLIND ANYMORE. . . !
A QUICK VICTORY ROLL. . .AND NOW IT'S BACK TO THE FALCONS!
THE GODS BLESS YOU, ENGLISH! THOSE TANKS WERE VITAL TO THE SURVIVAL OF LENINGRAD. . . AND YOU HAVE SAVED THEM!
ER, EXCUSE ME, COMRADE SERGEANT. . . !
WHAT SHALL I DO ABOUT THE COMMISSAR'S REPORT ON THE ENGLISH PILOT? HE GAVE ME ORDERS TO GET IT TO HEAD QUARTERS!
BEFORE THE SHELL GOT HIM, EH? LET ME SEE IT.
BUT THIS TELLS OF A MADMAN WHO FIGHTS WITH THE FALCONS. . . IN A PLANE THAT THE BRITISH HAD PRESUMED LOST IN A CONVOY ACTION! THERE IS BOUND TO BE AN INVESTIGATION!
BUT WHY DOES H.Q. HAVE TO KNOW, COMRADE? BECAUSE OF THIS 'MAD-MAN', OUR CHILDREN HAVE FOOD! OUR MEN HAVE WEAPONS TO FIGHT WITH!
PERHAPS YOU ARE RIGHT, OLD ONE! PERHAPS WE HAVE NEVER HEARD OF THIS JOHNNY RED. . . !
. . .SO LET HIM RETURN TO THE FALCONS! LET HIM FIGHT HIS WAR IN HIS OWN WAY — THE WAY HE HAS CHOSEN!

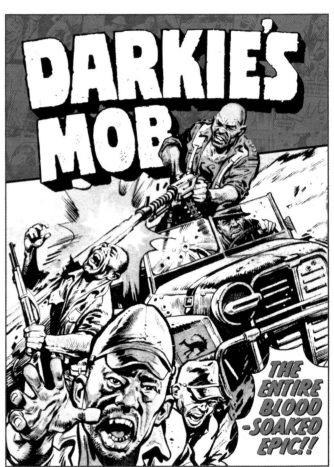